D1594816

Unless Recalled Earlier
DATE DUE

Demco, Inc. 38-293

STUDIES IN CULTURAL HISTORY

Avant-Garde Florence

Avant-Garde Florence

From Modernism to Fascism

Walter L. Adamson

RECEIVED JUN 23 1995 MSU - LIBRARY

Harvard University Press
Cambridge, Massachusetts
London, England 1993

DG
735.6
.A33
1993

Copyright © 1993 by the President and Fellows of Harvard College
All rights reserved
Printed in the United States of America

This book is printed on acid-free paper, and its binding materials have been chosen for strength and durability.

Library of Congress Cataloging-in-Publication Data
Adamson, Walter L.
  Avant-garde Florence : from Modernism to Fascism / Walter L. Adamson.
    p.   cm.—(Studies in cultural history)
  Includes bibliographical references and index.
  ISBN 0-674-05525-X
  1. Florence (Italy)—Intellectual life. 2. Modernism (Art)—Italy—Florence. 3. Fascism
and culture—Italy—Florence. 4. Avant-garde (Aesthetics)—Italy—Florence. I. Title.
II. Series.
DG735.6.A33   1993
945'.51—dc20
93-8062
   CIP

To Daniel and Thomas

Acknowledgments

Although the writing of this book sometimes seemed nearly a monastic experience, I was continually sustained by the memories of the many friends, new and old, whose kindness, generosity, moral support, and intellectual stimulation made the research out of which it grew such a pleasure. Some of them have continued to aid me in turning my manuscript into what lies between these covers.

The idea for the book arose from conversations in 1980–81 with a dear colleague, Arthur Evans, whose deep interest in the connection between European high culture and the advent of fascism as well as his wide knowledge of Italian literature and history were so immensely stimulating and helpful. Sadly, Arthur's death in 1992 makes belated my public appreciation of his inspiration and support.

Among the many other colleagues, former colleagues, and students at Emory who have meant so much over the years, I especially want to thank Cristina de la Torre, Jeffrey Herf, Bobby Hill, Miller Jones, Rudi Makkreel, Stefan Meller, Gwen Sell, Stefano Tani, Erdmann Waniek, and Steve Whitaker. Bobby's criticisms of my research as it stood after a seminar presentation in 1986 were of inestimable value; Stefano's support, which included sharing his house in Florence with me on my research trips there as well as his deep knowledge of all things Italian, has been unflagging; and Jeffrey was among those who read large portions of the manuscript and gave me the benefit of his sharp critical eye. Yet even those who have contributed in less material ways have had a greater impact on what follows than they are likely to realize.

Among other far-flung colleagues who have never ceased to be near when I needed them, I want to thank Jack Diggins, Ed Jacobitti, Mark Poster, Hayden White, and especially Richard Bellamy, Emilio Gentile, Martin Jay, and Robert Wohl, each of whom offered me the results of a scrupulous reading of the manuscript. Diana Rüesch was also of immense help, not only in introducing me to the treasures of the Archivio Prezzolini in Lugano, where she serves as principal archivist, but also in generously answering my many questions and even sending me books over several years of transatlantic correspondence. Finally, I would also like to thank the helpful staff of Emory's interlibrary loan office—Marie Hansen, Julia Jones, and Margaret Whittier—as well as the archivists in Florence—Maria Cristina Chiesi, Gloria Manghetti, and Manuela Scotti—without whom the research for the book would simply not have been possible.

I also owe a debt of a very special kind to Giuliano Prezzolini. Besides being a gracious host in Florence and an indefatigable correspondent who has freely shared his memories of his father and of what his father told him of "the days of *La Voce*," he has generously provided me with copies of many of the photos that appear in this book and helped me to get in touch with Anna Casini Paszkowski and Valeria Giaccai, who have been similarly generous.

Institutions have also benevolently extended support. The George A. and Eliza Gardner Howard Foundation provided me with the luxury of a year's leave from teaching in 1984–85, when the research was in its formative stages. Similarly, Emory University's Research Committee freed me for a semester in 1988, when the present book took definite shape; and the American Council of Learned Societies supported a leave for the 1991–92 academic year, during which the bulk of the writing was completed. In addition, the National Endowment for the Humanities provided both a 1991 summer stipend and a travel award that allowed a final trip to the European archives.

Finally, though of course not least, I thank my family. Lauren was supportive in every way, including taking the time to give me her reading of the manuscript. Daniel and Thomas were immensely helpful simply by being a constant source of brightness in my life. To them I dedicate the book, both out of my love for them and out of a vague but gnawing sense that the presently rising generation could do worse than to contemplate the experience and fate of their exact counterparts a century ago.

Atlanta
July 1993

Contents

Illustrations

Avant-Garde Florence

Introduction

A group of *young people*, eager for liberation, yearning for universality, aspiring to a superior intellectual life, has gathered together in Florence under the auspicious symbolic name *Leonardo* in order to stimulate our existence, elevate our thoughts, celebrate our art.

In *Life* we are *pagans* and *individualists*—lovers of beauty and intelligence, worshippers of profound nature and full life, enemies of every form of Nazarene sheepishness and plebeian servitude.

In *Thought* we are *personalists* and *idealists*, that is, superior to every system and all limits, convinced that every philosophy is nothing but a personal way of life and that there is no existence outside thought.

In *Art* we love the ideal transfiguration of life, combat the inferior forms of it, and aspire to beauty as the suggestive figuration and revelation of a profound and serene life.[1]

So declared the opening manifesto of *Leonardo* in 1903, just below an elaborate *art nouveau* masthead featuring a knight on horseback charging through clouds and just above a lead article by Giovanni Papini, "The Imperialist Ideal." The agenda was one of Promethean daring, synthetic in its political, artistic, cultural, and philosophical aims, generational in its self-conception and audience, at once cosmopolitan and self-consciously Florentine. While it may have appeared ludicrous to the political and intellectual élites of Florence at the time, in view of the humble origins of its youthful collaborators and the meager resources available to them, it inaugurated an avant-garde cultural movement that, over the next dozen years, reshaped the political culture not only of Florence but of all Italy.

This book tells the story of the world of *Leonardo* and its successors, *La Voce* and *Lacerba*, of the men and (in a few cases) women who wrote for their pages, and of their cultural politics and its consequences. Giovanni Papini, Giuseppe Prezzolini, Ardengo Soffici—these names have receded into relative obscurity, even in Italy. But in the first decades of this century, they dazzled readers in Florence quite as much as those of Gabriele D'Annunzio or Filippo Tommaso Marinetti, and even today one is hard pressed to find an early edition of one of their works in a Florentine bookshop. Papini was perhaps the most widely read Italian writer of his generation, at least in Italy, and although he never produced the great philosophical work he believed he had in him, his autobiographical and biographical prose, as well as his essays, exhibits a bulk, intellectual range, and conceptual power second in his era only to the work of Benedetto Croce, and Papini wrote keen-edged poetry as well. Prezzolini was an editor and journalist of tremendous energy and wit; *La Voce*, which he edited for much of its eight-year existence, and his long correspondence with Croce stand as cultural monuments to the prewar era. Soffici was both a painter of considerable talent and a writer who moved deftly between mordant polemic and charming aphorism; his memoirs of a decade in Paris with Picasso, Apollinaire, and other avant-gardists are as rich a source on that life as we have.

Yet for readers of English as well as for non-Italian audiences on the continent, their story is less a world forgotten than one never known. More than most national histories in the modern period, and certainly more than those of England, France, and Germany, the history of Italy tends to be treated as a world apart. Few comparative studies of modern Europe, whether historical, philosophical, or literary, include Italy; and topical studies of its political or literary movements, or of developments in science, philosophy, psychology, and the like also tend to ignore Italians. This book responds to that deficit by taking up one of the central anxieties of modern life—the death of God proclaimed by Nietzsche and the subsequent *fin-de-siècle* malaise in Europe—and showing how a generation of young intellectuals in Florence sought to overcome that condition by building a culture of sufficient spiritual depth to offset, or at least to complement, a social life based increasingly on industrialism, urbanization, science, and technology—that is, sought to overcome the crisis in much the same way as did its "modernist" counterparts elsewhere in Europe.

Because my focus is this avant-garde and its modernist outlook, I do not attempt a definitive history of Florentine culture in the period. Rather I present what amounts to a group portrait of the people and institutions central to the Florentine avant-garde, which burst upon the cultural scene in what has become known as the "Giolittian era," after Prime Minister Giovanni Giolitti, the political leader who dominated the decade and a half before Italy's entry into the First World War. To construct this portrait, I explore the avant-garde's perceptions of the city and region in which they worked, their estimation of the problems of Italian national life and, indeed, of modern life more generally, and their relations with the larger European modernist movement, with which they identified and collaborated, and which they sought to extend to Italy. I examine closely the aims, activities, and cultural-political environment of the prewar journals in which they embodied their aspirations, as well as the personal backgrounds, experiences, and intellectual itineraries of key figures. Finally, I consider how, in the specifically Italian political context in which they worked, they contributed, however unwittingly, to the cultural basis of early fascism.

In order to explore the interconnections between the modernist culture of Florence and Italian fascist ideology, I pay close attention to the political implications of Florentine avant-garde rhetoric in the first four chapters.[2] Then, in Chapter 5 I take up the connections between prewar culture, its politicization during the war, and the development of a specifically Tuscan fascism in the postwar period. In the Conclusion I consider some continuities between Florentine prewar journals like *Leonardo* and its successors, *La Voce* and *Lacerba*, on the one hand, and Mussolini's rhetoric in the period of fascism's ascendance (1918–1922) on the other. While these discussions do not pretend to "explain" or even fully to describe fascist rhetoric, they help make clear how that rhetoric could be created almost overnight.

Studies integrating the histories of cultural movements with the rise of radical political ideologies, and particularly studies of the cultural origins of fascism in Germany and France, have become more frequent in recent years.[3] In most studies of Italy, however, the traditional separation of cultural and political history has persisted. Thus, despite many studies of Italian intellectual and cultural traditions, most notably of *decadentismo,* about which there is a voluminous literature, and many studies of Italian political movements and ideologies, most notably fascism, few writers have connected *decadentismo* with fascism, even though connections between the two were clearly recognized by Italian intellectuals of the period.[4] Thus Benedetto Croce, despite his characterization of fascism as a "parenthesis" in Italian history, implicated *fin-de-siècle decadentismo* in its rise.[5] A decade earlier, the younger liberal Piero Gobetti had already seen that the generation born in the 1880s "was irreparably romantic, confusedly lost in the fray, insufficiently steady to be realistic; fascism was anticipated before the war by this intellectual futurism."[6] Nor was the point lost on important intellectual adherents of fascism. Giovanni Gentile argued in 1924 that fascism's deepest origins lay in the antipositivist intellectual climate of the fifteen years before the war in which he had been a principal player.[7]

This book also seeks to fill a gap with respect to Italian modernism. Despite ample cultural-historical scholarship in recent years on the various modernist movements in European cities—prominent examples include Carl Schorske on Vienna, Mary Gluck on Budapest, Peter Jelavich on Munich, and Jerrold Seigel on Paris—no Italian city has been so studied. What little attention has been paid to avant-garde culture in Italy has been focused on Milanese futurism, as if it were the only Italian avant-garde movement of the prewar period. Although Milanese futurism did have the largest international impact of any Italian cultural movement in the period, my research has convinced me that the Florentine avant-garde had a greater cultural and political impact in Italy. Of course the two movements were not completely isolated from one another, and their interrelations will be explored at appropriate points.

My decision to write about the Florentine avant-garde, then, is based in part on its political importance for Italy. Not only did its cultural politics provide a spawning ground for fascist ideology and rhetoric, but, as we will see in Chapter 4, its leaders played a significant role in catapulting Italy into the First World War. Yet the decision also reflects my sense of its intrinsic importance—its not inconsiderable influence abroad and its intellectual vitality. This vitality has long been recognized by the Italians themselves, who generally treat the Florentine avant-garde movement as the key opening chapter in the intellectual history of their *Novecento*.

Before turning to this history, however, a few words are necessary about the way I have conceptualized and contextualized it. My greatest debt in this regard is to the cultural sociology of Pierre Bourdieu, which is now just beginning to be extended to intellectual and cultural history.[8] While I cannot here consider Bourdieu's complex and subtle method in any detail, I do want to evoke a few of his key concepts to show how they provide the methodological foundation for the present work.

Bourdieu's central preoccupation in his reflections on method is to overcome all dichotomies based on subject and object, ideas and experience, or text and reality. Bourdieu thinks of agents, both individual and collective or institutional, as embedded in a *habitus* or web of *dispositions* that reflects the experiences, attitudes, habits, prejudices, and unconscious assumptions or *doxa*—those things that "go without saying"—of their society. From within this *habitus* agents articulate views *(prises de position)*, which then register themselves as *positions* that can be objectively mapped within the overall *field* of current positions. Thus a position-taking or *prise de position* mediates between *habitus* and position and, by extension, the overall field of positions. To speak publicly is to engage in a practice that both structures and is structured by the material and social world in which it takes place.

Even more crucial for Bourdieu than the origin of his concepts of position and position-taking in the social habitus is the relation of positions to one another. Bourdieu's method is relentlessly relational and intersubjective, a characteristic he shares with Jürgen Habermas and other contemporary thinkers who aim to break with the Cartesian tradition of the philosophy of consciousness. In Bourdieu's world, agents who take positions compete for the prize of having their position regarded as the most intellectually and culturally legitimate. They also always articulate a position within an already constituted field of positions, and each new position can be understood only in relation to the existing field. Ideas, then, are interdefined and positionally situated; to understand them we must understand not only the agents and their backgrounds but also the relations between cultural positions and the contours of the positional field as a whole.

It follows that the primary task of the intellectual historian is to reconstruct the field of positions in the society and epoch under consideration and, further, to reconstruct its *space of the possibles*—the universe of potential position options that an agent within that society might have been able to conceive given the existing field or space of positions. Yet matters are still more complex than this, since all modern societies consist of multiple, interrelated fields. Bourdieu speaks of the intellectual field, the political field, the field of class positions, and so forth. He also speaks of different forms of *capital,* principally of economic forms and symbolic or cultural forms, the former being generally dominant over the latter in the modern world. Thus the field of class positions is dispersed between the two poles represented by those rich and those poor in economic capital. The political field is inscribed within this field—toward the rich or dominant pole—and the intellectual field is in turn inscribed within the political field—toward the pole poor in economic capital but rich in symbolic capital, a positioning that leads Bourdieu to refer to modern intellectuals in general as the "dominated fraction of the dominant class."[9] It follows from all this that after reconstructing the intellectual field, the intellectual historian needs to go on to reconstruct the political and overall class fields in order to grasp how position-takings in the intellectual field may relate to positions in the other fields. Indeed, since the amount and variety of capital possessed by agents offer important clues to the positions they take, there are often *homologies* between the position-takings of agents in different fields with roughly the same sorts of capital. Moreover, position-takings in one field often have ideological effects in another or lead to alliances with homologous positions in another.

In considering Florence, then, I have attempted to reconstruct the general position of Prezzolini, Papini, Soffici, and their generation in terms of existing positions in both the cultural and political fields. As will become clear in Chapters 1 and 2, the major positions to which theirs in general was related were those of the local academic establishment, the "art-for-art's-sake" aestheticists (commonly at least half a generation older), the socialist movement, and the national political establishment represented above all by Giolitti. Of course the entry of any new position affects the interrelation among, and may prompt the redefinition of, all existing positions. Thus, in Chapter 4 we consider how the emergence of Milanese futurism after 1909 forced the Florentines to rethink their positions, diminished the centrality of their long-standing confrontation with aestheticism, and ultimately increased the divisions within their ranks. Similarly, the outbreak of a major crisis will force a reassessment of all positions and may therefore have the effect of redefining both the positions themselves and their interrelations. In Chapter 3 we consider how the outbreak of the Libyan War in 1911 tended to fracture the tenuous unity of those involved with *La Voce*, a unity made possible more by a common antipathy for Giolitti than by a shared set of political values, visions, and goals.

Yet if Bourdieu's great merit is to have shown how any position-taking must always be understood in relation to the overall field of positions rather than as the straightforward emanation of a particular mind, he by no means suggests that we should regard particular texts as corresponding in any simple, reductive way to positions in a field. On the contrary, texts—especially those with complex, "worklike" features, as against those with mere documentary value—may themselves be regarded as force fields homologous to larger fields.[10] That is, complex texts characteristically embody contradictory or contesting impulses that tend to mirror larger social and ideological conflicts. Nor is there any assumption in Bourdieu's theory that institutions manifest unified or linearly determinable systems of beliefs. As we will see, *Leonardo*, and especially *La Voce* and *Lacerba*, were all force fields of competing visions, desires, and goals. Similarly, although Papini, Prezzolini, Soffici, and their friends often faced off as a group against common opposing positions, each of them can also be understood as occupying a competing position within the field of Florentine modernism.

It is now time to say a few words about the general phenomenon of European modernism, a concept that was nowhere utilized by the intellectuals to whom it retrospectively refers but that, nonetheless, has proved immensely useful in understanding the commonalities in their aims, visions, and methods. As I understand it and use it in the following pages, modernism was the central project of the intellectual generation entering the European cultural scene between 1900 and 1914: that of a "cultural regeneration" through the secular-religious quest for "new values." In referring to the avant-garde modernist movement, then, I mean those organized cultural groups of intellectuals that sought to advance this project of cultural regeneration, most often through journals but also through publicly staged events, and who in order to advance this project took positions against both those who promoted the bourgeois establishment and those who withdrew from it in a privatistic, art-for-art's-sake retreat. Thus the Florentines of *Leonardo* and *La Voce* rejected the "decadent" and "aestheticist" posture associated for them above all with D'Annunzio and organized themselves as a collective voice asserting the need for a spiritual revolution against the cultural and political status quo.

Modernism, then, was by no means an embrace of the modernity of industry, science, and technology. It was, on the contrary, an "adversary culture" or "other modernity" that challenged the "modernizing" forces of science, commerce, and industry, usually in the name of some more "spiritual" alternative.[11] As Stephen Spender suggested in a classic account, modernism was a "sensibility of style and form" that developed because of the "unprecedented modern situation" in which "life-memory" is threatened with destruction.[12] The modernists were an "international inter-arts alliance" aiming at "the transformation of the whole of civilization within a revolutionary vision inspired by art." To restore life-memory, they turned to the past, but, because they sought revolutionary transformation, their approach was never one of simple retrieval but rather of sifting the past for remnants of primal—especially mythic—elements of culture.[13] Like the romantics eighty years earlier, the modernists were repulsed by the idea that the imagination should be placed in the service of a rationalist or utilitarian view of life, yet for them there was no hope of a simple return to "nature." Rather, they exalted artifice and the artistic imagination in hopes of shaping a new secular-religious framework integrating elements from religious tradition, poetic tradition, and contemporary philosophy and art. In short, they aimed to create a "new art" that would, in turn, establish a "pattern of hope" and the "symbolism of a shared life." The world would be "pacified and ennobled" in a "revolution of the word."[14]

As a trans-European description, Spender's ideal-typical portrait captures extremely well the social and artistic outlook of the generation of intellectuals who came to maturity between 1900 and 1914 and, to a lesser extent, the postwar generation. No doubt this is why many good recent studies have continued to build upon his approach.[15] In particular, his portrayal of modernism's "revolution of the word" is acutely sensitive to the aspect of the movement that continues to attract the most attention: its recognition of a nonmimetic, performative concept of language—language as a system of signs within which worlds are actively shaped and reshaped, not simply reflected. Here I wish to elaborate upon his understanding in four points.

First, the origin of what European modernists perceived as the need for cultural regeneration lay in their sense that civilization had "covered over" what is most basic to human existence—thus the importance of recreating the mythic, legendary, and "primal" forces of cultural life.[16] While the word *civilization* here refers to what might now be thought of as the forces of modernization, the modernists opposed not modernization per se but the positivism and materialism that were its cultural concomitants. Unlike many romantics, the modernists rarely thought in terms of a simple return to the past. Rather they sought a kind of Vichian *ricorso*, or Nietzschean transvaluation of values, or Sorelian heroic regeneration, in which technological, industrial, and (sometimes) national power would be infused with a new spirituality.

Second, in seeking cultural and spiritual enrichment for the dynamic world of modern productive forces, modernists were faced with the perplexing problem of how to reconcile the seemingly contradictory imperatives of form and fluidity, order and constant change. As Baudelaire had famously written already in 1860, modernity was "the ephemeral, the fugitive, the contingent, the half of art whose other half is the eternal and the immutable"; a genuinely modern art would somehow have to fuse the two halves.[17] Nietzsche, too, had insisted in *The Birth of Tragedy* that genuine art necessarily fused a form-giving or Apollonian element and a fluid, Dionysian one. But how this fusion could be achieved, how the representation of the eternal and immutable was still possible in a world whose only bedrock was Bergsonian flux, was a problem that could not be solved simply by reading Baudelaire, Nietzsche, or Bergson and that yet demanded a creative resolution in every modernist effort at cultural and spiritual regeneration. Not surprisingly, such resolutions commonly rested less upon logic than upon a messianic mood of frenzy, despair, and apocalyptic hope.

Third, the practical strategy of modernism depended on an active social role for art. Although modernist views of art ran the gamut from expressionism to idealist moralism, all stressed the importance of creativity, rejecting or at least strongly questioning any view of art as mimesis, asserting the central role of art in the project of cultural regeneration, and resolutely denying any normative boundary between the "arts" and society. Precisely because they rejected the romantic notion that the basis for a mythic and spiritual dimension of life could be recovered from pre-industrial, folk traditions, the modernists necessarily set great store by their own unfettered creativity as the main hope for reshaping modern life.

Finally, modernists stipulated a central role for intellectuals—that is, for themselves—in the creation and organization of a regenerated culture. Modernists experienced the new world of science and industry as a cultural void, believed that some solid cultural counterpart to it needed to be created, and appointed themselves to the task. Not infrequently, this took the form of an attempt to forge the intellectuals into a kind of "great party," organized around a journal, which published internal debates and manifestos for the edification of the masses. In this sense, modernists tended toward avant-gardism. It might even be said that modernism in the prewar period recast avant-gardism by suggesting that an avant-garde can be strictly cultural, with no mandated political aim or organization besides its self-appointed and autonomous role as the "party of intellectuals."[18] During and after the war, however, modernist avant-gardism did become politicized, moving away from the notion that art and writing by themselves have the power to change human beings and social life. In Florence, as we will see, this transition had profoundly negative consequences.

Yet modernism was far from uniform everywhere, if only because the local fields of positions into which it inserted itself were always different. For example, as we will see in Chapter 2, some Florentine modernists— especially Soffici—became attached to an ideal of *toscanità*, an ideal based on reverence for Tuscan peasant life and the uniquely spiritual beauty of its rural landscape, and thus, in general terms, more romantic than modernist. Yet Soffici saw no contradiction between this ideal and his embrace of avant-garde modernism. Indeed, of all the Florentines his was the most radical effort to insert himself into the Parisian scene. For him *toscanità* was precisely the element that could lend distinctiveness to his position within the field of modernist positions in Paris, and he went so far as to suggest that Arthur Rimbaud, that most radical of late nineteenth-century French avant-gardists, shared more with his own *toscanità* than he did with cultural ideals drawn from life in Paris.

Despite its *toscanità*, however, the Florentine modernist movement took place in a city. In pondering this fact, I have found it fruitful to consider the urban space of Florence in relation to Bourdieu's concept of social space, even though Bourdieu's social space is a theoretical field of positions, not literally a geographic space. If we think of Bourdieu's social space as a mapping of class positions and then consider the distribution of social groups in geographic space (where they live, work, and spend leisure time), two extremes emerge: either the various groups composing that social field or space tend to inhabit different sectors of geographic space, or the various groups of the social space tend to intermingle in geographic space. In the following pages I refer to *public space* when social relations approach the latter extreme, and to *civil society* when a public space has been extended, formally or informally, into a forum for public discussion.[19]

During the last four decades of the nineteenth century Florence moved from being a city with at least some elements of public space (albeit with sharp hierarchies of class and gender) to being a city increasingly segregated by class. To the young intellectuals at the turn of the century, Florentine public space appeared to be under siege, increasingly managed and yet inefficiently so, increasingly controlled by a bourgeois aesthetic or non-aesthetic that was deeply offensive, and ultimately threatened with chaos by the new political movements of the working class. These intellectuals experienced themselves as atomized individuals living in an urban space that had become nonsocial, a mere thoroughfare, increasingly deficient in common life. Yet while they sought to use their journals to build a civil society of educated interaction and elevated common purpose, they remained unsure that they could really raise the *popolo* to their level, and thus forever fearful of a new worker-dominated urban space in which they would be no less excluded than in the current one. These fears would reach an intense pitch in early September 1902, when a working-class movement demonstrated that it could, at least briefly, entirely disrupt the life of Florence, bringing its trams and public services to a halt, forcing many of its stores to close, and making everyone outside its own ranks fear to walk the streets.

In a famous essay written in the year in which *Leonardo* was founded, the sociologist Georg Simmel located the central modern problem in the individual's desire not to be "swallowed up in the social-technological mechanism."[20] He considered the modern city essentially a place of "distantiation" and reserve created by the abundance of calculative (monetary and clock-bound) relationships with others, as well as by the intensification of emotional life that arises out of pure scale, yet one that also permitted much greater expression of individuality than did the small town. Friedrich Nietzsche, he wrote, hated cities because of their quantitative, schematized character, and lived in small towns as the lonely genius, the better to escape their stifling conformity. Like Nietzsche, members of the Florentine avant-garde sought refuge in periods of countrified isolation, but they could not leave the city for long precisely for the reason Simmel identified. They were ultimately dissatisfied with the role of the lone genius, even though they initially dramatized themselves by invoking such an ideal, and they sought always to recreate the city and its cultural life in their own image. Inspired by the cosmopolitan dynamism and creative daring of Paris as well as by the premodern beauty of Italian cities such as Venice, which Soffici once called the most beautiful city in the world, they never forgot that any possibility for creating a new culture would inevitably arise in cities.[21]

This acknowledgment did not necessarily entail a commitment to Florence. Prezzolini himself was born in Perugia, though of an originally Tuscan family, and he had come to Florence only in 1899 at the age of seventeen. Many of the important later writers for *La Voce* came from still more distant Italian regions and at later dates: Scipio Slataper, Giani Stuparich, and Italo Tavolato from Trieste; Giovanni Boine from Porto Maurizio (Liguria); Giovanni Amendola from Naples; Luigi Ambrosini from Fano (the Marches); and Renato Serra from Cesena (Emilia-Romagna). Yet just as there is something very Milanese in the pomp and excess of futurism, so there is something unmistakably Florentine about the exacting prose and intensely critical spirit of *Leonardo* and *La Voce*. After the demise of *Leonardo* in 1907, Prezzolini, Papini, and Soffici did try to launch a new journal, called *Il Commento,* in Milan; but it failed after one issue, and the next spring they returned to Florence, acknowledging that it was in Tuscany that they felt their deepest roots.

Much as they sought to reinvigorate the public life of their own city, the central aspiration of the Florentine avant-gardists was to produce a new political culture for Italy, indeed a "new Italy" altogether. But a key aspect of their vision of a new Italy was that it should build on the nation's regional strengths, knitting them together in a more federalized state, rather than suppressing their vitality and attempting to control everything from the center in the manner of Napoleonic France. The latter strategy, which had been the basis of the Kingdom of Piedmont's unification of Italy in 1861, had succeeded, in their view, only in producing an élitist politics of compromise and pettiness, a system of bureaucratic and parliamentary patronage known as *trasformismo*, a political system incapable of dealing with the country's deep social and economic problems or of involving the masses in political life.

The newly unified nation had faced humbling problems everywhere it turned. Politically, it suffered from a long history of territorial division and subjugation, a minuscule and corrupt political élite without much experience in self-government, and the lack of an established civil society and culture, even of a common language. Italy's social ills were reflected in high levels of illiteracy, low levels of technical knowledge and skill, divisive cultural antagonisms among regions, and, especially in the south, widespread lawlessness and brigandage. Economically, it confronted an antiquated agricultural system, rampant mismanagement in agriculture and railroads, a pronounced gap in development between north and south, paltry natural resources, and tremendous debt after three wars with Austria and a civil war in the south (1860–1865). Thus, as Italy moved from the ecstatic expectations of the Risorgimento to the sober realities of independence, many experienced the change as an "age of poetry" giving way to an "age of prose."[22] This sense of the transition was heightened by the decidedly unheroic manner in which Rome was annexed in 1870, a symbolic moment that would become a virtual obsession among spiritual-nationalist writers of the next several generations. As we will see, the avant-garde in Florence built upon the tradition established by these writers, extending from Francesco De Sanctis and Giosuè Carducci to Alfredo Oriani and Benedetto Croce, and believed, as they had, that only through a reinvigorated culture could any of the nation's problems be resolved.

Looking back upon the decades after 1861 from the vantage point of 1915, spiritual nationalists such as the writers for *La Voce* would have reconstructed the historical logic of their political situation in something like the following terms. Confronted with reactionary, bickering local élites and illiterate masses in the various regions of Italy, especially in the south, Cavour and the Piedmontese had created a centralized state and organized it into fifty-nine roughly equal provinces (sixty-nine after Venetia and Rome were acquired), each governed by a prefect appointed by the minister of the interior, who was himself ultimately responsible to the king. This arrangement allowed the imposition of centralized rule, but only at the cost of a corrupt system of patronage (the notorious *trasformismo*) through which local élites and parliamentary deputies could be kept in line. In this way, the system could avoid having to incorporate the masses and the difficult job of "making Italians" (as former Piedmontese prime minister Massimo D'Azeglio had famously called it) that such incorporation would involve. Indeed, in the years after 1900, with the eruption of socialist and, to a lesser extent, Catholic masses into society, Giolitti had shown how the system of *trasformismo* could be extended even to them. The result was a political system, supposedly open to true parliamentary democracy, inside a social system essentially unchanged from the one that had existed through centuries of aristocratic paternalism and foreign rule. When Giolitti took the momentous step of establishing near-universal manhood suffrage in 1911–12, the masses were completely unprepared, and the only alternative to a still more reactionary leadership like that of old conservatives such as Antonio Salandra (who did in fact take control in March 1914), became the social-revolutionary propulsion of Italy into the First World War. By failing to create the civil society and culture that could support its institutions, liberal Italy had sealed its own doom.

To begin to build the civil society and culture that might have permitted a genuine mass politics in Italy had been the Florentine avant-garde aim, especially in *La Voce*. But like earlier writers in the spiritual-nationalist tradition, their goals were rent by contradiction. Most of their efforts did not really address a mass audience but an alternative élite. In part, this élitism reflected their own strivings for cultural preeminence, but it also represented their realization, no less than that of their foe Giolitti, that efforts to do decades' worth of mass education in a few years risked mobilizing the masses for a politics either far more traditionalist or socialist than they themselves could ever support.

Yet the Florentines never limited themselves to local-regional or even spiritual-nationalist aims, but always sought above all else to link the avant-garde culture of Florence to the broader movement of European modernism. They were responding not simply to Florentine or Italian problems but to a crisis of values in European civilization, to Nietzsche's proclamation of nihilism and the death of God. Certainly they were not the first Italian intellectuals to sense this civilizational crisis. There were intimations of it already in the 1870s, both in the intellectual culture of Milan that produced the literatures of *scapigliatura* (bohemianism) and *verismo* (roughly, Italian naturalism), and in the moralizing literary culture that sought to confront the post-romantic situation with a more classicist sensibility. The major figure in the former tradition was the novelist Giovanni Verga, a Sicilian living the 1870s and 1880s in Milan's bohemian Brera district, and in the latter, the poet Carducci, a Tuscan then living in Bologna. In Florence itself, the first steps toward overcoming the isolation of literary intellectuals by establishing a collective, avant-garde movement, had been taken in 1896 with the founding of *Il Marzocco*, a luxuriantly decadent review in the D'Annunzian style. But within a few years, *Il Marzocco* had devolved into mere style and had lost most of its initial avant-garde zeal. Only with the founding of *Leonardo* in 1903 did Florentine avant-gardism take full root, becoming institutionally established (albeit precariously until *La Voce*), genuinely philosophical, and extensively interconnected with the center of the European modernist movement in Paris.

1 Sources of Avant-Gardism in Nineteenth-Century Florence

In the spring and summer of 1910, Giuseppe Prezzolini published three articles on the people of Florence in *La Voce* that display a deep ambivalence about the life of the city and the surrounding region of Tuscany.[1] The articles were received with unusual interest, and there is good reason to believe that his attitude was widely shared among writers in the Florentine avant-garde, certainly by his close friends Giovanni Papini and Ardengo Soffici, both of whom wrote congratulating him on the articles.[2] Prezzolini and his friends all had great affection for the Tuscan landscape and for the simple virtues of its traditional, peasant-based culture, but they also saw the defects of that culture in sharp relief and were especially contemptuous both of the changes that had been imposed upon Florence by a poorly conducted modernizing process during the three decades in which they had grown up and of the inability of the old aristocracy in power to cope with these changes.

In the first of the articles, Prezzolini takes us on a typical day's walk through the city, a device that both personalizes his vision and draws us into it. He celebrates the "spectacle of the crowd" of "my" Florentines, with its wonderful mix of classes. At the same time he holds himself distant from them in Baudelairian fashion—"I don't believe I lost any time looking at them"—and much of his affection is poured into the landscape, into following "those winding streets that lead to Maiano and Settignano and Monte Ceceri, through pine forests and holly groves, and terraced hills of olive trees."

One still finds the old Tuscan character that Stendhal had described nearly a century before, he observes, and promptly cites several passages from the touring Frenchman's diary entries of January 1817, including the following gem: "The Florentine is the politest of mortals, the most meticulous, the most obedient to his painstaking calculations of prosperity and economy. In the street, his aspect is that of a clerk, employed at a salary of eighteen hundred francs a year, who, having just brushed his suit with careful affection and polished his own boots, is now hurrying off to his counting-house, so as to be punctual to the minute at his desk; nor has he forgotten his umbrella, for the weather is decidedly unsettled, and nothing ruins a good hat so readily as a heavy shower of rain."[3] But whereas Stendhal's tone is amused if somewhat patronizing, Prezzolini's gloss on his description seems more negative; the old Tuscan, he remarks, is characterized by "dryness of spirit, avarice, and fickleness." Of course by now there are also new Tuscans, immigrants from "the country and neighboring regions such as Romagna and Lombardy, even the south," who are, on the whole, more aggressive in advancing themselves and more generally active than the older type. Yet this new type does not seem to have fundamentally changed the culture of the city. Today's Florentine still "whistles well and makes cute little skips and jumps through the woods, but is not made for the peaks where snow and sky become confused for one another." More significantly, the long-standing local political order corresponding to this carefree ethos, one based on the "political moderation" (moderatismo) of an old Tuscan aristocracy that is far more passive than its Milanese counterpart, remains intact. It is an order that introduces small doses of practical reform in an effort to preserve traditional ways and the traditional structure of political and social power rooted in Florence's old families. It is an order "symptomatic of a spirit that is dry, ungenerous, little given to fantasy, more capable of epigrams, more skilled in understanding than in giving itself over to a cause." It is a paternalistic order, but a mild one—"without pitchforks or clubs and with comfortable jails."

Yet as we read further, we begin to sense that for Prezzolini a change did take place in this older aristocracy and the political order based upon it, one roughly coinciding with the incorporation of Rome into the newly independent nation in 1870:

> The mentality of the old Florentine is, however, always that of those days. He voted for the moderates, the great names of the aristocracy . . . who were a bit cliquish, if you like, but not profiteers, not ambitious, and very tight on matters of public spending. Certainly their mentality was in general rather petty, and they failed to comprehend, as their fathers in the Risorgimento had, the future of the country, and they had no conception at all of the problems

of a big city, such as water supply, sewers, trolley lines, railway stations, public health, and so on; and they did not understand later on—and this is their greatest fault—the workers' movement, which was building itself while the old élites, tied politically to high officials and once important but now retired functionaries, were unable to perceive the gathering storm of rebellion.

Never very aggressive or ambitious, the old aristocratic political class had functioned reasonably well in the era before mass politics and the problems brought on by urban modernization, much less well thereafter.

Turning to culture, Prezzolini finds a generally pervasive "narrow-minded philistinism and provincial pettiness" among the Florentines. "There are probably people more boorish," he writes, "but none who are so visibly boorish. Cursing, insolent, scoffing, boring with women and, behind their backs, ironic regurgitators of the abominable Anglicized or Frenchified Italian of the hotels, guidebooks, and travel dictionaries." Public life certainly exists but it is superficial, resting mostly on a great deal of public display, and full of nastiness. Florence is a place where one necessarily bargains for everything one buys so as not to robbed, he remarks, yet where, having concluded a purchase at half the original price, one is still likely to feel cheated.

Despite (or even because of) its magnificent cultural heritage, contemporary Florence is a city without artistic taste. People go to the galleries "not to see the paintings but to watch people looking at paintings," and the prevailing public taste is simply imposed by "academicians." The daily newspapers mirror the "general poverty of spirit, the bad taste of the traditionalist academy, and the lack of character and political passion that is fervid and generous." The best of these, *La Nazione*, is "decent, clean, sound," since at least it tells the truth, but it is written at a lamentably low intellectual level despite its origins in the Florentine élite culture of *moderatismo*. The only real alternative to it, *La Fieramosca*, "should have tried to become truly the 'newspaper of the people,'" but utterly failed to do so. "The *Fieramosca* is neither fish nor fowl, not popular enough to be enjoyed for its neighborhood gossip, and certainly not intelligent enough to be read with profit by an educated person." Moreover, in its pages no less than in *La Nazione*, we find perpetuated that pervasive myth of Tuscany as the region that lives "idyllically with 'harmony among classes,'" a myth based on complete hypocrisy. The Florentines, he declares, were simply "not born to engage in political opposition." They are too lazy and indifferent to their circumstances to become sufficiently aroused.

Despite the despairing tone in this last assessment, one that would appear far less often with the onset of the Libyan War a year later, it is clear that Prezzolini and his friends in the Florentine avant-garde sought to change this attitude fundamentally, to educate their contemporaries for political opposition, and simultaneously to begin to raise the level of cultural life to that of Paris, Vienna, or Berlin. By 1910 this avant-garde's activities, in publications such as *Leonardo* and *La Voce*, were entering their eighth year. Thus, despite a certain measure of disappointment evident at the progress made to date, these articles help to explain why the Florentine avant-garde arose in the first place. In this regard, Prezzolini's catalogue of complaints may be read as a list of clues: the establishment "myth of Tuscany" as a happy and prosperous place in no need of improvement; the nature of Florentine intellectual and university life, including the disproportionate role of foreign visitors and residents in the city's culture; the "modernization" of the city after 1864, which for many was extremely disruptive; the rise of socialism and other forms of working-class activism, as well as distinctly working-class quarters, in the 1890s; and the cultural atmosphere of "decadence" that immediately preceded the formation of an avant-garde.

The Myth of Tuscany and the Problem of the Post-Risorgimento

For no region of Italy was there so strong a myth regarding the "moderate" eighteenth- and nineteenth-century past as in Tuscany. Freed from the last of the Medici in 1737, Florence and Tuscany came under the benign rule of a collateral line in the Habsburg Empire, so the myth went, and entered a reformist golden age under Grand Duke Pietro Leopoldo, who ruled from 1765 until 1790, when his older brother, Joseph II, died and he was called to the throne in Vienna. During that quarter-century Pietro Leopoldo had overhauled the duchy's administrative structure, liberalized its trade policy, improved its semideserted and malaria-infested coastal lands (the Maremma), and launched an ambitious program of agricultural reform based on physiocratic principles. This reform aimed to increase agricultural production by converting formerly uncultivated state property to smallholdings and improving contracts and taxation within the traditional sharecropping *(mezzadria)* system. In this system, which dated from the late Middle Ages, landlord and tenant shared equally in the fruits of agricultural labor, the former providing the working capital (usually quite modest) and the latter the labor.[4] Its weakness was that it created severe limits on production and made tenants overly dependent on landlords, especially in years of bad weather. Still, *mezzadria* undoubtedly also had a certain genius, for it allowed the landlord to retain ultimate control of the wealth while making the tenant feel sufficiently secure and prosperous (and so separated by physical distance from his fellows) as to have no need to revolt. But aggressive versions of the myth went so far as to claim that the system was flexible enough to permit economic modernization without altering the traditional social structure, as Bettino Ricasoli was supposed to have proved at Brolio in the 1840s and 1850s. Even the myth's basic version was tendentious in interpreting peasant submission as a sign of contentedness.

Like most myths, however, this one contained enough truth to be plausible, especially to those who had experienced the political ravages of the agrarian system in less "enlightened" regions of Italy. It was true, for example, that institutions such as the Accademia dei Georgofili—the paternalistic and physiocratic society of landlords that had been founded in 1753—had improved the practice of agriculture in the region, even if it had also blocked the thoroughgoing commercialization necessary to make it competitive in the long term. It was also true that the House of Lorraine, under Pietro Leopoldo and, in the wake of the Congress of Vienna, under Ferdinando III (1815–1824) and especially Leopoldo II (1824–1859), had achieved a relatively nonrepressive form of political rule. Tuscany, famously, had in 1786 become the first Italian state to abolish the death penalty.[5] In the era of Grand Duke Leopoldo II it had become a liberal haven and the home of *Antologia* (1821–1832), the leading cultural journal of the day in all of Italy. Even when the Austrians were finally ousted in 1859, Leopoldo II had left Florence without the firing of a shot and with respectful farewells from many common citizens, who doffed their hats before his departing carriage. Yet the weaknesses of the myth were abundantly clear almost from its inception.

To finance his reformist projects without antagonizing the local aristocracy, Pietro Leopoldo had expropriated church funds and undercut the parish houses that had traditionally provided social services. His free-trade policy, which was at least partly motivated by the major British presence in the port of Livorno, had the effect of raising food prices and producing local shortages. Although little peasant opposition to him was apparent during his rule, the forcefulness of the "Viva Maria!" rebellion of 1799 against the French occupation made clear that peasant resentment had been seething for years.[6] That reaction also reflected underlying poverty and disease never effectively dealt with by Pietro Leopoldo. As a British agronomist, traveling in Tuscany on the eve of the French Revolution, wrote:

I was assured that these *metayers* [*mezzadri*] are (especially near Florence) much at their ease; that on holidays they are dressed remarkably well, and not without objects of luxury, as silver, gold, and silk; and live well, on plenty of bread, wine and legumes. In some instances this may possibly be the case, but the general fact is contrary. It is absurd to think that *metayers,* upon such a farm as is cultivated by a pair of oxen, can be at their ease; and a clear proof of their poverty is this, that the landlord, who provides half the live stock, is often obliged to lend the peasant money to enable him to procure his half; but they hire farms with very little money, which is the story of France; and indeed poverty and miserable agriculture are the sure attendants upon this way of letting land. The *metayers,* not in the vicinity of the city, are so poor, that landlords even lend them corn to eat: their food is black bread, made of a mixture with vetches; and their drink is very little wine, mixed with water called *aquarolle;* meat on Sundays only; their dress very ordinary.[7]

Such conditions worsened during the French occupation and persisted into the nineteenth century. Indeed, after independence the contradictions between the developing world market in agriculture and the Tuscan system intensified to the breaking point.[8] *Mezzadri* found it increasingly difficult to maintain the large extended families and other traditional arrangements the system required, and in 1881 the number of landless day laborers in the region increased to about 110,000, roughly the population of the city of Florence.[9] In such an atmosphere, the fear of the upper classes—both aristocrats and intellectuals—for the peasant masses was so integral a part of life as to be almost instinctual. The myth of Tuscany tacitly acknowledged that fear even as it sought to portray peasant submissiveness as a genuinely happy social order. The increasing emptiness of the myth would be fully revealed in 1921, in the explosion of peasant support for the fascists in the Tuscan countryside.

The disparity in Tuscan social life between surface calm and underlying disorder—punctuated now and then by strikes, food riots, and similar manifestations of discontent—is fully evident in Prezzolini's analysis of 1910. Yet it is also notable that he and his fellow *vociani,* as the writers for *La Voce* were generally called, did accept certain aspects of the myth. In an article on the Tuscany of Grand Duke Leopoldo II later that year, for example, Antonio Anzilotti referred to it wistfully as a "world of practical intelligence" and to Leopoldine Florence as "a moral center for Italy, a point of intersection, a place that had gathered and integrated the various activities" of the "cultivated classes."[10] Nostalgia for pre-independence cultural life, a belief that the peasantry had appreciated and been well served by the paternalistic politics of the Grand Duchy, a celebration of the life of the common people coupled with a subterranean fear of and contempt for them—these were weaknesses to which many of the *vociani* sometimes succumbed. But they emphatically parted company with the myth in their estimation of the Tuscan élite and their sense of the deterioration of life under that élite after 1870. Despite their occasional nostalgia, none of them believed that it was either possible or desirable to return to an earlier era. They aspired to a modern culture that worked spiritually as well as technically, one that gave full expression to human creativity and purpose. That no such culture existed—indeed, that it seemed less likely with every passing decade to become a reality—was in their view above all the result of a failure of leadership.

On this point their analysis of Tuscany's culture and history converged with their estimation of post-Risorgimento Italy as a whole. Although the Italian independence movement had lacked a mass base, it had possessed, in their view, a vision of a dynamic polity with a genuine civic culture, above all in Giuseppe Mazzini. As intellectuals such as Francesco De Sanctis and Giosuè Carducci had perceived, in the early years of the new nation the political class had simply lacked the will to "make Italians," preferring to buy good will through patronage and to get rich through profiteering. Yet most of the members of this political class came not from a newly rising bourgeoisie but from the traditional large landowners and old aristocratic families. Again and again in their writings in *Leonardo* and *La Voce*, the young Florentine intellectuals had meditated on this failure of leadership, often by reflecting on the ideals associated with men such as Mazzini, De Sanctis, and Carducci.

At twenty-two, Mazzini had sent to the Florentine journal *Antologia* an article claiming that Dante's *Monarchia* had been a call for Italian unification.[11] The journal's editors judged the argument too daring and rejected it, and four years later, in 1831, Mazzini moved from Savona (near his native Genoa) into his long exile. Among Italian exile organizations, Mazzini's Giovine Italia lay between the extremes of the secret societies of the Carbonari and the Parisian group around Filippo Buonarroti. Unlike the former, Mazzini was unionist and republican; unlike the latter, he was anti-Jacobin and less egalitarian, although he shared Buonarroti's commitments to popular sovereignty, mass education, and political participation. His great fear was that Italy would become Piedmontized rather than genuinely unified, and when this was borne out by events, he became bitter and disillusioned. In 1870, just as Rome was being incorporated into the new Italian nation, he wrote privately that "the Italy I see before me is nothing but a corpse."[12]

It was this late, disillusioned Mazzini who most attracted the Florentine avant-garde. In 1906, for example, Papini reminded his readers that "Mazzini had dreamed of a Third Rome—in a somewhat too spiritualist, revolutionary, and Lammenais-like manner, but a noble and grand Rome nonetheless. Mazzini's Third Rome ended up somewhere between Giovanni Bovio's sallies of anticlerical rhetoric and its actual existence as a quarter for petty clerks and foreigners. The ideal Third Rome should be born of our will and our work, and if my contemporaries do not begin to feel this necessity strongly they can simply leave me be."[13] Later, in his autobiography of 1912, Papini recalled that in the era of *Leonardo* "I had asked myself what was the role, the mission of Italy in the world. And I could find no answer. It was then that I began, with Mazzini's disregard for proper timing, my 'campaign for a reawakening through force' . . . I wanted my country to do something of her own, to play her part among nations. I wanted Italians to throw away the rhetoric of past *risorgimenti* and to propose for themselves a great common cause. After 1860 there had no longer been any Italian national sentiment or common thinking. It was time to get back on that road. A nation that does not feel in itself a messianic passion is destined to collapse."[14]

Although Papini chided Mazzini for his inefficacy, and although neither he nor his friends shared Mazzini's republicanism or his concept of unification by centralization, they did appreciate his belief in the need for a secular religion of spiritualized nationalism. They also shared his sense of the sanctity of the nation, his aim of creating interclass social solidarity, and his appeal to youth to forge a new Italy. Moreover, they conceived of themselves quite explicitly as present-day Mazzinis leading a revival of his hopes.[15] Specifically, their aim was to spark the "intellectual and moral reform" Mazzini had called for in one of his last published writings, a reform that would educate Italians for citizenship as well as (in their view) the Nietzschean world of the death of God.[16]

Formulated by Ernest Renan in 1871 amid the double shock of the Prussian victory and the insurgent Paris Commune, the concept of an "intellectual and moral reform" made as major an impact on the political climate of the early post-Risorgimento as it had in France.[17] In addition to Mazzini's essay, it inspired a number of important essays by De Sanctis in the 1870s.[18] Though most famous for his *Storia della letteratura italiana nel secolo XIX*, De Sanctis was as much politician and political critic as literary historian, having served as a parliamentary deputy and three times as minister of education in the 1860s. What he and Mazzini found in Renan was not so much a political program—indeed, Mazzini explicitly warned against what he regarded as Renan's reactionary tendencies—but a general project and a moralizing temperament and outlook perfectly fitted to the Italian national problem. In one of his most famous appropriations of Renan's idea, which Prezzolini would later deploy as the epigraph to his review of *La Voce*'s first year, De Sanctis had proclaimed: "There remains a final program: political unification is in vain without intellectual and moral redemption. This program was not given to Mazzini, nor is it for the present generation to fulfill; it remains entrusted to the new generation."[19]

Like Mazzini, De Sanctis had been severely disappointed by the development of post-Risorgimento politics. In countless speeches and essays, he castigated the Italian ruling class as morally weak and inept, sometimes corrupt. Born in a small village near Naples, and a battle-scarred veteran of the Neapolitan revolution of 1848 who suffered in prison for thirty-three months after its close, De Sanctis was particularly embittered by the repeated use of extraconstitutional martial law to put down the civil war in the south in the 1860s. "I condemn private individuals who break the law," De Sanctis declared in a parliamentary speech of November 1862, "but there is nothing worse than a Government, whose duty it is to defend the law, using the immense power given it by the country to violate the law."[20]

The tendency of the government to rule by force, however, was simply the logical correlative of its failure to pursue a politics of civic and moral education, especially as the years wore on. It was this greater failure which preoccupied De Sanctis in his Renan-inspired essays of the 1870s. In a passage from his best-known essay, one that brings to mind similar reflections by Max Weber on "science as a vocation" half a century later, he declared:

I hear it said that science has made Germany great . . . The qualities that make peoples great are not created by science; it finds them already in place. It can analyze them, look for their origins, follow their development, determine their effects; it can also moderate them, correct them, turn them to this or that end. One thing it cannot do: it cannot produce them, and where it finds them wearied and worn, it cannot replace them. No, it cannot say, where the religious sentiment languishes: "I am religion." Nor can it say, where art has become sterile: "I am art." It can give you a philosophy of history, of language, of man, of the state, but it cannot give you history, language, man, the state. It gives you the knowledge of life but not life itself; it gives form but not material; taste but not inspiration; intelligence but not genius.[21]

One could not hope to build a modern Italy simply by investing in science. Nor could one build the nation simply by investing in economic infrastructure or pursuing more rational economic policies, important as those might be. The fundamental requirements were civic and moral: the nurturing of religious faith and an education in such virtues as "moral courage, sincerity, initiative, and discipline."[22]

De Sanctis was a philosophical-minded man, a somewhat unorthodox Hegelian in the Neapolitan idealist tradition of Vico, and this historicism had a salutary effect on his thought, buffering him against the pessimism his view of the post-Risorgimento might otherwise have provoked. By intellectual disposition he was much more moderate and philosophically high-flown than Carducci, the other great literary figure of his era in Italy. The latter was also much more rebellious in temperment and in ideals—a self-conscious "pagan" who sang hymns to Satan and who had no use for idealism or historicism. Yet Carducci's virtues were remarkably similar to De Sanctis'. As Papini would write in *Leonardo*, Carducci possessed "certain qualities that are rare among us: pride and daring, dislike of small talk, sincerity and a sense for the grand."[23] It was for these qualities, rather than for his poetry and literary-critical talents, that he seemed exemplary to the young Florentines of Papini's generation.

Born in 1835 in Valdicastello, a hamlet just north of the port of Viareggio, Carducci grew up somewhat farther south, in the Maremma, the poor, peasant-dominated area of coastal Tuscany, and came to Florence when he was twenty-one. Four years later he took a professorship at the University of Bologna, where he remained until three years before his death in 1907. Though not of peasant origin, Carducci strongly identified with the common people and never lost his sense for their way of life. "I enjoy . . . being a plebeian at the right time and place, in my concepts and forms, in my vocabulary itself and in my images, in language and style, poetry and prose, just as Aristophanes the conservative, Dante the gentleman of Roman blood, Montaigne, and Saint-Simon were plebeians."[24] Commenting upon this passage, Papini wrote that Carducci's plebeianism did not undercut his refinement as a man of culture, but rather made him a "man of nature" in the Nietzschean sense, for whom "Christianity is . . . a long and debilitating illness" from which we can recover only by recommitting ourselves to a pre-Socratic form of reason in tune with the naturalness of spirit.[25] In Papini's view, Carducci's Tuscan origins gave him access to such a reason and were the key to understanding his preferences for paganism over Christianity and classicism over romanticism.

In his early work, Carducci sought primarily to stimulate nationalistic pride through recovering the classical traditions of Rome and the Italian Renaissance. At times this project tempted him to assert the "primacy" of Italian culture over that of other European nations, and much of his writing is resolutely antiforeign.[26] Although this attitude became more moderate in later writings, Carducci never tired of bemoaning the unfortunate influence on Italian youth of foreign writers, above all French ones, whom he regarded as "decadent." In a typically anguished pronouncement of 1894, he declared: "From foreign literatures, Italians today read only recent French writers; in literature we have become a French *département* . . . Our criticism has been reduced to the rapidly changing nomenclature of this new country of ephemeral writers: Parnassians, realists, naturalists, decadents, symbolists, mystics. A young Florentine asked me if it did not seem to me that Dante was a decadent. [I replied that] to me all of you seem decadent. You whimper about the ideals you lack . . . But you should hold your tongue rather than utter your worthless, immature pronouncements."[27] Yet the decadents were merely taking to an extreme attitudes that had prevailed for decades in European romanticism. While Carducci himself was not without some romantic tendencies, above all in his yearning for the spiritual rejuvenation of his nation and in his belief that the best art had deep roots in folk expression, he believed that the romantic tradition was far too tainted by individualism, sentimentalism, and privatism to be appropriate to the cultural needs of contemporary Italy.

To judge from his aesthetic attitudes, one might imagine that Carducci was an active political opponent of post-Risorgimento politics. Yet although he had held Mazzinian republican sentiments in his youth, he reluctantly surrendered them in the years after 1870. Similarly, although he had led a short-lived avant-garde circle in his years in Florence (1856–1860) called, ironically, the Amici Pedanti (Friends of Pedantry), after 1860 he declared:

because my desire that the people speak of me is by now exhausted . . . and recognizing that the present age is completely "Alexandrine," as much in its craving for criticism and erudition that in the end kill art and emotion as in its tiny, troubled rivulet through which art, philosophy, and even politics are advancing, I feel like doing little or nothing. And for me to act means to conceive and imagine beautiful things and ideas with beautiful forms, that is, poetry . . . The age of poetry will return, certainly; but it is dead for us, and dead for the whole of this old Europe and this weary and faint-hearted society. After the last great poets, Goethe, Byron, and Leopardi, who mourned the old philosophy, the old aristocracy, the old individualism, there can be no more poetry until the new age, of faith, of the people, of social freedom. Between these two ages there can be neither poetry nor art: to look back at the past is useless, to look forward to the future can appear mad. So then? Erudition, criticism, philosophy, in short Alexandrinism [*alessandrinismo*].[28]

For the *vociani* this complex of attitudes was flawed in two related ways. First, insofar as Carducci was political, he suffered from the "democratic illusions" of Mazzinian republicanism, although, since his political formation predated the discoveries of élite theorists such as Gaetano Mosca and Vilfredo Pareto, he himself was perhaps not culpable. "The scientific and historical critique of the illusion of democracy," wrote Papini on the eve of fascist ascendancy, "came too late to show Carducci that reason does not always result in justice or at least that if an insufficient reason leads us toward the rule of the many, an adequate form of reason leads us toward rule by the few."[29] Second, insofar as he gave up on both politics and poetry out of "Alexandrinism," Carducci himself came dangerously close to the decadence he so forcefully decried. As Prezzolini recalled in 1912, his own generation had been born into a world in which "art had devolved into sensualism and aestheticism without faith or belief; from Carducci, whom our fathers read accompanied by Tuscan wine and cigars bought from street vendors, one passed on to D'Annunzio, the idol of our dandyish older brothers."[30] Yet on this point, too, they were not inclined to hold Carducci personally liable.

Carducci used his belief that he had been born "between two ages" to justify what he recognized as his descent into philological obscurities and cultural-political quietism. Prezzolini, Papini, and their friends likewise saw themselves as living "between two worlds."[31] But they drew much more activist consequences from this view, believing that they had the freedom and the obligation to bring the "new world" into being. In part their greater aggressiveness reflected their sense of Carducci's fate. His Alexandrine posture had led to his being canonized by the cultural establishment and made into an icon of academism, even though his true message was that "the poet should be the fighter against the bullies and cowards, the derider of the vicious, the castigator of clowns, the champion of the nation, the advocate of the people, the defender of the lower classes . . . that is to say, civic, patriotic, and moralist . . . the instrument for straightening out and improving Italy."[32] The problem Carducci came to symbolize for them was how to "revive the Carduccian spirit" while castigating the false academic "cult" that had so shamefully misappropriated him.[33]

The charitableness of the Florentine avant-garde toward Carducci had at least three sources. First, they felt personally close to him, both because he was a Tuscan and because they had encountered him while growing up. Papini, for example, recalled that as a boy he had been so intensely drawn to Carducci's *Confessioni e battaglie* that he had made it the model of his polemical style of *stroncature,* and that when he had actually laid eyes on Carducci in the Biblioteca Nazionale in Florence in 1897, "I rose to my feet, completely dumbfounded, like a newly recruited infantryman who sees his general pass."[34] Similarly, Soffici remembered having seen him on the street in "1898 or 1899" with his "grey head of hair ruffled under a black bowler hat, no longer leonine but shaky and humbled, though still indicative of an ancient fierceness and with flashing small eyes that were dark and almost ferocious."[35] For Prezzolini Carducci's image was no less heroic, but it was balanced by the intimacy of having actually met the man, who was a friend of his father, several times while growing up.[36]

Second, Carducci was dear to the generation of 1880 as the latest major exemplar of the "good" Italian literary tradition—the "plebeian," "realist," and "masculine" tradition of Dante—as against the "elegant," "empty," and "feminine" tradition of Petrarch, most recently embodied in D'Annunzio and other "decadents."[37] For Papini in particular, resurrecting the moral virtues of Carducci and overturning this Petrarchan tradition assumed the character of a triumphal return of a repressed "masculine" culture of "stone," and a dethroning of the prevailing "feminine" culture of "honey."[38] Despite his quietistic behavior, Carducci had a "ferocious" spirit that made him a most important ally in this key cultural struggle. Their older brothers had not perceived this spirit because, as is perhaps inevitable in the swing of generations, they had been too busy reacting to it. Less involved in overcoming Carducci, the new generation could perceive his spirit and, more important, link it to the form of action Carducci himself had failed to undertake.[39]

Finally, even if Carducci had to some extent capitulated to the academic conformism and quietism of post-Risorgimento intellectual life, the generation of 1880 recognized that he had resolutely maintained his personal independence and had never allowed himself to be absorbed into the ranks of the reigning élite culture of *moderatismo*. Moreover, his Amici Pedanti was arguably the only group in the entire history of Florence before 1890 that the new cultural avant-gardists could regard as an ancestor of their own efforts.

Intellectual Life, the University, and Foreigners

While Florentine high culture during and after the Risorgimento was certainly among the most liberal and progressive in Italy, it was still only cautiously reformist and always closely tied to the city's old families. Perhaps its most notable achievement in the first half of the nineteenth century was the establishment of *Antologia*, a dignified and sophisticated monthly review cofounded by a young bourgeois from Geneva, Gian Pietro Vieusseux, and an aristocrat from one of the city's best-known families, Gino Capponi. Capponi had gone on a European grand tour at the end of 1818 and, over the next two years, had developed a passionate ideal of Europeanism as well as a specific model for its cultural dissemination based on the *Edinburgh Review*. Meanwhile, after some years as a merchant in Oneglia, Vieusseux had applied his business and organizational talents to journalism. In 1818 and 1819 he had worked on the Milanese *Conciliatore*, and had come to Florence in early 1820 when it was suppressed by the Austrians. Together, Capponi and Vieusseux assembled a group of contributors from throughout Italy, including leading literary figures such as Ugo Foscolo and Giacomo Leopardi, and from France (including Alphonse de Lamartine) and England as well. Although its print run never exceeded 800 copies, *Antologia* was soon recognized as the finest Italian review of the day.[40] Its articles covered a wide range of topics in ancient, foreign, and contemporary Italian literature, moral philosophy, history, economics, geography, education, and even natural science, archaeology, agriculture, and medicine. As Mazzini discovered, however, it rarely touched politically sensitive themes, and never directly engaged political issues. The caution seems to have been fully warranted: the Grand Duke Leopoldo II suppressed the journal in a moment of crisis early in 1833.

In addition to *Antologia*, Vieusseux founded a library, the Gabinetto Vieusseux, which quickly became one of the most important cultural institutions in the city and was sufficiently enduring to be honored with a place on the main floor of the beautiful Palazzo Strozzi when the latter was finally restored in 1937. The library served diverse purposes. Dostoyevsky is supposed to have gone there daily to read Russian newspapers during the nine months he spent in Florence in 1868–69 while finishing *The Idiot*.[41] It played an equally significant role for young autodidacts like Prezzolini and Papini, for whom books were as difficult to obtain as they were urgent. But although Vieusseux's influence on Florentine culture lingered with the library, the liberal Enlightenment culture he represented became more and more remote from the popular life of the Risorgimento era. Some years after the last issue of *Antologia*, the Grand Duke did allow Vieusseux and Capponi to collaborate again on the important *Archivio storico italiano*, but as the title suggests, this was a more specialized enterprise safely removed even from the mildly reformist ambition of influencing public opinion or politically educating an élite.

In the tumultuous days of February 1848, the Grand Duke granted a constitution, modeled on the French constitution of 1830, in order to support moderate elements over more radical ones. But he was unable to control the political situation, which devolved from moderate governments (the last of them led by Capponi) into a much more radical one, and finally into the Jacobin-style dictatorship of a onetime novelist from Livorno, Francesco Domenico Guerrazzi. Even before this last government, Leopold was forced in February 1849 to seek refuge at the pope's residence at Gaeta, on the Mediterranean coast south of Rome. His restoration two months later, solely as a result of a decisive victory by the Austrian army over Piedmont, together with the dashed hopes of self-rule, made the 1850s a dismal decade for Tuscany and set the stage for the one radical cultural experiment of the era, Carducci's Amici Pedanti. The group had a brief existence, from 1856 to 1858, while events again reversed direction, pushing Tuscany and then Italy to full independence. The cultural hegemony of *moderatismo*, never seriously threatened, was fully restored after Tuscany achieved independence on April 27, 1859.

No event better symbolized the connection between independence and Tuscany's élite culture than the establishment that July of *La Nazione,* which remained virtually unchallenged thereafter as Florence's leading daily newspaper. *La Nazione* was established at the behest of Bettino Ricasoli, leader of the newly independent state until he became prime minister of Italy in June 1861. Ricasoli was primarily concerned that traditionalist sentiment would support the ideal of a "Toscanina" (Little Tuscany) in opposition to any absorption of Tuscany into a united Italy. As the paper's name (which he suggested) implied, *La Nazione* was established specifically in order to champion the idea of a united Italy, although its editors also hoped to use it to make Florence visible as the cultural capital of the new nation.[42]

Shortly after the founding of *La Nazione,* Florence saw the birth of a cultural and scholarly monthly that soon rivaled it in quality and impact. The *Nuova Antologia* was launched in 1866 by Francesco Protonotari, a professor of political economy at the University of Pisa. Like the model from which it derived its name, it aimed to raise élite culture to a cosmopolitan level even as it steered clear of the politically controversial. As Protonotari wrote in an impassioned but politically guarded and somewhat ambiguous prologue to the first issue:

We know very well that the old *Antologia* was an enterprise no less civil than literary, and that today Italy is rising up to the realization of its national and political destinies with other means and along other roads. To this we say that any literary enterprise that is neither commercial nor frivolous should be a great source of civilization. And if in earlier days science and letters were already bursting with the heat of coming events, today we should take up our task not very differently, preparing with new ideas new and difficult measures of social improvement. If the danger has ceased, and boldness today is of a different nature, the germs of a modern thought that we cultivate can still be almost as valuable and fruitful. No sensible man can foresee much good in a political *risorgimento* when an intellectual movement fails to accompany it or to follow close behind. Today in Italy there is a justified desire for and a painful and impatient expectation of such a movement.[43]

Nuova Antologia, then, would take up the enterprise of "intellectual and moral redemption," as De Sanctis would soon call it, but it would do so while carefully avoiding political passion. Although the journal did run a regular article-length survey of national politics, Protonotari was careful simply to have this cast as an objective review, one that raised questions but avoided polemic and strong views. Moreover, when he did run an article on a political subject, especially in the early issues, he sometimes inserted an introductory note justifying the piece in the interest of advancing "wide and fertile discussion of those ideas that can divide the country."[44]

Like that of its predecessor, the educational strategy of *Nuova Antologia* was to present massive amounts of information on every imaginable artistic, literary, historical, natural scientific, and social scientific topic. One consequence, intended or not, was that in volumes running 2,500 pages per year or about 200 pages per monthly issue, the personalities and views of individual authors inevitably became submerged by the weight of the whole. Nonetheless, the journal did have prominent contributors. Carducci wrote a number of literary articles for it in its early years, although he was dissuaded from pursuing more political themes.[45] De Sanctis also wrote for it, especially during the four years (1867–1871) he lived in Florence. But for him these were years of "absolute and complete dedication to study, with no public activity, neither cultural . . . nor political," and most of his articles for *Nuova Antologia* were merely drafts for chapters of the *Storia della letteratura italiana* on which he was busily engaged.[46]

From an internal point of view, the review's chief problem in its early years was financial. So long as it was located in Florence, Protonotari was simply unable to avoid falling into debt, and by 1878 he felt compelled to move it to Rome and make it a biweekly. Although it has remained at the center of establishment cultural life in Italy ever since, Florence and Tuscany would arguably never replace it.

Yet in that same year, as if to do just that, there emerged the *Rassegna settimanale*, edited by two conservative landowners of Tuscan-Jewish background, Sidney Sonnino and Leopoldo Franchetti. This review, however, was actually quite different from Protonotari's, though no less distinguished. Sonnino and Franchetti had made their mark earlier in the decade with a sociological study comparing the agricultural system of the Italian south with the Tuscan version.[47] Together with other contributors, including Pasquale Villari, a distinguished Neapolitan historian of Renaissance Florence who had immigrated to Florence and was teaching at the university, and Giustino Fortunato, a landowner from Basilicata who served as the review's Naples correspondent, Sonnino and Franchetti hoped their efforts would unsettle the complacency and opportunism with which the northern political élite's pursuit of laissez-faire, *trasformismo,* and related policies of self-enrichment willfully overlooked oppressive conditions in the south. Fervent believers in the "myth of Tuscany" and its system of *mezzadria,* they were motivated in part by paternalistic moral concern for the south but, above all, by a desire to educate the general public so that it might develop, or at least support, a more reasonable alternative to the ruling élite. As they wrote in a joint editorial in the very first issue, their goal was "to make sure the Italian public is continuously informed on those great questions of a scientific and literary sort that are debated among the other civilized nations. At present, the echo of their discussions reaches us too late, and even then is heard only by the learned and the specialists, not by the educated public in general."[48]

Although the editors of the *Rassegna settimanale* would persevere at or near the center of local and national politics for decades to come, the journal itself lasted less than a year in Florence and, even after moving to Rome, came to an end in 1882. In the 1880s Florentine alternatives to the establishment press, though plentiful—police records indicate that eighty-three journals existed in Florence in 1889—were mostly either low-level tabloids or small, financially weak, and correspondingly erratic and short-lived reviews.[49] Of the first variety, the most noteworthy was the *Fieramosca,* which Prezzolini would lampoon as the newspaper for "doorkeepers and maids" that was too blind to its own nature to recognize itself as such.[50] Yet during the three decades after its founding in 1881, it represented the only real threat to the local circulation of *La Nazione.* Typical of the second variety was the anarchist *Questioni sociali,* edited by Errico Malatesta in Florence from December 1883 until May 1884, and then for another six months four years later at Pisa. On the literary-cultural front, there were by the end of the decade some incipient avant-garde efforts such as *Vita nuova,* which during its brief existence (1889–1891) published articles by such future luminaries as Benedetto Croce and Luigi Pirandello, as well as a steady diet of somewhat "Alexandrine" literary criticism from the young men of its own circle. A few years later the same group would develop the much more ambitious and successful *Il Marzocco* (1896–1932). But even to the extent that the journals of this second type endured, they were either too partisan and extremist or too withdrawn and intellectualist to create a sense of genuine public discourse or public space.

Nor was such a space opened by the creation in 1859 of a Florentine university, the Istituto di Studi Superiori Pratici e di Perfezionamento, although this institution would ultimately produce effects unintended by its founders.[51] Like *La Nazione*, the Istituto was created at Ricasoli's initiative to meet a specific political objective, in this case the need for an élite educational institution for professional training and scientific research on the model of the Collège de France.[52] Initially the Istituto contained four divisions: law, philology and philosophy, medicine and surgery, and natural sciences. In 1875 a division of social science was added. In each of the divisions the leading figures were frequently positivists such as the historian Pasquale Villari. Ironically, leading positivists from Europe's intellectual centers, such as the German chemist Ugo Schiff and the Russian Darwinian biologist Alexis Herzen, were recruited precisely at the moment that the positivist ideal was there entering its most profound crisis. Naturally, however, not every faculty member was a positivist. At the turn of the century, students and "auditors" (such as the young Giovanni Papini) enjoyed lectures by Felice Tocco, an idealist philosopher who had been a student of Bertrando Spaventa.[53] But idealists were far more common in the student body, which in 1897–98 included such future leading lights as Giovanni Gentile, Rodolfo Mondolfo, and Giuseppe Lombardo-Radice.

Despite its élitist aspirations, however, the cultural impact of the Istituto on Florence was a complex matter that cannot be reduced to a typical "town–gown" split, with élitism and positivism on the one side and a traditionalist, antiscientific popular culture on the other. Nor did the division between professoriate and average citizens exactly reproduce the political division between aristocratic *moderatismo* and a peasant-oriented traditionalism yearning for a "Toscanina." Although it is likely that the élitism and prestige of the professoriate made them appear aloof, even disdainful, to Stendhal's old Florentine, it is not clear that this attitude provoked much in the way of genuinely populist reaction. More obviously, its effect was to stimulate an intense rivalry between the professoriate and groups of non-university intellectuals, especially the struggling petit-bourgeois variety of the café, who felt unfairly denigrated and excluded by the academy. The effect of this rivalry, however, was hardly to encourage the latter group to cultivate popular favor. On the contrary, it probably reinforced decadentist tendencies toward withdrawal and, in some cases, toward reactionary politics. As Eugenio Garin astutely observed:

> From 1870 on, there is frequently present in Florence an extreme tension between the learned men of the Istituto and non-university intellectual groups. But if in this dialectic it may seem at times that the non-academics are the more audacious, in reality closure and conservatism reveal themselves behind their rebellious poses, whereas the culture of the professors appears the more open-minded even on the terrain of politics. Nor is this a strange thing: many of the professors, who were neither Florentine nor Tuscan, had been among the intellectual promoters of the national revolution. They had come out of the school of De Sanctis, like Villari, and they had seen teachers and friends imprisoned or killed by monarchical reactions. The revolutionary experience had not happened in vain for them: exiled, in contact with the most open-minded intellectual outlooks in Europe, they had become men of European resonance, anxious, now that national unity had been achieved, to continue on the path toward human emancipation.[54]

This division was certainly evident in a viciously ironic attack on Villari by Prezzolini in *Leonardo* in 1905.[55] Yet, interestingly, something very much like it would reappear within the ranks of *La Voce* when the intensely political and left-leaning Gaetano Salvemini, who had come to Florence to study with Villari at the Istituto and who remained his loyal pupil even while never embracing positivism, came into sharp conflict with the more artistic and nationalistic Papini and Soffici in the days leading up to the Libyan War of 1911.

Moreover, the university may have more directly stimulated the formation of an avant-garde by bringing to the city a great number of the best and brightest young students from throughout Italy. Not only did they account for a significant number of the subscribers to the Florentine journals, but many would eventually be counted among its contributors. In addition to Gentile, Lombardo-Radice, and Salvemini, university students later active in the city's avant-garde included Antonio Anzilotti from Pisa, Giuseppe Antonio Borgese from Palermo, and Scipio Slataper and Italo Tavolato from Trieste. On balance, then, it seems that what initially appeared as another indication of the enormous chasm that separated the dominant culture of aristocratic *moderatismo* from everyday life may have contributed, both indirectly and directly, to the avant-garde effort to create a greater sense of public space in the Giolittian era.

Foreigners, and foreign-born artists and poets in particular, also played a surprisingly significant role in the city's cultural life. Foreigners in Florence had always come in two basic varieties. There were, first, those who came to the city, especially in spring and summer, as an obligatory stop on the grand tour or, already in the early nineteenth century, as middle-class tourists. But there were also many foreigners who, attracted to Florence by its picturesque surroundings and leisurely pace of life, stayed for many months or even for years, developing separate "colonies" with their own institutions and ways of life. The largest of these was the English colony, which numbered perhaps 30,000 and was quartered primarily in the hilly Bellosguardo section, south of the Arno River. The colony had its own churches, cemeteries, schools, doctors, tailors, pharmacies, and grocers (with medicines and foodstuffs imported from England). There were also smaller communities from elsewhere in Europe, including Russia, Poland, and Hungary.

When Stendhal visited the city in 1817, he found an abundance of both foreign types. "The displeasing aspect of these gardens [the *Cascine*]," he wrote, "is that I find them constantly encumbered with some six hundred or so foreign visitors, English and Russian predominating. Florence is nothing better than a vast museum full of foreign tourists." As for the English colony, he declared that "the English, with their rigid caste-system, their meticulous observance of it and their firm resolve never to depart from it, even by a hair's breath, provide the material for countless satirical anecdotes."[56] Later French visitors to the city, such as the Goncourt brothers, who arrived in 1856, concurred in finding Florence "an entirely English town" and, as such, insufferable, except for its art museums.[57] Yet there is little evidence that the presence of so many English bothered the nineteenth-century Florentines themselves. Poets such as Robert and Elizabeth Barrett Browning and, to a lesser extent, Walter Savage Landor, all of whom lived for many years in Florence before the latter two died there in the early 1860s, felt warmly received and passionately involved in local life, even if their social contacts remained largely confined to its English and American residents and, insofar as they did involve native Florentines, tended to be restricted to its élite. Such assessments as we have from Florentines suggest that they regarded the English in particular as aloof and odd curiosities, but not as wholly unwelcome ones. Though written later, the evocation of late nineteenth-century British Florence by the poet and sometime *vociano* Aldo Palazzeschi is not atypical in its attitude:

> They lived a countrified life within the old city walls. Their customs were simple and dignified, their houses tastefully decorated with beautiful and authentic Tuscan items, chosen or unearthed with loving care when they were not yet appreciated among us. Among them one might meet some old impec-

cably dressed gentleman and some slightly evanescent young person who would hold polite conversations at tea time, laughing at the top of their voices at witticisms, wisecracks, or insignificant compliments (always among the guests was an officially recognized dog with a little monogrammed handkerchief in the small pocket of his jacket) or seriously discussing matters that not everyone present recognized as serious. They lived without really eating, filling themselves with trifles, candies, fruits, vegetables, and jams; their style of dress was what the mood had inspired; and when the gentle and slightly lazy observer among them became lost, it was not difficult to determine from which of the various churches and galleries, museums and chapels he had come.[58]

Not all the British in Florence were such idle bourgeois types, however, and native Florentines could hardly doubt that they made a contribution to the cultural and political life of the city. Perhaps the city's most famous English-born citizen of the late nineteenth century was Jessie White Mario, who at the age of twenty-three had met Garibaldi in Nice and become an impassioned fighter for Italian independence. In 1865 she chose Italy's new capital, Florence, as the place to pursue a more scholarly life. Among her accomplishments there in the four decades before she died in 1906 was a well-known biography of the Italian who had first inspired her.[59]

Most prominent among Russian émigrés was the anarchist Mikhail Bakunin, who chose Florence as his residence for fourteen of his first sixteen months in Italy in 1864–1865, perhaps because of its Russian exile community. That his was not an isolated existence, however, is clear from the fact that his initial residence was with Giuseppe Dolfi, a humble baker who had been the popular hero in the overthrow of the House of Lorraine in 1859. Bakunin moved from Florence to the warmer political climate of Naples in June 1865, but he left a devoted following among native Florentines that would eventually produce one of the city's first socialist organizations.[60]

Still more prominent in Florentine life were foreign-born writers, poets, and artists. Many of them, of course, merely passed through—like Oscar Wilde, who commemorated his Italian vacation in 1875 with a poem about the church of San Miniato; or Rainer Maria Rilke, who while vacationing in the summer of 1898 had encountered Stefan George in the Boboli Gardens entirely by chance; or André Gide, whose journal reports an absolutely typical tourist circuit in Florence in 1895, except that he was joined at the Caffè Gambrinus by the then more accomplished Italian novelist, Gabriele D'Annunzio.[61] Others stayed longer but made little contact with local intellectuals. Dostoyevsky appears to fall into this category. So too does Georg Lukács, who, after many visits to

Florence between 1908 and 1910, tried to publish a Hungarian-language journal, *A Szellem,* in the city in 1911, but who seems to have paid no attention to the *vociani,* then at the height of their influence and prestige.[62] But among the many who took up permanent residence in the city, perhaps the most influential at the turn of the century was Arnold Böcklin, the German-Swiss painter of huge, mystical, satyr-filled canvases, who lived in a villa at San Domenico with that most famous view of the city afforded by the hills to its north. Soffici would later recall how Böcklin had "lived among us" when Soffici was a student artist of nineteen and had been an important influence in his own early efforts to mix sensual and spiritual themes.[63]

Still, it is perhaps not surprising to read how the overwhelming cultural presence of foreigners in Florence could be experienced as humiliating, and indicative of a certain decadence in its way of life, by another of Soffici's compatriots in the Florentine avant-garde. At the futurist *serata* (evening) of December 12, 1913, Papini would castigate his native city on precisely this ground:

> Like Rome and Venice, Florence is put to shame by the fact that it is a city that does not live off the honest earnings of its living citizens, but off the indecent and miserly exploitation of the genius of its ancestors and the curiosity of foreigners. We need to have the courage to cry out, "We live on the backs of the dead and the barbarians. We are the caretakers of the mortuaries and the servants of exotic vagabonds" . . . Half of Florence lives directly off the backs of foreigners, and the other half lives off those who live off foreigners. If tomorrow the tastes and sympathies of these idiots from France, England, America, Germany, Russia, and Scandinavia who come here to make fools of themselves in front of Michelangelo, Giotto, and Botticelli were to change, our city would be ruined. In Florence, as soon as the people begin to suffer even a little, they say: "We lacked foreigners this year" . . . But all hope is not lost. When a city like ours goes out of its way to smother every vestige of vigorous life with its provincial narrow-mindedness and traditionalist [*passatista*] bigotry and yet manages to produce a group of young writers who, in *Leonardo, Il Regno, La Voce,* and *Lacerba,* have made Florence the spiritual center of Italy, this means that it is not completely screwed up.[64]

While the harshness and vulgarity of Papini's indictment were no doubt stimulated by its futurist setting, the idea that the weakness of the city's public life and its pervasive cultural complacency could be traced to an overwhelming presence of foreigners was widespread in the Florentine avant-garde. At the same time, their answer to that presence generally involved not xenophobic withdrawals into an exclusivistic *italianità*, but rather efforts at cultural renewal involving the education of the public to the level of comparable European cities and thus overcoming the "provincial narrow-mindedness and traditionalist bigotry" that the foreign presence paradoxically reinforced.

Modernizing Florence

In the catalogue of complaints found in Prezzolini's 1910 articles on Florence, the one regarding its intellectual life pertained at least to the entire previous century, as did the generalized lament about the lack of a genuine public life, the hegemony of a timid and restrictive *moderatismo*, the failure of the city's old families to exert forceful leadership, and the atmosphere of complacency typified by the myth of Tuscany. But Prezzolini clearly believed that the city had taken a turn for the worse after independence. Part of this can perhaps be explained by the fact that the city's new university life, far from helping to create a more extensive public space, had actually appeared to constrict further what little public space existed. The most dramatic changes in city life during this period, however, had to do with its brief and unhappy experience as the nation's capital and the efforts to "modernize" the city with which this experience was initially linked.

At the beginning of the fourteenth century, Florence had a population of about 100,000; five and a half centuries later, this figure had increased only modestly to about 135,000.[65] Nor had the character of economic life in the city changed fundamentally. A detailed survey of the businesses and trades within the city walls in 1865 reveals a mix of artisanal industry and commercial shops—grocers, wine merchants, shoemakers, tailors, and so forth—that would have contained few surprises for the inhabitants of 1300.[66] Significant development of modern industries was still three decades away. Nor was the city's physical aspect very different from the one it had attained at the height of its Renaissance building boom. Its look remained medieval, with its turreted houses, its narrow and dark streets filled with wagons, peddlers, and gamblers, and its lovely walls and gates, which shaped the city into two rough-hewn triangles north and south of the Arno. Beyond the walls lay peasants' fields still nourished as they had been for centuries from waterwheels driven by blindfolded donkeys. There, too, were the few industries—tanneries, candlemaking shops, varnish and paint factories—whose odors and other side effects prohibited a city location.

But if much remained traditional, population and resource pressures had begun to create a need for more space already in the 1830s, when a few remaining fields inside the city were converted to residential areas. An outbreak of cholera in 1835 and another in 1853 showed, however, that still more would have to be done to alleviate overcrowding, particu-

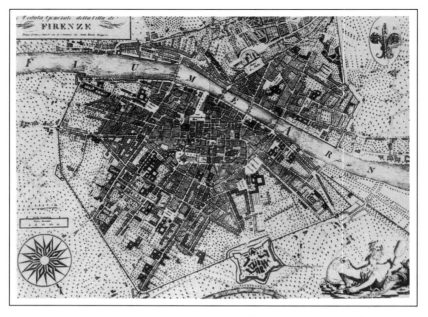

1. A map of Florence in 1826, when the city's walls and gates were still intact.

larly in view of the city's traditionally problematic water supply. Increasingly, the choice came to be perceived as one between converting remaining inner-city green space (mostly small parks and squares) into residences, or razing the walls so that the city could spread out into the countryside. It was a choice that would very shortly be made not by the Florentines themselves but by political forces at the national and international level.

In 1864 Napoleon III, who still held Rome, agreed to withdraw his troops from the city gradually over two years in return for a transfer of the capital from Turin to Florence, a city presumed to be more favorable to the pope. The Italian government accepted the proposal, and on the September day on which the announcement was made, thirty people died in rioting in Turin. But the protests were to no avail. On May 21, 1865, the minister of the interior arrived at the Palazzo Medici-Riccardi in Florence to supervise a transition involving 15,000–20,000 federal employees.

No public protests greeted the new government in Florence, but the move was not popular with its citizens either, as parliamentary elections the following October would show. In those elections, moderate deputies such as Ricasoli and Ubaldino Peruzzi, who were identified with the national government that had made the move even though they did not personally support the transfer, were voted out in favor of lesser-known radicals. Ironically, not a single member of the new government housed in the city was a Florentine. Fearing that it might delay rather than advance the day when Rome would be capital and strengthen "Toscanina" sentiments in the process, Ricasoli had called it a "cup of poison."[67] In a sense both he and the Florentines who had voted against him were right: the next five years would be a fiscal and architectural disaster for the city. Its treasury would be plundered so mercilessly that it would take a hundred years to recover. Its museums, palaces, and convents would be converted at great expense to governmental uses and then could not be converted back in 1871 for lack of funds. Worst of all, the city would be forced to craft a new master plan in a mere two months, with consequences that would be dire and irreparable.[68]

In order to create housing for 50,000 new inhabitants, the plan called, not surprisingly, for the destruction of the city walls and their replacement by wide boulevards (viali) of the sort already constructed in similar projects in Paris and Vienna. Begun in 1865 and finished four years later by the English "Florence Land and Public Works Company," the demolition used mines as well as picks to level the walls, then reused many of the stones as the bed for the new roadways. In the process a number of important monuments along the walls were destroyed. Once the roads were in place, new residential districts were built in the fields that had formerly stretched from the walls into the countryside. While most of these districts were bourgeois and of an unprecedentedly pure residential sort (one of which would later house Prezzolini and, for a time, the editorial offices of La Voce), at least one of them involved prefabricated housing for those former inner-city poor who could no longer afford the newly escalating rents. This housing was, however, of such poor quality that much of it was abandoned in 1871 when the government moved to Rome.

One consequence of these developments was a fundamental reorientation of the very concept of Florentine urban space. Until 1865 the walls had sharply defined "city" in relation to "country"; thereafter, as a continuous vista from the historic center to the hills south and north was opened up, the distinction became blurred. Indeed, new boulevards, such as the Viale dei Colli and the Viale Giuseppe Poggi (named after the main architect of the new master plan), were built to provide easy access from the city to the hills from which it could be viewed. More and more, the hills came to be identified as recreation areas (for Sunday outings and the like), the inner city for "business," and the areas in between for "residence," a tripartite division inspired by bourgeois life and quite unknown to pre-capital Florence. Rather than city and country, people began to speak more and more in terms of center and periphery.

A number of further changes followed from this fundamental one. To contend with the new distances, a horse-drawn "omnibus" service was established in 1865 by a firm from Bologna; a few years later a second such service arrived, courtesy of a firm from Hungary. Meanwhile, old buildings along the Arno were cleared to make way for new, wide pedestrian walkways *(lungarni),* which were completed in 1872. These were to function as promenades for the evening walk or for suburban dwellers who came into town on Sunday. In 1885, in part because of increasing complaints from "respectable" citizens about the dirt, crime, and disease in the area of the old market just south and east of the Palazzo Strozzi in the city center, the market was destroyed and replaced by a new square, the Piazza Vittorio Emanuele (now the Piazza della Repubblica) and, in 1902, by a new post office as well. The old market's major architectural monument, Vasari's Loggia del Pesce (fishmarket), was dismantled and then reconstructed farther away in the Piazza dei Ciompi. Alongside the new square, formidably barren except for an equestrian statue of King Vittorio Emanuele II at the center, were built the cafés that would become the city's most fashionable at the turn of the century: the Gambrinus, the Paszkowski, and the Giubbe Rosse. The symbolism of the change was unmistakable: in place of a lively (if also archaic and increasingly unhealthy) commercial center, whose shops were run by the people who lived in them and which drew crowds that mixed every social class, had come a stark square symbolizing the newly unified Italy and an entertainment district for foreigners and the local rich. Although the Florentine avant-garde would, on the whole, deplore this change, it was perhaps indicative of the contradictoriness of their position that the back room of the Giubbe Rosse would later serve as *Lacerba's* only true editorial office.

In a matter of two decades, then, the look and feel of Florence changed more than in the previous three or four centuries. From the tightly constricted space of a medieval walled city, it became a sprawling set of spaces, each increasingly identified with a use and, in many cases, a social class. While reasonable observers could and did disagree about whether this change had been inevitable and to what extent wise or unwise, clearly the costs had been high. Some very beautiful things had been lost, and it was difficult to deny that at least some of them might have been spared by a more gradually implemented and thoughtful urban plan. And why all the haste anyway? It had been justified only in order to facilitate an eventuality—the coming of the capital—that few wanted, that did not last in any case, and that left the city financially ravaged and its public life disrupted for years to come. In retrospect, it was clear as well that the changes had been made in a reactive and haphazard fashion, ungoverned by any overall concept of how public life in the new city was supposed to function, and that they had been motivated at least as much by private enrichment (primarily through speculation in real estate) as by public enhancement. Painfully little had been done to minimize the disruption, even devastation, that many of the city's poorer residents had suffered as their consequence.

Not surprisingly, the public mood of the late 1880s was one of some weariness and considerable nostalgia. After the demolition of the central market, a number of smaller projects of the same sort were abandoned. Yet, despite the widespread sense that too much had happened too fast, the changes that would occur in the next two decades were even greater than those of the previous two. For if the years from 1865 to 1885 had irreparably altered the city's traditional character, only in the two following decades would a modern character begin to replace it. These were the years of Florence's first streetcars, automobiles, electric street lights, telephones, and modern industries.[69] With the last of these came many other novelties: ideas like socialism, a human type called the industrial worker, and unprecedented possibilities of disruption when ideas and human types converged in the new political phenomena of strikes and general strikes.

The Impact of Socialism and Aestheticism

During the 1890s new working-class quarters sprang up throughout the city: in the east along the river near the old Porta Aretina, in the south near the old Porta Romana, and in the west and northwest, where the fields that had formerly stretched toward Prato now contained the most concentrated worker settlements at Pignone, Rifredi, and farther out in the new suburban town of Sesto Fiorentino. While the population of these areas was initially modest, it rose steadily, and by 1901 industrial workers accounted for 15.5 percent of the overall work force in the Florence area, three times what they had been only eight years before.[70] The industries in which they labored were a mix of new ones, such as chemical and steel, and modernized traditional ones such as textiles, ceramics, mining, and cement making. In terms of electoral politics, this industrial presence was unfelt until 1897, when Giuseppe Pescetti was elected to parliament as the city's first socialist deputy. In the years immediately thereafter, it remained for the most part a minor factor. But its effect was quite different at the level of street politics. From 1898 through 1904, a wave of political *sovversivismo* (subversion), which had been stimulated by recession and by the unbending *moderatismo* of the established political order, would raise the temperature of fear within that order to unprecedented levels.

There was little about the appearance of Florentine politics in early 1898, however, to suggest that the city was on the verge of crisis.[71] The mayor was a man from one of the city's old families, the Torrigiani. The city's leading political organization remained the monarchist "King, Country, Liberty, and Progress," founded in 1882 by Count Luigi Guglielmo de Cambray-Digny, still led by him as he neared the age of eighty, and in every way the "true living symbol of the traditions of Tuscan *moderatismo.*"[72] Still, the local socialists, no doubt stimulated by their success at the national level in mounting a unified Italian Socialist Party in 1892, had managed to bring together the remnants of Bakunin's anarchists and the more extreme republicans and radicals with the "republican-legalitarian" groups led by Pescetti into a new Florentine Socialist Union. Signs were also at hand that the polarizing effect of the Dreyfus Affair in France would have its local counterpart, above all as demonstrations by university students against French militarism. Complaints about the "lack of discipline" among university students were also becoming more insistent.[73] But only in the economic world were there clear signs of impending crisis. Despite emerging industrialization, the local economy was still overwhelmingly dependent on agriculture, and a bad harvest in 1897 had cut local income at the same time that the price of grain (and thus bread) had risen precipitously.

Whether city officials recognized that the state of the economy might provoke unrest is unclear, but the government in Rome did respond to the economic problem late in January 1898, offering to lower the excise taxes on grain and flour. Far from easing tension, however, the measure provoked hostility, the most visible manifestation of which in Florence was a stone-throwing attack on the offices of the liberal but pro-government *Fieramosca.* Such expressions of discontent, however, do not appear to have been understood by either the local or national élites. Although matters worsened still further in early spring, as the Spanish-American War disrupted oceanic trade and local rains brought flood waters from the Arno into many of the poorer neighborhoods toward Pignone on the west and Pontassieve on the east, little was done either in terms of economic policies aimed at reducing unemployment and easing prices or in terms of disaster relief. In May, on the day after four people were killed and ten wounded by police in Sesto Fiorentino during protests against the mounting price of bread, the largest demonstrations ever seen in the city were held. The official response, however, was repression rather than dialogue. From the *Fieramosca* and *La Nazione* came intensified criticism of Pescetti and other socialist leaders; from the prefect representing the national government, a ban on Florence's intransigent-Catholic newspaper, *L'Unità cattolica;* from city officials, the cementing of a liberal-monarchist alliance; from the police, more shooting and more deaths.[74] The climate of fear in Florence mounted still further as reports drifted in about a "revolution in Milan."[75]

Although the panic evident in the government response would cause the cabinet of Antonio di Rudinì to fall in June, the climate of fear behind that panic did not dissipate. On the contrary, it became a permanent feature of national life in the next decade. While Florence was certainly not Milan, its unrest seemed quite grave to most Florentines, especially in view of the myth of Tuscan political tranquility. In this persistent climate of crisis, the liberal-monarchist alliance proved difficult to hold together and suffered many brief periods of disarray over the next decade.

During May 1898 public services in Florence had been paralyzed for several days, and shattered street lights made the night seem especially perilous for many more. But the disruption was even worse during the next major political explosion at the end of August 1902. A labor dispute in Pignone, in which twenty-two metal workers were fired, quickly became a strike, and then escalated into a general strike with pickets *(squadre di vigilanza)* conducting open warfare in the streets and *piazze* of Florence. Shops were smashed and looted, especially on the most fashionable bourgeois streets, such as the Via Tornabuoni; railway and gas lines were severely damaged; streetcars came to a standstill except to transport soldiers; and all the newspapers were forced to shut down. The after-effects of six days of violence would be evident for weeks in the lingering piles of trash and debris. In retrospect it would be clear that the threat of socialism had reached a new level, marking the dawn of the era of general strikes and syndicalist violence.[76]

Two years earlier—and just days before King Umberto I was assassinated by an anarchist bullet at Monza—elections were held in which socialist candidates ran for parliament in three of the four Florentine districts, a radical republican in the other. Of the three socialists, one was Pescetti, the man who had given them their first victory in 1897; the second was Gaetano Pieraccini, a man little known and soon to be forgotten; the third was none other than Gabriele D'Annunzio.

Born into a family of bourgeois landowners in Pescara in 1863, D'Annunzio had gone to secondary school in Prato, just a few miles from Florence, and had published a book of poems, *Primo vere* (1879), while still an adolescent. During the 1880s, which he spent in Rome as a poetic importer of French "decadentist" fashion, his reputation as the rising star of Italian verse became consolidated. In the next decade he turned to a different genre. From 1889, when his highly acclaimed *Il piacere* appeared, until 1900, when the chronicle of his soured love affair with Eleanora Duse was issued as *Il fuoco,* he wrote six novels. Each centered on a male protagonist in search of spiritual meaning, mostly by means of sensual pleasure. Initially, in *Il piacere,* the hero was isolated, self-absorbed, and weak-willed, more romantically involved than but otherwise similar to his counterpart in Joris-Karl Huysmans' *A Rebours* (1884). Then, in 1892, D'Annunzio discovered Nietzsche through extracts in the Parisian *Revue Blanche,* and thereafter the aesthetic of his novels began to shift increasingly toward the celebration of action, violence, misogyny, and the myth of the superior man "beyond good and evil."[77] Both the novels and the occasional articles of this period make it plain that Nietzsche's ideas of the superman and will-to-power were understood biologistically and as doctrines.[78] The result was a myth of "two races"—nobles and plebes—scripted as the story of the noble artist-creator who mesmerizes, violates, and then discards the plebeian masses much as he does women.[79] Although D'Annunzio also flirted with the Wagnerian notion of the artist as the creator of a new secular-religious faith, his cultural stance remained individualist and aloof rather than avant-gardist.

Nonetheless, like Maurice Barrès in France, D'Annunzio was too absorbed by his own public image to isolate himself from politics entirely. Whether inspired by his Nietzscheanism or not, he had sought and won a parliamentary seat in 1897 as a conservative from Ortona in his native Abruzzo. That he was no ordinary conservative became clear, however, when, in March 1900, during angry debate in the Chamber of Deputies over a government measure curtailing civil liberties, he made the declaration that appeared to move him (and, in political practice, did move him), famously, to the opposite side of the aisle: "On one side I recognize many moribund men who scream and, on the other, a few men who are lively and eloquent: as a man of intellect, I go toward life."[80] In retrospect, D'Annunzio's "move toward life" appears as an early sign of a new Italian right, one that would combine traditionally conservative themes with a rhetoric of violence seemingly borrowed from the left. At the time, however, it appeared as a move toward defeat, given the failure of his reelection campaign under the socialist banner in Florence that June.

To run for his second term in Florence had made sense to D'Annunzio because he had moved in March 1898 to an old Capponi family villa, "La Capponcina," in the hills of Settignano southeast of Fiesole and a few doors away from the modest rented room of "la Duse." But although she was perhaps the city's main attraction for him, she was not the only one. The art critic and curator Angelo Conti, with whom he had become close friends in Rome, had moved to Florence in 1893 to take a position at the Uffizi Gallery. Together they were among the main inspirers of *Il Marzocco*, the aestheticist journal that was the most immediate precursor of the Florentine avant-garde.

The opulent and refined *Il Marzocco* was financed by Leone Orvieto, a wealthy Florentine from an old Jewish family whose two sons, Angiolo and Adolfo, were its first editors. Published by a prestigious firm on the Via Tornabuoni, it had an unprecedentedly elegant typeface and generally represented the standpoint of what passed in Florence for an aristocratic bohemia. Its title, chosen by D'Annunzio, was local in origin—it referred to the heraldic lion of Florence as represented by Donatello—but alongside the lion on the frontispiece was a Latin motto: *multa renascentur* (may many things be reborn). Its main contributors, who besides the Orvieto brothers, D'Annunzio, and Conti included Diego Garoglio, Giuseppe Saverio Gargàno, Mario Morasso, and Enrico Corradini, were all members of the generation of the 1860s and had been inspired by the poetics of decadence and aestheticism developed by the poet Giovanni Pascoli and, above all, by D'Annunzio himself.[81] Typical in this respect was Conti, who wrote under the pen name of Doctor Mysticus and was known to his comrades as the *dolce filosofo* (sweet philosopher).[82]

The journal's program was an unabashed defense of "art for art's sake" or "pure beauty," as they themselves called it. The "prologue" to the first issue, cowritten by D'Annunzio and Gargàno, declared:

> We have meditated for a long time about whether it would be worth starting an enterprise like the one upon which we are embarking, in which we will oppose with all our energies that production of literary and, more generally, artistic work that has its origins outside the pursuit of pure beauty [*pura bellezza*]. For a long time we have witnessed those usurpations that material interest or an unbridled desire for fame have made in the closed confines of art, without a voice of protest being raised to throw these modern barbarians far from our midst . . . And we hope that the work of a few solitary adorers of beauty might make new and powerful words heard once again.[83]

Readers with a taste for irony might have noticed the acuity with which the writers characterized the sins of their unnamed opponents, but the politics of nostalgia this aestheticism supported was clearly genuine.[84] For not only did *Il Marzocco*'s writers continually hark back to those Renaissance glories so enticingly interpreted by Walter Pater, and follow the "religion of beauty" developed by John Ruskin and the British pre-Raphaelites; they also wrote insistently about the ills of Florentine modernization. Early issues invoked the ideal of *pura bellezza* to condemn the coming of telephone lines, trams, and automobiles, the use of funiculars on mountainsides, the new pervasiveness of commercial advertising, and the omnipresence of smoke from factories.[85] No less than for its foreign visitors, Florence for these aesthetic "noble spirits," as Pascoli had aptly called them, was "ancient Florence"—"monuments, houses, traces of the past"—the city that was Europe's "cradle of art."[86] After the shameless excesses of what had passed in recent decades for urban renewal, it was now necessary to restore the city's older architectural monuments to their former glory and to make the people more aware of their significance. Thus, in 1900 the journal launched a regular column called "Dentro la cerchia antica" (Inside the Ancient City Walls), which it allied with a new civic organization, the Amici dei Monumenti (Friends of the Monuments).[87]

In a journal in which most of the articles celebrated ideals of sensualism, mysticism, and *pura bellezza*, this campaign for consciousness and restoration of the city's architectural and artistic heritage appeared as a natural translation of that ethos into a cultural politics. Yet from the beginning there was a second, more radical position struggling to overcome the nostalgic one. Associated primarily with Morasso and Corradini, it emerged most noticeably during the years Corradini served as editor (1897–1900). In this more avant-garde view, a proper cultural politics should go beyond specific campaigns to make the environment safe for art and seek to alter mass culture and politics generally in a direction congenial to intellectuals. Not surprisingly, this direction was often expressed in the language of nationalism and imperialism.[88] But it came to the fore initially in two articles Morasso wrote on the intelligentsia itself during the congressional campaign of 1897, in which D'Annunzio, not coincidentally, was seeking office.[89] Accusing his fellows of allowing their disgust with political corruption and the electoral process to produce "absenteeism" and "culpable fakirism" *(fakirismo)*, Morasso called for an open confrontation with "the hegemony of the older generation" of politicians in which the young generation of intellectuals would prove its "superiority" over them as a political class. It should do so, moreover, in the name of individuality and "genius," thus positioning itself between the reigning conservatism and *moderatismo* on the one hand, and the emerging socialist forces on the other.

But this argument never made much headway in the world of pure beauty and sweet philosophy. Adolfo Orvieto and Garoglio replied immediately, attacking Morasso himself for hypocrisy and his proposal for its infeasibility. In a particularly revealing passage, Garoglio pointed to the incompatibility between Morasso's proposal and the ideal of life most of them as aesthetes were actually living:

> Men who feel an irresistible impulse toward action display an energy a hundred times stronger than we do, continually preoccupied as we are with examining all sides of a problem, with navigating through an atmosphere of regrets and dreams, or with losing ourselves in the contemplation of nature . . . It is useless to delude ourselves: however great the strength of a man, even an extremely brilliant man, in comparison with the masses, that strength is always very limited in relation to the efforts that he must expend to reach excellence in his intellectual creations and to have them exert a strong, visible social influence. Because of fatal mechanical laws, that which is gained through extension is lost in intensity, and he who consumes a fortune in political struggle without saving his energies will search for them thereafter and fail to find them when they are needed for artistic creation. The result is that he may be deprived of them precisely in those supreme moments when having them might allow him to create a master work.[90]

With Corradini as editor, however, the controversy did not end there. Readers were invited to submit their views on whether literary intellectuals should take part in politics, and, assuming an affirmative answer, what that precise role should be.[91] But despite the further controversy this prompted, the answer of most of the *marzocchisti* was never in doubt, and while Corradini continued at least nominally as editor for nearly three more years, both he and Morasso would part ways with the journal at the dawn of the new century.

Interestingly, when Prezzolini looked back on this dispute and the early *Il Marzocco* in 1909, he sided not with Morasso and Corradini, as one might have expected given their apparently greater proximity to the ideals of *Leonardo* and *La Voce*, but with Conti, Garoglio, and the Orvieto brothers. True, he was disposed in this direction by personal biases. After an initial collaboration with Corradini, he and his fellow *leonardiani* had had a falling out with him around 1905, and Prezzolini probably retained an affection for Garoglio, in particular, because he had been a mentor and close friend of Papini from 1898 until 1902, and something of a friend to Prezzolini himself.[92] Still, his reasoning appears to go deeper. Aesthetes such as "the warm-souled Conti, *Il Marzocco*'s Apollo," the "Tolstoyan and Buddhist Angiolo Orvieto," and the "hard-working and severe Garoglio" were highly cultured men who had done much to combat the superficial, fashion-conscious culture of "the salon" that so dominated Florence. Conti, in particular, "had reawakened works of art and the souls of men: he was always ready with invective against the erudites, and he knew how to shake with rage against the legalistic coldness of the historians of art, and to raise a fervent protest against the profaning of Dante that was acted out weekly by the professors of Orsanmichele." The problem with Conti was only that his ideal of beauty was "of a past time, perhaps of no time," and this meant he could offer no guidance to the younger generation, who "want to go forward, while his gospel is one of retreat." But the problem with Corradini was far worse: he suffered even more from Conti's defects while having much less genuine "culture." Corradini was an "egoist" whose "nationalism is airy and abstract . . . resting on mere words . . . like Rome, *romanità*, Caesar, Virgil, etc., etc."[93] Morasso, too, only pretended to be more modern and activist than his fellow *marzocchisti*. In an earlier review of one of Morasso's books, Prezzolini had written: "Why, then, does Mario Morasso, so enamored of action, act so rarely? Because he, who deals in workshops of words for discussion, is such a furious forger of sentences? Because he publishes so many books and writes articles on top of articles? I have never seen his name in an automobile race and I am told that, far from having a car, he doesn't even have a lowly motorcycle. Morasso, then, for those who don't know, is the latest Italian Petrarchist; just as Petrarch loved Laura in sonnets, and Italy in songs, Morasso drives a car in his articles."[94]

Despite its inability to locate its aesthetic ideals in reality and develop a genuinely modernist position, Prezzolini continued, the early *Il Marzocco* had much to commend it. Insofar as it had steered clear of the empty rhetoric and cultural vulgarity of Corradini, as well as the pretentious hypocrisy of Morasso, it had played an important role in challenging the "snobbism and socialite culture that is still the characteristic defect of the cultured class of our city." Its early issues overflowed with "faith, enthusiasm, life, true youthfulness, and open, even imprudent, sincerity." Yet after 1900 it had become steadily corrupted. By 1909 it had moved full circle to become one of the leading exemplars of the defect it had aimed to condemn. Above all, it displayed "unconscionable servility toward of the Istituto di Studi Superiori and in general toward any person with a university title who is widely recognized. Such people could send *Il Marzocco* their laundry lists and get them published in large type on the front page."

Why, then, had self-betrayal been *Il Marzocco*'s fate? As the generation after Carducci, the *marzocchisti* had retained his early emphasis on Italian cultural primacy and his paganism, even in some ways his classicism, although he would certainly have judged their manner of celebrating the Renaissance, for example, as utter decadence. But they had self-consciously broken with him over his critique of individualism and of the softening of the virtues in modern life. Like their masters D'Annunzio and Pascoli, the *marzocchisti* were clearly in that "second" tradition of Italian literature that Papini labeled "elegant," "empty," and "feminine." For Papini and Prezzolini, the problem with this tradition lay not so much in its individualism—they were themselves unabashed individualists in their *Leonardo* days—as in its conception of the virtues, which was not only contemptible in itself but also, as Prezzolini especially had recognized, ultimately self-contradictory. For the soft virtues of aestheticism led to a sensualist inertia that ultimately undermined all faith and belief, and because aestheticist criticism lacked a philosophical standpoint beyond its own corporeal and contemplative pleasure, its convictions could not endure.[95]

Although in his articles on *Il Marzocco* Prezzolini did not trace this nihilistic trajectory back to D'Annunzio, it is clear from his later recollections, as well as from those of his fellow Florentine avant-gardists, that they all tended to hold D'Annunzio accountable for the failures of avant-gardism in the previous generation.

In their earliest attitudes toward and encounters with D'Annunzio, at least some of the young men of the generation of 1880 who would soon build a cultural avant-garde appeared to regard him as an inspiring model for their own enterprise. Soffici, for example, would later recall an incident in 1899, when he, Prezzolini, and Papini (whom he, however, did not yet know) witnessed D'Annunzio giving a political speech about "beauty" outside a working-class laundry and were entirely swept away by it.[96] Shortly afterward Soffici had established a periodical, *La Fiamma* (The Flame), which had "something of the air of *Il Marzocco*." It proved short-lived, but in one of its three issues, he had written a highly celebratory article on D'Annunzio's tragic drama, *La Gioconda*.[97]

By November 1900 Soffici had gone to Paris, but Prezzolini and Papini, who were becoming fast friends, stayed behind. Their attitude toward D'Annunzio was quite different from Soffici's, as the following incident from around that time, recalled by Prezzolini in his memoirs, shows. Walking in the woods not far from D'Annunzio's villa at Settignano, he and some friends had seen the famous poet suddenly "appear from afar, elegantly dressed with a monacle, riding a white horse." But, as Prezzolini commented, "knowing full well who he was, we didn't want to give him the satisfaction of looking at him in the face and recognizing him . . . for this [refusal] gave a tone of independence to our lives."[98]

Similarly, Papini recalled that his attitude toward D'Annunzio in the days before *Leonardo* was one of rebellious disdain. So intense were his feelings that a proper contempt for D'Annunzio became a test of friendship. He recalled that he and Prezzolini had split in 1900 with their two closest friends, Alfredo Mori and Ercole Luigi Morselli, because "Prezzolini and I could no longer remain tied to men who put aesthetics before thought and defended D'Annunzio's art to the death."[99] Papini expressed this antipathy directly in 1903 when he was launching *Leonardo*. Hearing of the new effort from a mutual friend, D'Annunzio apparently sent Papini his best wishes, offering both money and assistance. Not only did Papini refuse the money, which he badly needed; he refused even to consider meeting with D'Annunzio—until, that is, he "could speak to him as an equal" and not "in the role of an unknown young man who pays homage to a famous man."[100]

Though active as novelist and dramatist respectively for many years to come, neither Mori nor Morselli participated in the Florentine avant-garde. Yet there were of course at least a few partisans of D'Annunzio who did. Adolfo De Karolis and Giovanni Costetti, the two artists who most frequently contributed *art nouveau* mastheads and drawings for *Leonardo*, were good friends of the poet (it was De Karolis who had brought Papini D'Annunzio's offer of financial support). The fact that they were half a decade older probably had something to do with their more positive attitude. Even more important was the fact that their inclinations were mainly artistic rather than philosophical, for it was when D'Annunzio was judged in philosophical terms—either for his thought or for what his life reflected about his lack of it—that he appeared most wanting. But even among those who were initially quite receptive to D'Annunzio, enthusiasm for him and for the style associated with him declined steadily with each year of the new century. Thus the critic Giuseppe Antonio Borgese, who was quite enthralled with D'Annunzio when he began as editor of the literary journal *Hermes* in 1904, held him in considerably lower estimation by the time he published a book on D'Annunzio in 1909.

Probably the most acute critical treatment of D'Annunzio and *D'Annunzianismo* during the early years of the Florentine avant-garde was Papini's chapter on the topic in *La coltura italiana*, a book he coauthored with Prezzolini in 1906.[101] Very much in the style of Oedipal revolt, Papini opened with a brisk dismissal of D'Annunzio as having already become a historical relic:

D'Annunzianism has lasted ten years: it began about 1895 and is now finished. It began when Melchior de Vogüé announced in the *Revue des Deux Mondes* the new Latin Renaissance; when [Enrico] Thovez launched the stupid campaign against [D'Annunzio's] plagiarism in the *Gazzetta letteraria;* when in

Florence *Il Marzocco*, not yet academic and officious, got excited about the new God of Italian literature. In those days there were many youthful enthusiasts who recited and imitated the *Poema paradisiaco* and the *Isotteo;* who did their spiritual exercises through Claudio Cantelmo's meditations; who tried to model their public and private life on that of Gabriele the Grand . . . D'Annunzianism began to be associated with certain tastes and attitudes like dandyism and over-refinement that already existed among us as they existed in every moderately civilized country. In every generation there are always a certain number of young people who search for originality in dress, speech, and theories; who love to put on an original and sought-after air . . . But this type of "early-model" D'Annunzian has died out little by little—it has become ridiculous, comical, provincial. It has become fused with the idea of the "superman," and the two together have by now almost vanished from Italian life except for lingering, like a caricature, in a few novels and comic dramas.[102]

D'Annunzio had sought to be the "national educator of Italy." His "mission," Papini continued, had been to "arouse and lead a new Italy less vile and commercial than the present one, a bold and refined Italy given to works of beauty and labors of conquest, an Italy that would be the enemy of mechanical civilization and greedy demagoguery." But he was simply not up to the task. "The means he had summoned up to realize his desires—speeches, writings, that is, words—had been soft, insufficient, impotent." Moreover, he was too removed from the two things that really move the masses: their immediate interests and their religious needs. He had no idea how to reconnect Italian culture and civilization with its rapid economic development and the spiritual crisis of modernity associated with that development. He was at a loss to arouse "that spirit deep in all of us, that spirit of faith" that might heal the wounds the process of modernization had opened. He had thought we could resolve the national crisis through aesthetic creation, yet we read his poems and tragedies and still had no idea how to build a new Italy. "Italy," Papini concluded in a revealing metaphor, "still waits for the whip that will make her run and for the wrist that will guide that whip."[103]

2 The *Leonardo* Years

Fin-de-Siècle Florence and the Myth of Paris

In the wintertime, when the sun was shining and the weather pleasant, my mother would take me to the Lungarno just before sunset to see the people coming back from a day in the Cascine [a large Florentine park]. In those days [the 1880s] the well-to-do and foreigners used to go every day, ritualistically, along the river up to the grave of the Indian prince, and then return all together toward the city. That festive return was one of the dearest spectacles for Florentines who then had little to be happy about . . . When my mother led me along the Lungarni, in that hour of magnificence, I was dressed much better than usual. She made me up that way, with pieces of old velvet and teased hair that enhanced the beauty of my curly, shoulder-length locks. My mother wanted very much for me to look like a rich boy, best of all a foreign one, and my blond hair and sky-blue eyes encouraged her in this innocent bit of mania or vanity . . . On one of these days there passed near us two tall men, undoubtedly foreigners. One of them, seeing me, stopped and stared. A bit astonished, I stared back at him so hard that I can still remember his strange figure. He wore thick glasses and an enormous mustache; his face was large and fleshy, but grave and a bit sad. Suddenly he reached out with his right hand, delicately and affectionately patted my blond curls, and said something to his companion. Then they both moved on and I could no longer see them . . . Many years later I happened to see in a book a portrait very closely resembling the unknown man who had stopped before me on that day long before. My heart leaped in amazement: it was a portrait of Friedrich Nietzsche.[1]

With this remarkable recollection, Giovanni Papini provides several important clues about his experience of childhood. Born in 1881 into a family of shopkeepers struggling to stay just above poverty, he seems to have come to regard himself as a spectator in his own city, foredoomed by frozen class divisions to watch the parade of the rich and powerful. "I never felt myself to have much chance in that in-grown and sleepy peacefulness."[2] Indeed, he frequently sought to escape it by retreating to the country "far away from its holy laws of daily humiliation."[3] Yet he refused to resign himself to subordination and, even while in the city, "sought anxiously to be able to breathe different air, breezier and more savage."[4] During childhood this meant seeking out exotic events like traveling circuses from Asia or Buffalo Bill's Wild West Show from America. However, it also appears that his sense of being imprisoned in an immobile social structure was to some degree just the public consequence of a peculiar and withdrawn personality. "I was never a boy, I never had a childhood," begins the autobiography he wrote at thirty. As a child he had been called "toad" and "old man" by the other boys, and while they played he tended just to watch, or retreated to the corner of the attic to be alone with books.[5] A few years later he would be lying about his age in a vain attempt to gain entry to a public library.[6]

Despite curly blond hair, blue eyes, and the fond attentions of his mother, Papini had an inescapably ugly face. It was long and thin, with a remarkably high forehead, deep-set eyes (later hidden behind spectacles as thick as soft-drink bottles), an overly prominent nose, and a wide, fleshy mouth. The combination of features was so unusual and expressive that André Gide later found him "almost beautiful," and Soffici, with the eye of a modernist painter, found Papini's "an ugliness that was beauty . . . at a higher level."[7] Yet Papini himself clearly felt marked by that ugliness and "at war with others" because of it.[8] Alberto Viviani, who would later become a close friend and his first biographer, wrote that Papini's physical being and early experience had implanted in him a "timidity that would grip him tenaciously throughout his life." The "apparent coldness and cruelty" that would mark his polemical style "were simply the result of this timidity."[9] Just as clearly, however, those characteristics made evident the deep resentment he felt for the foreigners and local rich who spent their afternoons in the Cascine and had never suffered as he had.

In part because of his tendency to withdraw, the parade at sundown did not propel Papini upon a political career. His father had run away at eighteen to fight with Garibaldi, and he remained an ardent republican until the day he died in 1902. Initially, the son had followed him in that republicanism, and he had experienced a welling up of nationalist emo-

2. Papini in 1910.

tion at the defeat of the Italian army before the Ethiopians at Adowa in 1896.[10] But when King Umberto I was assassinated four years later, Papini thought it a "fact of little or no importance, at most suggesting certain anthropological and sociological reflections."[11] Yet if he lacked interest in active politics, he certainly still wanted to rise in the world, even to change it. In these latter respects, the parade had undoubtedly had an effect. It was as if the touch of the German cultural prophet had anointed an Italian heir, had appointed him to the task of bringing Italy fully into the ranks of the European modernist movement.

Although he lacked the means to pursue a university degree, the young Papini launched himself upon an intellectual career with manic intensity. Already at the age of fifteen, he was producing his first, carefully handwritten journals. Soon thereafter he vowed to know "everything" and to record the results in his own encyclopedia.[12] Before turning twenty he was scheduling his days to the minute to ensure at least ten hours of intellectual work.[13] His new dream was to become the leader of a "party of intellectuals," and he outlined in detail the means such a party might deploy to "improve humanity."[14]

The first person to encourage the young intellectual was Diego Garoglio, who taught him during his final year of secondary school (1898–99) and, when not rushing home to write for *Il Marzocco*, took him after school to the Caffè Gambrinus for further intellectual conversation.[15] Despite the difference in their ages, they became fast friends. During the following year he made similar friendships with two university students, Alfredo Mori and Ercole Luigi Morselli, who encouraged him to audit classes. But the person to whom he felt most akin when they met in 1899, and with whom he, Mori, and Morselli soon became an "inseparable quartet," was Giuseppe Prezzolini.[16]

Prezzolini had grown up in a much more comfortable, even privileged environment. His father, Luigi Prezzolini, was a prefect (a local representative of the national government) stationed at Perugia when Giuseppe was born in 1882. Thereafter the family moved frequently to similar regional towns, residing in elegant houses provided by the government. A literary intellectual as well, Luigi Prezzolini found those residences always wanting in only one respect: their lack of adequate shelf space for his considerable library.[17] Yet despite being surrounded by such amenities, the young Giuseppe did not enjoy an intimate home life in his early years. His mother died when he was only three; later in his diary he wrote that "I remember nothing of my mother except that when she died they would not allow me to enter the room where my parents slept."[18] He also felt somewhat estranged from his father and older brother because of great differences in age: forty-five years in the first case, nine in the second.[19]

In 1899 the three Prezzolinis had come to Florence, and in the fall of that year Giuseppe met Giovanni, beginning a personal friendship and intellectual companionship that, despite later trials, would be unceasing through six decades. Many years later he would vividly recall the early days of that friendship and its context in his life:

I was then a rebellious high school student. I had abandoned school because I did not like Latin, could not write Italian themes, was annoyed by the way history was taught, and was satisfied only by mathematics . . . The encounter with Papini was for me the opening of a new world, through which Florence, where I had lived for a year somewhat heedlessly, now took definite shape and became the cocoon out of which I would take off . . . So began the great adventure of an autodidact, in search of personal cultivation, without practical purpose, without aspiring to a diploma and—in my view at least—without ambition. Notoriety did not attract me; rather research, ideas, novelty, and logical truth were my passions. I lived in intellectual communion with Papini until 1903 in an artificially closed atmosphere in which social conflicts and the events of the time almost did not penetrate. For us the discovery of idealism (the world made by the human spirit, without independent reality) was more important than the assassination of Umberto I. We were poor, unknown, solitary, and yet the world appeared to be ours. When we traveled outside the city in search of some point of view from which to gaze at all the dwellings where there lived that swarm of people ignorant of what they had discovered the day before, we glanced through the gates at the villas and whispered to each other that no one understood how beautiful they were, and that in reality they belonged more to us than to their owners who had enclosed them with iron fences and walls for fear of losing them or sharing them with others. Florence also seemed to be ours, and Papini, a most Florentine son of a family of republican artisans, was my first teacher of *fiorentinismo* . . .[20]

The Prezzolini of 1900 was rather ordinary looking, short, slight, dark-haired, but with pleasant features that, when depicted by a skilled artist, could make him appear quite handsome. Such a portrait was in fact executed by his friend Armando Spadini and appeared in the November 1904 issue of *Leonardo* under the title "Portrait of an Unknown." Yet what struck those who met Prezzolini in these years was less his physical being than his intriguingly contradictory personal qualities. In 1900 Papini found in him "a complete absence of sentimentality" but also "a lack of self-control"; "an extremely warm and irrepressible love of liberty and independence" but also a "lack of faith in himself"; and, in general, a rebelliousness that rendered him "smiling, cool, careless, and bored."[21] After meeting him in Paris a decade later, Romain Rolland sensed similar contradictions: Prezzolini appeared "at once brusque and affectionate, his eyes intelligent, shielded by a pince-nez, his face bearing an expression that is resolute and irresolute at the same time."[22]

Prezzolini had in fact matured considerably during that decade, moving from a deep insecurity and an unfocused rebelliousness through a philosophical phase of romantic individualism and, finally, into a more balanced cultural politics with self-conscious commitments to social betterment, cultural renewal, and a Crocean-idealist view of ethics and history. But the initial rebelliousness was etched too deeply in his character ever to fade entirely. Only months after arriving in Florence, Prezzolini's father had died, and the young man of eighteen felt com-

3. Prezzolini in 1905 while he lived in Perugia.

pletely cut off from his past. Later that year he wrote in his diary: "I have found that it is best for me to withdraw as much as I can from the world, aiming to have as little contact with other people as possible, since these usually end up as collisions without clear purpose. Fortunately, this will not involve any great sacrifice for me: glory, money, women do not attract me. My most lively desire at the moment is to know and admire, that is, to enjoy nature and art."[23]

With an inheritance that allowed him to live "modestly but independently," Prezzolini set out on a journey of intellectual exploration in which the only real-life intimacy was his friendship with Papini.[24] He became "Giuliano il Sofista" (Julian the Sophist), naming himself after two earlier rebels, Julien Sorel and Julian the Apostate, while Papini, with his cutting wit and hawklike face, became "Gian Falco" (Janus-Falcon).[25] Together they took on Florence:

> Our contempt for the crowd of *endimanchés* [bourgeois Sunday dressers] was expressed one festival day when we turned our jackets inside out and, so sheathed, walked against the oncoming crowd after a Cathedral mass. One evening we had to go to the hospital of Santa Maria Novella because—following Baudelaire—we had taken too much marijuana, and the testimony of the examining doctor who had had to check his manual to find out what to do for that then quite new mode of intoxication is probably still there. But beyond these signs of protest, I learned to turn our rebelliousness into invectives, sophisms, contests, caricatures, attacks and polemics.[26]

Without the resentment but no less intensely than "Gianfalco," "Giuliano" expressed his contempt for his adopted city, a contempt that at this point was registered more in bohemian frivolity than in political or cultural commitments. Yet behind the adolescent silliness was a budding intellectual of nearly Papini's Promethean ambition, and an equally acute intelligence, less poetic perhaps but no less interested in art and culture and, in those years, more philosophical.

One of the enthusiasms the two renegade intellectuals shared was the culture of France, especially as expressed by the Parisian avant-garde. Papini studied the French language diligently, writing a number of his early diary entries in it, but he lacked the means to travel to perfect it among native speakers.[27] Here Prezzolini was more fortunate. In 1901 he set out for Grenoble to learn French firsthand; a year later he spent six weeks in Paris, whiling away the hours in libraries over Henri Bergson and the *Revue de Métaphysique et de Morale,* and puzzling over how he might "become a Catholic without being a Christian."[28] Prezzolini appears to have been without real companionship in Paris, the one local address in his possession for a Florentine of his generation having proved erroneous or perhaps outdated.[29] This was a pity, for the young man in question, who later became a close friend and an assiduous collaborator on *La Voce,* was already deeply immersed in the Parisian scene that Prezzolini was only reading and dreaming about.

Two years before Papini and three before Prezzolini, Ardengo Soffici was born near the town of Rignano sull'Arno, some twenty miles upriver from the center of Florence, the son of a *fattore* (farm manager). As *fattore,* his father enforced landlord interests over several *mezzadri,* a job that offered some prestige, but at the price of many unpleasant duties and an ambiguous and somewhat tenuous class position for his family.

His mother came from a more prosperous family that owned a silk mill near the town of Poggio a Caiano, about the same distance from Florence as Rignano but to the west. The young Ardengo grew up, then, in the heart of the Tuscan countryside. But in 1892, when Ardengo was thirteen, his father's contract as *fattore* was not renewed, and the family moved to Florence. Shortly thereafter they were running a wholesale wine business south of the river near the Porta Romana.

A handsome young man with well-defined, delicate features, Ardengo showed an early interest and talent in art and design, in which he was already taking private lessons during his first years in Florence. These were interrupted in 1897 when his father was struck by paralysis (he would die two years later), and Ardengo moved in with his mother's relatives at Poggio. But he managed to return to Florence the following year, living with his mother in a rented room and attending the Accademia di Belle Arti, where he soon became a student of the foremost Florentine painter of the day, Giovanni Fattori.[30] His evenings were spent at the Gambrinus with other young painters such as Costetti, De Karolis, Spadini, a young Frenchman named Henri des Pruraux, and the elder statesman of the group, Arnold Böcklin.

Poetry was an early passion as well. Soffici was an enthusiast of *Il Marzocco* from its first issues, and under its stimulus read Baudelaire, Verlaine, and Mallarmé.[31] Even more important for him in these years were the art and poetry of the British pre-Raphaelites, whose leading journal, *The Studio*, was quite popular in Florence because, like Böcklin's painting, it sought to probe the primal depths of myth and the human unconscious.[32] It was under their influence, especially, that he would publish some early sonnets, both in his own *La Fiamma* and in another fledgling Florentine review, *La Bohème*.[33] Moreover, the importance of both the pre-Raphaelites and Böcklin would remain paramount for Soffici well into the next decade. He would even credit them as the fundamental sources for the early Pablo Picasso, who lived in Paris but "was not essentially French-influenced [*afrancesado*]."[34]

When Soffici himself left for Paris on November 6, 1900, his immediate aim was to visit the recently opened Universal Exposition, but clearly he and his friends were drawn more generally by the "myth of Paris" they had been absorbing for half a decade.[35] One important stimulus in this respect had been an international art exhibition in Florence in 1896–97, which included canvases by French painters such as Pierre Puvis de Chavannes, and in which Soffici had been especially struck by Léon Joseph Bonnat's portrait of Ernst Renan.[36] Another had been the stories of Henri des Pruraux, who, "before coming to our school, had been, together with his friend Gauguin, among the painters Emile

Bernard, Maximilien Luce, Maurice Denis, and [Paul] Sérusier, who had gathered in the famous restaurant of Pont-Aven in Brittany."[37] As Soffici later reflected: "All these texts, these echoes, these visions [of Paris and the French avant-garde], the bits of news and the voices that arrived from there of revolutionary schools, artistic and literary struggles, intellectual and artistic ferment, threw even us into motion, excited us, pushed us to think and explore, inspired us and gave us reason to hope. Above all they increased our intolerance for all the mediocrity and vulgarity that we saw around us and that contaminated the works of even the best Italian writers and poets of the day. They threw us into a manic frenzy, a longing, a burning desire, though for precisely what we did not know."[38] Or as Costetti put it more succinctly: "For some time now I have had no other desire or vision or mirage than Paris, a Paris that will be our salvation or our death."[39]

When Soffici, Costetti, and several other friends arrived at the Gare de Lyon just before midnight on November 8, it was the latter possibility that loomed larger. Through the station door the city outside appeared magical, so brightly lit and teeming with activity that "the swarms of people leaving the theater and hurrying to packed cafés, bars, and elegant restaurants appeared to us to be starting their day."[40] But the tired travelers would end theirs in a shockingly rundown hotel on the Rue Dauphine, and for many days thereafter, in dingy rooms on the Rue de Buci and the Rue Ancienne de la Comédie, their lives would be sober and hard, filled more with "squalid ugliness" than with magic.[41] Even the Universal Exposition for which they had come, and which did not disappoint them, proved to be too expensive to attend very often.

Gradually, however, Soffici's charming manner and considerable talent won him a place in the left-bank world of artists' studios and avant-garde reviews. Indeed, his progress from 1901 through the late spring of 1903, when he returned briefly to Florence, was little short of miraculous. Already in 1901 his freehand drawings and *art nouveau* designs were gracing the covers of the highly regarded *Revue Blanche* and various lesser satirical reviews such as *L'Assiette au Beurre* (born that April), *Le Rire, Gil Blas, La Caricature,* and *Frou-Frou*.[42] He also designed the cover for a self-consciously decadent novel by Louis Dumont, *La Chimère*, which, because it was published by the Editions de la Plume, also appeared as the November 1901 cover of the journal *La Plume*.

Not long thereafter Soffici would become a friend of the editor, Karl Boès, and be invited to join in the celebrated "soirées de *La Plume*" that Boès gave at the Caveau du Soleil d'Or on the Place Saint-Michel. There Soffici met poets such as Paul Fort, Guillaume Apollinaire, Alfred Jarry, and Mécislas Golberg, a Jewish anarchist from Poland with whom he was very much taken, as well as the elder statesman of the symbolist movement, Jean Moréas.[43] When the Editions de la Plume reissued the latter's book of poetry, *Les Cantilènes*, in August 1902, Soffici designed the cover. Indeed, his design had appeared already as the cover of the April 15 *La Plume*, the same issue in which Golberg, perhaps not quite coincidentally, published an essay on Arnold Böcklin.[44]

By early 1902 Soffici had met Auguste Rodin, joined the Société des Artistes Indépendants, and participated in their spring exhibition with seven of his works.[45] Later that year, while working for yet another journal, the *Cri de Paris*, he would meet Pablo Picasso and Max Jacob, both of whom would become good friends in the years around 1905 when they resided in the famous "Bateau-Lavoir" on the Rue Ravignan.[46] In general, Soffici's contact with Parisian intellectual life came through artists and poets; only in 1910 would he make the acquaintance of the French philosopher Henri Bergson, who was already creating a stir among his future friends in Florence.[47]

Yet as Soffici became more and more deeply immersed in Parisian cultural life, he did not turn his back on Florence and Tuscany. His private drawings showed signs of some nostalgia for his native region, and from his arguments about art with Costetti, he appeared to be struggling with the issue of how art might be simultaneously modern and yet rooted in the landscape, people, and customs of one's own region. One particularly revealing argument of this sort pitted Costetti's championing of Puvis de Chavannes, who was known for large murals often idealizing the ancient world, against Soffici's enthusiasm for Paul Cézanne.[48] When, in early 1903, he received the first issues of *Leonardo*, which struck him with its "fresh look and novelty of thought, form of presentation, tone, and modes of expression," he not only plugged the new Florentine review in *La Plume* but also used the occasion to separate himself from *Il Marzocco*, with which in his mind Costetti remained identified. "A number of courageous young painters and writers," he wrote, "have come together to found a journal called *Leonardo*, which, overturning the last remaining debris of an exasperating past, pursues the march forward opened by *Il Marzocco*, itself no longer sufficient to the needs of the day."[49] That spring he and Papini began correspondence, and by the end of May, with his expenses born by *La Plume*, Soffici returned to Florence for a two-month summer sojourn.[50]

Once in Florence he did an enormous quantity of drawings and woodcuts depicting Tuscan scenes and people. In effect, Monte Ceceri near Fiesole became his Mont Sainte-Victoire. He also sought out Papini, learned firsthand about *Leonardo*, and emerged even more impressed. As a recent student of Soffici's avant-gardism has remarked: "When

Soffici returned the first time from Paris to Florence, he finally understood how to choose his friends. Paris had taught him to distinguish those Italians who were more European from those who were irremediably provincial or who merely mimicked foreign things."[51]

The summer of 1903 brought one more event of the greatest importance for Soffici: an encounter at the Gambrinus with the elegant Hélène d'Oettingen, herself an aspiring poet and artist, who was visiting, conveniently enough, from Paris. The event sparked a love affair that would endure, with brief interruptions, for half a decade.[52] Known in Paris as "La Baronne," Hélène was of mysterious origin, but indisputably lovely and well-to-do.[53] Referred to variously as Polish or Russian, she may in fact have been the daughter of the Austrian-Hungarian Emperor Francis Joseph.[54] Through her, Soffici soon met her brother, Serge Jastrebzoff, who was also a painter and who went by the pseudonym of Serge Férat, although the difficulty of his real name would lead Picasso to dub him "Serge Apostrophe."[55] He would become one of Soffici's closest friends.

When the three returned to Paris in August, Soffici's position in the Parisian avant-garde would take another major leap forward because the apartment on the Boulevard Raspail in Montparnasse that Hélène and Serge shared was fast becoming one of its central gathering places. Photographs of Soffici in this period depict an unabashed dandy who

4. Soffici in 1903 in Paris.

looked remarkably like the young Baudelaire, with whom he was in fact often compared.[56] Yet this was also a period of intense reflection for him, as he sought to work out a theoretical orientation for modern art. In an article for *L'Europe Artiste* late in 1904, he wrote: "After [ancient] Greece and the Italy of the Renaissance it is a third Beauty that we pursue. A profound, meditative, and interior Beauty. A Beauty without pomp, without draperies. Muscles that bend to support psychical movements, fabrics that wrap around passions, landscapes that harmonize with heartbeats."[57] This "third beauty" must be "modern" both in the sense that it is based on "our" subjectivity, our perception of the world, and in the sense that it does not flee the present world in favor of some abstract *pura bellezza*. It does not grow, then, from a simple embrace of subjectivity but from an attempt to link our subjective experience with the external reality we find in landscape, the body, and daily life. When the linkage is successfully made, art becomes not a retreat into interiority but the depiction of reality on a higher plane, at once intensely personal and yet "mathematical" in its sense of order.[58]

In an article the following year in *La Plume*, Apollinaire would portray Picasso's concept of art in similar terms, and in his memoirs Soffici would remember fondly his intellectual friendship with Apollinaire in this period, a friendship that would become even more significant for the later story of "futurism in Florence." From 1904 through 1906, however, Soffici became increasingly ill-at-ease with Parisian life and returned to Tuscany every summer for an extended visit. In January 1904 he was writing Papini: "Next summer I hope to get to know you more intimately and to spend some beautiful days with you in the hills and valleys of our beautiful Tuscany."[59] A year later, again prior to his summer sojourn, he wrote: "I live a rather secluded existence here in small measure because of the distance that separates me from the center, but much more because of the great disgust I harbor for my friends."[60] This remark would become even more apt when *La Plume* ceased publication later that same summer, after which Soffici's activity level both for the reviews and in the intellectual life of the cafés became much less intense. In retrospect it would appear that, by late 1905 and 1906, Soffici was in the midst of a shift of focus: from the idea of educating himself as a European artist in its most cosmopolitan urban center, and participating in the international inter-arts alliance centered there, to becoming a European artist and writer in Tuscany and adding Tuscany to the range of cultures represented in the international avant-garde.

After the 1905 visit home, Soffici's contributions to *Leonardo*, though still relatively sparse, became more significant, especially in their insistence on a kind of born-again *toscanità*. Perhaps his best-known and certainly his most interesting woodcut of this period, depicting "Don Quixote in Tuscany," appeared as the cover of the August 1906 issue. Although Soffici remained in close touch with certain particular individuals in Paris such as Apollinaire, by January 1907 he had published a renunciation of his Parisian life in *Leonardo*, with the implication that he intended to return home soon and for good.[61] In fact his intentions were not quite so clear, as is evident from a letter to Papini of early 1907 in which he indicated he would go next to Spain.[62] Yet with respect to his seven years in Paris, the exhibit of large, brightly colored oil paintings of Tuscan peasants that he had at the Salon des Indépendants later that spring appeared to bring him full circle: from his flight to Paris to escape the "mediocrity and vulgarity we saw all around us" to his return to Florence in search of the roots without which he could not create a genuine modern art.

The Birth of *Leonardo* and the Search for Secular Religion

For Papini and Prezzolini, the odyssey of the new century had begun more slowly; the frenzy of *Leonardo* would begin only in 1903. At first, theirs remained largely a private world of country walks, intellectual conversation, and voracious reading, enlivened by their ever-present contempt—sometimes lighthearted, sometimes deeply embittered—for what they saw as the bourgeois provincialism of their city. Papini's dream of a "party of intellectuals" merged with Prezzolini's fantasies about "revolts and wars" and "burning down everything old in the world."[63] But neither of them showed much inclination to go beyond dreams and fantasies. During the summer of 1901 they did venture on to Rome, only to make the disillusioning discovery that it was as backward as Florence, if not more so. They found its streets completely lacking in the bustle of public life or in signs of technological progress, and Papini later wrote that he "had never imagined that the capital of a nation could be like this."[64] After the trip the two appeared to become more convinced that the social problems they saw before them—complacency in public life, corruption and disruption in political life, mindless specialization in academic life, decadence in what passed for avant-garde cultural life— could not be escaped and would have to be actively confronted by them and their generation. Still, lacking any concrete sense of how to act, they left unaltered their daily pattern of libraries and conversation for most of 1902.

Or perhaps the source of their inaction lay one level deeper. As Papini wrote in his diary early in 1900:

In us [our generation] there is a distrust for the men of the ruling generation that is both strong and well founded, yet we recognize that we are no better than they. We lack a unity of philosophical doctrine; we lack faith and steadfastness. Some take refuge in utilitarianism, others in aristocratic art, others in old, outmoded political ideals. But nowhere is there unity, action, or a goal. We are skeptics and pessimists, indifferent or feckless optimists; we are neurotic, strange, abnormal products of generations who have done too much, thought too much, enjoyed too much. Introspection torments us, external observation nauseates us, faith does not attract us, and love for us is simply a carnal pastime. What is to be done? That is the terrible question reaching us from the Russian steppes and finding an echo in our souls. But no one knows the answer. It is the twilight of souls, perhaps even their dead of night. Will the dawn come? and when? and where? Or will this night perhaps be eternal? A mystery.[65]

The problems of public life in Florence and post-Risorgimento Italy generally begged to be confronted, yet Papini felt that he and his generation were ill prepared to do so because of their lack of a "faith," of some overall outlook suited to modern life through which the moral virtues needed to face its problems might be nurtured. The initial task, then, would have to be to find or develop a faith.

In early October 1902, Papini's father became gravely ill in Turin and died after a harrowing three-week ordeal. One can only speculate about the role this event played in sparking Papini to launch *Leonardo*, but the fact is that in a matter of days, despite Prezzolini's absence, he was busy meeting with Costetti, Spadini, De Karolis, and various others about the idea of a new journal. As he wrote to Prezzolini in Paris on November 17: "In a few days we will have assembled a group of about thirty young people, all of them full of passion and hope, and who can become the first nucleus of that party of intellectuals I have been thinking about for a long time."[66] Later, however, he would confess that at the time of *Leonardo*'s inception he had lacked any "definite idea about what we ought to be doing, defending, attacking" and had "had no idea where to begin."[67] Nor did he have any sense of a potential audience outside his own group. He knew only that he wanted *Leonardo* to be philosophical in order that it might find the faith their generation so badly needed, in contrast to *Il Marzocco*, which in its blind devotion to art and poetry had either not sought such a faith or had been even further debilitated by the decadentist nihilism that it found.

While they were busy plotting late in 1902, Papini and his friends had met in *piazze*, but by the time they set out to produce *Leonardo*'s first issue in the first days of the new year, they had managed to rent an "editorial office" in the once magnificent, but by then internally dilapidated, Palazzo Davanzati, on the edge of what had been the old central market. The room they acquired had been used, most recently, as a factory for producing cricket cages, but with some impromptu refurnishing and the hanging of proper photographs—"the nude women of Titian, the dignified old men of Leonardo, and dancing figures of malicious fawns and foppish Apollos"—they were ready to write.[68] The first issue hit the streets on January 4, 1903.

In their opening manifesto (quoted at the beginning of the Introduction) the *leonardiani* made clear their strong generational sense, their intellectual ideals and commitments in life, their sense of the indivisibility of thought and life, and their rootedness in Florence. To emphasize their individuality, they used pseudonyms as self-conscious masks, and sometimes symbols instead of signatures.[69] To emphasize their creativity, they used a rough, handmade paper and original woodcuts of their own making. To emphasize their rejection of specialization, especially in intellectual matters, they made a point of abolishing any strict division of labor: "poets wrote on philosophy, philosophers did artistic design, scholars expounded their metaphysical ideas in verse, and painters tried their hand at critique and theory."[70] Moreover, they chose as the eponym of their review the Tuscan Leonardo da Vinci, "the man who had painted enigmatic souls, rocks, flowers, and skies better than the best painters before him; who had looked patiently for truth, in machines and cadavers, better than the best scientists; and who had written about life and beauty with words more profound and images more exacting than the best professional writers."[71] Though skilled at art, science, and literature, Leonardo was never the narrow professional. Rather he was a perfect exemplar of "the complete interior man . . . who loves solitary work and feels himself diminished by men . . . one of those rare men who are wholly self-sufficient."[72]

Already by mid-December the original *leonardiani* were joined by Prezzolini, who would soon confess that he was "happy to have left my solitude and to have joined the group."[73] A few months later he was noticing what had been apparent to Papini from the beginning: "We are joined here on *Leonardo* more by hatreds than by common ends . . . and we are united more by the forces of the enemy arrayed against us than by our own. Positivism, erudition, naturalist [*verista*] art, historical method, materialism, bourgeois and collectivist varieties of democracy— this entire stench of poisonous acid, flabbiness, and vanity, of the sweat of the people, this screeching of machines, this commercial bustle, this clatter of advertising—all of these things are tied together not only rationally but by human hands and emotions. If they were farther away

CONTIENE:

GIULIANO IL SOFISTA — IL DAVID DELLA FILOSOFIA INGLESE
(F. C. S. Schiller).
GIAN FALCO — MARTA E MARIA (Dalla contemplazione all'azione).
ETTORE REGÀLIA — DOLORE E AZIONE.
GIULIANO IL SOFISTA — UN CALUNNIATORE DELL'UOMO (G. Sergi).
ORTENSIO — IL PELLEGRINO.
G. IL S. — MANIPOLI (Elogio delle parole).
MARCELLUS — ELOGIO DELLA SOLITUDINE.
GIAN FALCO — UN PITTORE DELL'ABBATTIMENTO (E. Zoir).
G. IL S. — PER UNA CRITICA.
ALLEATI E NEMICI — (Una voce dal profondo, P. Eremita — La filosofia
in Italia, G. F. — La mitologia della scienza, G. il S. — La vendita di
Nietzsche al minuto. G. F. — Lo spiritualismo scientifico, G. il S.)— (Re-
censioni di O. Ewald, P. Lombroso, A. Martin, Allodoli, Corradini, Leo-
nardo da Vinci, Bourdel, C. Busse, Bateson, Botticelli).
SCHERMAGLIE — (Notizie meravigliose — Quarta Pagina Filosofica).
PALLE AL BALZO — (Per P. Orano, D. Garoglio, F. Gaeta, R. Forster,
G. A. Borgese, G. Prezzolini, L. Dami, G. Papini.)

DIREZIONE E AMMINISTRAZIONE:
FIRENZE — 10, VIA DEI BARDI, 10 — FIRENZE

Abbonamento annuo . . . . . · L. 5.00
Un numero . . . . „ 0.50

Questo Numero doppio costa L. 1.00

5. The March 1904 issue of *Leonardo* with a drawing by Giovanni Costetti, who had
studied with Auguste Rodin in Paris. The issue featured an article by Prezzolini on
the British pragmatist philosopher F. C. S. Schiller.

they might simply be disdained, but because they are so close they must
be actively hated instead."[74]

As we will see, this emphasis on "active hatred" and fighting "enemies" was a key aspect of Florentine avant-garde rhetoric. Before approaching that rhetoric, however, we need to recognize the way in which
Prezzolini's characterization of their mode of cohesion was an overstate-

ment. However strong their hatreds, the *leonardiani* shared a sense that modernity had opened up a spiritual abyss and that a new secular religion was desperately needed to repair the damage. However numerous and influential their enemies, they also had allies in this effort and, even more important, intellectual *maestri* to inspire them and, perhaps, to help fulfill their longing for a secular faith. Three of the most important of these *maestri* were Benedetto Croce, Henri Bergson, and William James.

Croce was a proudly independent scholar in a long and genteel Neapolitan tradition, who ranged across an astonishingly vast intellectual landscape that included philosophy, political thought, literary criticism, and cultural and political history. Born in 1866, and thus a decade and a half older than the generation of Papini and Prezzolini, he was an established presence in Italian intellectual life already in the 1890s. Yet it was with two acts early in this century that he caused his greatest stir within the emerging Italian avant-gardes: the publication of his *Estetica* in 1902 and the establishment a year later of *La Critica*, the review that he would produce almost single-handedly over the next four decades.

In launching *La Critica*, Croce saw himself as the rightful heir of De Sanctis, pursuing the project of the "intellectual and moral redemption" of Italy.[75] Not only did the review make available the resources of the European and specifically Italian cultural traditions; it also propounded an original philosophical standpoint that aimed at being adequate to the requirements of modern life and, by virtue of its presentation in short and simply written essays, accessible to the average educated person. Such a philosophy was necessary, in Croce's view, because of the great failing of modern industrial society and the positivism that underlay it: the fact that in this context our "religious need" remains "unsatisfied."[76] In light of the magnitude of his objective, however, the concept of philosophy that he actually developed in *La Critica*, and in the major philosophical tomes on aesthetics, logic, history, and practical life that his essays there distilled, was surprisingly modest. Philosophy could not offer a full and rational comprehension of reality, as Hegel most famously had imagined, but only an overall orientation or faith for the proper conduct of life. Such a faith, Croce argued, could be predicated neither on the God of traditional theology nor on empirical existence per se (as in the pragmatism of William James) but rather on empirical existence understood as possessing the divine (or absolute) within it. In other words, Croce sought to develop a worldview in which a sense of the absolute would be preserved without any claim to knowledge outside human experience.

The implications of this way of conceiving faith were complex. On the one hand, human action was all that produced historical experience, and our creativity therefore was nearly godlike. But on the other hand, our action was necessarily also constrained by past human action, whose results presented themselves as obstacles and limits for us. Moreover, our ability to understand this action and experience could never be absolute, indeed remained all too human. Certainly there was no possibility of grasping the historical unfolding of spirit as a panlogism in the Hegelian manner whereby certain moments of human action were seen as subordinate to others and philosophical knowledge could thereby be reconstructed in a grand synthesis. In Croce the various modes of human action—aesthetic, logical or scientific, practical, and ethical—were, rather, distinct moments whose interrelation might be appreciated contemplatively but could not be understood as a dialectic on the Hegelian model. One crucial consequence of this was that, while Croce's faith could make sense out of past human action, it could offer no gnostic hope of worldly fulfillment in an "end of history" through which present uncertainty might be overcome.

This insistence on the limitations of human existence, however, emerged more slowly in Croce's writings than did the theme of creative human action. In the *Estetica*, humanity appeared as a spectacularly creative species with vast powers of intuition that enabled it to make history in the way poets made poetry, and artists, art. Moreover, the fact that human action generally was conceived on the model of artistic intuition made art (rather than positivistic science) appear as the preeminent spiritual activity, and the artist or creative intellectual as the supreme human being. Indeed, the fact that there was no Hegelian *Weltgeist* in Croce's world, far from being understood as a limitation on human knowledge, appeared to many of his younger readers to make his faith still more attractive. For if only individuals existed, then all creative action was necessarily individual, and their own efforts, necessarily redeemed. From such a proposition to the view that human creativity itself could become the basis of a new "lay religion" was a very short leap.

So interpreted, the *Estetica* exploded like a bombshell among the young Florentine intellectuals, as it did among their counterparts elsewhere in Italy. Croce became "our *maestro* not our professor," who offered the enticing combination of a secular "faith" in human creativity as a source of the divine, genuine "philosophical intoxication," and a role model suggesting that they, Italy's young intellectuals, the class in whom the new faith was destined to take initial root, were thereby also Italy's future saviors.[77] Prezzolini, in particular, exulted in the view that Croce had discovered a new secular religion in which "man" had become a "man-god [*uomo dio*]," "unique in existence, the creator of the world, universal, infinite and eternal, capable of miracles, master of truth, lord of the world by means of science, prophet of the future."[78] But Papini also was initially full of praise for a philosopher he saw as "warm, courageous, and talented, even wildly so," and who seemed to promise a road out of the "mystery" that so preoccupied him.[79]

Croce appears to have done much to encourage this adulation, despite the fact that within a very few years he would be working hard to discredit the philosophical stance behind it as an embarrassing misunderstanding of his position. The Florentine review had come to his attention almost immediately after its inception, and not only had he praised it lavishly in *La Critica;* he had actually stopped in at Palazzo Davanzati in 1903 to visit with the young writers.[80] Signs of trouble began only the following year when Papini visited Croce in Naples. According to the account Papini later gave a biographer, he and Croce went to a theater to hear music, but Croce, instead of listening, spent the evening with his head buried in a ponderous tome of German philosophy.[81] A year later, Papini had begun a polemical exchange with him that would endure for a decade, one that would become especially raucous (albeit one-sidedly so) in the *Lacerba* years (1913–1915), when Croce was made symbolic of all that ailed modern rationalist civilization.[82] Yet it was significant that this polemic began over Croce's publication of his *Logica,* the book in which he first appeared to back away from the radical voluntarism of the *Estetica.* Indeed, Papini's position in 1905 remained very close to his reading of what Croce had said in 1902, although by then he was grounding his position in Jamesian pragmatism rather than in his earlier idealism. Prezzolini, too, seems to have lost his enthusiasm for the *Estetica* by 1905, but, unlike Papini, he remained largely faithful to Croce's views as they evolved and was openly embracing the Crocean "system" by 1908.

In his initial review of *Leonardo* Croce had written that its "writers are tied together by a philosophical conception, an idealism, especially close to the form given it by one of the subtlest contemporary French thinkers, Bergson." This was not false modesty; Bergson was indeed even more central than Croce in the initial outlook of the review, especially in Prezzolini's contributions. For not only was he engaged, like Croce, in developing a properly modern philosophical outlook; he was also far more interested than Croce in exploring its depth-psychological ramifications. This was the discovery that Prezzolini, to his great delight, had made in the libraries of Paris and, even more dramatically, in Bergson's lectures at the Collège de France. Years later he would remember that in those days, "I thought that I had found in his thought the key to the universe; I felt myself in possession of a liberating, religious knowledge that could unchain the soul from the cogwheels of determinism, and make man, and man alone, the beginning of spiritual liberty."[83]

Although Bergson would become a cultural sensation in Paris only after the appearance in 1907 of his *L'Evolution créatrice*, with its provocative concept of an *élan vital*, he had already made a considerable mark by the time Prezzolini discovered him in the fall of 1902.[84] In his doctoral dissertation on the "immediate givens of consciousness," published in 1889 when he was thirty, Bergson had already established his most fundamental thesis, namely, that time is not simply a convenient system of measurement but a lived experience, a "duration," a reality within which all experience takes place.[85] It was a thesis he explored not only through philosophical analysis but also through psychological investigation into processes of hypnotic suggestion and memory, processes that were attracting widespread attention in the wake of Jean Martin Charcot's pathbreaking experiments in hypnosis at Paris' Salpêtrière Hospital. In 1896 Bergson published a second, more psychological book on "matter and memory" that further explored his thesis; and by 1901, as a professor at the Collège de France, he had turned to an examination of its implications for two particular phenomena in human experience, jokes and dreaming, precisely the same phenomena to which Sigmund Freud, under the same influence, was also devoting himself in these years.[86]

In what became known as his "philosophy of contingency," Bergson maintained that there were two fundamental modes of human knowing, intuition and analysis, the one absolute and in harmony with reality, the other relative and conceptual, a mere tool for manipulating reality for human ends. Although his mode of expression was unwaveringly poised and coolly matter-of-fact, Bergson's polemical intent in favor of intuition was never in doubt. Nor were its implications for artistic creation, which made his philosophy appear to be no less a secular religion than Croce's *Estetica*. In Bergson's view, those who wrote or painted as if the world existed independently of our consciousness, like the naturalists, were clearly inferior to those, like the symbolists, who understood that the world is apprehended differently by each of us, and that at the center of all genuine art must lie a vision at once personal and interior, intimate and individual. At the same time, artists in touch with reality through intuition understood that there is no selfhood in the sense of a fixed persona, but that our experience of ourselves, like our experience generally, has about it a fluidity that defies concrete representation. Two of the key implications of this view were that reality as revealed by intuition is perceived as discontinuous and psychically mediated—like dreams—

and that "characters" are in fact "masks" we construct rather than realities we live out.

When Papini wrote to Prezzolini in Paris about *Leonardo,* he asked him for an article about Bergson, and the result was "Life Triumphant," which appeared in the journal's inaugural issue. Here, Prezzolini summed up the philosophy of contingency in two magnificently ornate sentences:

> It teaches us that under the hardened and cracked crust that we present to ourselves as ourselves, there runs, like a torrent of burning hot liquid lava, life itself, continuous, tumultuous, heterogeneous, and indivisibly unified, without ever repeating itself, always new and always tirelessly creative, an astonishing wellspring of harmony, which we can reach through profound action and introspection, and through disdaining logic, abandoning the practical metaphysic of common sense (the most dangerous because the most unconscious), and rejecting science as incapable of producing the real. An apology for the intimate life, a vindication of the power of the individual over the external world, a reduction of science to a convenient language, to an instrument of action, to a coinage capable of storing up the purchases of the past and permitting their exchange among men—such are the main features of the new philosophy.[87]

For Prezzolini, then, the main import of Bergson's ideas was his concept of life, through which fundamental oppositions—reason and faith, science and art, cosmos and psyche—could be overcome in a new synthesis, with implications of the most fundamental religious sort.

Yet Bergson was important, too, because through him life itself could be rediscovered in the sense that Oscar Wilde had recognized when he wrote that "mystery lies not in the invisible but in the visible," a phrase Prezzolini used as an epigraph to his article. In his book *Vita intima,* which he wrote immediately afterward, Prezzolini played at greater length with these implications in such propositions as "A lie is not only a mask of intimate life, but also a multiplier of the self" or "Irony is a beautiful mask and always a sign of pride, a strong feeling of one's superiority" over those many who fear to use it.[88] In a final bit of self-referential irony, Giuliano il Sofista reviewed the book for *Leonardo,* finding it "a mix of notes and thoughts, digressions and remembrances, citations and discussions, without any order or goal" and thus "impossible to read and of no utility . . . entertaining perhaps for the author who wrote it, but not for the reader."[89]

Still, however important Bergson may have been to Prezzolini as a *maestro,* it is remarkable how much of what he wrote in these years simply used Bergson to put a stamp of legitimacy on attitudes that he had long held and that would appear to have derived more from his life in Florence than from serious study. For example, Bergson was invoked to support the notion that the good life is that of "a solitary spectator, a creator of internal values" who takes "logic [as] my primary enemy, my hostile demon," and the notion that "we can affirm two things: (1) that we do not understand other people, and (2) that they do not understand us."[90] It becomes difficult to escape the impression that Prezzolini found in Bergson mostly what he wanted to find, and that what he gained from him was less a "new faith" than an affirmation of what he had already been trying very hard to believe.

In a sense this use of Bergson was in perfect keeping with a central insight that Prezzolini had appropriated from him, namely, that true philosophy involves not the acquisition of new knowledge but the revelation of what we at some deep level already know. Its model is autobiography or poetry, not the scientific treatise. Yet when one looks at the main works Prezzolini produced in the five years he spent primarily under Bergson's spell—five short philosophical works more or less in a Bergsonian vein, a study of the German mystics, and a volume on Italian culture coauthored with Papini—it becomes clear that Bergson's philosophy had led him into a self-indulgent egoism that was bound to prove ultimately unsatisfying for someone in search of a new faith to sustain his rather fragile sense of identity. Prezzolini's hope, as revealed in an essay he wrote on Novalis, had been for a "magical idealism" in which the nature of the world itself privileged fantasy over reason, creative imagination over scientific investigation, and the occult and secret powers of the "intimate life" over the false and corrupting powers of the public life.[91] Yet under Bergson's influence he proved unable to move beyond a kind of magical solipsism and to find the world, whether in the sense of cosmos or in the sense of collective creation with others. On the latter point, Prezzolini would come to appreciate only somewhat later the way Bergsonian insights were already being linked to social theory by such French thinkers as Georges Sorel and Charles Péguy.[92]

Papini never became quite the devotee of Bergson that Prezzolini was, but he shared the latter's initial enthusiasm as well as the quest for a "magical idealism" that underlay it. He read the *Introduction to Metaphysics* as soon as it appeared in early 1903, judged it "revolutionary," and struck up a correspondence with Bergson later in the year. In September 1904 he ventured outside Italy for the first time in order to meet Bergson at the International Congress of Philosophy in Geneva.[93] Yet although the meeting there undoubtedly reflected admiration for his work, it also seems to have been motivated by Bergson's ties to the publishing house of Félix Alcan in Paris, where Papini aspired to publish a volume on pragmatism.[94] It was, in any case, pragmatism and its then current *maestro,* William James, rather than Bergson's philosophy of contingency, which figured by late 1904 as the central hope in his own quest for secular-religious inspiration.

Born in 1842, and thus old enough to be the father of Croce or Bergson and the grandfather of Papini or Prezzolini, William James had turned his attention to philosophy only in the twilight of his career. Trained in medicine at Harvard, he had spent two decades working out the foundations of a scientific psychology, which culminated in his *Principles of Psychology* of 1890. Temperamentally, however, James was far from a rigorous scientist, and when, in the wake of the book, he recognized that he had grown tired of its project, he turned increasingly to philosophy, especially to the pragmatism of his friend Charles Sanders Peirce.

However, unlike Peirce, who was interested primarily in the logic of scientific investigation, James gave pragmatism a much more moral and speculative, even literary shape. Where Peirce had sought to use "practical consequences," above all the empirical results of science, as a basis for distinguishing meaningful and meaningless statements, that is, as a means for arriving at meaning, James developed the simpler argument that the meaning of a statement is identical with its practical consequences. The implication—that there is no meaning or truth independent of human actions—was unlike anything Peirce believed. Moreover, Peirce was essentially a logician and philosopher of science, James a humanist concerned with human experience in everyday life and the role of ideas and beliefs in that experience. Indeed, James sometimes felt constrained even by speculative philosophy in his understanding of life and compelled to think beyond the limits of reason.

In a lecture of 1896, which became a famous essay, James argued that we have a "freedom to believe," and thus a justifiable "will to believe," whatever is "live enough to tempt our will."[95] For not only does reason fail to answer our most fundamental religious and metaphysical questions, questions about which we must have an answer in order to live properly, but it is often insufficient even in the course of our everyday affairs. For example, in the midst of action we often lack the evidence necessary to make a rational judgment about what to do next, and yet we have no choice but to make some judgment. In such circumstances, James suggested, we should exercise our "will to believe," an idea quite similar to Bergson's notion of following intuition rather than intellect.[96]

It was above all this essay that brought James to the attention of philosophers everywhere who had tired of positivism and neo-idealist metaphysics and who sought something more daring to go beyond both. In England, the most prominent was the Oxford philosopher F. C. S.

Schiller, who had long been a critic of closed neo-idealist systems like that of his senior colleague F. H. Bradley, and who now, under the stimulus of James's notion of a will to believe, began to argue that reality and truth are wholly man-made in a way that is open, pluralistic in direction, and never finished. It was a conclusion still more radical than that of his mentor. For while James had gone so far as to argue that our categories for thinking are man-made and that, in this sense, there is no truth independent of our actions, he also viewed physical reality as almost stubbornly independent of us. James, who never gave up strong links to the empiricist tradition, tended to start with objective facts and claims about them, while Schiller's starting point was the unabashedly subjective one of individuals and their beliefs. His object was not simply to provide the modern individual with strong humanist beliefs but to forge a philosophy of humanism that could "stir us to activity" by inspiring complete confidence in our ability to remake the world.[97]

Like Schiller, Papini was deeply inspired by James's essay "The Will to Believe" but sought to go beyond James by making pragmatism into a secular religion in celebration of human action.[98] Moreover, he was quite familiar with Schiller, who had been discovered by Prezzolini and extolled in the pages of *Leonardo* as the English "David" who was then slaying the contemporary neo-Hegelian Goliaths.[99] Apparently, Prezzolini's enthusiasm for Bergson had whetted his appetite for pragmatism as well, and for a year, beginning in late 1903, he might even be said to have taken the lead in importing pragmatism into Florence. In a 1904 review of James's *The Varieties of Religious Experience*, he went so far as to call its author "the greatest and most original philosopher alive today."[100] The attraction, however, was relatively short-lived; by 1905 Prezzolini had returned full-force to Bergson.

In addition to the attractions Prezzolini may have found in pragmatism's concept of philosophy, it is clear that his brief embrace of it was also motivated by his conviction that it represented a rejection of academic philosophy. In his review of *Varieties*, for example, he lamented that its Italian edition should have a preface by "that doctrinaire pontiff of Italian positivism, R[oberto] Ardigò, a preface that shows either that the old theologian has not read or has not understood the book." In Prezzolini's vocabulary, which in this respect was also the vocabulary of *Leonardo* generally, positivism was associated with the doctrinaire, outmoded, and academic, pragmatism with the exciting, novel, and avant-garde. "I am perhaps a badly educated philosopher," he had written a few issues before, "but I am not a failed student or a paid hack."[101] Similarly, Papini wrote in the same issue that "the philosopher today does not know how to love or hate . . . he is a eunuch who no longer knows how to impregnate the world."[102] While we have ever more books on philosophy, he continued, "thought has become a profession" in which "there is no longer any lightning flash, any scream, any explosion"— precisely why "we" intend to revitalize it, even if ours should be a "solitary road."

Nonetheless, Prezzolini and Papini were quite cognizant of the need to legitimize their review philosophically, given their own lack of "professional" credentials. To this end they recruited two more senior and certified philosophers, Giovanni Vailati and Mario Calderoni, to write for their pages. Both were pragmatists but of a Peircean stripe, a fact that no doubt made the review's founding figures appear the more ecumenical, but that also provided for quite a number of spirited polemics. For the "logical pragmatism" of Vailati and Calderoni focused somewhat narrowly on countering positivism without much reforming its rationalistic ends, while the "magical pragmatism" of Prezzolini and, especially, Papini was an openly irrationalist effort at transforming the world. As Papini wrote in his memoirs: "For me pragmatism was not a principle of research, a cautionary procedure, or a refinement of method. I was looking well beyond that. For I was then seized by the dream of attaining magical powers: the need, the desire to purify and strengthen the spirit in order to make it capable of acting without instruments and intermediaries and so to achieve miracles and omnipotence. Through the 'will to believe' I sought a 'will to act.'"[103] If, in finding a "will to act," one somewhat relaxed the rigors of evidence or logic of proof, what did that matter? "Why not declare openly that philosophy is an invention, a form of play [giuoco], a spiritual exercise, a mystical edifice, a poetry of concepts that we need in order to feel, live, love, create, overturn, confound, and excite—for the pleasure of those who are solitary and despite the merchants?"[104]

The attractions of Jamesian pragmatism for Papini, whose development of it took most of his energy between 1904 and mid-1907, were essentially two. First, it offered a justification for an activism at once social and cosmic in which emotional and practical interests, as the conditions for action, were empowered to "change the world" and create the truth.[105] Pragmatism "teaches us how to gain convictions (the 'will to believe') . . . and how to use them to transform reality"; it is "a faith that creates its own verification."[106] Moreover, it was a faith that aimed to fulfill both the general need of humanity for a modern religion and the specific needs of individuals in all their irreducible particularity.[107]

Second, pragmatism offered the possibility of liberating thought, of founding a new, nonprofessional and avant-garde form of philosophy based on what Papini called "play":

Having seen the vanity of the philosophical work that has now come to an end, we can no longer take philosophy seriously, think with faith, construct in the spirit of gravity . . . But there will still be aristocratic spirits who, knowing that their meditations and constructs have no rational or universal value, delight in composing new metaphysics, new theories of consciousness, new moral formulas or to adapt and transform in various ways those that already exist. In this way they are doing "philosophical play" [*giuochi filosofici*]. For them a manual is necessary. We will make one, perhaps by displaying some of the rules of speculative play: variety, complication, contradiction.[108]

The special beauty of this play, for Papini, was its pluralism. As he wrote in a passage that James would later cite as an exemplary articulation of pragmatism's outlook: "For some pragmatism leads to mysticism and devotion, for others it leads to immoralism, for everyone to skepticism . . . [Pragmatism] is, then, a 'corridor theory'—the corridor of a grand hotel where there are a hundred doors opening into a hundred rooms," each of which has people very differently engaged inside, but "all [of whom] use the same corridor" to enter and leave.[109]

Yet although James himself was unfailingly pleased by the way Papini appropriated and expanded upon his philosophy, there were in fact considerable differences in emphasis between their respective views. James had spoken of the importance of belief in provoking the action that would lead to the realization of one's goals; Papini spoke of action that produced belief, which then retrospectively justified the action. In James it was belief that was most fundamental to modifying reality, in Papini, action. "Faith," wrote the latter, "does not create directly. Faith can arise from action and produce it, but it is action that, forming habits, creates new ones and modifies old ones."[110] Furthermore, whereas James spoke of belief as a complement to reason, Papini saw in action, even irrational action, a substitute for reason. In James's "will to believe," the goal was not to show how a person might acquire more power over the world but how he or she might deal with the limits of reason in the face of our need to know beyond it. In Papini, the idea was reversed: faith in the beyond became the "magic" that grounded otherwise meaningless action. In short, the Jamesian "will to believe" became more like a Nietzschean "will to power."[111]

When the two men met at the Fifth International Congress of Psychology in Rome, James was sixty-three, Papini a mere twenty-four. Clearly, James enjoyed the attentions of the younger man and was strongly drawn by his combination of intellectual sophistication and grandiose purpose, the latter putting him in stark contrast to James's more mundane academic colleagues. A year later in the *Journal of Philosophy*, he was hailing Papini as a "genius" and "the most radical conceiver of pragmatism to be found anywhere" whose writings should be consulted by all "American students" of pragmatism.[112] But perhaps the supreme compliment came in one of many private letters to Papini he wrote in this period:

> I have just been reading your *Crepuscolo dei filosofi* and the February number of *Leonardo*, and great is the resultant fortification of my soul. What a thing is genius! and you are a real genius! Here have I, with my intellectual timidity and conscientiousness, been painfully trying to clear a few steps of the pathway that leads to the systematized new *Weltanschauung* and you with a pair of bold strides get out in a moment beyond the pathway altogether into the freedom of the whole system, into the open country. It is your temper of carelessness, quite as much as your particular formulas, that has had such an emancipating effect on my intelligence. You will be accused of extravagance, and *correctly* accused; you will be called the Cyrano de Bergerac of Pragmatism, etc., but the abstract program of it must be sketched extravagantly.[113]

One might think, then, that life's prospects must have appeared quite good to Papini in 1906. He was being hailed as a *Wunderkind* by one of the foremost philosophers of the day, and it looked as though his book on pragmatism would soon be published by Alcan. More important, he seemed to have found the modern faith he had been so desperately seeking six years before when he first articulated his "terrible question" from the "Russian steppes."[114] Yet, despite all the recognition and apparent philosophical gain, Papini gave up on pragmatism by mid-1907. The book contract with Alcan never materialized, and in any case pragmatism was apparently also unable to satisfy his longing for an activist faith.[115] Perhaps, like Prezzolini's experience of disillusionment with Bergson that same year, he had found that philosophical "magic" could not sustain itself without a more concrete indication of its relevance to collective human problems. Yet unlike Prezzolini, Papini did not turn away from individualism toward social commitment but only away from philosophy, a pursuit he came to regard as inherently a source of false hopes.[116] As he lamented at the close of his 1912 autobiography, if "I am a failure," then "I am nothing because I tried to be everything."[117] Like the young Karl Marx, who had exhorted the workers to be revolutionary with a strikingly similar phrase—"I am nothing and I should be everything"—the young Papini had sought to overcome philosophy by realizing it.[118] But the result, for him, was that he felt unfulfilled by philosophy without any apparent benefit—worldly or otherwise—from having played the philosophical game.

The goal of using the most radical philosophical currents of the day to forge a secular religion was the principal feature of *Leonardo*. Croce, Bergson, and James had all inspired the *leonardiani* in their cult of the individual creative mind or genius, who feels excluded from society (or above it) by virtue of the independence of his intuitive beliefs and his heroic will to self-realization, and who wishes to transform the world with a philosophy that sustains mythos over logos. In the end, none of them was able to provide the new mythos the *leonardiani* were seeking. But the quest that these three *maestri* represented for their youthful epigoni hardly exhausts the importance of *Leonardo* for the present story.

The Rhetoric of Cultural Renewal

Despite the deeply personal nature of Papini's and Prezzolini's quests for faith, both justified their philosophical efforts as central to a collective project of cultural renewal. No word was more important to the message of *Leonardo*, or recurred more often in its pages, than "renewal" and its various equivalents: "rebirth," "reawakening," "renaissance," "regeneration," "resurgence," "resurrection." Nor was any attitude more deprecated there than the one that simply contemplated the world rather than remaking it.[119] The philosophical quest for faith in *Leonardo* was, for its writers, neither privatistic nor passive. It was an activist effort to fulfill De Sanctis' project of "intellectual and moral redemption," and to produce from their own midst the new cultural Mazzinis that might allow Italy to unify at a spiritual level rather than merely at a political one. Moreover, as Papini wrote in *Leonardo* in 1905, it aimed to go beyond the Italian case to the modern situation as a whole: "Only the minimum program of Mazzini (that of the unity and independence of Italy, which ought to have been the means for another, grander program) has been followed for good or for ill, while the other one, the one that referred not just to Italy but to all humanity, not only to political unity but also to a spiritual one, not only to independence from foreigners but also to freedom from misery and unhappiness, still remains a solitary dream . . . The third Rome, which should begin a new spiritual era of humanity, is still to come . . . The new religion that should succeed Christianity and substitute people for man has still not triumphed."[120]

It was because of this activism, this desire to have a cultural and intellectual impact that would "remake the world," that *Leonardo* can be thought of as an avant-garde review, arguably the only such review in the Florence of its day. Enrico Corradini's *Il Regno* may have had a comparable or even a greater social impact, but its focus was so narrowly protonationalist as to make it appear to be just another sectarian instrument, like journals of socialist or Catholic persuasion.[121] Similarly, the focus of Giuseppe Borgese's *Hermes* was literary rather than broadly cultural, and in its approach, subject matter, tastes, and goals it was rather like *Il Marzocco*'s younger brother, a literary review for the next generation, but not an effort to reshape it as a group of new cultural Mazzinis.[122]

Nowhere does *Leonardo*'s distinctively avant-garde approach to culture emerge with greater clarity than in an article Papini wrote late in 1905, which soon became the introduction to *La coltura italiana*, a book that he and Prezzolini coauthored and that represented in many ways the culmination of their efforts in this period.[123] In a brief preface to the article, they wrote: "We propose, with this volume, not just to react against the misery and baseness of this culture but also to put forward the problem of culture to our fellow citizens today as the most important problem facing contemporary Italy, assuming we want to be an actor in the world and not simply a choirboy." Then, in the article itself, Papini explained that although they were unsure whether a real Italian culture still existed, they were sure that what usually passed for it had become moribund. They smelled "bad intellectual air." Its source was in the generation that had followed the Risorgimento, a generation that had built only an enormous bureaucracy on a disastrously centralized Napoleonic model, the consequences of which were "ignorance in the people [*popolo*]" and "absurd specialization" in the universities. This bleakness was nearly unrelieved: "the few autodidacts who arise here and there . . . are regarded with pity by the ignorant, since they lack official positions and fixed salaries, and with scorn by the stamped and certified scholars, since they lack titles and specializations." In short, Papini concluded in a typically aggressive metaphor, "the sons of the political liberators were not intellectual liberators; to the contrary, they have even . . . added new strands to the ropes that have tied down Italian culture for a very long time and that we today must cut with long knives we have sharpened."[124]

The Italian problem, however, was not simply one of bad government or a corrupt élite. The Italian people, in Papini's view, had fallen asleep from the end of the Renaissance until the early nineteenth century. They had lost the virtue of "courage" in the broad sense of loving adventure, initiative, and risk. Fortunately, Napoleon had reawakened them politically, and the Risorgimento had provided the foundation for an economic reawakening in subsequent decades, but only now had the moment of "intellectual resurrection" arrived. To seize it, Italian culture would have to bring itself into greater contact with the "foreign cultures that have surpassed us for two or three centuries" and, somehow, muster the courage to break the "atmosphere of moral servitude" that enveloped it.

The Italian spirit "has become restricted, prudent, timid, fearful, cowardly, in love with compromises, hypocrisies, halfway phrases, honeyed language, polite formulas, precautions, sweetness, and the enemy of things said openly, of risk, of reckless enterprises, of overly new ideas, of irregular things, of insults, of violence."[125] What was needed was a new "spiritual virility."[126]

In his contributions to the book, Prezzolini echoed many of the same ideas—the importance of courage as a moral virtue, the impotence ("eunuchism") and mediocrity of academic culture, the need to reassert the cultural vitality of Italy's regions against state centralization—but he also added an element that was at once cautionary and apocalyptical. On the one hand, he claimed to have no illusions that the work of *Leonardo* would overthrow the cultural predominance of the professors or "change the people." Nor did he imagine that he would "see the libraries improved, the school of Dantean pedants flushed down the toilet, [Cesare] Lombroso's [positivist] charlatanism exposed, or the flies swatted away from [Alessandro] Manzoni's carcass." On the other hand, he expressed hope that Italy's "lack of revolutions" might soon be overcome and that a "third great Italy" might be created, "not the Italy of the popes nor of the emperors, but the Italy of the thinkers."[127]

Given his supposed lack of illusions, was this vision of a "third Italy" simply a chimera? Perhaps, but Prezzolini did at least have a broad sense of what its source in reality might be. "The culture of a nation," he wrote, "is much vaster than its schools"; it comprises not only what artists, writers, and scientists say, but also the "sentiments" and "political and religious theories" that common people hold, as well as their "moral visions, their mode of considering life, and their personal philosophies." Vibrant cultures, moreover, do not emerge from schools; rather, good schools emerge from vibrant cultures.[128] One can read countless learned essays about Dante and fail to comprehend him if one's culture lacks the spiritual resources of Dante's culture. By the same token, if one's culture has those resources, it will not need scholarly essays for the task. Indeed, it may well regard such essays as so much dross covering over what remains alive in the original work.

For the early Prezzolini, then, cultural renewal was a matter of discarding overrefinement at the same time as one sought spiritual depth in philosophical thought. The same idea had been expressed by Papini in *Leonardo* earlier in the year, for whom it appears to have had a Nietzschean origin. The culture of Romanticism, he argued there, had already "stripped man of everything that had developed in him that prevents life from continually renewing itself," giving us back the "nudity of man." The post-Romantic problem was whether "to return to the human past (neoclassicism, tradition, etc.) or to the animal past (to the beasts, as Rémy de Gourmont proposes), or to create new clothes, that is, new rules and constraints or, finally, to resolve to remain nude and to act more powerfully without the need for instruments and restraints." For Papini the first solution was too backward-looking, the second too inhibiting; only the last offered the possibility of real cultural renewal for only it would unleash the "subliminal self," the "power that is personal, secret, awe-inspiring, quick-moving, that resides in every person."[129]

In both Prezzolini and Papini, then, cultural renewal was conceived in precisely the terms common to the European modernist movement in this period, namely, as an uncovering of the primal self buried beneath the debilitating incrustations of a decadent civilization. Yet, supposing that the common people were so liberated, would they in fact produce a genuine cultural renewal? This was the great source of doubt that plagued the project of *Leonardo*. On the one hand, as we have just seen, the language of the *leonardiani* frequently implied a kind of cultural populism. The falseness and corruption of Italian cultural life was portrayed mostly in terms of its control by the academy, and the hope for renewal, in terms of liberating the "personal philosophies" or "subliminal selves" of the common people. Moreover, such language was even stronger in Soffici than in Prezzolini and Papini. For him, the vigor and quiet strength of the Tuscan *popolo*, in contrast with the decadence of Paris, was a cardinal point of faith, one that he communicated repeatedly in his letters.[130] Yet on the other hand there was a pervasive fear in their writings of a "sleeping" and "ignorant" people that might never be "awakened" or "changed" to meet the challenges of modern life. Correspondingly, much of their early writing invoked an ideal of solitude that seemed aimed at consoling them, as it had Nietzsche's Zarathustra, for their inability to reach the unblinking herd. Thus, for example, they had pictured Leonardo as loving "solitary work," Bergson as having conceived the good life as that of the "solitary spectator," and Gide as being "one of the companions in solitude whom we love for his simple and profound spirit."[131]

Even when they idealized the common people, the *leonardiani* regarded them from a distance as creatures quite unlike themselves.[132] Although they might address their "fellow citizens" in an article or book, there was never a sense of a public space shared with them, of any real interaction with those uneducated or less educated persons who might happen upon their writings, or of any influence by them on those writings.[133] Moreover, they frankly acknowledged this state of affairs. In a 1906 article announcing "a campaign for a reawakening by force,"

Papini was perfectly clear about his audience: "I speak neither to Humanity nor even to the Italian people; I speak to a few hundred of the young people born in Italy around 1880, in other words to a part of that generation that began to think and act at the turn of the century . . . My wish is for a part, a small part, of the latest Italian generation to free themselves of certain tendencies, certain tastes, certain weaknesses and to acquire other characters, new passions and preoccupations. To modify men, to reshape and enlarge souls, to transform spirits: that is my favorite art."[134] It was the old dream of the "party of intellectuals," one that was now at the center of his correspondence with both Prezzolini and Soffici, and that was now theirs too.[135] Yet what none of them understood was how the new party might engage the "Italy" it sought to renew.

No doubt their lack of any concrete notion of how to engage the common people reflected an attitude of impatience with, even contempt for, "politics" among the *leonardiani,* an activity they identified with corruption, outmoded ideologies, and decadence. Their activities were for the most part self-consciously "spiritual," that is, on a higher plane than "mere" politics. Yet Prezzolini and Papini did in fact think a good deal more about politics than their self-descriptions at the time would lead one to believe. Each wrote several expressly political articles during the first year of *Leonardo,* and when Corradini founded his political journal *Il Regno* late in 1903, both contributed substantially to that effort; indeed, Papini served as its first editor. Moreover, Papini devoted considerable time in 1904 to giving a speech in various towns and cities on his "nationalist program."[136] All of this suggests that the failure of the *leonardiani* to conceive how they might connect themselves to a popular audience and build a movement reflected not a lack of effort in this respect, but the particular nature of their political views.

Although they may have paid no attention to the assassination of Umberto I, two factors arose subsequently that made them pay greater attention to politics. Of these, the more important initially was the rise of socialism across northern Italy, and specifically in Florence, where the general strike of August–September 1902 had had such a shocking effect. All their more political articles in *Leonardo* in 1903 focused on the need to defend the city from the effects of such strikes and on countering what in their view were the pretensions of socialist ideology.[137] In general, the strategy of these articles was to suggest that socialism, far from being a genuine countermovement to the bourgeoisie, was actually only the same old bourgeois humanitarianism in the service of an emerging but equally decadent, rival political class.

The form of the argument may already suggest the second and more enduring source of their early politics: the "élite theory" that was then being put forward by Gaetano Mosca and Vilfredo Pareto, especially the version of it that the latter had published in 1902 as *Les Systèmes socialistes*. In general, such theories claimed scientific foundation for the notion that all politics were based on domination by some "political class" (Mosca's phrase) or "élite" (Pareto's), and thus on a "circulation of élites" rather than on the democratic rule of the people that parliamentarism purported to institutionalize. Moreover, such theories traced Italy's problems to the decadence of its existing "political class" and thus posited the need to produce a new one. Pareto's book took the additional step of showing how the theory could be utilized as a critique of socialism, one that appeared to undermine its utopian pretensions at the same time that it cast similar aspersions on the "bourgeois" politics of the status quo.

In one of his memoirs Prezzolini recalled that he had first encountered Pareto's ideas "on a cold day in the winter of 1900 while leafing through a French review in the icy reading room of the Biblioteca Nazionale in Florence."[138] But even if the recollection is accurate, Pareto did not appear to have much impact on his thinking until 1903. What is certain is that by the end of that year, when Prezzolini wrote his first major article for *Il Regno*, he was intimately familiar with both Mosca and Pareto, and particularly enthralled with the latter's critique of socialism.[139] As he wrote years later about Pareto: "What was new that he appeared to us to have brought out was his interpretation of the history of political life as a series of aristocracies, which succeeded one another when those that were dominant became soft, humanitarian, incapable of combat."[140] Socialism, in this perspective, was only an effort to mount another such aristocracy, but one that did not know itself as such, and was therefore self-deluded as well as decadent like the bourgeois élite it sought to replace. What was historically required, by implication, was a genuine "new aristocracy," one in full possession of heroic and martial virtues.

When the article appeared, Prezzolini sent a copy of it to Pareto in Lausanne, where he was a professor of political economy. The latter replied immediately in a long letter at once praising Prezzolini's analysis and replying to his one criticism of it, namely, his rejection of the notion that a "new aristocracy" could arise from "the part of the working class that is most educated and specialized."[141] In a published reply, Prezzolini reaffirmed his claim that any "socialist victory would only be a victory of a bourgeois minority" and therefore no significant departure from the status quo. The only genuine source of a new aristocracy, he added, would be a group like that around *Il Regno*, "a minority of heretics that has the courage to scoff at the sacred beliefs of the humanitarian religion, to scorn the softness of the pacifiers, and to try to bring back the sympathy for force that the bourgeoisie has lost." As a distinguished man of science, Pareto, in his view, had seen in "the theory of aristocracies only a scientific theory" and had therefore failed to understand how it should be applied in the present context. As an engaged activist, Prezzolini claimed to "see it rather as a scientific justification for a present political necessity." Moreover, Prezzolini insisted that any new aristocracy would have to be forged by a single forceful leader and was therefore unlikely to arise out of a mass-based, egalitarian movement: "What the Italian bourgeoisie up to now has lacked is an example and a forceful voice . . . that is, *a man*. We believe strongly in the power of individuals in the history of peoples."[142]

For Papini, too, Pareto's political thinking had been a major inspiration, and when in September 1904 he went to the International Congress of Philosophy in Geneva to meet Bergson, he made a point of stopping at Pareto's house in Céligny on the way.[143] Impressed as much by the demeanor of the man as by what he said, Papini would come to regard his élite theory as a scientific demonstration of the impossibility of democracy in the sense of direct rule by the people.[144] The point seemed to him to clinch the argument against the republicanism still maintained in the generation of his father and Carducci. But perhaps more important, for both Papini and Prezzolini, the acceptance of élite theory served to deflect attention from their lack of a sense for how to engage the *popolo*. From this perspective, such an effort appeared unimportant, especially in contrast with the need to develop a "new aristocracy" that was a genuine alternative to "bourgeois humanitarianism," one that cultivated a warrior spirit with corresponding moral virtues of inner strength, hardness, and discipline. Once such an aristocracy was firmly established, they seemed to be thinking, the problem of engaging the *popolo* would take care of itself.

Pareto's theoretical writings offered one additional feature that seems to have been quite significant for the *leonardiani*. This was his conviction, reflected continuously in his language, that major forms of politics such as monarchy, democracy, and socialism were tantamount to "religions" and that to replace a dominant one required mounting an essentially religious alternative. Thus, in his first letter to Prezzolini Pareto had written that "for any hope of success against socialism, which is a faith and a religion, one can only oppose another faith and religion," which is what he suggested the "nationalism" of Prezzolini and his friends finally was.[145] This perception not only fit perfectly with their self-understanding but also provided the conceptual link they had hitherto lacked between their philosophical and political activities. In the Paretian perspective they adopted, the search for a new secular religion became the necessary philosophical grounding for the politics of a new aristocracy.

Out of their encounter with Pareto, then, came the basic elements of their political position in the *Leonardo* years, one that in essential respects endured through the subsequent years of *La Voce* and into the First World War. One of these was certainly the idea of a new aristocracy with which they characterized their own aspirations and those of other intellectuals in their generation. It is noteworthy that the key chapter, "The New Aristocracy," of novelist and political historian Alfredo Oriani's 1908 *La rivolta ideale*—an immensely popular book that would come to epitomize for many the call for a spiritual revolution against liberal Italy—had already appeared a year earlier in *Leonardo*.[146] Yet there were at least three other key concepts that emerged out of their reception of élite theory.

The first of these concepts, and the most important in terms of its mythic import for the later *prises de position* of the Florentine avant-garde, was Prezzolini's characterization of the "two Italies" and of a rising "second Italy" in an article that appeared in *Il Regno* in the spring of 1904.[147] Rhetorically, the article rests on an elaborate binary opposition between the "state," the "superficial" and "exterior manifestation" of Italy, and the "nation" or "vital part" of Italy—the one decadent, oratorical, ineffectual, the other forward-looking, active, creative.[148] The state is a "crust" or "shell," a "mechanism" based on "words" that emanate from "offices"; the nation is "the part that produces," an "intimate, working" group of people, based on "deeds" conceived in "living rooms." In the concluding paragraph Prezzolini declared: "Between these two Italies—one which repeats in its somnolent life the daily intrigues and sterile formulas of the old generation; the other which acts, grows, expands the nation, but does not know itself, lacks grand goals, is poor in politics, poor in art, poor in thought—between these two Italies, one of profiteering and sophistical, rhetorical habits, the other of fertile unconsciousness, with energies but without direction, we ought to be both the force that destroys the first and the light that illuminates the second; we ought to be a torch that both burns and brightens." In this conceptualization, then, Italy's problem was the domination of a decadent "first Italy" and the inchoateness of the emerging "second Italy," which does not yet "know itself." The role of the "we," the avant-garde of the "new" generation or "new aristocracy," is to "burn and to brighten," to destroy the first Italy as it educates the second.

One of the advantages of this sort of formulation, apart from the sheer drama in its mythic image of confrontation, was that it was vague enough to allow apparently political forces to be portrayed in philosophical and psychological terms. Thus, for example, Prezzolini could write of the first Italy of "parliamentarism" as based on "a rationalist and optimistic concept of man" and the emerging second Italy as incorporating "the nonrational, sentimental, instinctive, passional motives" of human life that the former repressed.[149] Similarly, Papini would write two years later of the need to oppose the "vile spirit of the existing Italy" based on "a fear of the grand" with "the spirit portrayed by a part of the youth of Italy . . . of the love of risk, adventure, and danger . . . that alone can found a new Italian civilization."[150]

Allied to the image of "two Italies" in confrontation was a second element derived from it: the concept of the "internal enemy" (nemico interno). Unlike the more benign image of a "third Italy" or "third Rome," which conjured up a historical succession of praiseworthy realms, the image of "two Italies" pitted two antagonists in a present-day struggle and thus depended implicitly upon the concept of an enemy. Still, Prezzolini's initial uses of it were cautious, as when he asserted in his reply to Pareto that the Italian bourgeoisie was its own worst "internal enemy": "the common reference point among the middle classes themselves, their internal enemy, has been their sure conviction of being condemned to cede everything to their enemy sooner or later; and this conviction has too often led them into cowardly inertia or the vice of concessions."[151] With his more combative temperament, Papini was the first to take the idea further, claiming that the "democratic mentality" was not only its own internal enemy but the internal enemy of the nation. "In order to love something deeply you have to hate something else," wrote Papini in 1904. "No good Christian can love God without loathing the devil." Similarly, no good Italian could love Italy without hating the "democratic mentality," which "one feels to be present, adversarial [nemica], dominating, and hostile in every event, at every moment."[152] A decade later when, in the midst of the campaign for Italian intervention, Papini wrote his famous article "Due nemici" in Benito Mussolini's newspaper Il Popolo d'Italia, his only real addition was explicitly to name as his "devil" the recently deposed prime minister, Giovanni Giolitti, and the political system of giolittismo associated with him. In the climate of war, his idea of an "internal enemy" more loathsome than any external enemy and, thus, the real object of the war effort, would catch national attention, becoming an anti-establishment myth that endured long into the war and the era of *squadrismo* that followed it.[153] In the period of *Leonardo*, the image was used more vaguely and innocently, but its provocativeness and potential to incite were certainly not lost on its youthful deployers.

Moreover, the *leonardiani* were already utilizing as well a third concept deriving from élite theory that made explicit what the notion of the "internal enemy" left implicit: the idea of war or violence as a necessary instrument in the molding of a successful new aristocracy. As early as February 1903, in the article in which he first attacked the socialists and their strikes, Prezzolini was writing: "to fail to react would mean to die shortly: we believe with Heraclitus in war as the queen mother of all things."[154] Given the context, Prezzolini's advocacy of violence might be understood as defensive. But a year later, in an article titled "Elegy on Violence," he made startlingly clear that his concept of violence was anything but defensive:

> To someone used to the calm meetings of the Accademia, and to the hypocritical gentility of their erudite polemics, our language seems violent . . . Yet so-called gentility, silence, politeness are very often just synonyms for cowardice, lack of arguments, weakness of mind . . . The violence that we employ has to do not with hatred for others but with love of ourselves; an injurious epithet is not so much a blow at the enemy as a mental improvement for us; a polemic that excites the competitive faculties and separates one profoundly from an adversary serves as gymnastic exercise for the intellectual limbs and as a deep moat we dig within the fortress of the self. To separate oneself, to cultivate solitude, to love war, these are the aims of every person who wants to feel himself profoundly. Violence is, then, a moral cure, an exercise that strengthens, a categorical imperative for all those who love themselves.[155]

For the early Prezzolini, then, violence and war were understood in regenerative terms, as a necessary moral educator for those wishing to be in touch with their deepest instincts and feelings. While this attitude appeared to moderate somewhat in the early years of *La Voce* (1908–1911), it returned full-force during the intervention campaign of 1914–15.

For the early Papini as well, the need for regenerative violence and war appeared self-evident. In an article in which he defended his "reactionary" views on the basis of "a love of country, war, expansionism, property and order," he set forth their underlying anthropology in terms reminiscent of Joseph de Maistre a century before:

Don't these [passions for country and war] correspond perhaps to instincts so powerful in the soul and flesh of man that they will not die out in the future just as they have not changed over all the many centuries of the past? . . . Man . . . is a battlefield. He has always sheltered many enemies in his soul. The most diverse instincts, the most opposed passions, the most contradictory wills are found and are jostled within his chest . . . From the days of Cain and Abel there have been born under the sun men who loved fireside calm and were full of the fear of God . . . and beside them, in every land, men who were more violent, more energetic, harder, more ferocious, who did not tremble in their hearts before the need for slaughter . . . Thus the opposition [we see today] between those men who want an energetic nationalist policy of conquest and those who want an internationalist policy of peace and humanitarianism is not an opposition of past and present . . . but of two types of spirit, two concepts of life, two groups of instincts.[156]

The problem was to give freer reign to the "more violent and energetic" types so that the modern spirit so dominated by lovers of "fireside calm" could be genuinely renewed.

Beside this political rhetoric of "two Italies" poised for combat, the one passive and small-minded, an "internal enemy" to be conquered, the other presently dormant but potentially aggressive because still open to expressing primal instincts of violence and war, lay a corresponding moral rhetoric whose elements are not hard to guess: the need to cultivate the "hard virtues," to overcome D'Annunzian "decadence," and to restore the spirituality of "interior man" as against the materialism of "external man." Yet this moral rhetoric did not flow directly from Pareto and élite theory as had the political one. Rather it owed more to the cultural-élitist and incipiently antifeminist attitudes that Papini developed, quite likely in part through a critical reading of Nietzsche, and that Prezzolini appropriated above all from *fin-de-siècle* Vienna's foremost philosophical prodigy, Otto Weininger.

Although their fullest discussions of the moral virtues of "hardness" and "discipline" would come only later in *La Voce*, their basic moral commitment to them was already quite clear in the era of *Leonardo*. Indeed, in the very first issue Papini inveighed against the humanitarian softness of democratic thought, even as he also sought to position the tough-minded "interiority" of his "spiritual imperialism" against the "materialist and exterior," but also softer, "literary and aesthetic" imperialism of Corradini and Morasso.[157] To do so, he invoked Nietzsche, though without elaborating his views. "Nietzsche's immoralism" also appeared in his early critique of socialism as the philosophical basis of a "new morality" that he hoped would overturn a "European spiritual climate too soaked through with Christianity" and its "reign of the weak."[158] By 1905, though in the name of Dante rather than Nietzsche, Papini was offering the related argument that Italy was suffering from a lack of "spiritual virility" whose source lay in the "soft" and "feminine" style of *D'Annunzianismo* followed by the likes of Corradini and Morasso.[159] At about the same time, he appeared to put these two points together in an argument that made Nietzsche an archetypal antidecadent and philosopher of masculine power, but he complemented this suggestion with a sharp criticism of the German as personally "weak" for failing to act on his convictions.[160] Half a decade later, he would retract the criticism in a highly sympathetic "prayer for Nietzsche."[161] Yet, however great Nietzsche's role in the development of Papini's moral views, there is no doubt that these views came to be increasingly centered upon a cultural "masculinism" that was, in turn, quite inseparable from his own notion of a new aristocracy.[162]

Prezzolini's early reading in Nietzsche was more limited and its effects less apparent.[163] But as early as 1904 he too was using a morality of "hardness" to separate himself from those he considered decadent.[164] Two years later a decisive event in the development of his moral rhetoric occurred when he pored through the turgid German of Weininger's *Sex and Character* (1903), a book that Papini would acknowledge only in 1908 and that would be translated into Italian only in 1912.

Weininger's book, which he completed just after taking a doctorate in philosophy and just before shooting himself fatally at the age of twenty-three, is a zany ride through a verbal thicket of purportedly interrelated claims about maleness and femaleness, homosexuals and prostitutes, geniuses and nihilists, Aryans and Jews. After a seemingly sophisticated opening in which, like the Freud of the same period, Weininger found both "male" and "female" tendencies (as well as homosexual and heterosexual ones) in all men and women, he went on to make such claims as: "woman is only sexual, man . . . partly sexual"; feminists are strongly "male" women; "true women" do not want emancipation; only men can be geniuses, whereas women have "universal passivity," "organic untruthfulness," and no "continuous memory" or "logic"; soft, feminine virtues such as "sympathy" should be rejected; Jewish men are more "female" than "Aryan" ones (excepting perhaps the English) and thus tend toward "nihilism"; and women, Jews, and Negroes should nonetheless be emancipated legally, even though they will never in fact be truly equal.[165]

In connection with his project on Novalis and German mysticism, Prezzolini had traveled to Munich for a two-month stay in the spring of 1906, during which he appears to have discovered Weininger. In an April letter to Croce, he referred to the "rebirth of idealism [in Germany] but in certain very curious forms, for example in Vaihinger [*sic*], whose work derives wholly from Fichte but is dedicated to the problem of eroticism."[166] Six months later, he wrote a long and very favorable review of the young "enemy of women" whose "curious moral suicide" had made him a cult figure among German-speaking youth. Although Prezzolini presented all of the book's principal points—and favorably, without a hint of reservation concerning its misogyny—what he seems to have found most praiseworthy in Weininger was his "strong self-presentation, in fine contrast to the contemporary generation of overly literary Germans," and his concept of "genius," which he himself exemplified. Weininger's identification of the "mediocre, base, vulgar, bad, dishonest, and stupid" with the feminine, and of the "great, beautiful, energetic, solemn, and intelligent" with the masculine, was above all a moral valuation and an indication of his personal willingness, fortified by his antipositivism, "always to battle reality, whether in constructing these ideas or in applying them."[167] As Prezzolini wrote later in a letter to Romain Rolland: Weininger, "like you, fought against all effeminate forms, all German decadentisms and charlatanisms, all voluptuous art and pornography."[168]

Odd as it may seem, the association in Prezzolini's mind between Weininger, the distraught Viennese Jew, and Rolland, a devout French Catholic of aristocratic bearing, is in fact quite helpful in understanding the sort of personal character and moral commitments that both he and Papini were advocating. In November 1906 Papini had traveled to Paris, where he had met Rolland's friends Péguy and Sorel and heard from them about an author he had already been reading for most of the year. Shortly thereafter, Prezzolini appears to have begun to read Rolland seriously, both his biographies of Beethoven and Michelangelo and the first installments of his *roman-fleuve*, *Jean-Christophe*, which had been appearing in Péguy's journal, *Cahiers de la Quinzaine*. Like the biographies, *Jean-Christophe* was a novel rich in poetic feeling whose hero, a musical genius, had only contempt for the academic intellectuals of Paris and lived a solitary life of spiritual moralism that, despite his constant depressions and self-doubts, made manifest an intimate link between art, genius, and morality. To Prezzolini, then, Weininger probably appeared very much like a real-life Jean-Christophe, and the latter was certainly quite like Rolland himself, who in turn soon came to exemplify (together with Péguy and Sorel) the sort of spiritual idealism and moralism he and Papini were striving to attain.

Another mark of the moral life the young Florentines held up as an ideal was, as we have seen, the virtue of courage. Courage for them meant avoiding the narrowness and smallness of the professors and politicians as well as the decadence of the D'Annunzians, which they associated both with a lack of virility and, even more, with a lack of sincerity. Because of the latter association, the virtue of sincerity was equally central to their moral position. Its meaning and its connection to courage are well expressed in the following passage written by Papini in 1906:

> Like courage, sincerity is necessary for us. Sincerity is a form of courage. We need it for the grandest of our enterprises: for the discovery of our internal secrets, our fate and our ends, and for climbing the high mountains of meditation. We know our own souls very little, and we think a great deal about ourselves—not about the little "me" who looks for a job or a wife but about the great "me" who no longer belongs to this house or this city, who thinks and rethinks the world and its significance, who thinks about life and its purpose. *We need to discover ourselves,* and, when we have done so, perhaps we can change our direction. To do this, courage, a great deal of courage, will be necessary.[169]

In fact the importance of sincerity had long been a hallmark of Péguy's rhetoric, and his *Cahiers* were dedicated to the "revolution of sincerity" he believed the French Socialist Party had become incapable of carrying out.[170] It was to the same value that Prezzolini would dedicate *La Voce,* one of the central models for which was the *Cahiers.*[171]

If to be sincere for the young Florentines meant "discovering one's internal secrets," such secrets often turned out in practice to lie among their roots in Florence and Tuscany. The worst of the D'Annunzian poses was that of the "cosmopolitan" equally at home in Rome, Florence, or Paris, and thus truly at home nowhere. For Papini and above all for Soffici, who returns to the center of our story in 1907, self-discovery meant rediscovering their *toscanità,* just as for Péguy, who lived as a non-academic intellectual in the shadows of the Sorbonne, it had meant remembering his roots in the French heartland near Orléans. Even for Prezzolini, whose family came from Tuscany but who was not himself native-born, and whose *toscanità* was less pronounced, the Tuscan landscape and people were an occasional source of inspiration and hope as he moved fitfully between Florence, Milan, Perugia, Munich, and the mountains of Tuscany near Consuma in the years from 1905 through 1908.

For Soffici and Papini, the discovery of the importance of *toscanità* was intimately connected with a crisis of values they and Prezzolini all had in 1907, a crisis that spelled the end of *Leonardo.* Before discussing that crisis and this final aspect of their moral rhetoric in the *Leonardo* years, however, it is worth encapsulating what the *Leonardo* experience meant as the initial stage in the development of Florentine avant-gardism.

In their writings for *Leonardo,* Papini, Prezzolini, and, in his more limited involvement, Soffici made evident a distinctive and precarious blend of commitments. Although their various positions were by no means identical, their differences in these years had mostly to do with personal choices of *maestri* and subjects of study, as well as with individual temperaments and styles, rather than with conflicts over ideas. Philosophically, they shared commitments to individualism and pluralism. Even in their search for a modern secular religion that would presumably have a collective application, they seemed to recognize that it could not have any single catechism, but would have to be flexible in the manner of Papini's "corridor theory" of pragmatism.[172] Certainly they understood that the kind of commitments to *romanità,* organic nationalism, and imperial grandeur they found in a Corradini were philosophically incompatible with their individualism and risked increasing their alienation from the bourgeois, materialist civilization of the present rather than relieving it. Politically, however, they were able to make common cause with Corradini, at least briefly, on the basis of their shared contempt for the existing political class and their common perception of the need to forge a new aristocracy. Through their collaboration on *Il Regno,* Papini and Prezzolini were able to take the political concerns that had animated some of their articles for *Leonardo* in 1903 and refine them into a distinctive political rhetoric, one that can be regarded, no less than Corradini's, as an important antecedent of Italian nationalism and fascism.

At the level of cultural ideology and moral commitment, however, they separated themselves sharply from Corradini and his generation. Papini and Prezzolini were anxious to overcome the provincialism of Italian intellectual life and to enlist the support of the European cultural avant-garde (with which Soffici was in such intimate contact) in their project of spiritual renewal. Although they remained cultural élitists and lacked any concrete sense for how to reinvigorate civil society, they were already fully committed to the European modernist project of this period: liberating the primal instincts that modern civilization had covered over and creating a new modern culture adequate to them, a project they believed would be impossible without the active involvement of intellectuals like themselves. Consequently, they argued that their generation would have to overcome the art-for-art's-sake privatism—the "decadentism"—of the previous one, and to live by a new set of moral virtues such as hardness, courage, and sincerity. Their generation would have to overcome the temptation toward "feminine" overrefinement and to steel itself for an as-yet-undefined campaign of regenerative violence and spiritual revolution.

Unfortunately, as its twenty-five issues came forth over the course of nearly five years, *Leonardo* looked more and more like a two-man show rather than an expression of an avant-garde group or intellectual generation. Although *Leonardo* had been conceived in a group effort, all the initial enthusiasts except Papini had soon drifted away, and although some new names became involved—Vailati and Calderoni in 1904, Soffici and Giovanni Amendola in 1905—the journal never succeeded in institutionalizing itself as a movement. Fully nine of its issues had appeared in its first five months, in contrast to only three or four in each of its last four years. At the same time, these issues became increasingly swollen in size, and thus incapable of delivering the kind of pointed message that would have been necessary to inspire others. Nor was any attempt made to provide a financial basis for the journal, either through advertising or through regularized subsidies from patrons. As Prezzolini came to recognize in 1905, despite their good intentions *Leonardo* was in fact becoming an increasingly "artificial" exercise in personal soul-searching rather than a genuine source of cultural renewal.[173]

Spiritual Crisis and the End of *Leonardo*

> He [Soffici] arrived from Paris in [June] 1907 looking years older but more up-to-date on literary life than Papini and I, who were formed and bound together by our five years of experience on *Leonardo*. He arrived surrounded by an aura of extraordinary, mysterious, and sinister voices, like the red light that tirelessly follows the singer on stage who plays the role of Mephistopheles. Shot through with the effects of a decadent and rebellious metropolis, and with a face that bore an extraordinary resemblance to Baudelaire's, he seemed to be bringing back into our midst the immorality, emphasis on will, disorder, and anarchy that we were trying to escape in our last issue of *Leonardo*.

So wrote Prezzolini in his memoirs about a man he had just met and who would play an increasingly large role in his life over the next decade.[174] The statement reflects quite faithfully the ambivalence Prezzolini's diary and correspondence show he felt toward Soffici in the first years of their relationship. On the one hand, Soffici was to be respected for his intimate knowledge of the most advanced intellectual world then in existence; on the other, he was to be feared for his probable effect on the Florentine intellectual world.

Yet for Soffici himself the Paris of 1907 had been a deeply disturbing place where "voices" rang out, not with the extraordinary or with mystery but with despair. For months, he recalled in his memoirs, he had been suffering a "spiritual crisis," a claim clearly corroborated by his "last letter to my friends" of January 1907. Indeed, at this point he may well have been close to suicide.[175] In an effort to escape depression and gain some enlightenment, he turned, with Papini's help, to the history of philosophy.[176] However, the book that made the deepest impression upon him was not a work of philosophy but *"Le Désespéré* by Léon Bloy, a novel of sad loves whose protagonist, Marchenoir, professed a very intransigent Catholic orthodoxy that allowed him in times of torment to act with such secure determination as to inspire my own move out of darkness."[177] As he wrote to Papini in March, "In these days I am making a magnificent discovery: Léon Bloy, about whom I knew almost nothing but sensed great things, is suddenly appearing to be marvelous, the only great man in our miserable times."[178] Soon thereafter he wrote directly to Bloy, who invited him for a visit to his home on the Rue Cortot in Montmartre. However, despite Bloy's reputation as a deeply spiritual Catholic convert who had successfully preached spiritual regeneration through suffering and poverty to a variety of Parisian intellectuals, the visit proved a disappointment. Bloy turned out to be narrow-minded, irascible, and so traditionalist and evangelical as to leave Soffici laughing inwardly as they parted.[179]

Although the visit did not lead to a Christian conversion, it did have an important effect on Soffici. Indeed, he would look back upon it as nothing less than a "perfect cure."[180] Responding to Bloy's questioning, he had clarified for himself the idea that "original sin is the pride that makes men believe they can discover truth by means of reason."[181] Religion, he and Bloy agreed, could not be based on reason; but whereas the latter sought its power in the virgin birth and in miracles, Soffici now recognized that he could find similar support in art, which came to "represent for me the true and supreme anchor of salvation."[182] A few months later he published a long article on sacred painting and sculpture in *Leonardo,* in which his principal theme was that "art is the lone, unique depository on earth of the divine secret, that is, of Truth."[183]

Written while he was still in Paris, the article reflected at length upon the art of ancient Egypt but made only a passing reference to contemporary Italy. Upon what in the latter context, the one in which he lived, might a "religion of art" be based? The answer, if not already clear to him, would not be long in coming. When he returned to his homeland in June, taking up residence in Poggio a Caiano, the *toscanità* that had for some time been his own strongest source of spiritual sustenance gave rise to an extraordinary emotional outpouring that showed quite clearly where the "divine secret" of his own art lay. Addressing himself to his readers as "your blood relative returning from afar," he portrayed his return as follows:

> Crossing the Alps, silent in their immaculate majesty, I wanted to interrupt their eternal silence with shouts and songs at the thought that I would soon see you again, embrace you, kiss you fraternally. But I cannot even express the jubilation that seized my gloomy soul when I saw again the blessed soil of Tuscany. Then, truly, the hope that lay dormant in me was set ablaze like a funeral pyre, and before the enchantment of her cheerful hills covered with olives that the sun put to sleep with its sweet, rosy caresses; before the terraces made green by ears of corn not yet ripe and made yellow by turnips in bloom, and smelling of young grapes or irrigated by rivers and streams running beside their damp and grassy banks in the midst of groves of tender reeds and accompanied on their wandering and sparkling trip by a double row of poplars swaying in the evening wind; before the knolls on which peasant houses lay surrounded by black cypresses, fig trees, and huge walnut trees with sparrows fluttering on their branches; before all these marvels of a land blessed by God, my hope was transformed into definite and absolute certainty.[184]

For Soffici, however, *toscanità* was more than a tonic bracing his sense of identity, more even than a wellspring of artistic creativity and the concrete foundation of his personal religion. It was at once the distinctive element in his concept of modernism, the inspiration for his art, and the link between his art and his collectivist impulse for cultural renewal. When Papini had trumpeted his "campaign for a reawakening by force" in *Leonardo*, Soffici had contributed a woodcut depicting "Don Quixote in Tuscany" for the issue's cover. The implication was that the campaign was being spearheaded by lone-crusading, idealist intellectuals who would eventually make contact with the peasant masses, bringing the "second Italy" they represented into national preeminence and, at the same time, restoring genuine spirituality to the world.

The "Don Quixote in Tuscany" motif continued to fascinate him, as it did Papini, over the next two years, apparently because, as Papini wrote in reference to Miguel de Unamuno's recently published *Vida de Don Quijote y Sancho*, Don Quixote was "an apostle of Spanishness [*Spagnolismo*] . . . which recognizes as virtues: a scorn for the comfortable life, for business deals, and for death, a love of adventure and poverty, and the courage of solitude and craziness—all of that, and not pessimism, is what Don Quixote teaches, according to Unamuno."[185] In short, not only was Unamuno fighting the same battle for moral regeneration as were the Florentines, and in similar circumstances, but he had conceived it in identical terms as a quest for secular religion linked to the cultivation of heroic virtues.[186]

Late in 1908 Soffici would publish a short story under the same title as his woodcut and begin a year-long correspondence with Unamuno.[187] However, his fullest articulation of the interrelation he felt between his religion of art, his Quixotian politics of cultural renewal, and his faith in the Tuscan people came in a letter he wrote to Papini in the midst of discussions the two of them were having with Prezzolini and others about their hopes for *La Voce*. Comparing the "religion of art" they should uphold with its "democratic" rival, he declared:

> The invisible idea is in Art and in Love and thus in *us;* the visible, palpable idea is in Democracy. And if you want to experience the signs of this idea, look at socialism—pure and innocent—where simple people embrace Sacrifice and enthusiastically welcome the children of the strikers and aid the strikers themselves with money and with the enthusiasm that their Faith gives them . . . Popular idealism! That is precisely what we ought to champion; but are *we* not ourselves a religious fact, the noblest and most solemn of religious facts, the custodians of the Flame? . . . The people [however] cannot believe in our God; their God is a master with a beard, good and terrible, an immense *Padrone* who watches over everything; a kind of dazzling Minos who judges and dispatches them as he wishes. If this God no longer commands belief, he is finished—and today he is no longer believed in, and that is good. But the people are never daunted, and when they find themselves without a God, they create Gods. Now they have in their hands various ones: Science, Political Economy, Progress generally, etc. It is for us to work to see that they cease this polytheism and atheism and become like us. Is this not perhaps the most ethical of purposes and the most beautiful hope in Culture?[188]

Although it is perhaps too much to say that the source of Soffici's fascism is already clear in 1908, the letter certainly helps us to appreciate why he might later have been tempted to see Italy's best hope in a political movement with a religious aura led by a charismatic former socialist.

The years 1906 and 1907 were ones of crisis for Papini and Prezzolini as well. For the former, a central factor was certainly his editorial responsibility for *Leonardo*, of which he appeared to be tiring already by the fall of 1905. The journal was fast becoming a place where he felt overwhelmed by "practical life in the bad sense of the word," a life of "intrigues, messes to clear up, and rivalries."[189] All this was taking a physical toll; for one three-week period in 1906 he was under doctor's orders to write nothing, not even personal letters.[190] Then, too, despite all his philosophical reflection in *Leonardo*, he confessed to Prezzolini that "I have still not understood what I really believe, what the interior foundations of my personality really are, not even (imagine!) the philosophical ones . . . I can see possible discoveries, awakening voices, blows not yet struck. But where? When? Poet or philosopher? Wizard? Hermit? Suicide? I am in a forest: the voices are infinite."[191] Finally, the "campaign for a reawakening by force" that he launched just after his confession to Prezzolini, perhaps in order to move him out of his doldrums, seemed to him almost immediately to have fallen on deaf ears. In the very next issue of *Leonardo*, he despaired that "the Italians have understood nothing." Italy still lacked a "fixed (or precise) national ideal," and it was showing "no capacity to forge one, either politically or intellectually."[192] His sense of impotence was such that he had come to feel, as he would graphically put it in his 1912 autobiography, "like a king who rules over a vast empire of maps."[193]

Another factor that certainly contributed to Papini's self-doubts and spells of depression in these years was his trip to Paris in late 1906, which he perceived as a dismal failure. Not only was he coldly received by the Alcan publishing house, which he had used for two years to symbolize his hopes for international intellectual distinction, but his modest means had forced him to stay in a dingy Latin-quarter hotel wholly out of character with his aspirations as a European writer. As he would write to Soffici upon his return, "the doubts and problems that tormented me in Paris have reappeared and they besiege and weary me day and night."[194]

Yet as the intimacy of the letter to Soffici also testified, the Paris trip had produced some positive results that would ultimately help Papini through his crisis. For not only had it deepened his friendship with Soffici, but the strength the latter derived from his *toscanità* would soon begin to rub off. A year later, Papini would write to Soffici that "I was covered with foreign crusts and scales and you turned me into a Tuscan," and to Prezzolini that he and Soffici shared "a love of Tuscany—an idealized Tuscany, naturally—seen through Dante, cypresses and Carducci."[195] Four years later, he would find in his "return to the earth" the source of his "rebirth" and delivery from despair.[196]

There was more to this "return to the earth," however, than the guidance of his artistic friend. Upon his return from Paris, Papini had fallen in love with Giacinta Giovagnoli, a plain but sweet girl from Bulciano, a tiny village north of Arezzo perched in the mountains above the Tiber River at the eastern edge of Tuscany. They would marry on August 22, and by 1908 they had built a home for themselves in Bulciano on a promontory with a 360-degree view of the mountains and river valley. No doubt the marriage helped considerably in repairing Papini's self-esteem. Yet in many ways it was Bulciano that proved to be the love of his life. Celebrated for its beauty in the opening lines of one of Carducci's most famous poems, Bulciano would be his home for large portions of every year thereafter, the place to which he would invite Prezzolini, Soffici, Serge Férat, and others for extended stays, and the birthplace of his first child in September 1908.[197] As he wrote in 1912:

> Finding myself meant, therefore, finding Tuscany in its countryside and its tradition. No longer for me the roads around Florence, enclosed between gray walls and the villa gates of the wealthy, but the paths of goatherds on the back of the Apennines, face to face with the sky and with the woods at my feet. No longer the urban heights of the Vial dei Colli or the Incontro, but the hump-backed hills of Pratomagno and the peaks of the Luna Alps. I found myself a hilltop hidden and unknown that lies both in the heart of and at the border of my Tuscany. It lies near the source of the Tiber, near the wood [at La Verna] where Saint Francis suffered, near the castle where Michelangelo was born and the village where Piero della Francesca was. A few feet from my house the republican Carducci came as a boy. And if I climb still higher I can glimpse the Romagna seacoast and the highlands of Umbria. On this rocky hilltop where the wind is never still, my spirit found peace and found itself.[198]

Florence, it will be recalled, had always appeared to Papini as a place "of in-grown and sleepy peacefulness" where he personally did not "have much chance." Although he would never entirely escape the need to live in Florence, it was in a remote corner of rural Tuscany—as rich in its intellectual associations as it was genuine in its *popolo*—that he found the sort of peacefulness he needed and could cherish.

It was to those "highlands of Umbria" that Prezzolini had gone in search of peace in March 1905 after his marriage to a young Milanese, Dolores Faconti. Perugia was "a town where I knew no one and where I could live in solitude with my wife, a few books, and no money-making occupation, just cultivating my mind and looking for faith."[199] Unfortunately, and through no fault of the marriage, which proved a happy one, Prezzolini's move not only brought no peace but deepened a spiritual crisis he reckoned had begun the previous November.[200] Barely twenty-three as he said his marriage vows, he had been forced to confess to the presiding priest that he "believed in nothing, but that I was desperate and hoped to open myself to a new life."[201] Thereafter, he turned to an intense period of reading in Saint Augustine and in the Spanish and German mystics, and wrote anguished letters to Papini full of questions such as the following:

> I would now like to know from you, in all sincerity, what is it that still holds you back from being a Christian, or from wanting to be one (let us leave aside the question of whether you can stand theological disputes about grace). And I would still like to know what you mean by Christianity. For me the *serious*

question about Christianity is this: if one's own salvation is in conflict with the good for other people (meaning a material good), should we sacrifice these people? And if we do sacrifice their welfare, do we lose our salvation? In short, for you is Christianity a matter of *faith* or of *works*, is it *solitude* or *love*, a desire for the divine alone or for benefit, charity, and giving to others, for asceticism or for practice? Don't answer me that it is *both* because I know they are often in conflict. In addition, is Christianity for you Catholicism . . . or only the Gospels interpreted in light of your conscience?[202]

Prezzolini asked the same questions of Croce, who visited him that summer and who then replied to him in some detail about his religious convictions.[203]

By 1906 Prezzolini appeared to Papini to have entered a period of "enormous psychic instability."[204] Clearly, he was unhappy in the intellectual isolation of Perugia. When he went to Munich that spring, he read widely in the contemporary German intellectual world and discovered, in addition to Weininger, such thinkers as Rudolf Kassner and Friedrich Hebbel. It was also at this point that he first came in touch with the writings of Sören Kierkegaard and with the religious poetry and autobiographical essays of Paul Claudel.[205] Moreover, he remained a devotee of Bergson, whose *L'Evolution créatrice* would soon appear. Yet none of this searching in exotic foreign sources ultimately led to the answers he so badly needed. Rather, it was in something that lay much closer to home that Prezzolini ultimately found the spiritual support he needed to launch *La Voce:* the moral and historical ideas of Benedetto Croce.

As with Papini, the other source of Prezzolini's sense of malaise was a mounting sense of dissatisfaction with *Leonardo,* one already clear in an essay on "The Experience of Christ" he published there in the spring of 1905. Referring to the concept of philosophy as "play" that Papini had developed in 1903, and that he had then championed as well, Prezzolini now wrote despondently: "The time for play is over. We have joked and run around so much, we have experimented with so many different spirits, we have spoken so many forms of jargon that we have arrived finally at a form of play that is no longer play."[206]

Thus, although Prezzolini was somewhat removed from *Leonardo* in this period, it is perhaps not surprising that when Papini suggested in the spring of 1907 that the journal be awarded a "death as beautiful and sudden as its birth," they would coauthor its published obituary notice.[207] In that declaration, they stoutly rejected any notion that *Leonardo* was dying for the usual reason avant-garde journals died: lack of money. Indeed, it was the imminent prospect of its financial success that they claimed to fear most, for "we have always written for the few."[208] The true reasons why "*Leonardo* is forced to kill itself" were threefold. First, it had become embarrassing to them because, to the extent that it had enjoyed success, that success had become somehow "superfluous." Second, the alliances they had made with other groups—with the protonationalists of Corradini's *Il Regno*, the literary critics of Borgese's *Hermes*, and their own Peircian pragmatists, Vailati and Calderoni—had all failed, and "it has not been possible, except for a brief period, to create an absolutely personal review, that is, one written entirely by the two of us." Finally, and most important, they confessed that they had failed in their main goal of "awakening and transforming souls," and that as a result they had lost their passion for the enterprise. "For us," they wrote in the article's most poignant passage,

> Leonardo has always been something necessary, personal, sentimental—the voice that we could not quiet in ourselves, the diary of our spiritual voyages as Wandering Jews of culture. From the beginning it has always been an eruption of passion, and, precisely because it has been such an eruption, it could not last for long. When the lava that descends becomes calm and is reduced to a slow trickle, the volcano becomes an object of laughter. By this we do not mean that we are extinct volcanos. We will continue to act, to think, to create, and even to publish. But we do feel the need to rethink problems that we imagined to have been dissolved in the air, to reexamine all the opinions we expressed with such easy confidence, to search out new solutions to problems that appeared settled, to revisit and confirm our judgments about people and things, in short, to recommence our intellectual life.

3 *La Voce:*
The Making
of a Florentine
Avant-Garde

New Departures, New Divisions

After the demise of *Leonardo,* Papini kept busy by writing literary articles for various newspapers and reviews, both mainstream and avant-garde.[1] One of them was the prestigious *Corriere della Sera* of Milan, whose literary editor, Ettore Janni, had given him some reason to believe he might land a permanent position on its staff. So, in the first days of 1908 he and Giacinta moved to the Lombard capital. His first impressions came in letters to Soffici: "The city is not poetic, but it is active. One feels everywhere the will to create, and that excites my own industriousness, which has languished so in these last months . . . Florence had become hateful to me. The only people it pains me to leave behind are you and Prezzolini. All the others bored me, and I could not succeed in working enough."[2]

Yet if to escape his spiritual crisis Papini had felt the need to escape Florence, Milan presented difficulties of its own. The position on the *Corriere* did not materialize, and the young couple's meager resources quickly proved inadequate to life in Italy's largest commercial center. Perhaps in part because of his sense of the added responsibilities children would bring (their first child was conceived at about this time), Papini was soon fearing a kind of bohemian regression. As he wrote to Prezzolini on January 9: "Despite all the love you and I have for the spiritual life, we do not want to live like ascetics in little monastic communities. You yourself enjoy a certain comfortableness, and since you have far more than I do, you want to earn a decent living so you can travel the world. I feel that I cannot live the lamentable life of the troubled bohemian . . . and that I need therefore to earn a decent living and to earn it with the work best suited to me, with intellectual work."[3] It was a specter familiar to idealistic young writers at least since Balzac had presented it a half-century before in *Lost Illusions,* although Papini seemed quite prepared to put his intellect to work for the literary establishment if only he could avoid financial ruin.

Today, if we turn our minds back to Milanese high culture in 1908, we are most likely to think of F. T. Marinetti, whose first futurist manifesto was then only a year away and who had been editing the lavishly produced journal *Poesia* since founding it early in 1905. Not unlike *Il Marzocco* in sensibility, but much more oriented toward France, *Poesia* mixed the work of an older generation of French symbolists such as Gustave Kahn, Henri de Régnier, and the Flemish poet Émile Verhaeren, with that of newer French avant-gardists such as Alfred Jarry, more familiar Italian symbolist poets such as Gian Pietro Lucini and Adolfo De Bosis, and the two major Italian aestheticists of the previous generation, D'Annunzio and Pascoli.[4] Mario Morasso's work also appeared in its pages, his book on the aesthetics of the modern machine having been as influential on Marinetti as it had been reprehensible to Prezzolini.[5] Not surprisingly perhaps, in view of the attitude toward Italian aestheticism that *Leonardo* had projected, neither Papini nor Soffici, who would soon join him in Milan, showed any interest in or even any awareness of Marinetti's group.[6]

What did interest them, especially Papini, was a very different kind of Milanese cultural movement, that of the Catholic modernists around the journal *Il Rinnovamento.* In Catholic terms, modernism referred to the organized effort to turn the church toward a doctrine incorporating modern science and philosophy as well as toward political support for progressive reform. In some cases, such as that of Romolo Murri, Catholic modernism was socialist or radical. The editors of *Il Rinnovamento*— A. A. Alfieri, Alessandro Casati, and Tommaso Gallarati Scotti—were all Milanese aristocrats far more moderate than Murri, but like him, they too would soon be excommunicated by Pope Pius X, who, unlike his predecessor Leo XIII, was not at all receptive to modernist ideas.[7]

The modernism of *Il Rinnovamento* struck Papini, in the words of one of his biographers, as being "more like a lecture hall than a temple," and although it certainly moved him closer to Catholicism than he had been, it did not produce the conversion experience he would have a decade later in the aftermath of the war.[8] Its wholly secular effect was rather to provide him with a concrete model for channeling his own diffuse "revolutionary" energies. In early February he, Soffici, and Casati began to walk the streets of Milan plotting how they might start another journal, one with the same general purpose as *Il Rinnovamento* but devoted to an avant-garde cultural audience rather a Catholic one. In a matter of days they were thinking through the first issue of something they called *Il Commento* and encouraging Prezzolini to come to Milan to join the new effort.

The first and, as it turned out, only issue of *Il Commento* appeared on February 16, 1908. Its prologue, written by Papini but like the rest of the articles unsigned, read as follows:

> It appears weekly. It costs ten cents. Subscriptions cannot be accepted. This issue and those that will follow are designed as an *essay*. Depending on their reception by others and our own desires, it may be continued or begun again. We seek to create a new type of journal—rapid, laconic, severe, sincere—that works at the *margins* of the great newspapers. We write without regard to what others may say. Our intentions are: to reawaken the consciousness of the good Italians faced with the stupidities, ugliness, and indignities of present Italian life, both civil and intellectual; to interest our fellow citizens in everything having to do with the life of the spirit; to teach them to think instead of gossiping and to say a lot in a few words.[9]

Many of the appeals in Papini's earlier rhetoric are apparent—to "sincerity," the "severe" virtues, cultural "reawakening," and the "good Italians" of the second Italy—but so, too, is its central contradiction: between addressing one's "fellow citizens" with respect as a principal source of hope and displaying open contempt for their lamentable habits and cultural level. What is new is the emphasis on rapid-fire presentation, pithiness of expression, and anonymity, an emphasis that might be seen as a faint anticipation of more recent commercial advertising and that is, in that respect, similar to some futurist writing a few years later. For reasons that these associations suggest, the new style would quickly become a source of friction between Papini and Soffici on the one hand and Prezzolini on the other.

Il Commento contained a number of provocative citations from famous, mostly foreign authors, a list of "books you should buy," and twenty-one short articles, fourteen of them by Papini, four by Soffici, two by Casati, and one by Prezzolini. Papini's efforts included an appraisal of the Catholic modernism of Alfred Loisy and a call for a new "Spiritual Party," while Soffici produced a rather vague "announcement to art critics" and a denunciation of "the ostrich nation." Unlike the other articles, Prezzolini's, which took up his new interest in Romain Rolland, was written from Florence. Whether he purposefully decided not to come to Milan because of reservations about the new journal is unclear, but we do know that he detested its first issue and that he continued to harbor a deep sense of bitterness about it for several months thereafter.[10] Prezzolini's view was that the new stylistic features of the review threatened to undermine the commitment to reasoned and clearly presented argument as well as to careful preparation of evidence that was crucial to any genuine educational mission. The point may seem relatively minor, yet it opened a wide breach.

At least two factors were involved in the tensions that surfaced when Prezzolini declined to become seriously involved in *Il Commento* and that continued to mount through the spring and early summer of 1908. The first, and probably the lesser of the two, was the arrival of Soffici as a kind of third force. One of Papini's biographers has suggested that Prezzolini was jealous of Papini's new relationship with Soffici, the "Paris intellectual," and that for someone like Prezzolini, so "serious, studious, and educated in accord with the rigorous ideals of his father the prefect, Soffici was too much the artist, too 'subversive' and too interested in the subversive art of France."[11] But this assessment overstates the difference between them. In much of his early work Prezzolini had shown a mystical bent that frequently overpowered his more rationalist one, and though not an artist himself, he did write on art and was interested in the Paris art scene, even if his tastes leaned more toward impressionism than toward Picasso.[12] Yet it is certainly true that Prezzolini renewed and intensified his commitment to the virtues of seriousness and rigor at just this point.

The second factor in provoking the tension was precisely this new intellectual departure by Prezzolini, which culminated in his becoming a "Crocean" after a visit to Naples in April 1908.[13] Unlike Soffici, whose 1907 spiritual crisis had resulted in no new intellectual allegiances, or Papini, whose own crisis had led only to short-lived and relatively superficial new interests in Catholic modernism and syndicalism, Prezzolini had shown signs of a basic reorientation as early as the winter of 1907. After his flirtation with Novalis and the tradition of German mysticism in 1906, which represented the final stop on his quest for a secular religion during the *Leonardo* years, Prezzolini had become interested in Catholic modernism and had begun a correspondence with Casati in March 1907. For much of the rest of the year he was engaged in two books on the Catholic modernist movement. Nonetheless, Prezzolini remained too much the skeptic to become a Catholic, even a modernist one, and what he retained from this experience was primarily his personal relationships with Casati, who would become the principal financial backer for *La Voce*, and with Giovanni Boine, a young participant on *Il Rinnovamento* whom Prezzolini met in Milan in March 1908 and who would become an important contributor to *La Voce* after the Milanese journal's demise at the end of 1909.

In an important self-assessment in the fall of 1908, Prezzolini summed up his experience in the previous two years as follows:

> *Leonardo* was the most beautiful expression of the arbitrary moment of individual consciousness when this consciousness, outfitted with the creativity that it recognizes in itself, becomes master of the world. This is a truly divine moment, which justifies the theory of the Man-God. But just as Heinrich Heine recognized one day that a God cannot have a stomach-ache, so, too, arbitrary consciousness recognizes that it is not alone in and separate from the world, but that it has in its inner depths a communication with the infinite from which all individuals are sent forth. One might say that all the merits and defects of arbitrary consciousness were reflected in *Leonardo*.[14]

Then, after a long list of the defects, including *Leonardo*'s tendency toward "sudden shifts that were not thought through," ill-considered claims of originality, an overly biographical approach to the history of philosophy, an overly emotional approach to art, and a "lack of discipline for serious study," he suggested that for him a "spiritual moment" had ended and a new one had been born, a moment of properly social consciousness.

Catholic modernism, he continued, looking back upon it as a finished chapter in his intellectual biography, had contributed to his new spiritual moment. "Studying this movement, I became fully conscious of the value of reason and overcame, I hope forever, my arbitrary moment. To the same movement I also owe a good deal both of the knowledge I have acquired about myself and of my possible function for the Italian public."[15] In 1905, it will be recalled, Prezzolini had posed for himself the question of whether Christianity was essentially "solitude or love." Two years later Catholic modernism had helped him to see that the latter was the better answer. Yet only the idealist philosophy of Benedetto Croce was capable of providing that answer with a foundation he could accept. As he wrote many years later, "curiously, through the philosophy of Croce I was able to find the sense of active life that I had not found in the church and that enabled me to become passionately involved in national problems."[16]

Although he had always been interested in Croce's philosophy, and had maintained an avid correspondence with him since early 1904, Prezzolini's conversion to Croceanism came very suddenly. As late as the final issue of *Leonardo*, he had criticized Croce for being intolerant toward the activism and apparent irrationalism of the younger generation.[17] Yet as it became clear that he wanted to adopt a more social orientation and that Catholic modernism would not provide it, Croceanism became the logical move. Bergson remained identified with individualism and "magic"—Prezzolini's "arbitrary moment"—and thus was more the source of his spiritual crisis than its solution. True, Georges Sorel was building his social philosophy of syndicalism on a Bergsonian foundation, and Prezzolini was quite interested in this effort; but whereas Sorel could use Bergson to explain the attractiveness of myth for the human psyche and thus its political usefulness, he himself did not have any such myth or faith to undergird his position. That was Croce's great strength. His system gave his followers confidence that human history is rational because humanly created, and thus faith that it will ultimately turn out for the good. Moreover, Croce's personal politics offered precisely the right combination of sophisticated scholarship and seriousness of purpose on the one hand with a contempt for mere scholarship on the other.[18]

In 1909 Prezzolini published two more books, one on Croce, the other on Sorel and syndicalism. Although he did not actually become a syndicalist, it is clear that he was attracted to Sorel because of the apparently more concrete politics he offered. It is also clear that Prezzolini viewed Sorel and Croce as mutually reinforcing perspectives.[19] Such appearances might lead one to wonder whether in fact Prezzolini's "new moment" involved a political left turn. This impression is intensified by other contextual factors: he developed a good relationship with the maverick socialist Gaetano Salvemini, whose activity on *La Voce* in its first three years was very conspicuous; he soon published a good deal by Romolo Murri there as well; and, most important, his own writing for *La Voce* in its first two years was clearly more sympathetic to arguments associated with the democratic left than his earlier writing had been.[20] Despite these developments, which will be considered in their proper context later in the chapter, two facts lead me to doubt that Prezzolini's new social consciousness involved any fundamental turn to the left. One is that he went out of his way to deny it in print.[21] The other is that Papini, whom no one thinks of as having moved left in this period, shared his interest in syndicalism.[22] Both Papini and Prezzolini in 1908 seem to have been looking seriously at all movements that appeared to promise any possibility of "real" change, as against the mere rhetoric of change they had so long identified with socialism. Hence their interest in Catholic modernism and in syndicalism, the prestige of which as a moral force was dramatically evident in the agricultural strikes at Parma that spring.[23]

Despite these similarities in position, however, an unprecedented tension became evident in the correspondence between Papini and Prezzolini after the failure of *Il Commento,* a tension that reflected Prezzolini's new intellectual direction and Papini's profound lack of sympathy for it. For Papini, the choice between "solitude or love" would always be for solitude. Indeed, not only did he never abandon the "magical" individualism expressed in *Leonardo,* but he seemed actually to reinforce it in the years after 1907 in which his allegiances shifted from philosophy toward poetry and, less dramatically but still significantly, from Florence toward Bulciano. In general terms, the same is true of Soffici. Despite all his *toscanità,* which might appear to imply a socially oriented philosophy, his main concern came to rest with his "religion of art," for which *toscanità* was simply the principal subject matter. Moreover, like Papini, he was dumbfounded by Prezzolini's adherence to a philosophical "system" that seemed so intellectually rigid, so antithetical to spiritual freedom and openness, so staid in relation to contemporary modernist experiments in art and literature.[24]

In a sense, then, the intense debate that weighed down the correspondence among the three men during the spring of 1908 might be seen as based upon a polarity of philosophy versus art. Yet, since Prezzolini was actually writing about art, was still receptive to artistic modernism, at least in its tamer forms, and was sometimes critical of Croce's attitudes in this regard, it might be better to see the conflict in terms of whether logos or mythos should be the central basis for a modernist culture. In any case it was, paradoxically, out of this extremely polemical correspondence that *La Voce* was born.

In his letters to Papini, who would return to Bulciano in April, Prezzolini took great care to preserve their friendship even as Papini was criticizing him sharply and speaking of "Soffici and I" as a force apart. At one point, for example, Prezzolini suggested a principle of tolerating differences that would later provide the basis for Papini's participation on *La Voce* as well as for the rather delicate internal balance of the journal more generally.[25] At the same time, however, he seemed to be trying to separate Papini from Soffici, and in an angry letter written while visiting Croce in Naples, he broke off relations with Soffici altogether.[26] A few weeks thereafter, and possibly also as a result of Croce's influence, Prezzolini would be inspired to draft a "Plan [*Progetto*] for a Journal of Thought in Italy" and to circulate it among a number of potential contributors, including Papini, Casati, Croce, Boine, Giovanni Amendola, and Romain Rolland.[27]

Of these figures, only Papini and Amendola would become major contributors in *La Voce*'s first years, although Casati and Croce would become two of its principal financial backers. Probably because he already sensed how important Papini would be to the effort's chance of success, Prezzolini put intense pressure on him to participate. In a letter sent with the *Progetto*, he wrote: "If you, for personal reasons, refuse to participate in this work, I will be very sorry (this matters little), but it seems to me that you would betray one of the principal duties you have, that of working in order to make the conditions of Italian intelligence improve. Unless you want to appear not to have the seriousness, honesty, and clarity of intentions and acts that raise you above the charlatanisms and irresponsibility of the present, I do not believe you can refuse."[28]

In the *Progetto* itself, Prezzolini articulated the character and goals of the review in terms quite reminiscent of *La coltura italiana*, the book he and Papini had coauthored in 1906. The review would be an "autonomous organ in which we can express the needs and movements of a predominantly philosophical and religious sort that concern and attract the spirits of our generation." It would be educational and, for that reason, favor progressive reform, but it would not be directly political. It would be Italian in focus, and so would concern itself with cities in addition to Florence (thereby making necessary a network of correspondents from those cities), but it would also pay close attention to cultural developments abroad. It would be written in plain language, open to polemic, and closed to the "dilettantish advertising" of mainstream or "bourgeois" magazines. Its principles would be "sufficiently broad to admit persons of very diverse views." The only obligatory commitment for its writers would be that "what they write is capable of rational defense and is not the titillation of their fantasies or the venting of their emotional needs." Finally, it would carefully cultivate its audience and make use of a subtle dialectic between tradition and modernity in order to do so:

A new review cannot then arise except by making use of . . . tradition. But at the same time it must prize highly the practical and theoretical lessons that are taking place in the present. A new review that wants to correct the errors of the past ought to begin by not allowing itself to be used as an outlet for writings and essays that, though certainly valuable, have no influence on the public, and that represent only a coterie or brotherhood of intellectual revelers. One creates a journal in order to act on the public, and it is hardly sincere to appear to be disdaining the very public for which one works and exerts energy. The first characteristic of the journal, then, will be the *contemporaneity of the objects* it uses to gain public attention.

Such a journal, he concluded, might be called *La Coltura italiana* or *L'Italia che pensa* (The Italy That Thinks).

It was the latter title, perhaps more than any other single indication, that encouraged Papini to read the *Progetto* as essentially Crocean in inspiration, a reading that seems quite reasonable despite Prezzolini's explicit rejection of it.[29] Nor was Papini necessarily off the mark in reading the discussion of the journal's commitment to rationally defended argument as a slap at Soffici. Yet Papini went far beyond these sorts of objections in his reply of more than sixty handwritten pages, the major thrust of which was to update Prezzolini on his intellectual position. As such, it was as much a personal confession as a response to Prezzolini's program. In particular, Papini recounted how he had developed his new, more intimate relationship with Soffici as a way of explaining his own emerging artistic side. He was, he said, "no longer a pragmatist," no longer interested in "pure speculation."

> In me, as you know, are mixed two tendencies of about equal force, the artistic and the philosophical, and however hard I try, I do not do well when I make one of them dominant . . . The third tendency in me is a *practical* one. I am driven to change things. I feel in myself in my best hours that intolerance for present conditions and that mania to change them that makes for missionaries and apostles. I want, in short, to make the life of men better by means of a preaching in the spiritual sense, but carried out above all through artistic means . . . You would say to me, I think, that it is enough to think about moral truths to be moral . . . For me the moralist should first know, but know in order to create. And to create, that is, to act on men, the simple and bare manifestation of thought is not enough. It is necessary also to have art, that is, something that moves and persuades people like us at a more universal level, and that is why I have decided to become a moral apostle, a thinking being . . . and an artistic being who uses passionate reasoning and aesthetic representation, fables and sermons, to move men forcefully and induce them to change their lives.[30]

In short, we need the power of art as our Sorelian myth mediating between pure thought and political practice. Prezzolini's program is too restricted, for while it is right to begin with thought, it is wrong to end there. To limit the means of persuasion to the merely cognitive is to deprive oneself of precisely those means most likely to excite and engage.

Despite a somewhat defensive tone in his response ten days later, Prezzolini appeared to accept this argument about the mediating power of art, at least when rephrased in Crocean terms as the importance of the first moment of "intuition" in preparing the way for the higher moment of "knowledge."[31] Moreover, in the same letter he reaffirmed his promise not to impose his own Crocean views on the new review, and the tone of his subsequent letters became increasingly upbeat as he continued to seek to assure Papini's participation in the effort. While Papini grumpily agreed to contribute, his attitude as expressed in letters to Soffici remained intensely critical of Prezzolini's "air of being the corrector and reformer of Italy and of thought."[32] Remarkably, however, on July 11, as Soffici was on his way home from Papini's house at Bulciano, he encountered Prezzolini, apparently by chance, when the coach in which he was riding stopped to change horses near the latter's summer residence in the mountain town of Consuma. The two men became immersed in conversation, Soffici allowed the coach to continue without him, and after a full day together they became reconciled to each other's views.[33] By early August Prezzolini had met face to face with Papini as well, and it was on his forty-mile walk back from Bulciano to Consuma that he had what he would later recall as the vision that gave birth to *La Voce.*

But the healing process that these face-to-face conversations encouraged was not quite complete. In particular, the sensitive issue of the new journal's name remained unresolved. Prezzolini now favored *Il Criterio,* a suggestion that proved no less objectionable to Papini than the ones offered earlier. Meanwhile, as active correspondence between Prezzolini and Soffici resumed, the latter sent a long list of possible titles, which, however, did not include the eventual choice.[34] Most likely the name *La Voce* was simply imposed by Prezzolini, who had used it previously as a chapter title in one of his books.[35] In any case, the three writers met together in mid-October and agreed to cooperate on the venture.[36] A few days later Papini wrote the circular that announced it publicly.[37] Yet even as the first issue appeared on December 20, for which Papini wrote the lead article and Soffici, a short polemic against Anatole France, many doubts remained about just how committed they were to an enterprise that, in Prezzolini's words, neither of them "ever understood or loved" and for which they wrote "out of friendship for me rather than conviction."[38]

Cultural Politics in Florence, 1909–1911

It is not clear to what extent the Florence into which *La Voce* was born had become "hateful" to Papini because of changes it (rather than he) was undergoing, but the city's transformation over the past five years had been significant in certain respects, and it is doubtful that he liked what had transpired. First and foremost, the cries of protest with which the working-class movement had earlier disrupted the town's quiet complacency were now being translated into political power. In 1908 Florence had a mayor, Francesco Sangiorgi, who, though not himself a socialist, certainly leaned to the left and had much socialist support. The following year, after new parliamentary elections, three of the city's four deputies (including Giuseppe Pescetti) were socialists. Moreover, the mounting strength of socialism at the national level had been demonstrated locally during the fall of 1908 when the city played host to a national convention of the Socialist Party that was attended by such well-known personalities as Filippo Turati and Anna Kuliscioff. Even the powerful speech delivered there by Salvemini on the problem of the "two Italies" probably would not have pleased Papini, since the two men shared little, despite the common support they were about to lend to *La Voce*.[39]

In cultural life, the biggest recent event in Florence had been the arrival in April 1906 of Buffalo Bill's Wild West Show with its troop of nearly a thousand entertainers and five hundred horses. While Papini may have attended out of nostalgia for his childhood, he could hardly have found in it any reason to believe that Florence was about to produce the "party of intellectuals" of his early dreams. Even more disturbing for him were the recent expressions of what passed for high culture in Florence, such as the plays of a working-class dramatist from Prato, Sem Benelli. Benelli's *La cena delle beffe* (Dinner of Jests), an antiquarian romance written in medieval language, was the stage hit of 1909, leading Papini to dub him the "the rag-and-bone man of our dramatic literature, a ragpicker and ragsorter, a man who washes and then redyes the foulest rags of poetry and history seen here in recent years."[40] Nor was there any consolation to be found in improved relations between the cultures of university and avant-garde. If anything, the gap between them had intensified, as would be most dramatically evident when a youthful participant on *La Voce*, Scipio Slataper, had his scholarship withdrawn because of his association with the journal.

When Papini chose to visit Florence in 1909, he spent much of his time at the Caffè Reininghaus or Giubbe Rosse, as it became known after the red smoking jackets worn by its waiters. He was joined there only rarely by Prezzolini, who disliked cafés; but Soffici was a frequent companion, at least on those two or three days a week when he came into the city from his house at Poggio a Caiano. During the warmer months the two would sit outside at one of the tables that stretched into the ghostly expanse of the Piazza Vittorio; otherwise they would sit in the café's "third room" in the rear, as far as possible from the heavily foreign crowd of lunchgoers. Now and then for a change of scene, Papini and Prezzolini would visit Soffici in Poggio, a feat that required taking

6. The Caffè Giubbe Rosse or Reininghaus on the Piazza Vittorio, the center of Florentine avant-garde life in the prewar era.

a steam-powered streetcar so embarrassingly primitive and inefficient that it came to symbolize for them the magnitude of the task of national renovation they faced.[41]

When Prezzolini again took up permanent residence in Florence after his years in Perugia, he rented an apartment on the Via dei della Robbia, one of the new streets just outside the historic center that had been created after the destruction of the city walls. Its four rooms stood on the top floor, some eighty steps up a winding staircase from the street. So arduous was the climb that when mail arrived it was placed in a basket attached to a long rope, which was then hauled up through a window. "That basket," Prezzolini later recalled, "proved invaluable when my study became the center of an international movement in mail and people, as well as the cause of a lot of complaints from our neighbors, who were all very quiet people without Don-Quixotian vocations like mine."[42]

The study itself, which doubled as the apartment's living room, contained "a wall of rather rickety wooden bookshelves that bore the signs of frequent repair and many moves, a couch in a red and yellow floral pattern, a desk with very weak legs, a small table on which sat a typewriter, and, added later, a painting by Soffici full of light and Tuscan springtime that was the only beautiful thing one could see."[43] It was here

7. The front page of *La Voce*'s first issue (20 December 1908), which featured an article by Papini on Italian intellectuals that Romain Rolland soon translated into French.

that *La Voce* was assembled just before being brought to the printshop every Thursday. The task would be repeated like clockwork for 263 consecutive weeks, until, exhausted and largely deserted, Prezzolini turned the journal into a biweekly in 1914.[44]

In contrast with *Leonardo*, *La Voce* presented itself rather austerely, its four folio-sized pages of small print largely unrelieved by artistic embellishments.[45] Gone were the handmade paper and elaborate *art nouveau* mastheads that had given the earlier review its distinctive flavor. In their place was a cleaner and denser look, suggesting that what was considered important was what was being written. Although avant-garde art did grace its pages from time to time—artists reproduced included Georges Braque, Paul Cézanne, Edgar Degas, Paul Gauguin, Hans von Marées, Pablo Picasso, Henri Rousseau, and Vincent van Gogh, as well as Italian natives such as Soffici, Medardo Rosso, Giovanni Fattori, and even the futurist Carlo Carrà—it almost invariably appeared in connection with an erudite discussion of their work rather than as a celebration of art for its own sake.

La Voce's seriousness of purpose was also communicated in its policy toward advertisements. Not only were they few in number, but they generally refrained from utilizing pictorial illustrations and were relegated to the last page. Usually they brought the reader's attention to books by the journal's own staff, or to a local bookseller, or perhaps to the furniture of the "Papini Brothers" (as the modest business of Giovanni's family was known). Sometimes they touted a foreign journal with similar aims such as *Der Sturm*, edited by Herwarth Walden in Berlin, or a local institution with international connections such as the language classes of the Istituto Francese.

Yet this seriousness was complemented by a real effort to establish a personal relationship with *La Voce*'s readers. By 1910 Prezzolini was printing his home telephone number in the journal, and "young readers" were being invited to call between two and four on Wednesday afternoon or to drop by his apartment during these "office hours."[46] The extent to which this approach succeeded is difficult to say, but there is no doubt that *La Voce*'s influence was strongly felt among the younger generation of intellectuals, as the example of Antonio Gramsci reminds us. From his fascist prison cell, Gramsci would make a very favorable assessment of the intellectual role that *La Voce* had played in building Italian civil society during his student years in Turin: "De Sanctis fought for the creation *ex novo* in Italy of a national high culture and against worn-out traditional ones . . . *La Voce* fought only to spread this same culture at an intermediate level and against such things as traditionalism. *La Voce* was an aspect of militant Croceanism, because it sought to democratize what had necessarily been aristocratic in De Sanctis and had remained aristocratic in Croce."[47]

If we look at more mundane measures of the journal's influence, such as subscription levels and total copies printed, its role in Italian cultural life appears less exalted. Even at its height in 1911, *La Voce* never published more than 5,000 copies of a single issue or had more than 2,000 subscribers.[48] Yet the pride with which Prezzolini reported these figures at the time suggests that they were quite good for that era and that, in any case, the journal had certainly not fallen into his nightmare of being only a self-enclosed "coterie or brotherhood of intellectual revelers." From the beginning it had a distribution network covering about a hundred Italian cities, and its price of ten cents an issue or five lire a year made it affordable to all but the nation's poorest citizens.[49]

Another contrast with *Leonardo* was the very large number and wide range of contributors *La Voce* had in its first five years. Certainly Prezzolini made by far the greatest single contribution, and it is perhaps not surprising that he was followed in this respect by Soffici and Papini. In addition, however, very substantial contributions were made in literature and religion by Scipio Slataper, Piero Jahier, and Emilio Cecchi; in politics and history by Salvemini, Amendola, Antonio Anzilotti, and Luigi Ambrosini; in philosophy by Croce and Boine; in music by Giannotto Bastianelli; and in psychiatry by Alberto Vedrani. Lesser but significant contributions were also made by Murri, Giovanni Gentile, Fernando Agnoletti, Roch Grey (the pen name of Hélène d'Oettingen, with whom Soffici had been romantically involved during his Paris years), Benito Mussolini, Margherita Sarfatti (who would later be romantically involved with Mussolini and who wrote for *La Voce* on the English suffragettes, among other topics), and many, many others.[50] All in all, *La Voce* involved more than 300 different writers, of very varied backgrounds, tastes, and outlooks, whose contributions ranged across nearly every field of thought and human endeavor. As Soffici would later remark, "*Il Marzocco* first, and then *Leonardo*, had created fresh air in their respective eras, but in particular fields; *La Voce* opened the windows to a view of the entire panorama of the spirit in its multiple manifestations; it was concerned not with this or that mental faculty of the individual but with, so to say, the whole person."[51] Considered as individuals, however, the only factor that seemed to hold *La Voce*'s contributors together was generation, most of them having been born in the 1880s.

In a book he wrote in 1912 but published only decades later, Prezzolini recalled:

In its first year, *La Voce* was a convention with many different kinds of people attending, different in terms of origin, age, aims, and cultural background. The encounters were often violent, the resolutions contradictory. Attitudes clashed. How was it, then, that the public saw a family atmosphere, a sense of unity, a mission that tied everyone together? It is not clear how this happened, but it did. Or to put the point more sharply: it is clear how it happened, since there really was this unity, this family, in comparison with the disorganization of the schools, political parties, religions, and all the rest. The previous generation was a generation of unbelievers, of skeptics. These new people from *La Voce* were different: they believed, badly or well, arbitrarily or rationally, pushing toward the universal or restricting themselves to the particular, with prejudices or without, with dogmas or more philosophical beliefs—but they believed. They felt that life was a serious matter, and they took it seriously . . . By the second year, *La Voce* was still a convention, but it had also become a group. And the group did not bore the convention, nor the convention the group. There was discussion, some dissent, but no misunderstandings and no separations.[52]

From the vantage point of 1912, this relative unity and identity as a group appeared as a brief moment now gone, one that, in Prezzolini's view, had been made possible by three fundamental agreements—on religion, art, and politics:

For the young generation belonging to *La Voce*, there was no doubt about the fundamental moral problem of their time. Religion had died; what new creation could take its place? Idealist philosophy had taught them to deny religion but also to justify it; to understand it and to exclude it. For this philosophy, to believe offered the promise of knowledge, to know meant completing one's belief: religion was the promise of philosophy, philosophy was religion grown full and mature . . . A movement ought to be joined together by and fully rooted in art, and not with art in general, but with that art that best appropriates an idealist way of seeing, with that art that has reduced the Ideal to the Real in the manner of the philosophy that has reduced God to man and religion to thought, with that art that has reduced the whole cosmos to a drop of water and can reveal the whole spirit in a clump of turf . . . an art that is popular because naive and interested in fables, that reacts against inherited rhetoric, against the academy, against aristocratic pretense . . . A movement ought to have practical effects, we might say even political effects, perhaps even becoming a party; but it needs to have depth, an ethical and metaphysical viewpoint, religious in a certain sense . . . And this movement, were it to be political, would be realist, practical, wary of labels, concrete, always making this or that problem precise, calling always for this or that solution, breaking fully with the formulas of the parties.[53]

Yet, while one need not go so far as to call Prezzolini's reconstruction of these fundamental agreements a myth, there is little doubt that the extent of the agreement is overstated. The *vociani* might well have agreed that the central problem of the age was religious, that avant-garde art was a necessary means of spiritual self-realization, and that their movement should have "practical effects" and should break "with the formulas of the parties" in doing so; but even in this early heyday they would not have agreed that idealist philosophy should be the new source of religious inspiration or the foundation of art, or that *La Voce* should expend its time and effort on practical political problems.

In fact the "convention" of *La Voce's* first year already contained in embryo the antagonisms, schisms, and defections of 1911, but it was able to lay them aside in favor of a common commitment to cultural modernism in part because of the orchestrating skill of its floor leader and in part because the convention took no votes. Thus Prezzolini, who clearly understood his position as that of a facilitator rather than a unifier, was careful to set out the journal's aims with broad and accommodating language quite in contrast to the more programmatic and ideological tone of the *Progetto*. In what amounted to the opening manifesto of *La Voce*, he wrote that the journal aimed to build the Italian character, to be "sincere, open, and serious," and to defend "the ethical character of intellectual life," but he avoided any more precise statements regarding its point of view.[54] Moreover, while discerning readers of the journal's early issues doubtless did see many statements about religion, art, and politics that reflected the agreements its editor would find retrospectively in 1912, what they more obviously found was an exhilaratingly diverse array of articles concerning the various manifestations of high culture then current across Europe, as well as many more culled discerningly from the Italian tradition. Thus, the very first issue featured a "letter from London" on Bernard Shaw; "notes" on Georges Sorel, the "ignorance of specialists," and Rudolf Eucken (who that year had won the Nobel Prize for literature); an interview with a German editor; a review of a book on Italian romanticism; and longer discussions of French cultural politics, of the cultural situation of Italy with respect to Europe, and of the need to pay greater attention to the art of the young generation.

Within this diversity, nonetheless, several common themes and emphases emerged. One was antipositivism, although in comparison with *Leonardo* there was far less pure philosophizing (such battles having become, for most of the *vociani*, either won or superseded) and far more attention to the philosophical underpinnings of other cultural studies. Thus the psychiatrist Vedrani took on the positivist psychology of Cesare Lombroso.[55] Another common theme—and, in terms of the conflict of generations, a related one—was a critique of Florentine cultural institutions, particularly the city's university life and its aestheticist journals such as *Il Marzocco*. At the same time there was also a keen interest in comparing the nature of Florentine culture with that of the various other cities and regions in Italy, such as Trieste, Venice, the Trentino, Emilia-Romagna, and the Italian south. For Prezzolini especially, such comparisons were important in "making Italians known to themselves" and thereby for fashioning a new Italian culture based on interconnections among regions, each of which should be encouraged to take pride in its own distinctive ways, rather than one based on attempts to suppress this diversity in the name of some fictitious culture of a homogeneous nation.[56]

Yet if any single set of issues could be described as the most central to the first years of *La Voce*, it would be that concerned with the relation between Italian and European culture. That Italian intellectual life was viewed by its northern neighbors as backward and, at least in recent decades, derivative was clearly a sore point among the *vociani*, and Papini made it the theme of the lead article for the journal's very first issue. There he argued that although "distinguished foreigners" had heavily influenced Italian culture until recently (Nietzsche was his central example), this tendency was now slowing considerably, and he himself felt a new freedom to speak. At the same time, he was careful not to push the national pride he felt in this liberation to the point of chauvinism. In his concluding paragraphs he wrote: "We should read Comte, but also Galileo; we should admire Loisy but also Sarpi; we should cite Hegel but also Bruno; we should translate Nietzsche, but we should also enjoy Machiavelli. Everyone says this is already being done, but it is not true. We always speak about the glories of our nation, and yet we read the latest foreign writers much more readily and frequently than the Italians of old. We need to give Italy again not only contact with European culture but also the historical consciousness of our own culture, which is certainly a significant part of European culture. I shall content myself with a few words: nationalists no, Italians yes!"[57]

As *La Voce* appeared week after week in 1909 and 1910, it was precisely this idea of expanding the reader's intellectual horizon to include both the best the rest of Europe had produced and the best of Italy's own tradition that seemed to be the most central principle of editorial policy. Yet attaining the proper balance always remained a delicate issue, as was most clearly evident in Soffici's articles. For although Soffici had spent much of the decade learning that only in Tuscany was he consistently able to realize an art based on the innovating aesthetic consciousness that Paris had excited in him, now that he was living in Tuscany fulltime the need he felt most keenly was to educate his readers about the art of France. That this could sometimes land him in hot water is evident from a concluding passage in his four-part article on French impressionism: "As I already have been and will again be speaking, here and elsewhere, of modern French painting with admiration and proposing it as a model for Italy, I do not want it to be thought that my intent is to bastardize our art, to corrupt it with forms and concepts of foreign origin and character; nor do I propose impressionism as a pictorial method to be followed blindly, as has been done with so many other artistic and literary theories that have come from outside and degenerated among us to the point of provoking eternal laughter—or tears." No, he continued, "as a heartfelt lover of the genius of our race, I do not await light from the north" but merely "recognize in impressionism's efforts the possibility of a vigorous [*virile*] education that, absorbed by our youth, might serve them as an impulse toward personal quests that can produce vital results while also being completely Italian."[58]

Although it was a sensitive point for Soffici's self-image and, perhaps, for *La Voce*'s readership, the idea that French culture was the world's most advanced and "revolutionary" remained virtually a given among the *vociani* themselves, even as their understanding of the relation between France and avant-garde culture became much more complex than it had been at the turn of the century. Then they were completely overwhelmed by the myth of Paris. Now there was a fuller sense that the avant-garde was a European phenomenon, and therefore that in educating the Italians they should look at all of the continent's many nationalities. Thus German expressionism and its antecedents excited the interest of Prezzolini and, even more intensely, of Slataper, whose background as a *triestino* gave him an edge in appropriating it. Moreover, when they informed *La Voce*'s readership about what reviews like their own were doing in other European countries, they were as likely to consider the Germans or even the English as they were the French. Finally, some of *La Voce*'s most successful issues were focused on a single theme in which contrasting perspectives from different intellectual traditions were set side by side. In one such issue on "the sexual question," a lead article by Sorel on "the social value of chastity" was followed by an inquiry into "Sigmund Freud's ideas on sexuality," the latter being one of the first such discussions to be published in Italy.[59]

A second way in which the Florentines had arrived at a fuller appreciation of the complex relation between French and avant-garde culture was that they were now much more able to see themselves as participants in an international avant-garde rather than as merely its spectators. In

1910, for example, Giannotto Bastianelli would introduce a new "revolutionary" Florentine musical ensemble to *La Voce*'s readers by writing, with evident irony, that "certainly in France, or more precisely in Paris, where they believe in all seriousness that they are the navel of the spiritual world . . . they are unaware of how in that old serene and apathetic Florence there is now silently emerging a world of music that is absolutely new and genuinely concrete."[60]

A final complexity in the understanding of avant-gardism held by the *vociani* was that French culture was no longer identified entirely with Paris. They had come to appreciate that much of what was important in the French intellectual world had been produced by intellectuals from the provinces, or by provincials who had moved to Paris but retained identities rooted in their native regions. Thus, Papini had written to Rolland in 1909 that for him Rolland had been the "revelation of the *good* France that consoled me after the horrible commercial bustle of Paris."[61]

Despite these complexities, however, when *La Voce* turned to Europe, as it did in virtually every issue, its most frequent focus was on France, and inevitably much of that was on Paris. Not surprisingly perhaps, when one looks at the whole of this discussion one discovers that, just as there were "two Frances" for Papini, so there were "two Parises" for *La Voce*. One might be called Soffici's Paris, the Paris of art and poetry. Although Soffici was by no means the only writer for *La Voce* to focus on this Paris, it was he who was most responsible for introducing its readers to the Paris art scene with early articles on Gustave Courbet, Henri Rousseau, Auguste Renoir, and Picasso, in addition to his topical pieces on impressionism; and it was also Soffici who provided their first introduction to French avant-garde poetry with his 1911 book on Arthur Rimbaud, the first book on Rimbaud published in Italy.

The other Paris was the Paris of philosophy and social thought, the Paris of Bergson, Sorel, Péguy, and Rolland—Prezzolini's Paris. Far more than Soffici's, this was a Paris of émigrés from the various regions of France: Sorel from Cherbourg on the Normandy coast, Péguy from Orléans, Rolland from Clamecy along the Yonne River; only Bergson had been born and raised in Paris. In part perhaps because of those provincial origins, this was a Paris of moralism and of high intellectual seriousness, of the Sorbonne rather than Montmartre. Unlike the Paris of the arts, which was mostly just written about in *La Voce*, this Paris actually contributed to the Florentine review, modestly but still significantly.[62] Moreover, the considerable interest that Rolland especially showed in the young Florentines sometimes provided fresh contacts for *La Voce* with their youthful counterparts in France, such as Rolland's protégé Jean-

Richard Bloch, who in June 1910 began the avant-garde journal *L'Effort* in Poitiers.[63]

When the Prezzolinis joined Soffici in Paris in March 1910 in order to make arrangements for an exhibition of impressionist painting in Florence that spring, the existence of these two rather different Parises and their relative isolation from each other became readily evident. Soffici, who had arrived several weeks before, had been spending his time with Serge Ferát, Max Jacob, Picasso, Apollinaire, and Medardo Rosso (who then had a studio on the Boulevard des Batignolles below Montmartre); but once Prezzolini arrived, his company changed rather abruptly to that of Péguy, Sorel, and Rolland.[64] Despite this difference, however, the two Florentines worked well together on the project that had brought them to the French capital, and it ultimately proved quite successful. From mid-April through mid-May the citizens of Florence were able to see an exhibition, billed as the first of its kind in Italy, that featured works by three artistic generations: that of Claude Monet, Camille Pissarro, Auguste Renoir, Cézanne, and Degas; that of Gauguin, van Gogh, Rosso, and Jean-Louis Forain; and that of Henri Matisse and Henri Toulouse-Lautrec.[65] In Prezzolini's estimation at least, the exhibition did not mark the end of the city's sluggish provincialism—the "red-tape of its bureaucracies, the diffidence of its powerful families"— but it had created, at least momentarily, the beginnings of a genuine public space in which the "good sense, generosity, firmness of will, and love of art" of the "second Italy" had been permitted expression.[66]

In the midst of all the cultural discussion, there was also embedded in the *La Voce* of these early years a moral rhetoric readily identifiable as *"vociano,"* despite the evident diversity of its many writers. In many ways this rhetoric simply continued the emphases already developed by Papini and Prezzolini in *Leonardo:* on the need to renew culture, to overcome "decadence," to allow the new generation to galvanize the "second Italy," and, thus, to cultivate virtues such as discipline, courage, and sincerity. Indeed, in one respect—the veneration for the antifeminism of Otto Weininger—the moral rhetoric of *La Voce* expanded and intensified the legacy of *Leonardo.* Where, earlier, Weininger had been more or less the private domain of Prezzolini, now he was taken up enthusiastically by a number of other *vociani,* including Papini and Slataper, despite the fact that *Sex and Character* would not be translated into Italian until the fall of 1912.[67] When this event finally occurred, Papini declared the book "a true masterpiece . . . the most important theoretical work that Germany has produced since the last books by Nietzsche."[68]

Although not everyone associated with *La Voce* shared the extremism of Papini's view of Weininger, which would reach even greater heights in 1914, it is notable that even those who dissented from it shared Weininger's central contention about the absoluteness of male-female difference. Thus, the feminist and sometime *vociana* Sibilla Aleramo, whose autobiographical novel *Una donna* (A Woman) had become one of the most sensational and celebrated books in Italy after it appeared in 1906, separated herself sharply from Weininger's argument that women were intellectually and creatively inferior.[69] Nonetheless, she read Weininger quite seriously and would even concede the influence of this "sad genius" when, in early 1914, she refashioned her feminism into one that stressed female difference as a source of artistic creativity.[70] Similarly, Soffici would argue in a review of Anna Gerebzova, a Russian artist living in exile in Paris whom he had known during his years there, that "the lack of discipline in the feminine soul, her instincts as an elemental creature, her spiritual anarchy, all things with which woman is stigmatized and upon which those who deny her creative capacities base their views, far from constituting an argument without appeal for her necessary impotence, seem to me so many favorable conditions for the creation of new and unusual accents, harmonies, and images."[71]

Yet it was not in controversy over Weininger that *La Voce* showed its most important breaks with the rhetoric of the *Leonardo* years, and these were in fact notable, arguably more notable than the continuities. One such change was the relative absence of the ideals of solitude and the solitary genius, although they would have a brief resurgence during Papini's seven months as *La Voce*'s interim editor in 1912, as well as in the journal *Lacerba* that he and Soffici would begin in 1913. Another change was that anxieties about the Italian *popolo* became much less evident, and in certain articles (above all those concerned with the politics of suffrage reform) they seemed positively overcome. Finally, the rhetoric of regenerative violence became much less pronounced than it had been in the *Leonardo* years. In the spring of 1911 *La Voce* (though not all the individuals associated with it) opposed the prospect of a war in Libya, and even in the fall when the military campaign was launched and *La Voce* reversed itself on the issue, the rhetoric of war was relatively restrained and instrumental in orientation.[72]

In general, these attitudes offer better clues to the nature of *La Voce*'s political rhetoric from 1909 through 1911 than do the rhetorical continuities with *Leonardo* such as Weiningerian antifeminism. Indeed, when one looks at this rhetoric, in which the causes championed included universal suffrage, support for the Italian south (or Mezzogiorno), free trade, and reforms in taxation, schools, and railroads, it appears so strikingly different from its counterparts in *Leonardo* and *Il Regno* that it is tempting to characterize *La Voce*'s first years as a kind of "democratic parenthesis" in the history of Florentine avant-gardism. While this would be misleading, in part because Prezzolini would not be an unambiguously committed democrat until two more decades had passed and in part because those like Papini and Soffici who remained the most vigorous antidemocrats chose mostly not to speak about politics in this period, it is certainly true that, owing to a number of contingencies, a political rhetoric developed in *La Voce* that would later be an inspiration not only to Gramsci but to many others on the left including the liberal Piero Gobetti. This development, however, was far from straightforward.

As we have seen, the fundamental idea behind *La Voce* was to become an institution of cultural education leading the spiritual rebirth of Italy by bringing it into relation with the avant-garde culture of Europe and the best of its own tradition. For this purpose, *La Voce* needed to present broadly reflective essays with serious intellectual content rather than technical discussions of particular social, economic, and political problems. At the same time, virtually everyone on *La Voce* believed, as Croce would argue in a landmark "interview" in the journal in 1911, that "socialism was dead" and that, more generally, the political ideologies inherited from the nineteenth century were either dead or dying.[73] In such a context, the only way to talk about political problems was to address specific issues and, inevitably, to propose specific (often technical) solutions to them.

Faced with this dilemma, Prezzolini might have overcome it simply by avoiding political rhetoric altogether, except that he was determined, as we have seen, to avoid the individualism and philosophical aloofness that had plagued *Leonardo* and to use *La Voce* to make a public impact. So, lacking this option, he fell initially into a somewhat ambivalent attitude. As he declared in its sixth issue, *La Voce* had not been intended as a "political journal—it cannot and will not make socialist, republican, or radical declarations—but it always remembers that the problems of our culture can be resolved only in relation to political and economic ones."[74] Yet the line here being drawn—between permitting articles that presented culture "in relation to political and economic problems" and prohibiting those that took up the latter by themselves—was almost no sooner articulated than crossed. As early as April 1909 Salvemini was offering overtly political commentary on the national government.[75] By the end of the year, when the government of Giovanni Giolitti fell after three and a half years in office, Prezzolini felt the need to exult in the event—and to herald Giolitti's replacement by local hero Sidney Sonnino—in a front-page lead.[76]

The rhetorical appeals underlying the critique of Giolitti, particularly in Prezzolini's version, were largely continuous with the journal's cultural and moral ideals. Thus, in the article just mentioned Prezzolini identified Giolitti with corruption, inefficiency, and dishonesty, called Sonnino "the only honest, cultured, and independent leader" in parliament, and ended with a ringing exhortation to the "young generation, which has moral force and a desire to do good, to abstain from the politics of the politicians and to create the higher politics of the common people who think and work: forget the government, parliamentary deputies, and bureaucrats; disregard the triple corruption that from Rome infects Italy; prepare a better Italy through study and moral self-improvement." Still, Prezzolini so obviously appeared to be crossing into previously forbidden territory that he had opened the article with yet another firm declaration that, "no, La Voce is not today becoming and will never become a journal of political criticism or propaganda." The reason for the appearances to the contrary, he continued, was simply that "in trying to deal with all the problems of Italian life, we cannot avoid occasionally occupying ourselves with politics," at least if we do not wish to suffer "that ruinous divorce between political activity and the other intellectual and moral activities of the human spirit . . . that has always been one of the greatest maladies in our country."[77]

In 1910 and 1911 this "occasional occupation with politics" became much more than occasional, even if the predominantly cultural character of the journal remained intact. Probably the foremost reason for this was the simple physical presence of Gaetano Salvemini. A decade older than Prezzolini and far more experienced in national life, Salvemini used his tenacious personality to gain a hold over La Voce's sometimes quite impressionable young editor that was far stronger than intrinsic support among journal associates for Salvemini's pro-south and reformist views would ever have produced by itself. Salvemini's influence was probably also increased by the fact that he was himself undergoing a transition in this period away from socialist politics and toward an as yet somewhat vague independent radicalism, and Prezzolini clearly wished to influence the speed and direction of this transition by giving Salvemini a significant editorial voice.

Once having allowed Salvemini's influence to move the journal in a more political direction, Prezzolini was encouraged to move tactically toward a "democratic" political rhetoric by two further contingent factors. One of these was that many of the issues Salvemini championed, and especially the interrelated democratic claims he advanced on behalf of the south and suffrage reform, appeared to provide a means of attacking that symbol of the liberal establishment whom Prezzolini had always hated, Giovanni Giolitti. Thus, in his article celebrating Giolitti's defeat in December 1909, Prezzolini had flatly predicted that "universal suffrage would destroy Giolitti's power base in parliament."[78] Although Giolitti ultimately proved agile enough to turn the suffrage issue to his advantage by bringing it forward himself, it did appear to be a thorn in his side until well into 1911.

The other contingent factor that encouraged a rhetoric of democracy in *La Voce* was the birth in Florence of the Italian Nationalist Association (ANI) in 1910. Although the *vociani* had themselves always been committed to some sort of nationalist outlook and program, and although they continued to champion the views of independent nationalist writers such as Alfredo Oriani, they were all firmly opposed to the Corradinian variety of nationalism that predominated in the ANI.[79] This opposition was based in part on personal animosities, the relationship between Corradini and Prezzolini in particular having deteriorated so far from the days of *Il Regno* that Prezzolini was publicly accusing Corradini of having attacked him with his walking stick on a Florentine street.[80] Yet those animosities were rooted in what seemed to the *vociani* to be profound differences in outlook. Corradini's was a nationalism that appeared antimodern, overly bombastic, and overly concerned with external appearances in its appeals to irredentism and the glories of the Roman imperial past. It was a "nationalism of literati" that, as Papini had remarked in 1909, "contaminated Julius Caesar with Maurice Barrès, a Latin song with a French refrain."[81] In order to mark their difference with this rhetoric and to establish their own modern and more "internal," spiritual orientation, some of the *vociani* had come to appreciate the usefulness of appealing to democracy. Thus, as Prezzolini would write in his most important political article of 1910, nationalism was dangerous because,

> with its vagueness and grandiloquent imprecision, it lends itself above all to our [nation's] rhetorical inclination and distances our thinking from those practical and specific internal problems that had begun to concern Italians and that unless resolved will prevent us from ever becoming a nation, problems such as the Italian south, education (primary, secondary, university, teacher training, professional), regional decentralization, and the relation of state and church . . . If on these four problems precise technical solutions were presented—some of which already exist, as in the cases of public instruction and the south—one would perhaps have a basis for developing a new party, one that would be both democratic and honest.[82]

None of the *vociani* were democrats in the sense of being fundamentally committed to parliamentarism or the rule of law, but some of them did want to broaden the base of political participation as a means of overturning the prevailing political élite and the corruption associated with it. Certainly they all agreed that no program of national renewal could be serious without engaging the masses. Yet the rhetoric of democracy in *La Voce* did not prevent the journal from being far more interested in political movements on the extreme right, such as Action Française, than in any democratic movement. Nor did democratic rhetoric endure once Giolitti moved to counter it with reforms and, even more significantly, once the mass demonstrations associated with the war in Libya indicated what appeared to be a much more effective way of awakening the second Italy. Before we examine this latter transformation, however, we need to become better acquainted with some of the more important new figures who joined the Florentine avant-garde with *La Voce* and the range of positions they represented within it.

A Widening Circle of Participants

Perhaps the major weakness of *Leonardo*, as we have seen, was that it failed to build an effective avant-garde group and became increasingly the private vehicle of Papini, Prezzolini, and, to a lesser extent, Soffici. Only with *La Voce* does one begin to see the development of a common position and some signs of genuine group solidarity. Although the solidarity was probably weakened by the fact that some of the *vociani* lived outside Florence, visiting the city infrequently, there were at least a dozen individuals who were publicly identified as central to the *La Voce* group, and many others who were associated with it on a regular basis. By the end of 1911, when the journal formally incorporated its small press, there were even bylaws, a board of directors, and meetings at which a formal record was kept.

Yet, even as they projected a common position vis-à-vis opponents such as the aestheticists of *Il Marzocco*, Corradini's nationalists, and Giolitti, from within the *vociani* remained a deeply contentious lot, and a wide field of positions was apparent at least to insiders. Essentially, this field ran in three dimensions: from those whose thinking was centered morally to those whose central concerns were aesthetic; from those concerned above all with philosophy to those concerned primarily with questions of history and society; and, finally, from those few whose thinking remained Catholic or Protestant to the majority who were secular in outlook. Still, there were many subtle complexities in this dispersed field as well as at least one particular mode of fusing apparently contradictory values that made otherwise discordant views appear similar.

One of the writers with the longest-standing ties to the circle around

Leonardo and *La Voce* was Giovanni Amendola. Born in 1882 into a poor family from Sarno in Campania, young Giovanni went to technical schools but showed a romantic, even mystical temper in his life outside school, becoming passionately involved in theosophy and other esoteric and occult philosophies while still in his teens. When the family moved to Rome so that his father could take a position as an attendant at the National Museum, Amendola joined the city's Theosophical Society. Soon thereafter he pursued philosophical studies, more formally though only briefly, at the University of Rome as well as at universities in Berlin and Leipzig.

An avid reader of the early *Leonardo*, Amendola began a correspondence with Papini in 1904 and was contributing by 1905. In July of that year, when Papini was in Rome, he encountered the "tall and handsome young man with dark skin and hair, black and powerful eyes, and a face that reminded me immediately of certain Hellenistic profiles."[83] Within a few weeks Amendola had also begun a correspondence with Prezzolini, one that would endure until just before Amendola's premature death in 1926 from the blows of fascist thugs.[84] In 1905, however, his relations with Papini were more important. It was Papini who put him in touch with William James and who advised him on how to get in touch with the symbolist circle in Moscow when Amendola had a chance to spend a few weeks there in the summer of 1906.[85]

It was after the visit to Moscow that Amendola went to Berlin to study philosophy, but he soon found the city "heavy and unpleasant, oppressive in its dead massiveness, and enlivened only very badly by a mercantile spirit that has been created almost ex-nihilo in only fifty years."[86] He thus moved on to Leipzig, which he found more "gemütlich" as well as more intellectually stimulating, largely because of the presence there of the neo-Kantian psychologist Wilhelm Wundt.[87] Yet Amendola was never sufficiently adapted to university life to realize his dream of a degree, and by year's end he had returned to Rome with a new bride, a Lithuanian by the name of Eva Kühn.

Eva and Giovanni had actually met four years before at the library of the Theosophical Society in Rome, where she had come to study comparative literature. Born in 1880 in Vilnius, and thus a native speaker of both Russian and German (to which she would later add English, French, and Italian), she grew up to be, in Papini's words, "a woman of passionate spirit, very cultured, who had written or was writing a quite original study on *Schopenhauer's Optimism*" at the moment early in 1910 when she joined her husband in Florence.[88] The two then struggled to support themselves and their two young children, she by doing translations into Italian (an anthology of passages from Dostoyevsky would appear from *La Voce*'s press in 1913), he by directing the library of the Theosophical Society and writing freelance journalism.

Already well established as a contributor to *La Voce* even before his arrival in Florence, Amendola distinguished himself among the *vociani* through his "profound moral seriousness" and the personal manner reflected by that seriousness—"the arching of his thick black eyebrows, the disdainful expressions of his lips, the dogmatic self-assurance of his speech."[89] The young Slataper was sufficiently impressed to see in him "the only man among us."[90] In later years Amendola would become very well known in Italian political life, first as the Rome correspondent for Luigi Albertini's *Corriere della Sera,* then as the democratic interventionist who joined the postwar cabinet of Francesco Nitti, as the parliamentary deputy from Salerno who organized the small but vocal liberal-democratic group in the Chamber of Deputies, as the leader of the constitutional opposition to fascism, and as a martyr to that cause when, after being severely beaten by fascists near Pistoia in July 1925, he went into exile in Cannes and then died some months later at forty-four. But these facts offer few clues about his life during the *La Voce* years. Although even then he had begun at least to write about politics, it was above all as a philosopher that he was known.

Like Prezzolini, Amendola had moved from the philosophical position he had held in the *Leonardo* years, in which intellect played only a very modest role in the immensity of "life," to one in which intellect was much more central. Yet his way of making this transition was very different than Prezzolini's. Rather than seeking to escape skepticism by adhering to a new rational metaphysics quite distant in spirit from his earlier life- philosophy, as Prezzolini had, Amendola sought to transform the latter by redefining its concept of will. In his early writing, he had conceived the will on the cosmic dimensions of Arthur Schopenhauer, but he now turned to the ideas of François-Pierre Maine de Biran, a Frenchman one generation older than Schopenhauer, in order to reconceive the will as the center of the human self. As such, the will for Amendola was both wholly rational and intimately connected to the emotional and spiritual.[91] As he wrote in 1911: "The rationality of the good is just this harmony and this cohesion of the human person, held in place by the will and thus raised above the chaos of the animal life to the order and clarity of the self."[92]

This position put Amendola somewhat at odds with Prezzolini, whose Croceanism he viewed as too narrow in its concept of reason and too dismissive of the emotional and spiritual dimensions of the human self. Indeed, in philosophical matters though not in moral or political ones, he seemed to be more comfortable with Papini, with whom in January

1911 he would launch *L'Anima*, a philosophical journal that offered the first clear sign of a potential splintering among the *vociani*.[93] Nonetheless, Amendola's influence on *La Voce* was for the most part steadying. According to Prezzolini, he alone on the journal had "no taste for polemic or scandal," and his conduct continually made manifest the same fundamental commitment to an ethics of spiritual discipline that underlay his thought.[94] Moreover, in terms of the internal politics of *La Voce*, his was as close to a middle ground as there was. Moralistic, philosophical, and secular, his position lay between the more aesthetic orientation of Papini and Soffici and the more social and historical one of Salvemini and Prezzolini. Yet, like Soffici, he was thoroughly international, a linguist almost as accomplished as his wife (with whom he corresponded in French), and a deep believer in culture as the central problem in renewing Italy and modern life more generally. At the same time, like Salvemini, he was adept in historical and political analysis as well as deeply committed to dealing with the particular problems of their native Mezzogiorno, although he was not yet the democrat he would become.

Salvemini, who was born at Molfetta in Puglia in 1873, had come to Florence much earlier and under quite different auspices than had Amendola. Though from an equally modest social background, he had won a scholarship to the Istituto di Studi Superiori, where he became the student of Pasquale Villari not long after his seventeenth birthday. He proved to have much in common with Villari, including what Prezzolini later called their love for "clarity and simplicity of thought"; but Salvemini was much more politically passionate than his teacher, and he allowed those passions to shape his historical thought.[95] After the Italian defeat at Adowa in 1896, he, like many other idealistic youths in his generation, became a socialist, and his early scholarship continually reflected that commitment. Among the topics of his early books were the class struggle in thirteenth-century Florence, the French Revolution, the nineteenth-century Milanese radicalism of Carlo Cattaneo, the military campaign in the south during the Risorgimento, and the thought of Giuseppe Mazzini. Moreover, Salvemini wrote frequently for socialist journals such as Turati's *Critica sociale*, and he chided its predominantly northern audience for what he saw as its lack of faith in the emancipatory potential of the working classes, particularly those in the south, and thus for its complacency and smugness.

When *Leonardo* made its debut in 1903, Salvemini was thirty and had already begun to look, as one of his colleagues on *L'Unità* later put it, "like an old Silenus: [with] a large skull, rendered wide by his baldness; small eyes, filled with kindness and intelligence; a snub nose; high cheekbones; a wide mouth which when he smiled showed a great fence of teeth; a pointed beard; wide shoulders; a thick-set figure; a heavy step—a man from the fields, not from literary drawing rooms."[96] It is thus not surprising that he was not drawn to write for *Leonardo*. Yet the journal did not escape his notice. Indeed, in one of his early letters to Prezzolini he even lamented its 1907 demise.[97] In the same letter Salvemini also told Prezzolini that his reading of the latter's *La coltura italiana* had led him "to believe that we are in agreement on many fundamental ideas," and it is not hard to see what he had in mind. Like Prezzolini and the other *vociani*, Salvemini had only contempt for the "first Italy" of the Italian political establishment, and he outdid them all in his condemnation of Giolittian politics as dead, dull, and morally reprehensible.[98] Moreover, although he wrote with great intensity of conviction, he was sometimes capable of a satirical style that helped make him more palatable to the young writers of *La Voce*. When tragedy struck him in the form of the Messina earthquake in late December 1908—it killed his wife and all five of his children—the *vociani* even became for a time his surrogate family, and he became, if not their patriarch, then at least their elder statesman.[99]

Yet, as we have seen, Salvemini never shared and probably never fully understood the concept of culture on which *La Voce* was based, and he was out of his element among so many who worried about the latest book or intellectual fashion from Paris or Vienna. What he had in common with the others was mostly an enemy *(giolittismo)* and a status—that of being an "individual on the margin of a group."[100] When tensions that had long percolated between him and his younger colleagues came to a head over the politics of the war in Libya, Salvemini moved quickly to establish his own strictly political voice, the journal *L'Unità*, and he never looked back.[101] Yet, unlike Amendola, who moved into political journalism at roughly the same time, Salvemini never ceased to indulge in a politics of idealism as a voice of conscience. Although this did not prevent him from making a brief excursion into practical politics—he served as a parliamentary deputy from 1919 to 1921—it did prevent him from ever being truly effective there. As Croce later wrote in his history of the period, Salvemini "nourished in the depths of his mind Mazzini's ideals of international justice and national good faith, and was prone to indulge in violent polemics of a moral character, half naive and half unjust, and tinged with utopianism."[102]

If Salvemini was *La Voce*'s elder statesman, then Scipio Slataper was the youngest of its many young Turks. Born in 1888 into a bourgeois family in Trieste, his mother Italian and his father Slavic, Scipio grew up torn between the natural beauty and the cultural and political tensions that surrounded him. Though under the control of Austria-Hungary, the population of Trieste was nearly two-thirds Italian, and the city had long been an object of irredentist fervor. One symbolic event that deeply impressed the young Slataper had come in 1882 when a twenty-four-year-old Italian *triestino* by the name of Guglielmo Oberdan was executed by the Austrians for allegedly plotting the assassination of the Emperor Francis Joseph. About Oberdan, whose martyrdom would later inspire many in the movement for Italian intervention in the First World War, Slataper wrote to Prezzolini in 1910: "Do you know that there is even an enormous physical resemblance between him and me? Sometimes I feel terribly close to him, as if he were the only real solution to my Trieste side."[103]

That the Italians of Trieste regarded union with Italy as the key to the city's spiritual survival was not lost on the Austrians, who developed Trieste as a port and an economic center but did not allow it a university.[104] Thus, in the fall of 1908 Slataper had gone to Florence to pursue a university degree. Almost as soon as he arrived, however, he discovered an early issue of *La Voce* in a Florentine bookstore and shifted his intellectual center of gravity to the *La Voce* circle, an association that ultimately cost him his university scholarship but not his degree, which he attained with a thesis on Henrik Ibsen in 1912.

Physically, Slataper was, as Soffici remembered him, "tall, with a big head of curly blond hair, a drooping mustache, and a nose red from the cold, wrapped in a black cape and moving his long legs in big strides beside Prezzolini, Papini, and me."[105] Similarly, his friend and fellow *triestino* Giani Stuparich recalled that "even in his walk he looked like a beautiful animal, heavy and agile at the same time."[106] Throughout his four years in Florence, Slataper had a series of passionate love affairs with girls from Trieste, the letters from which survive as vivid literary documents of the prewar era in Italy.[107] Yet what truly distinguished him among the *vociani* was neither the intensity with which he lived his private life nor his relative youth but the extreme passion and dogged determination that infused his intellectual pursuits.

Foremost among those pursuits, initially, was an effort to make more widely known both the glories and the plight of his native region. In 1909 his "letters from Trieste" appeared in *La Voce* as a seven-part series. Far from being (as their title might imply) a mere travelogue for the curious Tuscan or Roman, these "letters" were anguished reflections on the failure of the city's intellectual and professional élites, caught as they were "in a terrible conflict" between their spiritual needs (their "Italian soul") and their economic dependence on Austria (their "commercial soul").[108] Yet Slataper's problem as a *triestino* was also in many ways only a special case of *La Voce*'s general commitment to renewing culture and to building an Italian civil society that would be both vigorous and genuine. As time passed, he became more and more focused on the modern world's loss of contact with the divine and on the need to develop some new secular-religious framework. He read Nietzsche and Croce, coming away ultimately dissatisfied with each but with a deepened sense of the way positivism "represents a tiredness, a lassitude, and a discordant pause in the 'work of humanity.'"[109] Yet Slataper was not finally drawn to philosophy; at least on a personal level, he placed his hopes on a new poetic art. As he wrote in his diary in 1911: "I know that if there is something to which I can give birth it is a form of art with new, moral, religious content. I need to be drenched in this new consciousness to be able to do something, and sacrifice is therefore necessary."[110]

Slataper's idea of developing a new poetic art was very much in line with Soffici's project, as well as with the ideals of cultural renewal and generational revolt that Papini and Prezzolini had long been championing. In 1909 he wrote what was perhaps the most passionate appeal to the latter ideals ever to appear in the pages of *La Voce*. Addressed "to the intelligent youth of Italy," his article built an emotional crescendo from the quiet, confessional tone with which it began—in praise of poetry and the virtues of courage and sincerity—to a broad-based criticism of Italian society, and then to an exhortation to the new generation to "become moderns" and "to liberate ourselves, and to try to liberate others, from the false culture" that surrounded them. By the end, the idea that avant-garde art was the only possible source of deliverance for modern society had become an angry scream:

> Even art has a morality all its own, a specific one, higher than human morality because it surpasses it and precedes it: sincerity, liberation of the spirit from all the moral judgments of the day, expansion of the unconscious so that it becomes like a warm ethereal vapor rising against the obstructing twist of material necessities, against all the standards that gag us, against the individual yearning for great orgies in which we are intoxicated with incense and gold. When art becomes a pulsating nervousness inside your soul, and you see that in the common opinion of the day art has become a commodities exchange where bankers and brokers haggle, you should feel your fingers tightly curl and tremble before the need to seize these filthy beasts by the neck: to strangle them.[111]

Slataper actively cultivated the anarchic and destructive attitude evident in this passage, and he was sometimes quite critical of the *vociani* in whom he did not find it. "The mistake of *La Voce*," he wrote to his future wife in 1911, "has been that it schematizes life . . . Prezzolini lacks above all a certain joyousness, a sense of abandon, an openness to outings in the country and to conversation that is casual or even a bit silly; Prezzolini is always serious."[112] "Life" for Slataper was instinctive and primitive, best lived "barbarously" as a quest for elemental values such as love, friendship, health, and spontaneous contact with nature.[113]

Yet balanced against his championing of frivolity and "abandon" was another aspect of "barbarism," one involving a deeply moralistic attitude, especially in its commitment to other elemental values such as sacrifice, discipline, and—above all—work. In an article written shortly after the one just quoted, Slataper spoke of a "soul of joyousness that is extremely efficacious for our work" and of a "form of work with strategic intent, one that spurs and invites, rather than one that promotes work for the sake of work."[114] As Stuparich would later write: "Do you understand what work means [for Slataper]? It means living, feeling oneself act freely against an external obstacle, changing one's life in some sense, convincing, teaching, loving, creating. A divine thing, friendship among people, happiness. Precisely happiness: work is the apparent renunciation that leads to happiness."[115]

What is most interesting about Slataper is the way his feeling for "life" led him to attempt to fuse the extremes of anarchy and order, lightheartedness and discipline, expression and renunciation, love and work—in short, the aesthetic and the moral. As Sibilla Aleramo perceived, Slataper had at once a "stone-hard character" and an abundant "capacity for joy," a combination that helps to explain how he could be simultaneously a friend of Soffici and an admirer of Amendola, two men who could not abide each other.[116] Moreover, just as Amendola was launching the philosophical L'Anima with Papini, Slataper and Papini were plotting the establishment of a journal of literature and poetry to be called Lirica. The idea never got off the ground, but in its relation to L'Anima it symbolizes how the moralism of La Voce could take both poetic and philosophical forms in the service of the same ends.

Despite his relative youth, Slataper was among the first vociani to recognize in himself and consciously to live out this dialectic of anarchy and order. Also despite his youth, Slataper was recognized for his intellectual leadership, twice serving as the journal's acting editor: in March 1910 while Prezzolini was in Paris, and again from December 1911 until March 1912. Yet once he finished his university degree, Slataper moved slowly away from the circle. He spent most of 1913 teaching Italian literature in Hamburg, and when he returned in September to marry, it was to Trieste. By early 1915 he and Gigetta had gone on to Rome to be at the center of the movement for Italian intervention. In May Slataper volunteered, and by early June he was at the front. Wounded almost immediately, he returned to the front in November only to be wounded again, this time mortally, from a bullet in the throat while he was out on patrol. On that third day of December 1915, Slataper was twenty-seven; he had just received news of the birth of his first child.

In death Slataper joined the great anonymous mass of victims in the mindless slaughter of the First World War. In life, however, his way of fusing two of the values central to the Florentine avant-garde experience—at the most general level those of creativity and control—was exemplary in showing that these values did not have to remain separate and irreconcilable. We have already noticed how Prezzolini moved from an early "Bergsonian" cultivation of the wellsprings of individual creativity to a more "Crocean" emphasis on historical rationality and social order—separate phases that were never reconciled. In coming chapters we will see how Soffici and Papini attempted their own fusions of anarchy and order, fusions that held together for a time but that would ultimately appear more like separate phases of aggressive assertion and a "recall to order." Yet Slataper was not entirely alone among the *vociani* in his moral outlook. There were at least two others whose lives and intellectual positions manifested equally steadfast versions of the same dialectic but in whom the principle of order was ultimately stronger, probably because it assumed in each case a more traditionally religious form.

Piero Jahier and Giovanni Boine were the *vociani* for whom the question of Christian faith was the most agonizing and who yet remained believers. In personal manner and appearance as well as in many other aspects of their outlooks, however, they could hardly have been more different. Jahier was the son of an evangelical Protestant minister from the Waldensian valley in the mountains of Piedmont; Boine, a Catholic from the seacoast of Liguria.[117] Jahier was heavyset, outgoing, and vigorous; Boine, broad-shouldered but rather thin, withdrawn, and sickly— he suffered from tuberculosis throughout his adult life. Jahier was a vociferous critic of the Italian ruling class who went so far as to write for Mussolini's *Il Popolo d'Italia* during the campaign for Italian intervention but who, after the war, became a democrat and a fierce opponent of fascism. Boine was a contemplative but also cantankerous writer with the political values of Joseph de Maistre who did not live to see fascism, but he was certainly never a democrat.[118] Still, both were poets who experimented with "fragmentist" styles and who wrote prose like poetry, and both were especially attracted by the French Catholic poet Paul Claudel.

Jahier had two decisive and interrelated experiences in his early life. The first derived from his father's suicide in 1897 because of guilt over having engaged in adultery. Only thirteen at the time, Piero, as the oldest of four boys and the second oldest of six children, had to work very hard to help his hitherto unemployed mother support the family in the relatively expensive environment of Florence, where they had moved two years before. After graduating from high school in Florence in 1902, Jahier attended the divinity school of the Waldensians, but he abandoned these studies in 1904 because of growing doubts about Calvinism. Although he would later take degrees in law and French literature at the universities of Urbino and Turin, Jahier began a lifelong career as an employee of the Italian state railroads in 1905, and his intellectual activity even for *La Voce* was always an evening affair.

The second decisive experience for Jahier came on one of those evenings late in 1911 when he discovered Claudel, whose life, he soon recognized, bore some striking similarities to his own.[119] A poet of the older symbolist generation who had participated in Mallarmé's circle in the early 1890s, Claudel was a fervent convert to Catholicism who nonetheless had had a torrid romance with a married Polish woman from 1900 until 1904, an episode that became the inspiration for his famous play of 1906, *Partage de Midi* (Break of Noon). In the play, the clash between the call of the flesh and the fear of eternal damnation is portrayed at both a human and a cosmic level, the events onstage activated by the four Aristotelian elements of earth, air, fire, and water. For obvious autobiographical reasons, Jahier was immediately captivated by the drama, which he translated into Italian in 1912.

Later that year Jahier became embroiled in a dispute with Soffici that centered on Claudel, in which Soffici attacked Claudel as a neoromantic like Gauguin who had been passé for a decade because of his failure to attend sufficiently to language in the search for primal experience, while Jahier celebrated him as one of the currently central figures in the Parisian avant-garde who nonetheless had not fallen prey to the desacralizing immoralism and destructive attitudes then being promoted by Parisian "futurists" such as Apollinaire.[120] In some ways the conflict was between the "two Parises," and it definitely prefigured the divergence between the aesthetic attitudes of those poets with a primary loyalty to *Lacerba* and those like Jahier who remained primarily loyal to *La Voce*. Still, Jahier's poetry in this period was no less rebellious and radically innovative than Soffici's, and it is also no less frequently described as "futurist." What did distinguish it from Soffici's was its deep and genuine identification with the *popolo*, an identification reinforced by its convincing deployment of the everyday language of the street.

More the philosopher, less the poet, and far less the populist than Jahier, Giovanni Boine was the son of a railroad stationmaster, a position that took the family from the coastal towns of Porto Maurizio and Final-marina, where Giovanni was born in 1887, to the mountain village of Modane (near the Waldensian valley), and then to Genoa, where he entered high school, and to Milan, where he graduated. Once in Milan, however, his parents separated, and Boine effectively lost his father just as Jahier had a few years before. Fortunately, however, he soon met the wealthy nobleman Alessandro Casati, who, recognizing his brilliance and seriousness of purpose, took him under his wing. Casati supported his studies at the University of Milan, brought him into the circle around *Il Rinnovamento,* and even financed a six-week trip to Paris late in 1907 so that his young protégé might attend the lectures of Henri Bergson.

Already as a university student, Boine was showing signs of what Papini would later call the "torment of a soul tearing itself to pieces, which seeks to lie down in a natural peace, in an unburdening contemplation, but is unable to so."[121] In a letter written at the age of nineteen, Boine expressed a mystical attachment to death as a way of being united with God, and soon thereafter he dedicated one of his first articles for *Il Rinnovamento* to the Spanish mystic San Juan de la Cruz.[122] He also began a brooding correspondence with Miguel de Unamuno and, upon his recommendation, read Kierkegaard, whose sensibility was indeed very close to the one emerging in Boine.[123] Arguably, however, it was his discovery of Claudel in the spring of 1910 that made the strongest and most enduring impact on his intellectual position. What he found in Claudel was "Bergson imbibed by a poet . . . a universal spirit who has inside himself the cosmic chaos of Walt Whitman but who expresses it more profoundly and harmoniously."[124] For Boine, Claudel's virtue was to have recognized the "chaos" and thus the mystery of the universe, as well as the depths of human sinfulness, at the same time that he also pursued the Catholic spiritual discipline through which our vision of the world could become ordered and our "sin" rendered capable of making life substantial and concrete.

Following Claudel, Boine developed a Catholic idealism in which the concept of sin—like the concept of work for Slataper—was what guaranteed individual expressiveness, kept people firmly anchored in reality, and prevented them from falling prey to abstractions. The fullest and aesthetically most interesting expression of this idea came in Boine's "fragmentist" novella of 1914, *Il peccato* (Sin), in which a central theme is that those who "do not know sin" are "pure in death but not in life," since one can only "arrive at purity with substance when one has sinned a great deal, when one has 'sinned strongly.'"[125]

But Boine was already deploying Claudelian allusions and insights with regularity in *La Voce*—and in a surprisingly wide variety of contexts.

The first of these presented itself when, just at the time he was discovering Claudel, he replied to a polemic by Prezzolini on the sorry state of contemporary Italy. Casting Prezzolini's position in its most Salveminian light (but not unfairly) as the claim that Italy's problem was essentially economic and the solution primarily technocratic, Boine argued in good *La Vocean* fashion that, on the contrary, Italy's problem was essentially moral. Then, in a Claudelian twist, he suggested that perhaps only the "sinfulness" of a good war could serve as a cure. Despite the fact that the idea of war was then, in his view, being vulgarized by nationalists who treated it as a means of national power and expansion, it was still, he thought, preferable to Prezzolini's equally vulgar notion of "maximizing economic well-being." War, for Boine, should mean "spiritual revival" and "national education"; it should serve to help a society overcome "moral, intellectual, and political lassitude." Yet since there was no immediate prospect for a good war in 1910, he argued that the most pressing need was for "one of us to write for Italy a book that would be for our civilization what Nietzsche's *Birth of Tragedy* was for the Greek," a book that would make Italians aware of the seriousness of their own moral and religious tradition and through which they might ultimately be led to heroic action.[126]

Two years later Boine turned his polemical edge against Crocean idealism, which for him was far too rationalist, secular, and "Hegelian."[127] Here again Claudel was invoked in support of a view of "the world not as an ordered succession of things, thoughts, objects, and actions with final conclusions, a linear succession in space and time of a more or less logical syllogism" but as "a hundred million actions and things present simultaneously with a hundred billion very diverse lives lived harmoniously in the present." In Boine's view, despite the fact that Croce adopted as his "criterion of the beautiful . . . the objective recognition of each particular expression of individuality," he had failed to take particularity with sufficient seriousness and was too willing to see it subsumed by a "logical" view of history and human reality. That was why, Boine remarked, "the artists all complain, curiously, in the face of the 'freedom'" that Croce accorded them.[128] And that, too, was why Boine himself sought to articulate a "postromantic revolution" in aesthetic expression that would take the particular—the word, the phrase, the fragment—with absolute seriousness.

Almost immediately after the polemic with Croce, Boine initiated one with Soffici over his autobiographical novel of 1912, *Lemmonio Boreo,* which Boine found derivative (a "*Jean-Christophe* for Italy") and without literary value.[129] Soffici did not reply directly, although it seems to have been partly to Boine that he was responding in his subsequent dispute with Jahier over Claudel. Yet Soffici's silence may have represented his sense that there was little need to reply, Boine having allowed his polemical tendencies to reinforce his increasing isolation within Florentine intellectual circles. As Prezzolini would later remark, Boine was "not an easy man to get along with," and the fact that he came to Florence only occasionally from his home in Porto Maurizio probably increased the strain still further.[130] This strain would reach its climax when, just as the European war was being declared, Boine lived out his concept of "strong sin" in a desperate love affair with Eva Kühn Amendola.

Despite this isolation and strain, Boine remained a vital presence in the pages of *La Voce* throughout 1913 and the first half of 1914. Surprisingly, however, in view of the aesthetic revolution he had called for in his polemic with Croce, Boine's greatest popular success as a writer was his *Discorsi militari*, a deeply felt but, from a literary point of view, utterly conventional book published late in 1914 by *La Voce*'s press and later widely distributed in the trenches. The *Discorsi* were a kind of meditation on the military code, a catechism for Italian soldiers on how they might bring "spiritual order" and "discipline" to their conduct of warfare. If we take the book together with Boine's *Il peccato* of the same year, it appears that he, no less than Slataper, had a dialectic of order and anarchy. Although in Boine these remained separate (if nearly simultaneous) moments that would never be integrated or reconciled, it is possible that a coming reconciliation was overtaken by events. Too enfeebled by sickness to volunteer for the war himself, Boine nonetheless entered it as a medic and was wounded in battle in November 1915. His greatest enemy, however, remained his sickness: on May 16, 1917, Boine died of tuberculosis, three months before his thirtieth birthday.

Despite their divergent personalities and positions, Amendola, Salvemini, Slataper, Jahier, and Boine were all central figures in what would prove to be *La Voce*'s heyday. This was not the case with Benito Mussolini, who contributed just two articles to the review and never lived in Florence or fraternized with members of the group.[131] Yet it is worth considering his position in relation to those of other writers for *La Voce*, both because he was already developing a very close personal relationship with Prezzolini and because of his obvious centrality to the fate of Florentine modernism after 1914.

Born in 1883 into a poor rural family in Dovia near the Romagna town of Forlì, the young Mussolini shared many experiences and cultural attitudes with his generational counterparts across the Apennines in Florence. Like them, he had gone abroad in the early years of the century—they to Paris, he to Lausanne (1902–1904)—in order to escape what they all regarded as the constricting cultural atmosphere in Italy and to learn about and participate in the controversies then current in European intellectual life. In his autobiography of 1912, Mussolini referred to his "bohemian" life in Lausanne, and he departed with enough esteem for French culture to think for a brief period about becoming a professor of French.[132] Like the Florentines too, he was drawn in this period to Nietzsche, to the religious socialism of Sorel, and to the élite theory of Pareto, whose lectures he attended while in Lausanne. He believed as they did that Italy needed a "new aristocracy," and he drew his concept from the same sources: Pareto and Oriani. Finally, like them, Mussolini worried intensely about the social implications of the "death of God," and his first long essay, finished in July 1904, bore the title *L'uomo e la divinità.*

There was also, of course, an important difference between Mussolini and the young men of *Leonardo:* his active interest in socialism and their vehement rejection of it. Yet we must not be misled by this difference. Mussolini was never strictly a Marxist, despite the efforts of friends such as Angelica Balabanoff to move him in that direction; and his socialism was more instinctive than doctrinaire, the first of several forms that his rebelliousness would take during the years before the fascist seizure of power.[133] Thus it is not surprising that when Mussolini returned to Italy in November 1904, he quickly became a reader of *Leonardo.* Apparently he was able to perceive the deep-seated generational rebelliousness beneath its antisocialist veneer, and he clearly admired both its anti-academic rhetoric and the way it canvassed new philosophical currents in search of a secular-religious faith.[134] From 1905 to 1908 Mussolini did very little socialist organizing or writing, and by the end of this period he was entirely devoting himself to intense intellectual reflection. During the second half of 1908 he wrote a number of cultural pieces for nonsocialist journals, including an essay on the poet Friedrich Klopstock, three briefer articles on poetry, and a long and quite good essay on Nietzsche. In that essay he characterized the crisis of the epoch in terms that hardly suggest orthodox Marxism or socialism: "The superman is a symbol, an index of this anguished and tragic period of crisis passing over the European consciousness in its search for new sources of pleasure, beauty, and ideals. He is the recognition of our weakness, but at the same time the hope for our redemption. He is the sunset—and the dawn."[135]

Even while Mussolini was in the Trentino in 1909, devoting much of his time to writing for the local socialist press, he underwent what one historian has called a "brief but intense exposure . . . to European decadentism, from Baudelaire to Verlaine, Wilde to D'Annunzio," and it is perhaps indicative that one of his major contributions to the socialist journal *Il Popolo* was a serialized historical novel, *Claudia Particella, l'amante del cardinale*.[136] It was also while in Trento that he became an avid reader of *La Voce*, even helping in its local distribution. From the beginning it was clear that he fully understood—and fully shared—*La Voce*'s agenda of spiritual and cultural renewal. As he wrote to Prezzolini in October 1909: "*La Voce*'s latest initiative is excellent: to make Italy known to Italians. Besides political unity, which is slowly but progressively becoming consolidated, it is necessary to forge the spiritual unity of the Italians. This is difficult work, given our history and temperament, but it is not impossible. To create the 'Italian' soul is a superb mission."[137] Many years later, in 1924, when Prezzolini credited Mussolini with "realizing many of the things that I wanted when I founded and directed *La Voce*," it was very likely this modernist project of spiritual and cultural renewal that he had most centrally in mind.[138]

Even though Mussolini wrote only two articles for *La Voce*, he tried unsuccessfully to interest Prezzolini in several others, and there were signs that he felt great kinship with a number of the *vociani*.[139] One such sign was a short article he wrote about *La Voce* for a journal in Trento in which he cited extensively from Papini and Prezzolini's *La coltura italiana* and was wholly enthusiastic about their enterprise:

> To create a culture it is not enough to educate; to create a party it is not enough to have a program, even a maximalist one; to justify a present permeated with what is base and vulgar it is not enough to have a glorious past; to assign a nation a mission in world history it is not enough to unify it politically—if there is not also the psychological unity that binds its will and directs its efforts. Italian intellectual life lacks courage, and *La Voce* seeks to inspire it. It seeks to resolve "the terrible problem" posed before our national soul: "either to have the courage to create the third great Italy, not the Italy of the popes nor of the emperors but the Italy of the thinkers, an Italy that has not yet existed—or to leave behind only a few signs of mediocrity that the wind can quickly blow away." That is *La Voce*'s program. A superb effort . . .[140]

Another sign of the kinship Mussolini felt for *La Voce* was the great enthusiasm with which he pursued his correspondence with Prezzolini. As he would confess later to a biographer:

> I first had the feeling of being called to announce a new epoch when my correspondence brought me close to the group around *La Voce*. My study of the Trentino had aroused a certain interest in Florence, and my articles on the publications of Papini and Prezzolini had provoked some curiosity in Trento . . . Of the *vociani* I loved above all Soffici, Slataper, and Jahier. I felt that

they were close to me in temperament: young, open, clearheaded. Soffici appeared to me even then as a chapter on faithfulness, just as Slataper appeared as a treatise on the magnificent life. Slataper and Oberdan; the images became blurred together. It seemed to me that Slataper had been destined to write what Oberdan had only been able to say. These poets announced a whole new world, while I limited myself to interpreting statistics and the minutes of meetings of syndicalist and working-class organizations in Trento, but while I also was translating Klopstock and Platen and calling them great poets![141]

Of course not all the *vociani* were focused on poetry, and Mussolini wrote more about syndicalism than dry memoranda. In 1909, when Prezzolini had published his book on syndicalism, Mussolini had reviewed it—favorably—for *Il Popolo*. While noting that he held syndicalist convictions that Prezzolini did not share, he nonetheless characterized syndicalism's weakness in a way that owed much to Prezzolini's analysis: "By now syndicalism is complete as doctrine; it lacks men. We must make them."[142] Moreover, although Mussolini had earlier often taken the orthodox syndicalist position that a "new aristocracy" could emerge out of a properly educated working class, he treated Prezzolini's contrary position with great respect and at some points seemed even to agree with it.[143] Over the next several years the political importance of "spiritual elevation," "culture," and "ideals" was so strongly emphasized in Mussolini's writing that Renzo De Felice has located the essence of his "revolutionary socialism" in its "conjunction with *La Voce*."[144]

When Mussolini broke with the Italian Socialist Party in October 1914, it was above all to the *vociani* that he turned for intellectual support.[145] Yet already in July 1912, at the height of his influence in the party, he had written Prezzolini plaintively that he felt "exiled" from his fellow socialists because of his own "religious concept of socialism" and their "philistine revolutionism," and he wondered if *La Voce* might have space for his "efforts at revisionism in a revolutionary sense." Clearly, Mussolini was casting about for an alternative to the party organ *Avanti!* that he then edited. By November 1913, when he founded the theoretical journal *Utopia*, he had given up the idea that the future élite would come from the working class alone by appealing in the manner of *La Voce* to "the younger generation today—socialist and nonsocialist alike—the as yet unrecognized intelligentsia."[146] In a brief note in *La Voce*, Prezzolini recognized *Utopia*'s kinship to the journal but nonetheless deemed it a "hopeless enterprise" to try to "revive the theoretical consciousness of socialism."[147]

Very shortly, Mussolini would come to agree with him. Yet, as Mussolini later told a biographer, he also "feared that the *vociani*, who had thrown open the library windows so as to allow the noble winds of fantasy to enter its stuffy rooms, might be forced to close them again before there could be produced from within this new culture not so much a renaissance of cultural themes involving liberty as the birth of a new sense of history."[148] From this point of view, fascism was the effort to keep those windows open—by whatever means necessary.

War in Libya and Simmering Discontent

Ever since the Italian army had suffered the humiliation of a defeat by the Ethiopians in 1896, the citizens of Italy had yearned to restore the nation's reputation through foreign conquest. One object of this interest, despite its dubious value as real estate, was the desert territory of Libya (Tripolitania and Cyrenaica), which the nationalists had come to call Italy's "fourth shore." Controlled in 1911 by the decaying Ottoman Empire, it appeared to be there for the taking, but the Italian government had nonetheless proceeded cautiously given the delicate interdependencies in European diplomacy that even an apparently small initiative by a secondary power might unravel. In the summer of 1911, however, the crisis in Morocco, fears that Italy might be "awarded" Libya as compensation for an Austrian advance in the Balkans, and mounting nationalist provocation at home combined to force Giolitti's hand. To the cheers of huge throngs in every major Italian city, the troops were deployed across the Mediterranean on September 29.

Despite widespread expectations of a quick victory, the conquest of Libya proved a difficult undertaking. Turkey did not surrender formally for more than a year, and the war dragged on for several more in inland areas poorly controlled from Constantinople. Indeed, the conquest and colonization of the "fourth shore" remained a live issue in Italian politics for another three decades.[149]

The conflict in Libya has its appointed place in the intricate history of the origins of the First World War, but the sea change it represented in Italian domestic politics is perhaps less appreciated. Events in Florence were typical. On September 27, a day before the last-minute ultimatum to Turkey and two days before the departure of the troops, tricolor flags were draped in every public square, while socialist opponents of the war called for a general strike. Despite a demonstration the next day by several thousand leftist protesters, however, the strike quickly fizzled, and an even larger counterdemonstration, with its Garibaldian banners and songs, moved late in the evening from the Duomo to the barracks of the Eighty-fourth Infantry Regiment, due to depart the next day. When the departure took place, Florence saluted with still another demonstration of unprecedented size and a banner headline in *La Nazione* predicting the imminent conquest of Tripoli.

In the coming days and weeks, as patriotic fervor and political animosities continued to mount, a new domestic mood became apparent, one in which the heightened pride and hopes of many citizens mixed apocalyptically with their equally heightened sense of danger.[150] In cultural life the passions of nationalism and the cult of violence had been set ablaze, and in politics it began to appear impossible that the established liberal order could survive unaltered. Social conflict between defenders of the new "Italy first" attitude and their socialist opponents reached new heights, yet both sides were driven by many of the same extremist attitudes. Even those who most fervently opposed the war, such as the radical wing of the Socialist Party that Mussolini would soon lead, began to sound ever shriller in their commitment to and celebrations of violence. Among more moderate political elements, significant reform now appeared certain (and near-universal male suffrage did arrive in 1913), but no one had any clear idea of how to transform the political system in a comprehensive way. As Amendola wrote in an important assessment of the national atmosphere late in the year: "We must certainly admit that we would not have hoped to see in so short a time such a sharp rise in the tone of our civic emotions . . . The problems and preoccupations that the war raises for the best-informed sectors of Italian public consciousness do not succeed in overpowering the sense of relief that pervades this consciousness and everywhere reanimates it . . . What most interests us in the war, what most interests the Italian people, is the moral drama that is being played out behind it in the soul of the nation."[151]

During the spring and summer of 1911, *La Voce* had been clear in its opposition to war in Libya, in part because of economic calculations that appeared unfavorable and in part because of the journal's contempt for *L'Idea Nazionale,* the nationalist weekly that Corradini had begun to edit from Rome in March and that was trumpeting its enthusiasm for the enterprise in every issue.[152] On the first of these points, Salvemini had been especially vehement; the second was a favorite of Prezzolini's. Yet there was also a deeper reason for *La Voce*'s opposition to the war, one involving its nearly automatic reflex against any government-sponsored initiative. After all, how could the "first and second Italies" ever be expected to make common cause? By early October, however, in the words of *La Voce*'s lead editorial, "the die was cast," and the enormous groundswell of popular support made all but the most politically idealistic among the *vociani*—like Salvemini—fall into line. As if to emphasize the parting of the ways between Salvemini and *La Voce*, the same front page on which appeared the editorial grudgingly accepting the war also contained a meditation by Slataper on the poet Carducci titled "And the Cypresses of San Guido?"—just the sort of piece that the new editor of *L'Unità* had always least understood and most detested.[153]

The politics of *La Voce* would change profoundly in the wake of Salvemini's departure and in the new atmosphere of the Libyan campaign. The democratic rhetoric that marked the early *La Voce* as a distinctive phase in the development of the Florentine avant-garde was put aside, never to return, although the rhetoric combining bellicosity and discipline that would replace it emerged only very gradually over the next two years. This was not because this latter rhetoric had to be entirely invented; something very much like it had already been developed in the *Leonardo* years, and a rhetoric of discipline shorn of the connection with violence had played a role in the early *La Voce*. Much of this legacy, however, had been appropriated by the nationalists in crassly materialist ways that the *vociani* found reprehensible. It would take time to develop a way of speaking about politics that was both intrinsically convincing and sufficiently "spiritual" that they would not appear to be joining the nationalist camp. Above all, it would take time to integrate the rhetoric of violence and discipline with the European modernist culture that it was always *La Voce*'s first task to diffuse and promote.

Among the *vociani* the one exception to this gradualism (though not to the antinationalism) was Papini, who was immediately overwhelmed by the war mood. In an article on October 19 on the coming "victorious war" he gloried in his long-standing advocacy of it, separating himself "sharply from Prezzolini and Salvemini" and proclaiming that "Italy is no longer the land of carnival, dreams, or Goethean lemon trees; it is becoming a fairytale kingdom, a country of marvels, a true *Dreamland*." He also made clear, somewhat ominously, that "one does not make national policy with calculation and reasoning" and that "the life and greatness of a nation may require what appears *useless* to cotton merchants." Yet even he took pains to point out that the present war was not "a serious war, a great war with a great nation like Austria or France, for example," and that the "great-war myth" Corradini had been spinning was therefore only that, a myth.[154]

In a reply in *La Voce*'s next issue, Amendola wrote not of the "victorious war" but of the "pitiful war" and cautioned that it "should not be a cause of bellicose rhetoric."[155] But by the end of the year, though still separating himself from "the advocates of war for its own sake," Amendola appeared to take a step toward Papini's position by identifying "the men of the war in Tripoli" with "the men of my generation" and by taking pride in the way they were now overthrowing the image held "by foreigners of a nation that does not fight, a nation of shrewd politicians and able businessmen, but therefore also a nation of passive and egotistical men without restraint or discipline."[156] Yet what distinguished Amendola's words from Papini's, and what marked them as one of the first indications of the new rhetoric of *La Voce*, was the closing emphasis on "restraint and discipline."

Over the next year, many writers for *La Voce* with quite diverse perspectives were pursuing and developing the connection between war and social "discipline." Thus, Antonio Anzilotti distinguished between the true "nationalism that is inconceivable without disciplined preparation"—such as that evidenced during the struggles of the Risorgimento—and the "imperialist megalomania" of the Italian nationalists.[157] In an editorial on "the discipline of the Italians," Riccardo Bacchelli wrote similarly that his people, despite being "so deplorably undisciplined, that is, so unsociable regarding the little things in life, are now showing great discipline in enduring the weight of war without the slightest grumbling."[158] By the end of the year Prezzolini had crystallized the point: "War is death, disease, destruction. We know that. We feel that . . . But war, for us, is above all something else. War is the *general examination* to which peoples are called every so often by history. When this occurs, everything that is healthy, even if hidden, is revealed; and what is rotten is also revealed . . . The winners are not [necessarily] the big or heavily populated states, but those with peoples who are constant, prepared, disciplined, faithful, believing, farsighted."[159]

Even before the heady days of 1914, then, Prezzolini and his fellow *vociani*, though still disavowing war for its own sake, were very close to advocating war for the sake of discipline, war for the sake of building civil society. From the Libyan episode, they had learned the value of war as an instrument of popular education, as a vehicle for awakening the "second Italy." War, they now understood, could mobilize a population through mass political demonstrations, military recruitment, and the experience of sacrifice shared by those left at home. Whether a particular war made sense as an economic proposition or as a way of increasing national power—the sources of their initial hesitations regarding Libya—now appeared to matter less than whether (and how well) a particular war could function as a spiritual educator.

It might appear, then, that the war in Libya had greatly strengthened the Florentine avant-garde by providing it with a new rhetoric and strategy. For even if the rhetoric owed a great deal to ideas already developed in the *Leonardo* years, it was now being amplified and refined in a very different context, one that had fired the passion of the nation and that, in so doing, had begun to create a public space, and thus the possibility of a vital civil society, which the *leonardiani* not only had never found but had been unable even to conceive. Yet this point sums up at most half the story, and probably not the more important half. By 1912 the Florentine avant-garde was also deeply divided and dispirited, so much so that Prezzolini had actually discussed *La Voce* in the past tense in the book he was then writing, *Italia 1912*.[160] This division and dejection owed something to the war in Libya as well, although its most important sources lay elsewhere.

We have seen that, from the beginning, Papini and Soffici were uncomfortable with *La Voce*. Although their many letters to Prezzolini during its early years certainly contained words of support and even solidarity with the enterprise, they also contained many expressions of dismay and, occasionally, of open hostility. The essential feeling of the two men was perhaps most succinctly and directly captured by Papini: "When I write for *La Voce* I do not feel free . . . If I make pure art, it doesn't fit in with *La Voce;* had I written philosophy, I would have collided immediately with your ideas, and I don't always feel like writing—and can't always be expected to write—articles of information."[161] In addition to having these same feelings, Soffici felt hamstrung by what he regarded as Prezzolini's incomprehension of the cutting edge of avant-garde art, such as the cubist designs of Picasso.[162] In short, both men dissented from *La Voce* on matters of taste, believing that the concept of culture and the specific ideas about culture that it transmitted were insufficiently radical, overly moralistic, and too wedded to logos rather than mythos.

But even though these principal *vociani* felt the greatest unease, hardly anyone in the group was wholly satisfied with the journal or felt it to be an adequate reflection of his or her personal views. Prezzolini complained in his diary about personal antagonisms between Amendola and himself as well as between Soffici and Slataper.[163] When at one point he thought of asking Amendola to replace him as editor, he feared such a move would mean the flight of Slataper, Jahier, and Soffici.[164] Virtually everyone complained about Prezzolini's Croceanism, and, as we have seen, Amendola and Papini began *L'Anima* largely in order to have an alternative outlet for philosophical writing. Some thought that *La Voce*'s politics were too leftist, particularly on the question of suffrage, and this issue would cost *La Voce* its principal financial backing when Casati withdrew over it in the spring of 1911.[165] Others, like Slataper, felt that the journal was too preoccupied with political issues, whatever their ideological valence, and that this preoccupation had caused it to sacrifice its true "function of spiritual unification." Such views tended to hold Salvemini responsible for the problem.[166]

One incident in July 1911 pushed the tension level among the *vociani* nearly to the breaking point. Since it involved the emerging relationship between the Florentine avant-garde and the futurists of Milan, a bit of background is necessary. Papini later recalled that he and Soffici were at the Giubbe Rosse when they read the first futurist manifesto in February 1909. At that time they had applauded the futurists' desire to rid Italy of "the weight of all the bad antiquarianism" but had disapproved of the "air of tragic clowns with which they presented themselves."[167] That "air" had moved Soffici to write his "recipe" for futurism in *La Voce:*

> Take a kilo of Verhaeren, two hundred grams of Alfred Jarry, one hundred of Laforgue, thirty of Laurent Tailhade, five of Vielé-Griffin, a dash of Morasso—yes, even some Morasso—a pinch of Pascoli, a small bottle of holy water. Then take fifteen automobiles, seven airplanes, four trains, two steamships, two bicycles, various electric batteries, a few burning caldrons; put in some of your own flower of impotence and pomposity; mix everything together in a lake of gray matter and aphrodisiac foam; boil the mixture in the emptiness of your soul, on a burner of American quackery, and then give it to the Italian public to drink.[168]

By June 1911, however, Soffici had begun to recognize the futurists as serious rivals in the business of importing Parisian avant-garde culture into Italy, and he shifted from a tone of lighthearted jest to one of caustic polemic and fierce *ad hominem* critique.[169] A few days after having written just the sort of article that Prezzolini had most feared when he was drafting his *Progetto* in 1908, Soffici was sitting with Medardo Rosso at one of the Giubbe Rosse's outside tables, enjoying the summer air and some military band music from the Piazza Vittorio.[170] Suddenly someone tapped him on the shoulder to ask if he were Soffici, and moments later a fist landed in his face. A punitive expedition of futurists—F. T. Marinetti and the painters Carlo Carrà, Luigi Russolo, and Umberto Boccioni (the striker of the first blow)—had arrived in Florence. After a rousing brawl in the piazza, Soffici took his revenge the next day by hiding at the train station with Prezzolini and Slataper and ambushing the futurists just as they were about to board for Milan.

A few days later Prezzolini exulted in their "victory" by publishing the following "warning" in *La Voce:*

> Recognizing that there have been attempts to overpower those who write for *La Voce* with violent fisticuffs, taking them by surprise and when they were at a physical disadvantage, the various collaborators, friends, and sympathizers of *La Voce* who reside in Florence have decided to rally together whenever similar events occur and to reciprocate with violence as quickly as possible and with the greatest possible assurance of superiority. And they warn that the lesson taught the futurists at the Florence train station, as they were leaving for Milan in the aftermath of the sort of incident just indicated, is only the first application of this system. A warning to those who come next.[171]

Not all the *vociani* were amused, however. Amendola was so incensed by the "warning" that he immediately submitted his "resignation" from *La Voce* in two angry letters to Prezzolini.[172] Only after much pleading did he agree not to make this separation a public matter.[173] Salvemini was perhaps even more incensed. "Soffici was not in the right," he wrote Prezzolini the day after the "warning" in *La Voce*. "He provoked the futurist painter, baiting him more or less directly. He who baits another man opens an unjust dispute and should be the one to forget it . . . Soffici criticized *a man in particular*, saying that his paintings were trash, just as once before he had said about some sculptures that they were the stuff of homosexuals. If in this case a person who has not just been criticized but who has been insulted reacts, it is Soffici who has to give in. *La Voce* has nothing to do with this."[174]

Initially Prezzolini did his best to shrug off the whole affair, telling Salvemini that "my function is to understand everyone, admire everyone, help everyone, and hold us all together. If I don't succeed, then goodby: I will go study or sell wine and olive oil."[175] But the letters of criticism from Amendola and Salvemini so shook him that by the day after his "warning" appeared, he was proposing that one of them take over as editor.[176] This conciliatory attitude succeeded in somewhat defusing the tension, and by autumn Amendola had taken back his "resignation," at least in practice. Indeed, during the first half of 1912 he once again became a regular contributor. Nonetheless, *La Voce* was in many ways still reeling from the "Soffici affair," as Salvemini had called it, when the situation in Libya exploded.

In mid-September, as an Italian invasion began to appear imminent, Salvemini became impatient with what he saw as *La Voce*'s failure to do enough to mobilize public opinion against it. As he wrote to Prezzolini on September 17: "Don't worry about doing too much politics and not enough culture. To explain to those Italian jackasses [the nationalists] what Tripoli means and what the dangers and potential ruin of '*tripolismo*' are is no less a matter of *culture* than speaking about Péguy or Picasso. Except for the fact that Péguy and Picasso can wait, while Tripoli cannot."[177] Discussing Tripoli was "true culture," he argued a few days later, whereas discussing Péguy and Picasso was mere "literature."[178] Yet none of the other *vociani*, including Prezzolini, were willing to redefine culture in this fashion. At the same time, they did their best to explain to Salvemini why his attitude was inappropriate for *La Voce*. Interestingly, in this enterprise it was the "former" *vociano* Amendola who took the lead.[179]

Yet Salvemini remained unalterably focused on what he saw as the tragedy in Libya. When the invasion occurred and Prezzolini and Amendola reluctantly decided to change course and support the government, Salvemini's departure from *La Voce* became only a matter of time. Nonetheless, even after this occurred on October 6, he honored an earlier commitment to serve on the governing board of *La Voce*'s press, the first meeting of which was held in Florence in November. For he was leaving the journal itself, as he wrote Prezzolini, only because he could not "sacrifice the central nucleus of his individuality" and despite the fact that the move would cause him "infinite pain."[180]

For *La Voce*, Salvemini's departure meant the end of one kind of political rhetoric and the beginning of another. Fittingly, Prezzolini actually used the latter in his letter bidding Salvemini farewell: "No, dear Salvemini, we do feel, yes, that there are things above politics, but these do not have to do with literature; they have to do with the moral life, discipline, historical judgment."[181] Yet the issue that Salvemini had raised concerning the relation between "culture" and "literature" would not only endure within the Florentine avant-garde but would become increasingly important for it, even if what came to stand behind these concepts was not quite the same as what Salvemini had understood by them. Should we aim to develop a culture through which the masses are genuinely educated for practical political action, even if this culture is not based on what passes for avant-garde "literature" in Paris? Or should we strive to create our new culture in the most avant-garde way, even if it does not engage the masses—or, more likely, if it *does* engage them but at an irrational and elemental level that conventional education tends to ignore or repress? If we choose the former, how can we continue to say that our concept of culture is truly modernist, especially given that a hallmark of modernist art, literature, and philosophy is the exploration of the irrational forces in human consciousness and life? If we choose the latter, how can we continue to say that our artistic, poetic, and philosophical efforts as individuals are really helping to produce a common culture and "the intellectual and moral redemption" of Italy? This was the fundamental issue that would be posed with increasing insistence in 1912 and that would mark the dividing line between *La Voce* and *Lacerba* after the founding of the latter in 1913.

Although these questions were very much in the air when Papini and Soffici were fighting with Prezzolini over the founding of *La Voce* in 1908, *La Voce* had survived as a "convention" during its first three years in large measure because such questions were never posed in its pages. The journal had simply heaped together artistic modernism, Crocean idealism, Salveminian politics, and discussions of the need to educate the "second Italy" and to provide an outlet for the "new generation." At an organizational level, there had been a sense that *La Voce* was moving toward some more organized form like Papini's "spiritual party" or "party of the intellectuals," although there was little enthusiasm for creating a party in the conventional political sense. As late as August 30, 1911, Amendola had written to Boine that plans were under way for "a convention of ten or fifteen people, absolutely private, to see if it is possible to specify some fundamental points of a political program for further *study*." But by November 7, in another letter to Boine, he had given up on this hope because of the events in Libya.[182]

Thereafter, it was clear to all that the organization of the Florentine avant-garde would be at most a kind of loose confederation of individuals and groups, each pursuing its own personal, intellectual itinerary. In 1913 it may have appeared that there were two loose confederations, one around *La Voce* and the other around *Lacerba*, one cultivating the philosophical sources of a new social discipline, the other celebrating art and poetry as the sources of an angry, boisterous anarchism. Yet the two always remained tied by *La Voce*'s press and, above all, by friendships, even if according to the definition Papini then proposed, "friends are only enemies with whom we have concluded a truce—one that, however, is not always honestly observed."[183] In 1915 just such a "friendship" would be in effect between the *vociani* and the *lacerbiani* as they pursued their common goal of Italian intervention in the First World War.

What ended in the fall of 1911, then, was not the Florentine avant-garde but rather the possibility of unifying it—either within *La Voce* or under some other, not yet available auspices. Yet if, by 1912, Florentine avant-gardism appeared to have been weakened in this way, it had also been radicalized by Libya and made more self-confident in its conviction that a new Italy was about to be born. This combination of organizational weakness and self-confident radicalization may appear paradoxical, but it is in fact what prevailed from 1912 through the spring of 1915. On balance, it was probably the worst of both worlds. For as the rhetoric became more virulent and as the audience for it increased dramatically in size, the Florentine avant-garde also became more and more divorced from any prospect of a unified organization capable of acting both forcefully and responsibly.

4 Culture Wars and War for Culture: The Years of Florentine Futurism

The excitement had been building for weeks. First the crates of paintings had begun to arrive at the train station from London, Paris, Berlin, Milan, and Moscow. Then the exhibition itself had been set up in the flat next to Gonnelli's Bookshop on the Via Cavour. Soon the public would be asked to pay a stiff fifty-cent entry fee to stand wide-eyed before what, according to its sponsors at *Lacerba*, was "the most important, the most modern and the newest art exhibit ever seen in this medieval city."[1] Few among those who entered, however, would be able to make any sense of it, and many left feeling cheated. A few blocks to the south something related was apparently under way among the futurists gathered at the Giubbe Rosse. According to one of the youngest among them, Alberto Viviani, the café "was literally besieged by curious onlookers who pressed their noses against the misted windows (the more fortunate were able to make it to the first row) in order to study our every move, almost as if we were manufacturing bombs or were dangerous conspirators."[2] Soon came the big announcement in leaflets handed out on street corners: the public was invited to the *grande serata futurista*— the grand futurist evening—to be held on December 12, 1913.

On the afternoon of the appointed day, crowds began to mill in the Piazza Santa Croce near the Verdi Theater, one of the city's largest. By the time the *lacerbiani* and their Milanese friends arrived at about eight o'clock, the Verdi was already

overflowing with a restless and electrified public. In the main hall and theater boxes more than six thousand people were packed like anchovies in a tin. One wing of the gallery was occupied by an entire boarding school run in Florence by Catholic priests. There were also bourgeois of every economic level, students, many members of the Liberal Union party, aristocrats both known and unknown, journalists, policemen, rowdies and hooligans [teppa]. Who had recruited them all would forever remain a mystery. In the partial obscurity of the theater the confused shouting of the crowd rose like the sad song of a people in chains yearning for freedom. One heard the somewhat timid sounds of metallic sirens and whistles, occasionally the deep-throated honk of an automobile trumpet-horn. Clearly the crowd had not come to listen. They had come to raise hell and for that alone.[3]

The evening's performers moved backstage and out of sight. According to the correspondent for *Il Corriere della Sera,*

> by nine o'clock the first projectiles—some beans, some acorns—began to rain on the [empty] stage. Soon it was being inundated with an incredible barrage of everything a well-supplied greengrocer would be likely to have . . . By ten past ten, Marinetti, Boccioni, Carrà, Soffici, Papini, Tavolato, and two other futurists [Filiberto Scarpelli and Francesco Cangiullo] came forward into the lights, and the hail of projectiles became still heavier. Undaunted, with their heads high, they remained frozen in their positions while the theater appeared to become an infernal madhouse. When for a moment there was silence, Marinetti turned to the crowd and shouted: "You have acted like the Turks at the Dardanelles; you have exhausted your projectiles but you have not hit us."[4]

A potato then struck him squarely in the eye. By the next morning it was not difficult to tell which one of these curious performers was the famous Marinetti.

But the night was still young. Although not a word of their inflated pronouncements and poetry could be heard above the constant clamor, the futurists droned on as if the fistfights in the gallery and the deluge of objects in the air were all part of the show. From the stage, according to Soffici, it looked like

> an inferno. Even before any of us opened his mouth to speak, the hall was boiling over, becoming agitated, resonating with savage voices, almost like a piazza full of people awaiting an execution. Marinetti's opening words were greeted with ironic applause mixed with insults, loud handclapping, and obscene invective, which then degenerated into a universal clamor of whistles, animalesque screams, and side-splitting laughter, while a cargo of vegetables and fruit was thrown at the speaker. Having entered after him when the tumult was already raging, I approached the front of the stage, papers in hand, when a huge raw potato from a theater box struck me atop the head, my baldness now completely shrouded in pulp . . . Carrà, who stood beside me, then got hit with a plateful of pasta . . . And yet we continued with our speeches. Papini

spoke against Florence, Carrà against criticism, Boccioni on plastic dynamism—always under this hurricane, with continual interruptions, our voices submerged in the general clamor.[5]

At one point, when Marinetti was reading from Aldo Palazzeschi's poem "Clock" and reached the line "Oh how beautiful to die with a red flower opening at the temples," a member of the audience happily offered him a pistol. Although Marinetti confined his immediate response to another shouted insult, some accounts report that he was indeed ready for battle when he appeared on the street after the show and that he had to be arrested for his own protection. Others say the streets were deserted by the time he arrived. In any case, Viviani remembered a strange, postbattle procession of futurists in the wee hours of the morning: "Followed by friends and sympathizers, we sang as we walked together toward the Giubbe Rosse, a logical and necessary goal after such an evening. Even Amalia Guglielminetti came with us despite the fact that her very elegant evening dress had been reduced to a pitiful condition by the juice of some enormous onions that had crashed right in front of our stage box, inundating the poet with spray."[6]

How many people actually attended the futurist *serata* in Florence? Estimates range downward from the seven thousand reported in the *Corriere della Sera* to Viviani's six thousand, *Lacerba*'s five thousand, and *La Nazione*'s twenty-two hundred. It is impossible to check theater records for a more exact tally since these were swept away in the flood of 1966. What is clear is that it was one of the largest and most violent of the many *serate* held in northern Italian towns at the time.

Who attended? About this we can be more certain. In addition to those already named, Aldo Palazzeschi, Florence's first futurist, was definitely present. In a letter to *Lacerba* he reported that he "had stayed for two hours last night, struck dumb and smiling before the unfolding of a human and divine spectacle as grand as nature herself."[7] Others in the audience included Theodor Däubler, the German poet from Trieste; *Lacerba*'s young publisher, Attilio Vallecchi; its chief distributor, the bookstore owner Ferrante Gonnelli; and a number of young Tuscan painters and poets, including two who would later become quite well known: Ottone Rosai and Primo Conti.

What had brought together the two grand old men of the Florentine avant-garde—Papini, now thirty-two; and Soffici, now thirty-four—with these futurists from Milan, with whom they had struggled so bitterly just two summers before? To what extent had their own recent doings created the atmosphere in which this newest form of culture war was being waged? These, too, are important questions, but they are less readily answered. Part of the response to them lies in the change in atmosphere produced by the war in Libya and the roughly contemporaneous conflicts within *La Voce*, which we have already considered. But for a fuller perspective we need to look more closely at the intellectual itineraries followed by Papini and Soffici between their encounters with the Milan of Casati's *Il Rinnovamento* and their alliance with the Milan of Marinetti's "Destruction of Syntax, Wireless Imagination, and Words in Freedom."[8]

The Politics of Autobiography

When Soffici returned to Paris in February 1910 to work on an impressionist exhibition for Florence, he had been away for nearly three years. Yet his desire to return had been mounting steadily since the summer of 1908. Although he had never wavered in his conviction that *toscanità* should be the primary subject matter for his "religion of art," he had become increasingly aware of how lacking he was—alone in his house at Poggio a Caiano—in the sort of theoretical and imaginative stimulation that he had earlier enjoyed in Paris. In January 1909 he began an intense correspondence with Picasso, just as the first issues of *La Voce* were appearing.[9] Later that year he was writing Papini that he had become engrossed in Rimbaud's letters and that this reading had awakened a desire "to go to Paris as soon as possible."[10] Not that he thought "Paris an El Dorado, but one always finds there some stimulus to do great things as well as much liberty and breadth of vision."[11] Once in the French capital, he became even more enthusiastic, writing Slataper that "instead of fussing about in that small, shabby, somnolent, and almost hopeless Florence, I think you should all spend at least a year in Paris. Not that one finds talent here on every streetcorner, but the spectacle of prodigious activity and the grandeur of the atmosphere itself would give you the courage necessary to be ruthless with traditional formulas, with yourselves, and with everyone else, and you would then return to the struggle for the good cause with your eyes more open, with a more generous heart, and with absolute fearlessness."[12]

Although Papini was his closest friend and intellectual ally in Tuscany, even he appeared to Soffici to be far too timid and conventional in aesthetic matters. In August 1908, just after his reconciliation with Prezzolini at Consuma, Soffici became engaged in a polemic with Papini in which he championed Baudelaire over Papini's Walt Whitman. Only by moving from subjective to objective poetry in the manner of *Les Fleurs du Mal*, claimed Soffici, could one hope to be true to poetry's religious essence rather than its merely decorative function.[13] What Baudelaire had understood was that there is a way of "becoming unknown to ourselves" (abandoning our sense of a fixed, bourgeois self-identity) by "plunging into the abyss" (merging with nature) and, in effect, learning to see reality *qua* reality and, thus, finding "the new" in both art and life. To take such a plunge was to transcend both romantic subjectivity and a realism of the naturalist sort, one too external and detached to permit more than intellectualistic description. To reenter the world in Baudelaire's immanent way was to become open to a new mythos, one that alone could provide a source of religious comfort in a world in which Christianity was long dead.

For the Papini of 1908, fresh from his own spiritual crisis, this sort of talk was "satanism" of the most dangerous sort, and he admonished his friend to remember that "we are Christian men living in Italy in 1908, and in this year and in this country Christianity is still a moral force one has to take into account."[14] Such reminders, however, only served to reinforce Soffici's conviction that he and Papini disagreed because "you have not experienced certain feelings and situations whose profound truth one can know only if one has lived in that inferno known as Paris."[15] And so he had moved on from Baudelaire to Rimbaud.

For much of the first half of 1910, Soffici was engaged in a book on the poet from Charleville (Ardennes), whose provincial origins and life-long oscillation between urban and country life were not the least of his many attractions.[16] Soffici's Rimbaud had grown up dreaming of Paris as "the faroff El Dorado, the promised land," and yet even after he had come to know its charms, he had always remained at heart a "a man from the country" *(un campagnolo),* a "simple plebeian." Indeed, this was his great advantage over more urban and aristocratic poets such as Mallarmé, whose pursuit of Baudelaire's magical realism led only to an "artifice of syntactic and grammatical contortions." Rimbaud's "plebeianism" gave his "paganism" real roots and ensured that his disgust with bourgeois, Christian society would have a positive yield in a poetry of "infinitely complex and interpenetrating sensations and images."[17]

Rimbaud's need to move continuously back and forth between his two life settings, neither of them fully satisfying by itself, stimulated his more general "mania for activity and life" and his becoming an "eternal vagabond"—not in the sense of a homeless romantic but of someone for whom the artful life meant the same complex mix of images and sensations as did the artful poem. It was as if Rimbaud had provided a poetic gloss on the young Marx: poets have only interpreted the world in various ways; the point is to live it poetically. Thus he had moved from writing poetry to renouncing it at only twenty—in order to take up a more practical life, eventually as an African trader. Yet even in his poetry, it was precisely Rimbaud's fusion of art and life that had enabled him to transcend Baudelaire:

> In Baudelaire, who in his "Voyage" sings magnificent, funereal psalms on the tragedy of being a man, of living, loving, and having to die, we find in the end only the same old saw from Ecclesiastes made even more desperate by a Catholic idealism; in Rimbaud, who makes his way through the world of sensations joyously, we find the sense of exhaustion after the orgy, in the depths of which, however, laughs the hope of the spiritualist and of the atheist who adores life as the exteriorization of his own ego, and who will immerse himself there tomorrow in order to play once again his appointed role—be it Hamlet or Yorick. The one truly asks for death; the other wants only a modicum of interior order and repose.[18]

For Rimbaud, then, life certainly meant a deregulation of sensory experience, and thus an "indiscipline," "an aversion to obedience," a spiritual anarchy. Yet he did not leave matters there, as had the young D'Annunzio. At sixteen he saw the Franco-Prussian War fought nearly at his doorstep, and the "intensely violent moral life" he led thereafter was always governed by "sincerity" and by the need "to destroy every weakness, to trample upon and harden everything delicate . . . to cultivate the most difficult form of courage." For Rimbaud understood, as D'Annunzio had not, that anarchy and order were dialectical twins, that he who, "in the words of Friedrich Nietzsche (who was almost his brother), 'has the hardest, the most frightening vision of reality, who has the "most profound thought," still does not find in it any objection against existence,'" and that to live so as to arm oneself with this knowledge was to take the only true path toward "interior order and repose."[19] In short, Rimbaud's anarchy was a willful anarchy lived with deeply moral and religious motives.

Inspired by Rimbaud, as well as by his Parisian friend Guillaume Apollinaire, Soffici wrote an increasing amount of poetry (and all of his best) during the *Lacerba* years (1913–1915), but his first love had always been painting. In painting, in his estimation, the revolution that Baudelaire and Rimbaud had accomplished in poetry had been undertaken by Cézanne and brought to fruition by Picasso. That was why Soffici had been so intent on having Picasso's latest works included in the Florence impressionist exhibition, as well as placed alongside his article on the Spaniard in the *La Voce* of 1911.[20]

Although Soffici succeeded in neither case, he took pains in his article to demonstrate Picasso's premier role as the theoretician of modernist art by situating his work in the general context of impressionism and postimpressionism. According to Soffici, the impressionists had been the first to vindicate the "panpoeticity" of things, and the possibility of genuine artistic creativity, by rejecting the received view of the world as a fixed, divinely created hierarchy. Yet even in the hands of a master such as Claude Monet, impressionism had remained too much a slave of the external world objectively understood. Cézanne's pioneering achievement was to become immanent to his landscape, to feel the solidity of objects, their volume, density, and chiaroscuro effects as part of his own body and soul, and to begin to plumb their depths for a pure logic of art. Only with Picasso, however, had the decisive step toward understanding that logic been taken. For it was Picasso who had turned to the art of ancient Egypt and Africa in order to learn again how artists might "interpret nature realistically by deforming it in response to an occult, lyrical necessity." Even if others such as Gauguin had looked to the same "primitive" sources, their appropriations of them had remained mired in intellectualism and thus merely decorative. Picasso had proceeded systematically, working through such technical problems as volume, design, and light, in order to grasp nature as a totality, as a set of essences, and then to "deform" it as art.

During the *Lacerba* years, Soffici broke with figurative art and followed Picasso into cubism. Indeed, his reverence for Picasso was so great that he never seems to have been tempted to follow futurist artists such as Boccioni despite their alliance with *Lacerba*.[21] From 1909 through 1911, however, Soffici's main creative efforts were neither in art nor in poetry but in literature, specifically in a kind of fictional autobiography.

In the first of two such autobiographies, a short fable about an "unknown Tuscan," the hero is not quite thirty, "tall and thin and dressed always in black," a former Paris bohemian who has "traveled through the world without a definite purpose but, it appeared, more in order to forget than to learn anything."[22] Although he is an "atheist" and a "nihilist," his wandering has reflected a spiritual effort to "consolidate the old religions now in ruins or to found new ones." Yet there is little in the story to suggest that he has ever engaged in collective action toward this end. Politics do not interest him, since "the spiritual man, in his view, could not have an opinion but only a faith, one that had as its object something beyond any social or political contingency." Although the text adds, tantalizingly, that "in his heart he secretly nourished a vibrant love of revolution, to which he attributed a profoundly mystical value," the only soul that he has had the time or will to care for is his own. On the final page we find that his body has returned to the earth on a hillside "between Florence and Pistoia," his tombstone proclaiming him "dead at thirty-five without regrets or hopes."[23]

Although a key model for Soffici's hero appears to have been Marchenoir, the protagonist of Léon Bloy's *Le Désespéré* (1886), the text suggests many other connections, including Don Quixote and, of course, Baudelaire and Rimbaud.[24] Indeed, its main point seems to be to offer the reader a symbol for the act of seeking spiritual enlightenment by renouncing one's identity as a traditional, bourgeois subject and then finding true identity in a literal merging with one's native ground. In this way, the mystical paganism of Rimbaud is made to serve as an avant-garde justification for *toscanità*.

This effort to position *toscanità* within avant-gardism is even more integral to Soffici's second fictional biography, the novel *Lemmonio Boreo*.[25] There, however, the hero, far from resting in spiritual peace once the path to it has become apparent to him, becomes critically engaged with the distance he finds between the ideal of Tuscany that he cherishes and contemporary Tuscan reality. While the opening premises are similar—the hero, "pallid, tall and dressed in black," has returned to Tuscany from ten years in Paris hoping "to live in harmony with things"—his first act after his arrival is not to wander but to retreat inside his house for three weeks of voracious reading. What he finds disturbs him: "insipid novels derived from this or that mediocre model, mostly French," and, more generally, an intellectual and moral world of corruption and "D'Annunzian rot." Moreover, he discovers that the two available alternatives—Catholic modernism and nationalism—are both self-deluded, the first because it holds that reason and faith can be reconciled, the second because it substitutes rhetorical images of "Roman eagles and the lion of Venice" for a genuine analysis of national ills. There follows the inevitable epiphany: "Now, then, he finally understood. Instinctively, perhaps without reflecting, the whole educated population of Italy had, out of weakness, self-interest, or for other reasons, become united by their silence in an enormous association, like a kind of freemasonry or intellectual and spiritual secret society," a realization that makes him "fly into a rage."[26]

Only then does Lemmonio begin to walk in the country, "always taking the branch of the road that leads higher." At first he comes upon some simple folk who still live close to the land and who remain uncorrupted and good, but, increasingly, his encounters are with the many others who have fallen into that "dark and murky abyss of ethical and psychological barbarism" that has begun to engulf the Tuscan landscape. His choice becomes clear and inescapable: "either to move into a cynical solitude, letting things take their course," or "to act, in any way whatsoever." As he mulls it over, he feels a "deep and mysterious love for his land and his people." Then a Don-Quixotian fantasy flashes before his mind: to become "a man who combines warrior and priest, with a grieved look on his face and a cudgel in his hand." To undertake "a long march from city to city and town to town," and "to rush in wherever some indignity or unclean act is being committed, clubbing everyone in sight, left and right. The image seduced him." Before long, Lemmonio has assembled his small band of blackshirts who spend their days "giving little lessons" to discourage the ignorance, wickedness, and decadence that they never cease to find about them.[27]

In the second half of the novel there are a number of violent and confrontational scenes—the disruption of a socialist rally and the heckling of a local mayor prominent among them—that have earned the book a reputation as "a true digest of fascism *ante litteram*."[28] Yet, as Eraldo Bellini has recently demonstrated, all the politically explicit episodes occur after Canto IX, the point at which the 1912 version ends. Thus, far from being "fascism *ante litteram*," they were actually added during the rapid ascendance of Tuscan fascism in 1920 and 1921.[29] Bellini, however, overreacts to his discovery when he writes that "the story that appeared in 1912 has the character of a pleasant jest in the short-story tradition of popular and anticlerical satire like those of Boccaccio or, perhaps better, of Sacchetti."[30] On the contrary, the predominant tone of the first half is no less embittered and full of disgust than that of the second, as Prezzolini's letter to Soffici of February 1912 helps to confirm: "Don Quixote makes us laugh, yes, but that is what Cervantes wanted. What is so momentous and troubling [about your book] is that you are behind Lemmonio and you take him seriously."[31] Indeed, what is remarkable about the 1921 version of the book is how naturally and effortlessly the narrative of the early chapters sets the stage for the more explicitly fascist scenes that follow.

What distinguished Soffici's position within the Florentine avant-garde of 1912 was not his notion of what needed to be done. The idea that Italy was in need of a spiritual revolution, one that would use the dormant sensibilities and energies of its regional, peasant-based cultures to overthrow the false and hypocritical culture that had recently become encrusted over them, was, as we have seen, a staple of Florentine avant-garde thinking. Nor was there anything original in his view that the avant-garde should work outside established political groups and institutions. What distinguished his position were two of its other aspects: his use of Rimbaud to ground his fervent and idealized *toscanità* and the decisionism of his ethics—the way he posed Lemmonio's choice as such a stark "either/or," the sense that his only true guides in making that choice were visceral feelings and imaginative projections, and the implication that to continue to engage in reasoned discussion and analysis would be—wittingly or unwittingly—to join that "enormous associa-tion" of educated Italians who had become united in a conspiracy of silence because they feared to act.

For Soffici, then, the creation of *Lacerba* and the alliance with futur-ism, though not explicitly prefigured in his pre-1913 writings, followed naturally from the irrationalist avant-gardism with which they were so deeply imbued. This was far less the case with Papini. As we have seen, Papini rejected Soffici's call for an anti-Christian and nihilist "religion of art." For him, Christianity was "the only moral force that can give hope for the destiny of humanity," since it alone offered both a deep rootedness in popular life and an appeal that was not narrowly intellec-tual but broadly spiritual.[32] Art was certainly important as a mode of communicating that spirituality, but once divorced from religion it would lose its power as a spiritual educator for the masses.

For much of 1908, this position appeared to be leading Papini to embrace Catholic modernism. Not only did the movement seem to cor-respond to his own ideas and to offer him a personal anchor at a vulnerable moment, but when Prezzolini moved away from it in favor of a secular faith in Crocean philosophy, Papini found it additionally useful as a way of combatting "the fundamental prejudice of the whole Hegelian race, the *rationalist* prejudice that consists in the belief that conceptual thought can fully know and definitively judge that which is not concep-tual thought." Religion, he argued, could reach people in a way philoso-phy never could, because it was "made up of an infinite number of personal realities" rather than "universal concepts, general terms, and abstractions."[33] However, the more Papini came to know Catholic mod-ernism, the less it appeared to correspond with his notion of what a religious movement should be, and the more he was forced to agree with Soffici that its real nature was closer to his conception of philosophy.[34] True Catholics, he would soon angrily conclude, had ceased to exist.[35]

In the Bulciano of 1909, then, Papini was isolated not only geographi-cally but also culturally. Each of the movements and ideals that might have made him feel connected to the larger world—Prezzolini's *La Voce,* Casati's Catholic modernism, and Soffici's secular religion of art—was at least partially suspect. Yet unlike Soffici, Papini had no Paris to which to turn. So, enticed by his majestic surroundings, he retreated into a kind of private "religion of nature," which he expressed above all through poetry. His own first poems celebrating Tuscan landscape and peasant life date from this period, and when he became *La Voce*'s interim editor in 1912, he publicly proclaimed his private religion in an article rever-ently titled "Give Us This Day Our Daily Poetry."[36]

Papini's religion of nature was also evident in some of his prose writing. Although he had given up philosophy in 1908, he seemed determined to show that the personal needs philosophy had always sought to meet could be addressed in a more concrete, intimate, and emotively oriented form of reflection. He spent long periods at work on a magnum opus, a "report on man" in which he would show for the first time the concrete potential of philosophical reflection. Not surprisingly, however, the book proved frustatingly difficult to complete.[37] When Papini moved back into Florence in the fall of 1910, he gravitated toward those, like Giovanni Amendola, who shared his sense that philosophy needed to move away from the conceptual and make greater room for sentiment, above all religious sentiment. This conviction was central to *L'Anima*, which he and Amendola coedited in 1911. It was also expressed in an article of that year on "Tuscany and Italian philosophy," in which Papini responded to the challenge that Tuscany had produced no great philosophers by arguing that it could do so only if it capitalized on its "love of concreteness" and aimed at personalist reflections on nature and human nature.[38]

Unfortunately, however, Papini was unable (or felt unable) to pursue his new religion of nature in *La Voce*, either as poetry or as prose, until rather late.[39] What he did contribute there in 1909–1911 was rather different: a discussion of the moral virtues most necessary for contemporary Italians and of how the Italian literary tradition might be appropriated for a fuller understanding of these virtues. Thus, he proclaimed the need for "sincerity" and "hardness," and he relentlessly championed the plebeian moralism of his Tuscan Carducci against the flatulent decadentism of D'Annunzio. But this effort represented only one side—the public side—of Papini's emerging outlook, and the frustrations he felt in not having an appropriate forum for his other, private side left him frustrated and increasingly depressed. His letters to Prezzolini and Soffici in this period reveal a man not yet thirty who had begun to doubt his creative powers and to contemplate seriously whether he had lived his life in vain.[40]

It was under these circumstances that Papini spent two years writing his autobiography, *Un uomo finito*, a title that played upon the double sense of "finished man" and "finite man." The result was a long and intimate confession, punctuated now and then by bright moments but focused primarily on his early life as a quest for the infinite—for encyclopedic knowledge and for an intellectual production that would "inaugurate a new era in human history"—which, precisely because it was so titanic and unbounded, had failed utterly.[41] From the vantage point of the spiritual crisis that followed, he had seen that his life had been based on the wish to be perfect, in effect to be God. And so he had realized the need to return to "concreteness," to his own body despite its "ugliness," to his own personal intellect in all its imperfection and finitude.[42] "I have rummaged everywhere, stirred up everything, grazed in and sniffed every field of knowledge, banged my head against the unknowable, but I have never got to the bottom of anything. There is no doctrine, art, or philosophy in which one might say I am truly an absolute master. I do not have my speciality, my field, small though it might be—the tiny garden plot that is truly my own—in which I can deal fully with whatever lies under my feet."[43]

But what could that garden plot be? What could he cultivate that would be properly his, that would express his own soul? In facing this question sincerely—and the book absolutely reeked of sincerity—Papini came hard upon a contradiction in his character. "I am, to say the whole thing in two words, a poet and a destroyer, a dreamer and a skeptic, a lyricist and a cynic. How these two souls of mine can exist and get along together would take too long to tell. But this is truly the foundation of my being."[44] In consequence, there lay before him not one but two paths—paths that were diametrically opposed: that of the religious man who lyrically celebrates life, who prays for his daily poetry; and that of the cynic who arrogantly laughs at life, who destroys its idols with polemic.

In the book Papini did not clearly signal which path he intended to follow. On the one hand, he wrote of *toscanità* as a "doctor's prescription" for the health of his soul. "I must start again from the beginning; I must be born again, reenter the womb again, not a womb of the flesh, my mother's, but a truer and greater one: my native land."[45] A decade later, in a book that reads like a sequel to *Un uomo finito*, Papini would reinstate the metaphor, describing his postwar conversion to Christianity as a "second birth."[46] Yet, on the other hand, in 1912 his "first birth" received at least equal attention, and it pointed in the other direction: "I was not born to the peaceful breathing of oxen and donkeys, and gentle shepherds did not come to me on the first day of my life. I was born a revolutionary." And, as a revolutionary, his "natural form of expression" was one of "protest"; his "natural disposition," one of "assault with bayonets"; his "favorite form of speech," one of "invective and insult."[47]

The fact that, in the short term, it was the latter path that Papini chose to follow probably had as much to do with circumstances as with conviction. Isolated from Prezzolini and, by 1913, from Amendola as well, he had only one close friend left—Soffici, and for Soffici of course the choice was a foregone conclusion. Late in 1915 Papini would come to know Domenico Giuliotti, a devout Catholic reactionary from Greve in Chianti who had edited the journal *La Torre* in Siena.[48] In the postwar years, the two would become the best of friends, but in 1913 there was no one like Giuliotti in Papini's life who might have supported his religious soul.

By the time *Un uomo finito* appeared, there was little doubt that Papini had thrown in his lot with Soffici. In an article of October 1912, he had defended the aim of "becoming a genius" in much the same way as he and Prezzolini had in *Leonardo* but with a new French accent: "The genius is in an absolute sense the redeemer of mankind . . . 'To desire every day to become the greatest of men': this proposition of Charles Baudelaire's ought to be the motto of our daily life."[49] And in the inaugural issue of *Lacerba*, which appeared on the first day of 1913, he had written: "Everything in the world amounts to nothing, except for the genius . . . Religions, moralities, laws have as their only excuse the weariness and meanness of men and their desire to reassure themselves and preserve their communities. But there is a higher level—of the lone man, intelligent and without prejudice—for whom everything is permitted and everything is legitimate."[50]

In this context it is not surprising that Papini's colleagues at *La Voce* read his autobiography unequivocally as a choice for *Lacerba* and against them. Thus, Giovanni Boine wrote that "*Lacerba* is an epigone, a re-echoing insofar as Papini is concerned, of *Un uomo finito*. In *Un uomo finito*, what is striking is this same exaggerated willfulness, this artificial and inhuman aridity. Above all, what strikes us there is this almost infantile mania for grandeur, this wanting to be great, this shouting in every breath: 'I want to be a genius.'"[51] Amendola's reaction was much the same, although he took the book more personally. As he wrote to Papini: "This [book] expresses moral and aesthetic values that are not mine, that are even at the south pole if I am at the north pole . . . My ethic is not that of caprice, and my aesthetic is left unsatisfied by a work such as yours. I am, dear Papini, in my morality as in everything else, classical and traditionalist [*passatista*] in quite an old-fashioned way."[52]

More personal still was Prezzolini's response. Although he was happy with the "beautiful chapter" that Papini had devoted to their early friendship, he refused to allow the book to be reviewed in *La Voce*, despite a letter from Papini nearly begging him to do so.[53] The reason for his refusal was suggested only at the end of 1914 when he criticized *Un uomo finito* in a general monograph on its author. "The book," he wrote, "was in the making for a long time, two years at least, but the final chapters were written in a moment in which the funereal and resigned spiritual state [he had been in] disappeared, giving rise to an affirmation of vitality."[54] This "affirmation of vitality" was at odds with the book as a whole, and the "revolutionary" conclusion to which it had led simply did not follow from the story the book had told. Had Papini dealt appropriately with his spiritual malaise, Prezzolini seemed to be saying, he would have been led into some new commitment, not necessarily Croceanism of course, but something equally serious and weighty. What Prezzolini clearly could not accept was that his friend had broken free from his malaise by taking up again the exuberant manner of the early *Leonardo* days but in a new nonphilosophical mode that merely celebrated irrationality and lived for nothing greater than individual "genius."

Lacerba and Futurism, 1913–1915

To begin to unravel the complex relationship between the creation of *Lacerba* and the arrival of futurism in Florence, we need to distinguish two senses of futurism: the strict sense, which refers to a movement led by Marinetti in Milan; and the broader sense, which refers to any movement proclaiming itself futurist and making use of the self-publicizing techniques that Marinetti pioneered in order to dramatize itself as avant-garde, however non-Marinettian or, indeed, anti-Marinettian its own ideals might be. *Lacerba* was never truly futurist in the first sense, although it was loosely allied with Marinetti's movement for about a year, from March 1913 until February 1914. But if we take futurism in the second sense, then it is clear that the story of the creation of *Lacerba* and the decision by Soffici and Papini to become futurists were very much intertwined. What the two men hoped to do with *Lacerba* was to demonstrate the existence of a Florentine avant-garde that was every bit as flamboyant and vital as any then present on the international stage.

When Soffici made his annual pilgrimage to Paris in March 1912, the city was still enthralled by two events of the previous month. One was the début of *Les Soirées de Paris,* an avant-garde monthly that his friend Apollinaire had begun and that he would soon be coediting with Soffici's closest friend in Paris, Serge Férat.[55] The other was the exhibition of Italian futurist paintings that had been at the Bernheim-Jeune Gallery and was about to travel to London, Brussels, The Hague, Amsterdam, and Munich. Since *Les Soirées* would quickly become one of Europe's leading avant-garde reviews and the futurist exhibit was one of the most widely discussed—and certainly the most scandalous—to have come to Paris in recent years, both events rekindled Soffici's desire to be closer to what he regarded as a truly avant-garde movement. But the futurist exhibit had a more specific effect as well. The fact that an Italian creation had, for the moment at least, captured center stage seemed to be a reassurance that Italians, too, could forge autonomous avant-garde expressions and could therefore work as equals with their Parisian counterparts. As Soffici put the point in an article in *La Voce* that July: "Who takes it [the art of the futurist movement] seriously? No one. But, still, it did manage to shatter the legend-truth of an Italy dead and buried under the stupidity of its conservatism and its academy." That was why, even if Italian futurism was mediocre as art, it was "excellent in its essence as a movement of renewal."[56]

As a result of his recognition of futurism's power as a style around which to shape an avant-garde movement, Soffici had written Papini while still in Paris that he was tempted to reconcile himself with his old antagonists at the Giubbe Rosse.[57] Over the next few months, as he became involved in polemics with Boine and Jahier over *Lemmonio Boreo*, he had still more reason to distance himself from *La Voce* and to turn his energies to something more audacious and provocative. Then, early in December, he got a letter from Papini recounting how "the other day I ran into that printer [Attilio Vallecchi], whom even you know since he did your *Ignoto toscano*, and when I told him of our desire to publish our own review, he replied that he would be happy to print and distribute it at his own expense for a year."[58] It was an offer they could hardly refuse. The first issue of *Lacerba* appeared less than three weeks later.

For Papini, this new move into avant-gardism was even more abrupt than it had been for Soffici. Although for many months he had felt the urge to take "all my mediocre, wretched, and boring plans for erudite and academic writing" and throw them "in the Arno," as late as November he was still finishing up as *La Voce*'s interim editor and making the final corrections to the proofs of *Un uomo finito*.[59] Indeed, there is little indication that he thought through the rationale for *Lacerba* prior to its first issue. Only after the appearance of that issue, with its dramatic opening manifesto, did he write to his friend and co-conspirator: "I agree with you about the opportunity [we have] to join in with the one avant-garde force that Italy has produced, but we must try to safeguard our freedom as much as we can."[60]

The note of caution in this remark was at least as significant as the hope it expressed, for although Papini would look back on his move into a futuristically styled avant-gardism as "an act of liberation," at the time he was much more sensitive to the danger of becoming a lowly lieutenant in Marinetti's Milanese army.[61] Thus, while he did join Marinetti on the stage of the Teatro Costanzi in Rome for a February *serata*, his speech entered at least as many reservations about futurism as it did plaudits, and it explicitly stated that he did not consider himself one of their number.[62] Moreover, any among the crowd who still read straitlaced journals such as *La Voce* might have surmised that Papini's reasons for taking the stage had as much to do with the failure of contemporary religious thought as with the triumph of its futurist alternative. "The religious literati," he had written in January, "have produced no great works, and one may rest assured that the human spirit—the liberated spirit that is by now becoming atheist in the largest sense of the word—will not allow itself to be lulled to sleep by the mysterious panegyrics of saints delivered from porticos."[63] Apparently, the bellicose rantings of futurist sinners delivered from theater stages offered more hope, but by a margin that was not nearly as wide as Papini would have liked.

Although the early issues of *Lacerba* certainly projected a flamboyant style, there was no hint of any alliance with the Milanese futurists until the sixth issue, and even then Papini offered an ironic counterpoint with a cover article entitled "Against Futurism."[64] The middle pages of the issue were devoted to aesthetic treatises by Boccioni and Carrà, as well as to the poems of their comrades Luciano Folgore, Corrado Govoni, and Marinetti himself, but the issue closed with more pieces by Papini, Soffici, and their Florentine friends. The overall impression was of a Milanese presence carefully sandwiched in Florentine bread, a bit of spicy filling for an avant-gardism firmly within local control.

Lacerba's Florentine location and Tuscan heritage were the implicit message of its title as well. When Soffici was hurriedly casting about for something suitable late the previous December, he remembered a four-teenth-century poem, "L'acerba," written by Cecco d'Ascoli, who, though not a native Tuscan, had lived in Florence for many years and had liberally embellished the poem with Tuscan vernacular, while also launching a vitriolic attack on the local literary establishment of the day, above all Dante. In case the unsuspecting or undereducated reader should miss the reference, the journal's masthead reproduced the poem's first line—"Here no one sings in the manner of toads"—as its epigraph.[65]

Lacerba pursued its project of an independent Florentine avant-gard-ism with considerable focus despite its wildly irreverent content, its slapdash writing, and its pointed refusal to put anyone in charge as editor.[66] Thus the opening manifesto set out the journal's commitments in sixteen sharply worded aphorisms.[67] Besides the celebration of gen-iuses and the claim that, for them, "everything is permitted," the mani-festo rejected "seriousness" and "rational demonstrations," promoted art as the "justification of the world," declared its preference for "the sketch over the composition, the potsherd over the statue, the aphorism over the treatise," and, in a move that recalled *Il Commento*, proclaimed that "the thought that cannot be expressed briefly does not deserve expression." It also rejected any idea of "instructing or of resolving the world's gravest questions through pontification." While much of this was a less than subtle venting of the tensions that had been building for years under the constraints of Prezzolini's *La Voce*, the emphases on genius and on unbounded "liberty" as "the elemental condition for the life of the spiritual person" were clearly inconsistent with any notion of becoming part of any larger movement the *lacerbiani* did not control.

Unlike *Leonardo* and *La Voce*, *Lacerba* had no true editorial office, Vallecchi's space being too cramped and noisy for such a purpose. Instead, on the several days a week when Soffici came in from Poggio, he, Papini, and their young and enthusiastic collaborators, Palazzeschi and Italo Tavolato, would work in the "third room" of the Giubbe Rosse, cheerfully reserved for them by its German-Swiss manager. Occasionally, especially late at night, they might move to Palazzeschi's apartment a block away on the Via Calimala. Then, every other week without fail, they would take their articles, poems, and illustrations ten blocks north to Vallecchi's shop on the Via Nazionale. In 1913 and 1914 *Lacerba*'s readers were able to rely on the fact that a dose of spiritual anarchism had been readied for them, with absolute regularity, on the first and fifteen day of every month. In 1915 it came weekly.[68]

For most of its first year, *Lacerba* used a rather conventional layout and typography, not unlike *La Voce*'s though with much larger print and somewhat smaller pages. Illustrations by Soffici, Picasso, Boccioni, Carrà, Férat, and a few others were only occasional, probably because of the added expense they entailed. Although Marinetti was certainly wealthy enough to have aided *Lacerba* in this respect, there is no evidence that his support was ever solicited. Nonetheless, by the last issues of 1913 and in 1914, the review took on a much more dramatic and experimental appearance. The masthead came to dominate the first page, with the title displayed in huge black letters. The typography became ever wilder, the illustrations more frequent, and the distinction between writing and illustration more and more blurred. Experimental forms, such as the *parole in libertà* (words in freedom) that Marinetti had theorized in 1912, became typical and, therefore, increasingly outrageous.

Articles for *Lacerba* mixed earnest declaration with playful, sometimes mordant polemic. Croce was the most frequent target, but Hegel, D'Annunzio, and the nationalists were not far behind. One regular feature was a column called "The Electric Chair," in which leading personalities like these, or their ideals, were "electrocuted"; another was a column of

LACERBA

ANNO II, N. 16 Periodico quindicinale	FIRENZE, 15 AGOSTO 1914 Via Ricasoli, 8	IL N. 2 SOLDI L'ANNO 4 LIRE

PAPINI. Il dovere dell'Italia - SOFFICI, Intorno alla gran bestia - PAPA. La secchia rapita

Se la guerra presente fosse soltanto politica ed economica, noi, pur non restando indifferenti, ce ne saremmo occupati piuttosto alla lontana. Ma siccome questa è guerra non soltanto di fucili e di navi, ma anche di cultura e di civiltà, ci teniamo a prender subito posizione e a seguire gli avvenimenti con tutta l'anima. Si tratta di salvaguardare e difendere tutto quello che c'è di più italiano nel mondo, anche se non tutto cresciuto in terra nostra. Non possiamo stare zitti. Forse questa è l'ora più decisiva della storia europea dopo la fine dell'impero romano.

Noi ci proponiamo di esprimere, in questo libero giornale di avanguardia, il nostro pensiero con tutta quella schiettezza che ci sarà possibile col rigore presente.

Noi sentiamo che questo pensiero è quello di tutta la gioventù intelligente italiana e anche della maggior parte del popolo. Noi vorremmo incanalare queste aspirazioni e queste forze per la necessaria rivincita dell'Italia.

A partire da questo numero "LACERBA" sarà soltanto politica e per ottenere maggior diffusione sarà venduta a due soldi. Riprenderemo la nostra attività teorica e artistica a cose finite.

PAPINI

Il dovere dell'Italia

1.

Cosa facciamo ? Qui non è tempo di ponzare. Decidere subito — e agire prestissimo. Cerchiamo, ancora una volta, di parlar chiaro quanto è possibile in mezzo a tante reticenze e prudenze di politici e di quotidiani. Nessuno ha il coraggio di parlare in tono maggiore. Eppure in quest'ora tremenda è necessario intenderci bene e non armeggiare coi sottintesi. Non ci vogliono piccole furberie buone in tempi normali ma grandi audacie quali richiedono gli avvenimenti. I quotidiani, per non intralciare l'opera del governo e per non turbare il popolo minuto, non si pronunziano. Le dimostrazioni pubbliche son proibite ed è bene.

Ma bisogna pure che si esca un giorno o l'altro da questa faticosa e paurosa incertezza. Io, anche a nome dei miei amici, espongo qui il

8. The first issue of *Lacerba* after the outbreak of the First World War, featuring Papini's article on "Italy's duty."

quotations from such "great authors" titled "The Nonsense Bin"; still another was a column by Palazzeschi labeled "Trash." Throughout the journal, anal humor became increasingly frequent and outrageous. While advertisements were rare—as in *La Voce,* most of them were for books and journals—some prominence was given to "Cooper Pills," a laxative sold by H. Roberts, an "English pharmacy" on the Via Tornabuoni and the only business accorded the honor of purchasing advertising space in *Lacerba*'s pages.

Increasingly, *Lacerba* aimed to cater to a mass taste, and in 1915 when it became a weekly and halved its price from four cents to two, it reportedly reached twenty thousand readers, 80 percent of them working-class.[69] As Vallecchi later recalled: "The vivacity of its expression, its use of paradox as a means of persuasion, and the lively intelligence embodied in all *Lacerba*'s articles gave it a clamorous success. All Italy awaited each new issue with so much anticipation that on publication days, hard as it may be to believe, people lined up outside the printshop to get it hot off the press—in the same way that later, during the war, they would line up outside bakeries to get bread."[70] Vallecchi himself was so amazed by the commercial power of *Lacerba*'s new futurist style that he sponsored several similar efforts by younger writers, such as the *Quartiere latino* of Ugo Tommei.[71]

If, as Vallecchi claimed, *Lacerba* used paradox to persuade, then its success in this persuasion was also somewhat paradoxical with respect to its own stated intentions. While its opening manifesto had indicated its commitment to frank talk readily comprehensible by everyone ("Everything shall be called by its name; things that one lacks the courage to speak frankly about are often the most important in everyone's life"), it had also been uncompromising in its refusal to aim at pleasing an audience: "This will be a journal that upsets, that is irritating, unpleasant, and personal. It will be an outlet for our benefit and for those who have not been made totally stupid by contemporary idealisms, reformisms, humanitarianisms, Christianisms, and moralisms." A key paradox of *Lacerba* was that while it explicitly gave up the Prezzolinian-Salveminian project—in its origin, the De Sanctian project—of going to the masses and elevating them, it managed to gain their attention far more effectively than had *La Voce* through audacious and sometimes shockingly avant-garde fare that was openly contemptuous of the intelligence of its consumers. Like futurism more generally, the *lacerbiani* pioneered in a new style of public relations that marketed a mass culture with visceral appeal while making its more seriously motivated competitors look patronizing.

Another paradox of *Lacerba* was that, while it had been quick to recall its Tuscan heritage in order to assert its independence from Milan, it expressed contempt for the Tuscans who made up the bulk of its readership. One of Soffici's main efforts for *Lacerba* in 1913 was a column titled "Giornale di bordo"—a "journal on the edge" or, literally, a "logbook" of a ship's voyage.[72] As such it was a hastily written and haphazard record of his impressions and tastes. In one of them, he wrote as follows of his fellow Tuscans: "On the tram. When I think that this fat and sweaty Tuscan middleman ought to be closer to me and more likeable than the Frenchman who wrote the book I have in my hands, a book that is the very mirror of my most intimate life, and that to save his skin and that of his children I should cut the throats of Guillaume Apollinaire, for example, or Max Jacob or my friend Picasso, then I say that patriotism is the very essence of idiocy."[73] Yet it was of course this same "fat and sweaty Tuscan" who was standing in line outside Vallecchi's printshop in order to buy what had been originally inspired by Soffici's Parisian friends.

The Parisians were also important contributors to the journal and responsible for no small measure of its prestige. As Soffici proudly recalled in his memoirs: "The writers Rémy de Gourmont, Guillaume Apollinaire, Max Jacob, and Roch Grey, and the artists Picasso, [Alexander] Archipenko, Anna Gerebzova, and [Mikhail] Larionov were all ours."[74] Yet as a final paradox, unlike *La Voce*, which also featured Parisian contributors even if not quite so prominently, *Lacerba* published their writings not in translation but in French, a language that few among its readers could penetrate. Only when foreign contributions came in a language such as German, which the *lacerbiani* themselves (Tavolato excepted) could not understand, was a translation made.

Of obvious personal importance to Soffici, the Paris connection was also a way for him and Papini to hold the Milanese futurists in check. It has even been suggested that one of the reasons the *lacerbiani* made a complete break with Marinetti in 1914 was that, with Apollinaire in tow, they no longer needed him.[75] Yet relations between Soffici and Apollinaire sometimes became nearly as prickly as the ones between Florence and Milan. When Apollinaire published a book on cubism in the spring of 1913, Soffici reviewed it quite unfavorably in *La Voce*— possibly because it was in competition with his own recent articles on the subject, which were then being assembled as a book.[76] Still more indicatively, when Apollinaire argued in February 1914 that Italian futurism owed "everything" to the French, above all to Alfred Jarry, Soffici counterattacked forcefully in *Lacerba* despite the fact that he and Papini were then in the midst of their break with Marinetti.[77] In the world of *Lacerba*, culture war was definitely fought on multiple fronts.

Despite all *Lacerba*'s "international relations," however, its essential life was always concentrated around a few blocks in the heart of Florence. During its first year, this life was so intense that Soffici even relinquished his now annual trip to Paris. During its second year, he did go to Paris but took with him, in addition to Papini, Boccioni, and Carrà, one of the new faces that had made the life of the new journal so interesting. This new face was one of the great poetic talents of his era in Italy, as well as one of the principal forces propelling *Lacerba*'s rising star.

Aldo Palazzeschi was only twenty-seven when Soffici and Papini made his acquaintance just a few weeks before *Lacerba*'s début, but he was already the author of four volumes of poetry and two novels. Born into a prosperous middle-class family in Florence, the young Palazzeschi had taken a high-school diploma in accounting, presumably to follow his father in business, but his true loves had always been theater and poetry. His father, whose work had taken the family for a few years to Paris when Aldo was small, was quite supportive of his son's decision to pursue a literary career. He even bore all his publication expenses until 1909, despite the fact that the works involved were frequently scandalous by the standards of the day. For example, his first novel was based upon an epistolary interchange between two men that made no secret of the author's sexual preferences. In 1909, however, Palazzeschi had made a leap to financial independence by writing Marinetti and convincing him of his talents. The last of Palazzeschi's four early volumes of poetry and his second novel, *Il codice di Perelà* (1911), would both appear from Marinetti's private press.

In futurism's first days, Palazzeschi was an enthusiastic follower, but his work was always unmistakably original and independent. It is, in fact, arguable that Marinetti exploited Palazzeschi's talents for the futurist cause (which had attracted far fewer good poets than it had artists) at least as much as the latter used him to launch a career. In 1913 Marinetti wrote an article on the young Florentine celebrating him as "the world's most sure-handed thrower of intellectual bombs," a "futurist poet" whose talent had "as its foundation a ferocious, demolitionary irony that knocks down all the sacred cows of romanticism: love, death, cult of the ideal woman, mysticism, and so on."[78] In reality, however, while all of Palazzeschi's art was deeply ironic, what distinguished it was not its "ferocity," but its playful and carnivalesque qualities, its celebration of "lightness" and of "the comic and grotesque."

Despite Palazzeschi's interest in Marinetti's innovations in language and syntax, as well as in the hyperbole of Marinettian characters such as "Mafarka il futurista," his poetry was actually much closer to the *crepuscularismo* ("twilight poetry") of poets such as Guido Gozzano, who had reacted in similar ways against the grandiloquent decadentism of D'Annunzio and the *dannunziani*. D'Annunzio's poetry, with its intimations of imperial conquest and its image of the poet as a superman, had rubbed the noses of the Italian bourgeoisie in the pettiness of their aspirations. The *crepuscolari* had countered with a poetry of amusement that celebrated the quiet virtues and offered acutely detailed natural descriptions. Like them, Palazzeschi strove for an unaffected and unadorned directness that matched his taste for nostalgia, simplicity, and amusement. But although Palazzeschi was no more comfortable than they were with D'Annunzio's pomposity or, for that matter, with the confrontational manner of the futurists, he was also less willing than they to leave poetry without a critical edge against bourgeois society. Thus, his poems sought to re-evoke a private world now lost in order to remind the bourgeoisie, with gentle irony, not so much of their limited aspirations as of the magnitude of their repressions. Forbidden words and forgotten characters—the crying child, the acrobat, the clown, and, most threateningly, the arsonist—became not merely emblems of nostalgia but instruments that undermined the drudging seriousness of a society based on work, in favor of an anarchic and pleasure-filled, if largely imaginary, society of play.

The protagonist of Palazzeschi's novel *Il codice di Perelà* (The Code of Perelà), which in its later editions carried the subtitle "man of smoke," is the same sort of character, and the result is a hilarious spoof of contemporary society. Perelà is a man who has lived in a chimney for thirty-two years only to spring himself suddenly upon the wider world. Though well received at first, he becomes threatening when it is intimated that he seeks to establish a new and quite utopian "code" of behavior, and he soon falls victim to a rigidly normed society that cannot understand why anyone would entertain such a wish. Once a pretext is finally found to arrest and imprison him, Perelà, like his wistful hopes for a new code, is dissolved in a puff of smoke. Yet if Perelà and his hopes cannot succeed, he has at least asserted his own laughter and idiosyncratic behavior as the necessary remedy for modern social ills, in a manner not unlike that explored by Italo Svevo's character Zeno in the postwar novel *La coscienza di Zeno* (The Confessions of Zeno).

Given Palazzeschi's attitudes and style, it is hardly surprising that he never contacted Prezzolini in the early days of *La Voce*. Yet the role that he came to play among the *lacerbiani,* and between them and the Milanese, was not unlike the mediating one that Prezzolini had tried to play as *La Voce*'s editor.[79] It is even possible that Prezzolini sensed an affinity with the poet after they met late in 1912, for when Soffici was moved to celebrate him as "the first [poet] among us since Leopardi who knows how to translate into lyrics the visions, emotions, and new excitement of our modern existence," he did so in the pages of *La Voce*.[80] Moreover, the article was allowed to stand despite the fact that Soffici had used Palazzeschi to make an implicit criticism of the journal and its editor. Commenting upon the last line of Palazzeschi's 1909 poem, "Chi sono?" ("Who Am I?"), in which the poet answers that he is "the acrobat of his own soul," Soffici wrote that to be "the acrobat of one's own artistic soul, for Palazzeschi, means to be absolutely open and unbounded by all the conventions, by all the extralyrical preoccupations and all the ridiculous didactic, civic, and humanistic preconceptions that tend to make the poet into something like an apostle, enlightener, consoler, or leader of peoples."

In 1913 Palazzeschi's poetry became a staple feature in *Lacerba*, but the contribution for which he was then most venerated was his "Against Pain: A Futurist Manifesto," which appeared early the following year.[81] The manifesto summed up in one short, clear, and exceedingly clever statement what the poetry had long been proclaiming. When people imagine God as a human figure, Palazzeschi suggested, they see a huge and terrible tyrant. But why not imagine him instead as a "little man" who "looks at us while splitting his sides with laughter"? God had created the world not in order to rule it despotically but because it amused him, and it is our first moral duty in life to learn to laugh. "We ought to educate our children to laugh," he wrote, and "to laugh in the most insolent and unrestrained way possible." To this end, hospitals should be transformed into circuses, funerals into masked processions led by jesters, and insane asylums into professional schools for the new generation. In general, cultural life should be detached from its moorings in romantic pessimism and melancholy and allowed to set sail into life-affirming seas.

Although Palazzeschi labeled this carnivalesque image of a mirthful society as "futurist," in reality it had none of futurism's harsher side—its misogyny, warmongering, and general shrillness of tone—that was so deeply entrenched in Marinetti's version. And in a matter of months Palazzeschi would break with Marinetti for reasons that he chose not to specify but that clearly had much to do with Marinetti's overwhelming similarity to the wrong conception of God.[82] In the aftermath of the break, Palazzeschi moved much closer to *La Voce*, even raising with Prezzolini the possibility of starting yet another new literary review.[83] Later in 1914, he moved still further away from the futurist orbit by declaring himself against the war.[84] Yet, far from renouncing his former futurist standpoint in doing so, his reasons followed directly from the life-affirming images of his manifesto. In taking his antiwar stand, Palazzeschi showed that the sentiments in his manifesto were genuine and deeply felt, despite its surface appearance of frivolity. Moreover, in proclaiming his stand in *Lacerba* he demonstrated considerable courage, for it was a move that left him entirely alone within the Florentine avant-garde.

Besides Palazzeschi, the most prominent new face on *Lacerba* was that of Italo Tavolato, whose work showed a very different side of the review. If Palazzeschi was the young *lacerbiano* most capable of mediating the journal's culture wars, Tavolato became one of its most trusted specialists in frontal assault. As tall and burly as Palazzeschi was short and squat, Tavolato was a *triestino* like Slataper but with a rhetoric of sensualism diametrically opposed to the latter's moralism. A year younger than Slataper, Tavolato too had come to Florence to study at the Istituto, though in his case after a brief stint at the University of Vienna, where he had gained a taste for Weininger and Karl Kraus.

Arriving in Florence in 1911 with his mother (his father had died when he was a small child), Tavolato took an apartment on the Viale Volta, a broad avenue that wound up the hill to Fiesole and left him about four kilometers from the city center. Although the main bus route into town passed right in front of his door, his need for money frequently led him to save the fare and to go to town on foot. Mostly for the same reason, he wrote and did translations for *La Voce*. But when *Lacerba* began, Tavolato found his labor of love and his true home. As he wrote on one of its pages in 1914, his home was neither his rented house, nor the piazza (which was only for "charlatans and other socialists"), nor the countryside ("among almond and peach trees in bloom I am neither a creature nor a creator") but the Giubbe Rosse, where his "own little corner of the third room" was truly "my warm nest, my home, and my castle."[85]

According to Tavolato's friend Alberto Viviani, his was a bohemian life of "complete disorder, full of orgies and late-night wanderings," in which he moved from reverie into depression so precipitously that he appeared to be "a certain candidate for suicide."[86] However, it was the high side of his mood swings that was mostly evident in his articles for *Lacerba*, which were little short of scandalous in their promotion of sensualism and libertinism. Of particular note were three pieces that appeared in the first half of 1913. Here Tavolato made the case for a transvaluation of sexual values in which fornication for its own sake, sadomasochism, sensuality, and prostitution were redefined as good, while sex for procreation, conventional sexuality, spiritual moralism, and chastity were viewed as evil.[87]

Apart from the scandal of the argument itself, the articles raised eyebrows because of the intensity of their attack on the Catholic church and because they invoked the notorious Valentine de Saint-Point, a great-granddaughter of Alphonse de Lamartine, who had recently issued a "Futurist Manifesto of Lust" in Paris. In that manifesto, Saint-Point had pushed the proposition that women were no less lustful than men—

and no less interested in war, the ultimate celebration of authentic sensualism.[88] As if this were not already scandalous enough, Tavolato cast himself in the last of his articles as a kind of antichrist, and his text as an antiscripture, with twelve heretical parables in celebration of prostitution. Reading it, the local authorities were so shocked that they had him arrested for public indecency. When his case finally came to trial just after the futurist *serata*, all of Florence watched as a skillful defense attorney managed to get him acquitted. Upon the announcement of the verdict, the largely futurist audience shook the courtroom with chants of "viva il futurismo!"[89]

Tavolato's quick rise from obscurity to celebrity appears to have stimulated Papini, who did not like to be outdone. Shortly after Tavolato's salacious "gloss on the futurist manifesto on luxury," Papini wrote a piece arguing that since "cemeteries, with their severe and luxurious majesty, encourage the widespread superstition that cadavers ought to be respected and that we owe the dead great reverence," they should be "suppressed" and cadavers put to more profitable use as fertilizer.[90] When Tavolato then wrote his even more salacious "praise for prostitution," the act for which he was indicted, Papini responded with a blasphemous piece on "Jesus as sinner," which also ultimately got him into legal trouble.[91] But Papini did not stop there. He pressed an attack against many of the other icons of the bourgeois and Christian moral order such as the family ("I believe and maintain that parents have, toward their children, every duty and no rights") and the school ("I hate schools whatever their species or nature; I believe them harmful and dangerous, useless and cruel").[92] In one spectacularly irreverent piece, he even called for "the massacre of women," an act that would not be "the massacre of innocents" but of "our enemies."[93]

A great deal of what appeared in *Lacerba*'s pages was poetry, personal anecdote, and harmless verbal fun—tendencies that Palazzeschi epitomized but in no way monopolized. Yet the journal clearly had a more shocking and deadly earnest side as well. At the end of its second year, Papini and Soffici summarized what *Lacerba* had been in terms of four "campaigns"—one against bourgeois sexuality, the others in favor of "the most advanced forms of modern art," futurism, and Italian intervention in the First World War—and, certainly, this sense of mission, this relentless activism, prodding, and disruptiveness, were all central to the life of the journal.[94] Yet the nature of its commitments emerges most clearly in its rhetoric.

Many aspects of *Lacerba*'s rhetoric recalled the world of *Leonardo*, though without the self-conscious philosophizing and programmatic attention to secular religion. There are the same quest for cultural renewal and modernity; the same hatred of the existing Italy, its academy, and other "internal enemies"; the same moral rhetoric of hardness, courage, and discipline; the same critique of decadence and feminism; the same cult of genius and cultivation of modernist art; the same longing for regenerative violence. But there are also new elements such as libertinism and a taste for public scandal, as well as a general heightening of the earlier rhetoric with new excess. Thus, the earlier animus against the academy has now been turned against all philosophy, all "seriousness," and even all rationality, while the earlier antifeminism has now been linked with the concept of the "internal enemy" to produce a flagrant misogyny. Although Papini's 1914 article was perhaps the single most extreme expression of this attitude, it was not atypical of what was at times the journal's openly declared war against women. "What is important," wrote Papini four months before the guns of August, "is that we have established the moral necessity of this massacre [of women]. Women must disappear. It is useless, my futurist friends, to preach scorn for women if we then continue to live together. Living together, one can hardly avoid loving them—and loving them, one can hardly avoid serving them—and serving them, we are cowards, the betrayers of our true destiny."[95]

In such a context, it is not surprising that the rhetoric of regenerative violence was also taken to new extremes, as when Papini declared nearly a year before the war that "blood is the wine of strong peoples; blood is the oil for the wheels of this enormous machine that is flying from the past into the future—because the future quickly becomes the past. Without the sacrifice of many men, humanity will go backward; without a holocaust of lives, death will defeat us."[96] Yet there is something rather ethereal and cavalier, if not innocent, about this rhetoric. Although it coexisted with those frequent calls to "revolution" that had always been popular among the Florentine avant-garde, it also coexisted with an intensified disdain for the actually existing public and for all the "politics" associated with them. "We don't give a damn about politics," Papini wrote in 1913.[97] It was a slogan that would come into wide circulation as a symbol of the alienation of avant-garde intellectuals from existing political parties and structures in Italy and that, under the pressures of war, would resound even among servicemen in the trenches and play a rhetorical role in fueling the postwar fascist movement. In 1913, however, its effect was to declare the isolation of élite culture from mass politics and, in this way, to give what would become a venomous notion the appearance of mere culture talk.

Arguably, the rhetoric of violence among the *lacerbiani* was just another aspect of their modernist commitment to uncovering the primal features of life. In every respect, theirs was a defense of "first nature"—savages, delinquents, the insane, geniuses, children, art, and dreams—against the "second nature" of civil authority, academicians, clerics, businessmen, adults, philosophy, and rational thought. Thus, like Soffici's Rimbaud, their most central rhetorical commitment was to "indiscipline" in the sense of an attack on the repressive controls of bourgeois life and a widening and deregulation of sensory experience. At the same time, however, they were absolutely committed to "discipline" in the sense of the relentless destruction of every weak form of life, the trampling of every residue of romanticism, the criticism of every tendency to withdraw into decadent privatism, and the cultivation of militarist virtues in everyday life. Moreover, this kind of discipline required overcoming indiscipline in a sense quite the opposite of the variety they embraced. As Papini expressed the point:

> Our upstart psychologists have confused the tendency to indiscipline with the spirit of revolt. These are two very different, if not opposite, things. The Italian may be indisciplined, individualist, and turbulent, but rarely in the depths of his soul is he revolutionary. His indiscipline derives from his desire to become decadent, not to give a damn, to work little or the bare minimum, doing everything at the last minute or being sly in order to have long periods of leisure. This indiscipline is individualist, whereas revolution is collectivist and requires a discipline both in thought (in the mind, with the guide of a first principle) and among men (in the group, with the guide of a leader). This indiscipline is a symptom of laziness, whereas revolution requires a force of criticism and of combat far greater than all others. The spirit of individual indiscipline, when theorized and blown out of proportion, can make for attempts at anarchism but not at real revolution. Italy, in fact, has produced more isolated anarchists than genuine revolutionaries.[98]

The effort to overcome this stereotypically Italian sort of indiscipline, while also embracing the indiscipline of European avant-garde modernism, lay at the very heart of *Lacerba*'s rhetorical universe. Papini's statement, written in the immediate aftermath of the decision by the *lacerbiani* to join forces with the Milanese futurists, also helps to explain why they did so. Strange as it may seem, for them, futurism was to have been a source of discipline—their first principle, their group—and thus their way of shaking modern life to its foundation in a genuine cultural revolution. The alliance of the *lacerbiani* with Milanese futurism was made on the basis of principle and despite the fact that they always had grave fears about losing their independence. Thus, as late as December 1913 Papini was trying to reassure himself in print that "Marinetti is a man of talent, an innovative poet, a brain that is perpetually boiling over, an excellent friend, an energetic organizer, an untiring apostle, but not a pontifex . . . not a despot."[99]

Three months later, Papini would be writing just the opposite: "Entering into futurism, I did not think I was joining a church but a group of revolutionary and open-minded artists who were looking above all to destroy and to be original."[100] Yet while there is no reason to doubt that the *lacerbiani* ultimately renounced their alliance with Marinetti because of the sectarian despotism they perceived in him, the fit between the two groups had never been good. The Florentines, and especially Soffici, had always blended their futurism with *toscanità*, a sure sign that even if they embraced modernity unequivocally, it did not mean for them, as it did for the Milanese, a suppression of all ancient and primordial associations. Florentine futurism never made any effort to cut its roots to the agrarian society of *mezzadrismo*, which the bard of Bulciano and the painter from Poggio celebrated in their work and where they spent many of their happiest days.

This difference was reflected in the two groups' contrasting concepts of taste, which surfaced not only in debates about art or aesthetic theory but also in their everyday lives. To take just one example, Soffici was utterly appalled when, on a September 1913 visit to Milan, he was confronted with the garish decorations of Marinetti's famous Casina Rossa (Little Red House).[101] Although he was personally more comfortable with some of the other members of the Milanese group, above all Carlo Carrà (who would also soon be distancing himself from Marinetti), he confessed in a letter to Carrà after the war that he had "aided the [futurist] movement because of its will to renew and its research. I *never* believed in the fertility of Marinetti's and Boccioni's ideas. The former does not know what art means, while Boccioni was neither a painter nor a sculptor exactly, but made of art a kind of political discipline."[102] For Soffici, the only Marinetti-oriented futurist who could be embraced without reservation was Palazzeschi, who was both homegrown and entirely independent of anyone's political control.

The break with the Milanese began in February 1914 and was complete by the time Papini, Soffici, and Palazzeschi returned from their trip to Paris that spring. Yet their move was an assertion of their right to pursue their own Florentine futurism independently rather than a rejection of the idea or the movement as a whole. Futurism in this larger sense had been bound up with the entire history and style of *Lacerba* as a cultural enterprise. For it was because the *lacerbiani* were futurists that they had isolated themselves as a self-conscious avant-garde, sought to attract large audiences in order to ridicule them and be ridiculed by them (as in a futurist *serata*), exulted in irrationalist modes of presentation, pressed their relentless attack on bourgeois symbols, and swaggered as cultural "hooligans" *(teppa/teppisti)* who loved nothing so much as daring the local authorities to try to silence them.[103] Moreover, even after the *lacerbiani* began to turn away from futurism in the broad and fundamental sense, the style they had created persisted with younger avant-gardists such as Ottone Rosai, many of whom continued to identify themselves loosely as futurists or *teppisti* long after anyone was painting like Boccioni.

The Words of a Modern Man

A few days after *La Voce*'s declaration of support for the Libyan campaign and Salvemini's defection from its ranks, Prezzolini wrote Romain Rolland in Paris: "Today I am back at my post, but I feel rather sad and austere. I no longer expect great things from myself and my friends, I work out of duty, and I am motivated more by a sense of honor than by a living faith." He no longer had "that beautiful confidence and bright outlook on the future." He felt himself "inferior to the challenge ahead" and hoped "for ten years of calm."[104]

In these last weeks of 1912 Prezzolini did all he could to keep Soffici and Papini within *La Voce*'s ranks, since for him their defection meant the loss of two of his most able and trustworthy contributors as well as a confirmation of his own increasing isolation within the Florentine avant-garde. One of his more subtle moves in this respect was to publish a piece by Rolland in *La Voce* called "The War of the Two Riverbanks."[105] Rolland's thesis was that there were "two great intellectual peoples": the cultural aristocrats, who pursued spiritual ideals but who tended to retreat into privatism when the social seas got rough; and the new cultural democrats of the "theaters, newspapers, and boulevards," who pursued less elevated, more mass-oriented goals but who also retreated less. These "two riverbanks," he argued, had become divided just at the moment when they needed most to unite against the "common enemy." Without such unity the avant-garde risked the failure of its modernist project of building one unified culture against the reigning nonculture of positivism and materialism.

But Rolland's plea went unheeded, at least in Florence, and when *Lacerba* actually appeared, Prezzolini did his best to act magnanimously.[106] In February 1913 he wrote Soffici that he was "happy with what you and Papini have written in *Acerba* [sic]: happy, you understand, with reservations."[107] In April he went so far as to do a special issue of *La Voce* on futurism, which featured numerous letters from Marinetti as well as paintings by Boccioni, Carrà, Soffici, and Gino Severini.[108]

In his short introduction to the issue, Prezzolini laid out his own view of the movement. Like his earlier letter to Soffici, the piece was surprisingly positive, if also brutally frank. Futurism, he argued, was "in part old-hat" and "in part empty," the product of a "man of little culture and much verbal exuberance: Marinetti." What was good about it was "its aspiration toward a modern art for Italy," even if the results it had so far produced were meager. But, he concluded, "the entrance of Papini and Soffici, not among the futurists themselves . . . but among futurism's sympathizers, should help to push futurism toward modern art and away from Marinetti's external—academic and rhetorical—version."[109]

By summer Prezzolini was distancing himself from *Lacerba*, but not until the beginning of 1914 did he launch a full-scale attack. In a three-part series, he blasted the journal as a product of a "new barbarism" that "uses its intelligence against intelligence," sees "everything in black and white," and values "an imbecile in its own camp more than a genius in the camp of its adversaries." Moreover, although Prezzolini had tried until then to keep his friendship with Papini and Soffici separate from his disagreement with their views, he now turned openly against both of them, and with particular harshness toward Papini: "The Papini of *Lacerba* is not a futurist or even an artist. The calamity of the Papini of *Lacerba* is that he is gross and vulgar success."[110]

The delay in this attack probably had less to do with any change of heart by Prezzolini than with the new confidence he felt early in 1914, having just given *La Voce* fresh definition as a "journal of militant idealism."[111] For much of 1913, *La Voce* had drifted between the artistic modernism that it shared with *Lacerba*—and that therefore threatened its identity, even if it was in little danger of being confused with its new rival—and the philosophical modernism of idealists such as Croce, Gentile, and their young devotee Guido De Ruggiero.[112] Although Prezzolini had himself been a Crocean for the entire life of *La Voce*, only in 1913 had he allowed his idealist convictions to be expressed uninhibitedly in the journal. Now that he had decided to take a further step and make of them *La Voce*'s exclusive direction, he had recovered not only a sense of purpose for the journal but a group of close collaborators as well.

Yet *La Voce*'s move into "militant idealism" was not simply a response to the creation of *Lacerba*. In 1912 Prezzolini, like Papini and Soffici, wrote a kind of autobiography, although because of Papini's resistance it had not been published. In that book, *Italia 1912*, Prezzolini reassessed the itineraries that he and his fellow intellectuals had been following in the previous decade and offered some analysis of the tasks remaining. This analysis, though not very explicit, was consistent with the direction that *La Voce* adopted in 1914 and sheds further light on Prezzolini's personal position in the aftermath of Libya.

Italia 1912 opened with a dramatic statement of its most essential premise:

> It is by now a commonplace: the war has renewed Italy, has revealed a new state of Italian consciousness to the European nations and to Italy itself. So much war fervor, so much calm when faced with possible international complications, a perfect organization from almost every point of view, a sense of trust and a profound discipline among the soldiers, a most praiseworthy caution among the officers leading them—these things would not have been possible twenty years ago, they were not possible ten years ago, they did not appear possible even at the outset of the war, and although they were naturally rejected by the opponents of colonial conquest, they were not even accepted by its enthusiasts. The war has been a revelation for everyone—as much for those who opposed it as for those who favored it, as much for foreigners as for Italians—that *there is a new Italy*. Long ago there was the Italy of brigands and carnival. Then came the Italy of organ players and figurine vendors. Yesterday was the Italy of Adowa and the Banca Romana. For all but a very few foreigners and not very many Italians, these Italies were still the only reality at the beginning of the war.[113]

But that had now changed. The old, first Italy had been replaced by the new, second Italy. Its leaders might not yet have realized the full implications of the change, but no one could doubt that it had occurred.

To all appearances, then, the mythic image of two Italies in confrontation that Prezzolini had first articulated nearly a decade before had now been completed. However, the analysis that followed was far less optimistic than such a notion would imply. Despite its recent gains, Italy continued to face grave problems, above all in the moral realm. Italy had been morally debilitated for centuries by the desire of foreigners to have an "archival Italy, a museum, a hotel, for honeymoon trips and recuperations for those with ailing spleens and lungs, an Italy of accordions, of serenades, gondola rides, full of tour guides, shoeshine boys, multilingual people, and puppet shows." More recently, its intellectual élite had been suffocated by positivism and aestheticism. While some intellectuals had reasserted themselves outside the university mainstream in such journals as *Leonardo* and *La Critica*, most of Italian journalism was now under the control of the big industrialists for whom what was important was the "news," news that "produces no controversy, compels no polemic, makes no one think," news that entertains but does not educate.[114]

Matters had been made still worse by the fact that the important opposition movements had either been defeated outright or morally compromised and then gradually incorporated into the Giolittian system. Catholic modernism was an example of the former plight, socialism and syndicalism of the latter. Ten years before, the socialists had been particularly popular and attractive, but their aura had now completely vanished and they were no longer winning adherents among the young. This was so because "once a party is close to power, it becomes internally upset by greed; the disillusioned, those rejected by other parties, those who have been unable to feed themselves from the plate of other parties, now come to the newcomer's table. If the new party lacks solidity, tough body armor, and impeccable character, it will be difficult to avoid this dangerous fattening process; and socialism, because it lacked the necessary body armor, suffered a calamity." In short, socialism had failed in Italy because it lacked moral rectitude, forceful leadership, and ideals that could inspire its adherents over a long term. For socialism "to have become a real force it would have been necessary to instruct and above all to educate and to discipline . . . to make the world of producers feel that there was a superior life . . . something beyond material well-being."[115]

So where was there alternative leadership for the second Italy? It would not come from the nationalists. They had been no less co-opted by Giolitti than had the socialists, since the war in Tripoli for which they had campaigned so hard had now been won and they had lacked the vision to articulate new and more fundamental issues. Nor, unfortunately, would it come from the *vociani*. Theirs was a convention that had broken up into too many small cabals. Although they had correctly understood the fundamental task as educational and moral, they had lacked the internal cohesion to carry it out.

Nonetheless, history had produced one of its not uncommon surprises: the war itself had provided precisely the moral education that was so badly needed. Or rather, it had provided it for the common soldier and his military superiors. It had not, however, educated a "new aristocracy" or alternative political élite. In 1904 Prezzolini had imagined that if a new aristocracy were created, the problem of renewing the *popolo* would take care of itself. Now just the opposite had occurred: the war had morally renewed the people but without creating a new aristocracy. Although Prezzolini did not draw out the implications of this analysis in *Italia 1912*, he had for the entire previous decade been guided by the Paretian assumption that the essential condition for building a new aristocracy was a secular religion to undergird it, and, for that, one needed to appropriate elements from the most advanced philosophies available. It followed that renewed attention to Crocean idealism, as well as to the still more activist idealism of his competitor Gentile, and perhaps even a new philosophical thrust of his own, were all very much warranted.

The new emphasis on idealist philosophy that pervaded *La Voce* in 1913 and then became encapsulated in its 1914 formula of "militant idealism" was Prezzolini's effort to educate a new leadership class, one that would be worthy of the "second Italy" that he believed was finally at hand. Thus, he insisted that the journal's idealism was poles apart from all the vague sentimentalisms so often associated with idealism in the common mind. Indeed, far from being incompatible with a hard-headed politics of realism and national interest, *La Voce*'s idealism offered the only true philosophical grounding for such a politics: "Idealism in philosophy necessarily implies realism in politics and the abandonment of all the sentimentalisms and political mists that, conversely, are bound up in philosophy with positivism and materialism."[116] These reputedly tough-minded philosophies had in fact supported political concepts such as "the rights of man" and, more generally, the politics of humanitarianism that had been so dominant in recent years. But that linkage had been forged by an "older generation," which had now largely passed from the scene. In the meantime the new generation, as well as the masses newly arrived in politics for whom they spoke, had turned away from positivism and toward idealism, which they recognized as the true foundation of a modern politics.

Armed with these convictions, Prezzolini devoted much of 1913 to formulating the basic tenets of a new lay religion in a five-part series titled "The Words of a Modern Man."[117] It opened with the declaration that although he wished "no offense to our Catholic friends and collaborators," it simply had to be recognized that in the modern world "the religious transcendent had been superseded by philosophy." Unfortunately, although this fact was evident from the erosion of the traditional faiths, "modern civilization" had not yet succeeded in creating a secular substitute: a new "set of beliefs, a faith, a modern myth." Therein lay the essence of its present crisis. The democracies, in particular, had nothing at all comparable to the catechism of the church, a deficiency they badly needed to correct. "When God no longer exists for a people," he wrote in a sentence even more prophetic than he could then have imagined, "He will necessarily be rediscovered."

In the next three articles Prezzolini elaborated his "modern myth" in formulations that recalled his celebration of the "man-god" in the *Leonardo* of a decade before, and that were similarly indebted to idealist forebears such as Croce, Gentile, and Hegel. The fundamental basis of this myth, he argued, was necessarily the creative capacity of human actors and, thus, the power of human action to make history. While he did not deny that this idea had become so familiar as to be almost banal, at least in secular thought, he claimed that its full consequences were rarely appreciated. Too often repressed, for example, was the Machiavellian corollary of any genuine faith in human action, namely, that knavery, outright immorality, and violence were a necessary and thus a legitimate price to be paid for human progress. Traditional Christianity had understood the point: it was the implicit message of the "magnificent legend" of the Garden of Eden, which had dramatized how "human procreation was tied to original sin," as well as the fundamental reason why Christianity preached the forgiveness of sin. But Christianity had been reluctant to declare the point boldly for fear of endorsing its manifestations. This fear, however, was groundless. For out of the necessary evils of human action had come a history that was divine, a "universal story." Setbacks in history were inevitable, but no one who had seriously contemplated its vicissitudes could doubt the essential "sanity of the world and the impossibility of permanent decadence and crisis." Indeed, Prezzolini went so far as to proclaim that a universal justice was immanent in history, a justice that guaranteed the meaningfulness of individual death as well as the ultimate attainment of a social world that was "full, serene, and secure."

Needless to say, these buoyant words of 1913 were hardly uttered before they were cast into the most profound doubt. Yet in the final article of the series, Prezzolini summed up his credo in a way that served as a bridge to the rhetoric of interventionism he would soon adopt. For the primary theme of his summation was "discipline," a concept long favored by many of *La Voce*'s moralists but to which he now gave a rare profundity.

During a recent trip to France, the article began, he had noticed that "discipline" was the one word on every important thinker's lips—from Protestants such as Georges Sorel to neo-Catholics such as Charles Maurras. Moreover, the lament connected with it was everywhere the same: that the sources of discipline had been eroded in secular society and that only Christianity had ever offered a discipline sufficiently profound to sustain the human world over the long term. For Prezzolini, however, the sad truth was that there was no turning back. Society had become irrevocably secular, and

for those who are not believers, Catholic discipline is useless. For nonbelievers to take refuge there, as some French conservatives now do and as certain of our own parrots of these French conservatives now also show signs of doing, is to create a new disorder that, unlike the modern one in which we live, is sterile . . . The modern world is the destruction of the old Catholic discipline and, in general, of every external tie and obligation. But it lives on the basis of an intimate hope in a future discipline now in formation that will certainly come and that will be of an entirely internal character. The modern world is preparing a vaster and more intimate Catholicism, more truly Catholic because more universal. Democracy today is not a reality but a messianism. It is a promise not a fact.

Moreover, in a sign that he knew the hearts of at least some of the *lacerbiani* to be not very far from his own on this point, Prezzolini declared that the fact that there was no turning back meant that the modernist anarchism of a Rimbaud was a far better guide to modern life than the positivist anti-Catholicism of an Anatole France. "Rimbaud is the man of tradition and of a discipline that is alive; Anatole France is a man of tradition and of a discipline that is dead." Rimbaud's is a "discipline of indiscipline," but it is also "the only discipline currently available."

In this final article, then, Prezzolini took the rhetoric of discipline one step further than it had previously been pressed either in his own writings or in those of *lacerbiani* such as Soffici and Papini or *vociani* such as Boine, Amendola, Slataper, and Jahier. For Prezzolini in 1913, discipline was not merely ethical, individual behavior rooted in spiritual faith—the overcoming of egotism or decadence, for example—nor was it merely efficient and enterprising social organization, as in a world where the trains run on time. Nor was discipline merely the application of military virtues to civilian life or its reinvigoration through a Rimbaudian "discipline of indiscipline." It was all of these things but something more fundamental as well: their grounding in a secular-religious faith. Discipline had become a term spanning the personal, social, military, artistic, and religious, in effect another name—the key name—for that great cultural project of reimbuing the institutions of modern life with a spiritual presence that had so preoccupied the Florentine avant-garde from its earliest days. That is why, in 1914, Prezzolini would think not of discipline for the sake of war but of war for the sake of discipline.

Despite the importance of the conceptual innovations and the message of Prezzolini's "Words of a Modern Man," it is notable that nowhere in these articles did he make any effort to justify his arguments philosophically, at least beyond the minimum necessary to render them intelligible. Instead he proceeded in the manner of a secular catechism, his aim being to provide a spiritual outlook for a new political class rather than to win the plaudits of philosophers or to stake out an original position within the idealist camp. From this point of view, the importance of his concept of discipline was the way it crystallized in a single imperative both what the new political class most needed to possess and how it might obtain it.

Nonetheless, there were some who sensed from these articles that Prezzolini had shifted his new philosophical viewpoint, or more exactly, that he had become impatient with his Croceanism and had moved much closer to Gentile's "actualism." Thus Boine, without in any way seeking to defend Croce, suggested that Prezzolini, in his haste to ensure that his "modern myth" would effect action and not only thought, was guilty of having collapsed the latter's cardinal distinction between theory and practice.[118]

As we saw in Chapter Two, Croce had certainly always been attentive to the religious needs of the modern world, but he had denied that philosophy could offer a fully rational comprehension of life and thus that it could substitute for the certainties of traditional religion. For him, philosophy could provide a faith—a faith that empirical existence contains the divine—but this was a faith without guarantees. Moreover, at least after the early *Estetica*, Croce had been increasingly careful not to reduce reality to the reality of the human subject nor to present human creativity as coterminous with divine creation. Philosophy could comprehend the historical past, but it could not hope to change the world simply by comprehending it.

In contrast, Gentile's "actualist" philosophy respected none of these limits. In his view, the human spirit should be approached not on the model of self-reflecting consciousness but on that of thought indissolubly bound up with human action. Human thought was the "pure act" through which the world itself and everything in it was constantly created and recreated. In this sense, thought was itself godlike or divine, and life—the living out of concrete lives in history—was, when properly understood, literally identical with the divine of traditional religion. Moreover, Gentile rejected any division of theory and practice; the "pure act" of thought was at the same time the most basic practical action. Thus the problems of life could be resolved directly through philosophical reflection, rather than simply clarified there and resolved one by one in the domain of practice, as at best they were for Croce. Gentile's philosophy, then, suggested the possibility of a much more potent secular religion than did Croce's, one that came with an unconditional guarantee not only that we could fully comprehend the world as our own creation but also that, in this comprehension, we could simultaneously create it anew with godlike power.

There is no doubt that there was much in Gentile's actualism that Prezzolini found attractive. In the way Prezzolini wrote of "a future discipline now in formation that will certainly come," there was the same grasping after absolute guarantees, the same effort to forge an equivalence between present intellectual pursuits and the Hegelian world spirit. Moreover, Boine was clearly right to claim that Prezzolini had tired of strict divisions between theory and practice. Whereas the early *La Voce* had proceeded in a Crocean manner, for the most part keeping its theoretical discussions of ideals and virtues distinct from its specific confrontations with concrete social problems, the *La Voce* of 1913 and 1914 discussed philosophical problems as if to do so was itself to change the social world. It was of course no coincidence that much of this latter ambience was created by contributors such as De Ruggiero and Lombardo-Radice who were unambiguously identified with Gentile.[119]

Nonetheless, Prezzolini did not publicly declare himself a Gentilian or "actualist," and although he did correspond with Gentile, their exchange was modest in comparison with the one he maintained with Croce. Moreover, the latter correspondence showed little in the way of philosophical dissension between them, even though by 1914 it contained plenty of political dissension. It appears that Prezzolini was doing his best to maintain his impartiality, for when Croce decided toward the end of 1913 to publicize for the first time his growing differences with his longtime collaborator on *La Critica*, Prezzolini showed no signs of favoritism in his correspondence with either of them. Quite likely he felt that he could only gain by keeping supporters of both sides in *La Voce*'s camp.

Still, the Gentilian notion that social problems could be resolved in philosophical reflection, and that any attempt to resolve them outside philosophical reflection was doomed to fail, was very much present, as we will see, in Prezzolini's highly cerebral approach to the question of Italian intervention in the First World War. Even in 1913 there was a new and distinctive feature in Prezzolini's writing that appears closely connected with Gentile's collapsing of the distinction between theory and practice. This was his enthusiasm for the idea of a spiritual revolution that would culminate in a new politics of lyricism and pageantry, in a "world as theater."[120] At the end of 1912 Prezzolini had recognized in war not only its virtue as a school of moral character but also its value as a "magnificent event" that "elevates all hearts" and restores a sense of "grandeur" to public life.[121] In the first of his "Words of a Modern Man," he extended this image into a more general conception of "spiritual revolution":

All of its [democracy's] efforts ought to be directed toward the spontaneous generation (as against the state-enforced imposition) of substitutes for the special, social functions of the church. Only by creating in modern society its myth, catechism, and priesthood will it be possible to bring about practical democratic reform. Spiritual revolutions precede political ones, and there is no technical program, however serious or complete, that will be accepted by the young and the new generations. One cannot speak with statistics and information. One cannot excite people with documents. And a poet with a lyricism so moving as to be almost an invitation to religious life, or a philosopher whose dialectic is the ascertainment of religious life, is worth more to a people than a sociologist. As for politicians, they are not important here; they come later. They put into effect, like the crowds that serve them, the ideas of the philosophers, the enthusiasm of the religious, the lyrics of the poets.

In 1914, in an article that attempted to define *La Voce*'s new "militant idealism," Prezzolini reiterated that "for us the *spiritually* fundamental fact of modern times and of European democracy is the substitution of the social, intellectual, and emotional functions carried out until the French Revolution by the church . . . The new times are necessarily about to create one or more substitutes for the Catholic church."[122] Militant idealism was essentially the effort to promote such a substitute, and Prezzolini tried hard to make *La Voce* contribute toward this end. Thus, for example, he published the long and obstruse philological meditations of Enrico Ruta, a friend of Croce's who sought to use Vico to promote a new mythology for modern public life.[123] But perhaps the most explicit and interesting statement of what a militant idealism might seek to be was an article by Rolland's young friend Jean-Richard Bloch on "democracy and festivals," which Prezzolini translated and published in *La Voce*, fittingly enough, just days before the outbreak of the war.[124]

Bloch's article put straightforwardly what was implicit in much of the militant-idealist *La Voce*: that the fundamental problem of modern life was its lack of public festivals, of ritual and theatrical elements that could restore an aura of grand spectacle to an increasingly impersonal and individualist world. Modern people had ceased to believe in Catholicism but had yet to find appropriate secular substitutes for its festivals. In the past, religious festivals such as Pentecost, or seasonal ones such as those of the harvest, had been "a breath of air between two sins, an open parenthesis that allowed a period of human liberty between efforts at enforcing moral restraint." Now, without such festivals, life had become "a sad world . . . lacking in liberty and fantasy." Only the taste for music was left. Yet, divorced from its place in public performance, music only increased the "inclination toward individual isolation and melancholy that was characteristic of our times." Thus, Bloch concluded, "Christian pessimism generated public joy, while democratic optimism creates a new form of popular sadness."

The Intervention Campaign

Two months before the outbreak of the European war, Italy underwent perhaps its deepest crisis of popular discontent in the Giolittian era. On June 7, police fired upon and killed three demonstrators at a socialist rally in Ancona, recently the host city for a Socialist Party congress. Sensing an opportunity, Mussolini and other radical-left leaders quickly called for a nationwide general strike, and uncoordinated revolts did break out immediately not only in Ancona (which was actually held by insurgent forces for a week) but also in Emilia-Romagna and, to a lesser extent, in Rome, Florence, and other major cities. During what soon became known as "Red Week," so much violence and destruction occurred that the government was forced to call up thousands of troops and to dig deeply into its supplies of munitions and equipment in order to restore order. Not least among the effects of the event was that it set the context for the initial posing of the question of Italian intervention in the war. For it showed clearly both that the army was quite unprepared for war (the event left it still more unprepared) and that far more hostility toward the government still existed among the masses, particularly northern agricultural workers, than most observers had imagined.

Among the many reflections in the wake of Red Week were those of Papini and Prezzolini. Interestingly, neither of them responded in the reflexively antisocialist way that they had to similar events at the turn of the century. Rather, both seized upon the occasion to point out how "sick" Italian civic life had become after years of neglect by the country's political class, so sick that revolution was now the only available means of making necessary changes.[125] To this end, both sought to appropriate Red Week for their own concepts of revolution rather than for those of the radical left. Prezzolini's reflections, however, were notable also for the way they moved his rhetoric of militant idealism much closer to the rhetoric of the *lacerbiani* by embracing, for the first time, the concept and practice of *teppismo*:

Idealism has no fear of revolutions. There is nothing less "conservative" than idealism . . . And that is why it has nothing against the *teppa*. What is all this shame about the *teppa* coming forth these days? One understands it when the honest merchants who had their windows broken protest, but when the "subversives" of the "parties of disorder" try to separate their own responsibilities from those of the *teppa*, they arouse more annoyance than compassion . . . For can one make revolutions without the *teppa*? We don't think so. One doesn't make revolutions either with scholars or with people who wear white gloves. A *teppista* counts for more than a university professor when one is trying to throw up a barricade or smash down the doors of a bank . . . "Respectable people" are the delight of every tyrant. With "respectable people" the world would not go forward. And if now and then the world needs a sudden jerk or an act of violence ("violence is the matrix of new societies," said Marx, and the cult of violence was taught by Sorel), whom [besides the *teppa*] can we call upon to carry it out? . . . The mad delirium of the *teppa* has therefore its own sense, its own reasons that go beyond the reason of far too many conservatives.[126]

In short, an Italian revolution that truly puts the "second Italy" in control can never come from leftist political parties, which are all too close to the world of professors and people who wear white gloves. It can come only from the spontaneous madness of *teppisti*, who, in the vision of "The Words of a Modern Man," do the Machiavellian work that alone can promote Hegelian history.

In making these remarks, Prezzolini was almost certainly trying to move Mussolini—whose leadership qualities he much admired and with whom he was by now engaged in a close, personal correspondence—out of the socialist camp and into that of "militant idealism." As we will shortly see, something like this combined effect was not far off. More immediately, however, the effect of his response to Red Week was to aid in healing the breach with his old friends at *Lacerba*. Indeed, it was one among a number of signs that, by the spring of 1914, Prezzolini was moving to close the gap between their modernism of *mythos* and his own modernism of *logos* and that he no longer gave great weight to the political differences between their respective standpoints. Thus, he and Papini had decided to reissue many of their old political articles of 1903 and 1904 as a coauthored book.[127] And Prezzolini's diary, as well as a brief article he did for *La Voce*, suggests that his personal relationships with Papini and Soffici warmed even more in July, when he paid visits to Poggio a Caiano and Bulciano in quick succession.[128]

On the eve of the war, then, Prezzolini, Papini, and Soffici were on better terms than they had been in half a decade and in substantial agreement about the prescriptions necessary for curing the ills around them: revolution, *teppismo*, and a "discipline of indiscipline." Thus when war finally broke out they were unanimous that these aims would be most advanced if Italy were to enter it on the side of the Entente. Although everyone (except Palazzeschi) who had ever participated on *La Voce* or *Lacerba* came to share this conviction, some among the *vociani* or ex-*vociani*—Amendola, Salvemini, and eventually Jahier—hoped that the war would renew Italy within the broad framework of democracy. In contrast, Prezzolini, Papini, and Soffici all immediately saw the war as a historic opportunity to revolutionize Italian political life, even if they were not clear precisely what form the reshaping would take. On the basis of this conviction, they moved quickly to demand Italian intervention and to establish themselves as among the first Italian intellectuals actively campaigning toward this end.

As German troops began their advance on Belgium, Soffici was on his way to the highlands of Bulciano, where he and Papini would read the first news reports from the front lines with a mixture of surprise and great expectation.[129] Then, on August 7, Papini received a letter from Attilio Vallecchi in Florence arguing that, under the circumstances, *Lacerba* should abandon its "*parole in libertà* and graphical experimentalism" and devote its next issue to a serious exploration of the "questions of the moment," advice that Papini quickly took to heart not only for that issue but for the rest of the journal's life. In a preface to the next issue, he proclaimed the journal's political turn, characterized the situation as "perhaps the most decisive for European history since the fall of the Roman Empire," and then used articles by Soffici and himself to present a detailed case for intervention. This move led to *Lacerba*'s becoming for the first time the target of government censors, who, in support of the Italian government's officially declared neutralism, blotted out all those lines (perhaps 20 percent of the total) that were judged so anti-German or anti-Austrian as to risk provoking an attack by those nations.[130] Two weeks later Prezzolini made a similar interventionist case in *La Voce*, but his article managed to escape the censors since, despite its provocative title "Let Us Make War," it lacked specific references to the evils of the Central Powers.[131]

Of the three responses, Soffici's was the crudest in its reasoning and the most abrupt in reaching its conclusion. While his subsequent articles during the fall found many new ways to be vituperative against German civilization and Italy's leaders, as argument they never moved very much beyond his initial reaction, which was perhaps best put in a letter to Prezzolini of August 15: "According to us [he claimed to speak also for Papini], Italy has but one duty: to merge all its forces with the civilized Europe represented by France, England, and Russia (yes, even Russia) in order to crush and silence once and for all the ugly Austrians and Germans, those two disgusting peoples who have always represented barbarism, imbecility, and ugliness."[132]

In contrast to Soffici's reaction, the initial responses of Papini and Prezzolini were less starkly decisionist and more open to reasoned discussion. Essentially, they made arguments of two kinds: that the war was a historic confrontation between two forms of culture—the French and the Germanic—which required Italy to make clear its support for the former as the more progressive and less rationalistic of the two, and that the war was necessary to cure the ills of Italian public life. Although both writers made both arguments, Papini was more preoccupied with the first of them, Prezzolini with the second.

In Papini's view, to remain neutral in the war threatened to degrade still further a "national spirit" that was already lamentably low, while simultaneously jeopardizing important national interests that, if achieved, would boost this spirit considerably. But he reserved his most spirited language for the cultural argument:

> The present war is not only about interests and racial groups but also about civilization. It pits one type of civilization against another, or better, some types of civilization against one lone type that has dominated Europe for forty years: the German. We are opposed to German civilization. German civilization is mechanical and abstract . . . German thought is not thought but formula and formalism. German science knows how to apply and develop but not to create. It makes manuals and supplies industries but it does not invent. German art does not exist outside music . . . The most brilliant Germans (Goethe, Schopenhauer, Heine, Nietzsche) have been ashamed of being German. Heaviness, rigidity, formalism, and mechanicity are the most salient characteristics of German life and civilization. The war between France and Germany is the war of genius against patience, lightness of spirit against pretentious stupidity, art against bad taste and the monkeyish; of advanced thought against conservative stolidity; of liberty against discipline; of invigorating wine against indigestible beer; of intelligence against the soldier and the priest.[133]

In short, to fail to fight Germany was to threaten to unseat the culture of avant-garde modernism that had been born and nurtured in France, in favor of a culture of pedestrian industriousness without distinction and with pronounced conservative tendencies. Interestingly, the argument was no different from the one that writers such as Thomas Mann would make in Germany—except that there France was cast as the rationalist villain and Germany as the authentic explorer of cultural depths.[134]

For Prezzolini, the war raised still more apocalyptic prospects. He saw it as potentially the culmination of the historic process through which the "second Italy" had been aroused and in which a new leadership class might now be forged that would consolidate the achievement. Thus, his article began: "The mystery of the birth of a new world is about to be completed. Dark forces sprung from the profundity of being are in torment, and the birth is occurring amid monstrous streams of blood and wailing sounds that make one tremble. We are not merely witnessing pain. Welcome to the new world! Will the war give us what many of our generations have expected from a revolution? Faced with the totality of the event that is being completed, the spirit is calm and we cannot have doubts about tomorrow. Civilization is not dying. It is only retreating in order to make a new forward thrust. It is plunging into barbarism in order to reinvigorate itself."[135] Faced with such a world-historical event, how could Italy not participate? Such events, Prezzolini argued, were tests of every nation's moral fiber and will. To opt out would be to fail the most elemental of history's examinations, and Italy could do so only at the peril of failing to complete the "making of Italians" and thus losing her national dignity, her sense of being a historic people. The war was a war for culture, and Italy risked eternal shame if she did not align herself with the national and international forces of cultural renewal.

Despite the tendency of these articles to comprehend the magnitude of the new events by reducing them to a simple moral story, their audience was too transfixed and overwhelmed by what was before them to react quickly. Debate on Italy's role in the war was suddenly everywhere, but it produced as much confusion as clarity and certainly no unambiguous mandate for action. One illustration of this early atmosphere of confusion lay in *La Voce* itself, specifically in Prezzolini's relations with one of the men he most admired in the nations now at war. Romain Rolland, who among Europe's intellectuals would soon become the best-known opponent of the war, wrote to Prezzolini on August 30 with a copy of a letter he had just sent to Gerhart Hauptmann protesting the German bombardment of historic sites in Leuven. Rolland asked Prezzolini to lend his name to an international "protest against this barbarism," but also indirectly to support the idea, as expressed in the letter to Hauptmann, that "the war is the result of the weakness of peoples and of their stupidity."[136] On September 4 Prezzolini telegrammed Paris with a positive response, and a week later he published Rolland's letter to Hauptmann with a supportive introduction.[137] This put Prezzolini in the peculiar position of being simultaneously in favor of Italian entry into the war and supportive of Rolland's internationalist pacifism, although Prezzolini appeared to try to limit his endorsement of Rolland to the specific issue of Leuven.

By October, however, the enduring reality of the war and of the Italian government's refusal to become involved had created a clear division in Italy between neutralists and interventionists, even if the majority of the population remained silent. Some, of course, would change sides, as Mussolini did in late October, and liberals went in both directions, but the camps roughly reflected what was then perceived as a kind of "insider and outsider" division in national life. On the one side were the Socialist Party, the Catholics, and those with a political stake in the established order; on the other were the far left of syndicalists, anarchists, republicans, and radical democrats, the far-right nationalists, and the less classifiable groups of futurists and other cultural modernists. Each side had the support of leading intellectual figures—Croce for the neutralists, Salvemini for the interventionists—and of the nation's leading dailies. Among the interventionist papers were Milan's *Il Corriere della Sera* and Bologna's *Il Resto del Carlino;* among the neutralist ones (until the decision to enter the war was taken in May 1915) was Florence's *La Nazione.*

Because of *La Nazione*'s politics, *Lacerba* and *La Voce* were able to play an especially important role in rallying interventionist support on the local level. Although as a strict percentage of the adult population this support was never large in Florence (a fact that was equally true across Italy, except in Milan and Rome), the presence of the avant-garde behind such interventionist sentiment as did exist ensured that it was highly vocal.[138] On October 15, in response to government claims that the Italian people were generally opposed to the war, *Lacerba* sponsored a "referendum" on the question and claimed to receive "thousands" of letters of fervent support for intervention, some of which were soon published as a special supplement.[139] On October 20 *Lacerba* and *La Voce* promoted the first major pro-intervention demonstration in Florence, held just outside the doors of the Giubbe Rosse in the Piazza Vittorio. The next few months would see many more demonstrations there, and although they probably never attracted more than a few hundred people, they invariably provoked brawls with socialists and sometimes led to violent reprisals against interventionists in working-class neighborhoods. They also led to the establishment in mid-December of the "Revolutionary Interventionist Florentine Fascio," an organization aimed at promoting and coordinating the city's interventionist movement and one of a number of such organizations across Italy.

The leader of the Florentine *fascio* was Fernando Agnoletti, a longtime contributor to *La Voce* and *Lacerba* and the only writer besides Prezzolini to place prowar articles in both journals. Born in Florence in 1875, Agnoletti had gone to Greece in 1897 to fight as a Garibaldian volunteer. Returning in 1898 to take his degree at the Istituto, he had then moved on to Glasgow, where he taught Italian at the university, wrote poetry, and edited a bilingual journal for the city's Italian immigrant community. In 1910 he had come back to Tuscany to run a dairy farm. As Prezzolini later recalled: "He professed to make money by selling pure milk rather than the adulterated version, wrote [for *La Voce*] with incisive and nervous clarity," and became "a bit the musketeer, a bit mysterious . . . a pinch of spice in the meatball" of Florentine avant-gardism.[140]

With the arrival of the war, Agnoletti hit his full stride, fusing war poetry, inflammatory articles, and political activism with great success. His most famous poem, "Song for Trento and Trieste," was set to a simple marching tune and published with its musical score in *Lacerba*, after which it became a kind of anthem for the Florentine interventionist movement.[141] Soffici later recalled singing it endlessly in the cafés at night, and Vallecchi remembered how, during the war, the song had "resounded through my house, when we became a kind of general barracks for those who stopped in Florence on some troop train or other, either coming from or departing for the front."[142]

Agnoletti fashioned himself a futurist poet who was at the same time a man of the people. While this was something of a pose, there is little doubt that his early war rhetoric had a real popular appeal. In contrast, the rhetoric of Papini and Prezzolini smacked of intellectual insularity. During the fall, Papini began to mix antisocialist and anti-ruling-class language into his articles, but his most persistent argument for the war remained the need to make the world safe for the culture of the Parisian avant-garde—and unsafe for the nonculture of Austrian bureaucratic conservatism.[143] Moreover, even when he raised the emotional pitch of his writing, it was not to celebrate the nation, Italian popular life, or his own feelings for either, but to sing the praises of war in the abstract. Thus, in "We Love War," his most infamous article of the entire period, he paid homage to war as a sacred rite of nature, as a purification ritual for modern culture:

Finally the day of wrath has arrived after a long twilight of fear. Finally they are paying the tithe of the soul for the recleansing of the earth. What was needed in the end was a warm bath of black blood after all the humid and lukewarm showers of mother's milk and fraternal tears. What was needed was a beautiful sprinkling of blood for the unbearable heat of August; and a jug of red wine for the September harvests; and a dampened wall for the September breezes. The long sleep of cowardice, diplomacy, hypocrisy, and peacefulness is over. Brothers are always prepared to kill brothers, and the civilized to turn back to savagery; men do not renounce the wild beasts who gave birth to them . . . We love war and imbibe it like gourmets as long as it lasts. War is frightening—and precisely because it is frightening and tremendous and terrible and destructive, we ought to love it with every bit of our masculine hearts.[144]

If the piece recalled the outrageousness of some of Papini's early *Lacerba* rhetoric (such as his proposal to use cadavers for fertilizer), its self-conscious spirituality and biblical aura also help us to understand how his ultimate reaction to the war would be an embrace of Catholicism.

Prezzolini's war rhetoric during the early fall was no less distant from the realities of everyday life and popular imagination. Even though he argued for Italian intervention in the war ultimately on domestic grounds, he continued to portray the war as a kind of world-historical drama of competing philosophical principles, rather than as something that might grip the souls of the Italian masses, allow them to express their communal solidarity, or allow him to express his own solidarity with them.[145] Moreover, his arguments took no more account than did Papini's macabre lyricisms of the hard realities in the situation, such as the degree of Italian military preparedness or popular enthusiasm for the war. As Croce chided him in a letter of October 8: "For goodness' sake, put some water in your wine and stop stirring up war . . . I am convinced that it is sheer foolishness and a crime to throw a people into war who are as unmilitary as the Italians have always been (from the battles of King Arduin to the war in Libya!) and who have an army so technically ill prepared and a society with such turbulent conflicts hidden only by a fictitious national enthusiasm . . . Bear in mind that the great majority of the nation *does not feel the war;* and if it has been said about the Germans (wrongly) that theirs was a *war of officials,* then ours should be called (rightly) a *war of journalists.*"[146]

Croce's characterization of the Italian political atmosphere as a "war of journalists" was even more apt than he knew, for at just this moment Prezzolini was casting his eye toward the editor of the socialist *Avanti!,* whose contradictory embrace of its official "absolute neutrality" and his own pro-French and anti-Austrian attitudes made him look like a potential convert to the interventionist camp. In an article of October 13, Prezzolini joined a newly formed chorus of writers challenging Mussolini to clarify his position.[147] Five days later, Mussolini obliged them with a long article in *Avanti!* in which he conceded that a policy of "absolute neutrality" was too inflexible and should not be maintained if it conflicted with Italy's national interest.[148] The article was a watershed. Within a few days Mussolini had submitted his resignation as editor of *Avanti!,* left the Socialist Party, and begun to take the steps that, less than a month later, would place him at the helm of a new interventionist daily, *Il Popolo d'Italia*—a daily that, though still socialist in principle, would throw open its doors to all the best writers in the prowar camp.

Among these writers, of course, was Prezzolini, whom Mussolini began to court immediately after his defection from the Socialist Party and who resigned as *La Voce*'s editor and moved to Rome as the capital correspondent for *Il Popolo d'Italia* almost as quickly as Mussolini made him an explicit invitation to do so.[149] To explain why Prezzolini made this move necessarily involves some conjecture, for what he wrote about it at the time was limited to a very brief diary entry and some laconic references in *La Voce*, most of which suggested that he was again under the spell of Mussolini "the man."[150] Later, in his memoirs, he added only that the move "appeared to me then to be a matter of carrying out a mission."[151] Yet it is doubtful that the "mission" of forcing the Italian government to abandon its neutrality required him to leave Florence and *La Voce*, and to gamble on the success of a new daily led by a renegade socialist.

Certainly there were factors internal to the cultural scene in Florence that might have induced Prezzolini to leave it at this time. It was clear, for example, that a number of writers who had played only relatively minor roles in the Florentine avant-garde—above all Agnoletti, but also Ugo Tommei and Ottone Rosai—were now coming to the fore as leaders of its interventionist movement. Although there is no hard evidence that Prezzolini felt his long-standing intellectual leadership under challenge, it was obvious that the concept of a journal of "militant idealism" no longer carried the same sense of urgency that it had before the war and that he was having some difficulty in adapting *La Voce* to its new role as an organ of interventionism. But what seems most indicative about Prezzolini's move to Rome was the significant role reversal it represented in his relationship with Mussolini. Until then, he had always been the "editor," and Mussolini the aspiring contributor. That Prezzolini made such a fundamental move for someone who had been very much the junior partner in their relationship suggests that he must have believed he was serving larger historical forces. In all likelihood, the "mission" that took him to Rome was the one that had engaged him ever since he had recognized in *Italia 1912* that the nation's key problem was its lack of a leadership class to guide the newly resurgent "second Italy." At this critical moment, Mussolini was the one man on the Italian public stage whose presence seemed to him sufficiently powerful to lead the country out of its moral and political quagmire.

Yet whatever Prezzolini's motive for going to Rome, the reality of his life there by late November was clearly expressed by the steady stream of political commentary and news reports that he was sending from the capital to the editorial offices of *Il Popolo d'Italia* in Milan. Every day brought some new revelation or controversy, and Prezzolini wrote excitedly to Soffici of a city under siege and of himself as "a man in battle."[152] While this excitement certainly reflected the fast-paced events he was covering, it also had to do with the paper's avant-garde efforts to affect them. Thus, in one dramatic headline early in 1915, it would call for a national gathering of all the "interventionist *fasci*" to force the government to enter the war, a tactic that would appear in retrospect to have been almost a dress rehearsal for the fall of 1922.[153]

Although Prezzolini remained quite intellectual in orientation and was appalled by the chaotic atmosphere and lack of proper reference materials at the paper, he was also thrilled to be writing for a national audience ten times as large as he had ever had at *La Voce* (and that would double in the "radiant days" of May 1915).[154] Not infrequently he wrote the paper's lead article or shared top billing with Mussolini, while the rest of the paper bulged with reports from the front, from the major European capitals, and from the interventionist movements around Italy. For a moment it even appeared as if Prezzolini might become *Il Popolo*'s correspondent in Paris.[155]

Although Prezzolini's political background was quite atypical for the paper, his rhetoric blended into it quite smoothly. The argument that he had pressed earlier in Florence was simply transferred to his new home. Thus, in a typical early effort, "Can Italy Become Great?," he argued that, while it was important to gain territory in the Adriatic and to prevent German hegemony in Europe, the main justification for Italian intervention should be to offer "glory" to her people.[156] Another article pursued the same point by celebrating Guglielmo Oberdan, the nationalist martyr from Trieste who had so fascinated the young Slataper and who was now fast becoming an important symbol in the interventionist movement throughout Italy.[157] Moreover, there were signs that Prezzolini's influence on the paper went beyond his own articles. For example, one of his longest-standing arguments about the deficiencies of Italian public life— that its people were far better than its leaders—quickly became one of Mussolini's favorite weapons, one that he could deploy both against the government and against his former comrades in the Socialist Party.[158]

Nonetheless, there was clearly also some disjunction between Prezzolini and *Il Popolo*. Most of its writers were former socialists or syndicalists like Agostino Lanzillo, Guido Dorso, and Sergio Panunzio, and much of its appearance and language—its subtitle, its Blanquist motto, its frequent references to a "proletarian" audience—was far too socialist for Prezzolini's taste. In an early letter to Soffici, he complained that "a hundred times a day I have reason to feel myself more cultured, solid, honest, pure, and decisive than all these people."[159] There was also a substantial amount of irredentist sentiment on the paper, and although at times Prezzolini seemed receptive to it, he remained contemptuous of any notion of using the war merely to acquire a few new pieces of Italian territory. For him, the purpose of entering the war should be to "make Italians" and to enhance Italy's position within Europe, not to gain petty material advantages.[160]

To some extent Prezzolini was able to buffer himself against these less agreeable aspects of his new atmosphere by encouraging his Florentine friends to join in as contributors, and Papini, Soffici, and Jahier would all oblige him.[161] Papini even managed a visit to Rome in January, just as *Lacerba* was becoming a weekly under his editorship. Moreover, although *Lacerba* absorbed most of Papini's effort in the period, he gave a good deal to *Il Popolo* as well. On February 9 he and Prezzolini shared its front page—almost as if the clock had been turned back to the days of *Leonardo*. But this time, rather than pursuing their enthusiasms for Bergson or Jamesian pragmatism, their problem was to explain the persistence of establishment neutralism in Italy, which they did by claiming that its central personification—Giolitti—was in the pay of the international bankers.[162]

At least in Papini's case, however, the significance of his article wholly transcended its immediate focus. For this was the article in which his futurist contempt for the Italian *popolo* exploded in his most thorough articulation yet of the concept of the "internal enemy," a concept that would come to assume a central role in the rhetoric of *Il Popolo d'Italia* not only for the remaining months of the Italian intervention debate, but for the war and postwar years as well.[163] To understand why Italy remained in the grip of neutralism, Papini argued, one first had to recognize that its *popolo* was "the most narrow-minded, petty, uncertain, and niggardly that lives and multiplies on the face of the earth." Italy was "the country of minorities," where everything good that had been attained (including its "modern movement in art and ideas") had been the result of some small coterie of activists. If Italy entered the war, it would likewise do so because of such a coterie. For the moment, however, it was another set of minorities that was holding the day:

These classes—made up of wealthy bourgeois, the new rich among businessmen, parliamentarians without soul, ambitious people without direction, shrewd financiers, industrialists with short horizons, lawyers, and legal agents for foreign interests and those of international consortia—are the true impediments that have prevented the leaders in charge from following the road that history, reason, national and human interests have marked out for us. These classes are represented and magnificently personified by their section leader, Giovanni Giolitti, king of Italy's political and profiteering canaille. We have, then, two true and diehard enemies, one external—Germany—and one internal—Giolitti . . . one that organizes brutality in Europe, the other, cowardice in Italy.[164]

In Papini's mind, then, to succeed in making Italy enter the war would be to kill two birds with one stone, since the war was at once the fundamental precondition for shaking the Italian people out of their malaise and for sweeping away the corrupt "internal enemy" that had encouraged their fall into it.

During the spring of 1915 Prezzolini and Papini continued to pour out a steady stream of articles in support of Italian intervention. And by late April, as Italy's foreign minister Sidney Sonnino negotiated secretly for his country's entry on the side of the Entente, public debate (and its spillover into street violence) reached new levels of intensity. On May 5 Gabriele D'Annunzio returned to Italy from France and delivered a famous call-to-arms speech before an audience of some 20,000 at Quarto near Genoa, the site whence Garibaldi had departed for Sicily in 1860 and where a monument to his expedition was now ceremonially unveiled.[165] It was during the ensuing "radiant days of May" that Prezzolini persuaded himself to supplement his work for *Il Popolo d'Italia* with a Rome edition of *La Voce*, which he called *La Voce politica*.[166] Though a short-lived enterprise, it was in these pages that he would proclaim an ecstatic message of triumph on May 22: the government's decision to enter the war (taken the day before) had been forced upon it by an "anti-Giolittian revolution," and the way was now clear for Italy to fight its still greater "war of reason and faith."[167] From Florence, in what Papini had already announced as *Lacerba's* last issue, came his equally ecstatic "We Have Won!"[168] For him too, the internal enemy was now defeated, and the time had come to engage new foes—in the language of bullets and bayonets.

The closing of *Lacerba* symbolized the end of an era, but Italy's entry into the war did little to heal the wounds that the relentless campaign for intervention had opened. Indeed, it was in early June, as the first 100,000 Italian troops entered their third week of combat, that Prezzolini chose to follow Papini's redeployment of the "internal enemy" theme. Incensed by what he regarded as a duplicitous attempt by some former neutralists to pretend that they had always been in favor of the war against Austria, and that they had opposed only the still undeclared confrontation with Germany, Prezzolini declared:

This is false: they never wanted the war. Reread their leaflets . . . They want us now to believe that they wanted the war when they would have avoided it in return for tiny territorial concessions, ones that would have left us powerless in the Adriatic and that would have abandoned Trieste to the Germans. Their claims are untrue. We do not forget. We can accept their silence; we cannot accept their hypocrisy. One of the neutralists wrote me that it pains him to have broken the alliance with the Central Powers . . . He is sincere. But his journal still reasons hypocritically. We cannot accept this. Stay silent. Work away at your jobs in your little towns. Go be soldiers. But enough of your tricks and lies. I would prefer that you crossed over the Alps and fell in with the Prussians. Every man has the nation that he chooses. Go. But don't get our goat anymore. Don't try to lead us astray and to make yourselves feel comfortable.[169]

Soon, however, this mood of recrimination became overlaid with more somber sentiments, as the full reality of a conflict that had engulfed much of the rest of Europe for nearly a year began to hit home. For months, Italians had suffered through food shortages and increased unemployment, but now they were being asked to sacrifice their sons as well, and for reasons that to most of them remained quite mysterious. For Prezzolini, these reasons should not have been mysterious, yet in July, just as he about to enter the officer corps, he wrote an open letter to *La Voce* describing the war not only as an opportunity for "the liberty of Italy" but also as entailing a grave "risk" that she would fail, that "we may find ourselves, at war's end, ten or twenty years behind" the rest of Europe.[170] It was a more foreboding and pensive note than he had struck in some time. Still more pensively, Papini wrote in *Il Resto del Carlino* on the war's first anniversary: "A year has passed. Twelve months. Millions are dead, millions suffer, billions have been spent. And there is no end in sight. No one is certain of victory. It appears that the true beginning has not yet arrived."[171]

5 The Fate of the Florentine Avant-Garde: The War Years and the Postwar Crisis

For the generation born in the 1880s that had built the Florentine avant-garde, Italy's intervention in the war brought a strange paradox. They had spent more than a decade in relentless pursuit of an ideal of "cultural renewal," one that required Italy to break out of its provincial isolation and to integrate itself with the modernist currents of art, literature, and philosophy that were then so influential across Europe. At the same time they had sought to make "cultural renewal" transcend all narrow intellectual bounds. From the beginning the ideal was tied to regenerative violence and to the cultivation of Nietzschean "hard virtues" such as courage and discipline. Over time it became increasingly focused on a longing for a war of epic proportion, for what Papini in 1911 had called "a true national war, a serious and dangerous war in which all our forces would come into play, with our whole army engaged and our whole people under arms."[1] From 1912 through 1914, this rhetoric of violence, discipline, and war had been pursued in two different styles—one more futurist and sensualist, the other more philosophical and moralist—but they were not as far apart as they sometimes appeared, and were even beginning to converge just as the "serious and dangerous war" the avant-garde had longed for finally exploded. At that point *Lacerba* dropped its sensualism and experimentalism and *La Voce* redirected its militant idealism as part of a common effort to force the Italian government to intervene. Although they lacked the coherence that might have allowed them to exercise real moral and political leadership, in a very real sense the Florentine avant-garde was reunited by the war in Europe, and Italy's ultimate entry into the conflict appeared as a magnificent fulfillment of their expectations.

Yet—and here lies the paradox—Italian intervention meant the instant death of the Florentine avant-garde, at least for the generation that had created it. According to one of its younger members, the tables at the Giubbe Rosse were empty already by January 1915, as their former occupants turned to the interventionist struggle or departed for the front as volunteers.[2] Once Italian armies were thrown into combat at the end of May, *La Voce* became a monthly shadow of its former self and *Lacerba* ended altogether. Had the war proved to be the reinvigorating and "revolutionary" event that the avant-garde had expected, these developments might not have mattered. But before Italian participation was many weeks old, it was clear to all the former avant-gardists that it was doing far more to kill than to realize the ideals with which they had invested it. Although they had imagined the war as the long-delayed fruit of a decade of cultural activism, it proved in reality to mark a new beginning in which each of the major participants in that activism would go his separate way and all common efforts would be abandoned. In short, what they thought was a wake-up call for Italy, a reveille announcing the replacement of its political class by a "second Italy," became a wake-up call for themselves and a taps for their earlier ideals—or, perhaps, the realization of those naive and mostly apolitical ideals in something infinitely more imposing and sinister.

The hour had arrived when talk about cultural ideals gave way to action, action that would reveal the concrete meaning of those ideals for life. Except for Papini, whose physical frailty and myopia excluded him from military service, all would soon depart for the front.[3] Yet although the life of the trenches would appear to confirm their analyses of the weaknesses of Italian leadership and, for some at least, to improve their image of the Italian people, it would also make abundantly clear the sheer folly of having believed that such a war could somehow automatically resolve the difficulties that Italy was experiencing as it sought to enter the modern world.

The Experience of War

According to one recent historian, the First World War was a mind-numbing, sense-dulling affair, and the diaries and letters of its participants consisted mostly of rather banal accounts of personal hardships and monotonous existence rather than genuine reflections on the relation between what they experienced and the larger historical forces at work.[4] Among the accounts to be considered here, that of Ottone Rosai conforms to this description in some ways, but the other two most assuredly do not.

Although some of the younger *lacerbiani* like Rosai, Viviani, and Tommei had gone off to war as volunteers even before Italian intervention, Prezzolini was the first among the avant-gardists of his generation to enter military service. After a month of officer training, he went to the front as a second lieutenant on August 27. As he quickly saw, the circumstances were extremely demanding. Until the Italian army collapsed at Caporetto in October 1917, its front against Austria-Hungary was an *s*-shaped curve stretching about 350 miles along the base of the mountains from the Adda River above Brescia on the west to the Isonzo River above Trieste on the east. Nearly everywhere, then, the advancing Italian troops faced an uphill fight. Moreover, when they massed the offensive power needed to take a mountain, they nearly always had to expose a flank to the well-situated enemy. Because they enjoyed numerical superiority, the Italians did make slow and steady progress, especially during the first year, but only by paying an enormous price in human lives and material resources.

Prezzolini's first letters from the front were frank about the difficulties, but they nonetheless exuded considerable élan, as well as optimism about the probable outcome. "I write you from a trench," he told Soffici in October, "where for three days I have learned to live, sleep, and eat in a half-meter of space. My legs are cramped, and I can't leave for the latrine from five in the morning until eight at night, but I am very happy. Our artillery pulverizes the Austrian trenches, and we see their wounded soldiers fleeing with bandages in hand."[5] In December, however, as Soffici was about to enter the fray, Prezzolini wrote advising him not to ask for front-line duty.[6] Prezzolini himself would spend most of 1916 as an instructor for new recruits in Pisa, Novara, and Vercelli, and in 1917 he would go to Rome with the Historical Records Office of the War Ministry.

Prezzolini's war diary, published only late in his life, makes it clear that privately he felt uneasy about the war and its probable effects on Italian society almost from the day he began officer training camp.[7] After only in a week in uniform, he was writing: "I came eager to learn, obey, work, but I succeed in nothing. They have us hanging around from morning until night. Our superiors have organized everything so that we are prevented from learning. They do not think much of us. Our inferiors agree that we are ignorant. The public makes fun of us as 'the terribles.' The most military thing that I have been ordered to do is to grow a mustache . . . A general has punished a soldier by sending him to the front. What an intelligent example! To defend your country is considered a punishment."[8]

When Prezzolini himself arrived at the front, he found that his troops had binoculars, maps, and weaponry that were much inferior to those of their enemies, as well as living conditions that appeared much more adverse ("the Austrians have electric heating and lights in their trenches"). Early in November, he had to take command of the company because its leading officer had been so overcome by fear that a doctor had declared him a victim of nervous shock. Six months later, he met the Italian commander-in-chief, Luigi Cadorna, but found him "a very sorry sight, with nervous movements, petulance, and bad humor, an ugly sneer on his face, troubled eyes, buck teeth, no heart, no warm words, petty observations." Even more painful was his dawning realization that, in part because of the inadequacies of equipment and leadership, the overwhelming majority of Italian soldiers "oppose the war and want only to return home." But the most bitter realization of all was that, because of their hatred of the war, the troops had it in for all those who had been interventionists in 1915. No doubt in part because of this attitude, as the war dragged on he spoke more and more of "interventionists" as if they were some alien group with which he himself had never been associated.[9]

In the summer of 1916 Prezzolini sent an article to the *Nuova Antologia* in which he tried valiantly to reassert his historicist faith against the grim realities of the enduring conflict. "It is our duty," he argued, "to purge the war insofar as possible of all the implications in it that seem to deny the moral and intellectual progress of humanity," and thus to hold fast to the belief that "so many years have not been in vain, so many centuries have not been lost." Yet in making such a call, he admitted that he was asking the reader to ignore important facts. The war had sown confusion, raised patriotism to a dangerously irrational fever pitch, and made Italians turn against the great German philosophers of historicism as enemies, just when their ideas were most needed to shore up the nation's resolve and spiritual discipline. Moreover, in a turn that in effect denied the validity of the expectations for the war he had held so firmly just a year before, he suggested that it was "certainly foolish to expect from external events like the war any interior [cultural] renewals." At best, the war might lead to the overcoming of certain myths—like that of "the corrupt France and the mandolin-esque Italy"— but no one could expect it to create "new attitudes in life and thought."[10]

Privately, however, this tone of grim determination in the face of unpleasant events had given way to open skepticism and fear. Even though the Bolshevik Revolution in Russia was still more than a year away, Prezzolini was already dreading what he regarded as the likelihood of a successful socialist revolution in Italy. With the hatred for the war now felt by Italy's illiterate peasant soldiers, how could one expect the political system that had thrown them into this débacle to survive? Indeed, a paradox had become a likely historical reality across all of Europe: "socialism, which did not want the war, will perhaps arrive by means of the war." For socialism could capitalize on base instincts like revenge, whereas his own earlier hopes for a spiritual revolution depended on educating the masses to new heights of rational awareness. Such education, he now saw, had never really been possible. "The chasms of ignorance, the pools of laziness, corruption, and twisted character, the lack of any sense of duty—there is nothing one can do about these. I didn't know my compatriots before I entered the army. Remaking the Italians will never succeed."[11]

Such admissions cut so deeply into the basic assumptions Prezzolini had held for his entire adult life that a full reassessment of his goals and intellectual position was hardly avoidable. Despite public indications that he was trying to shore up his idealist historicism, in the privacy of his diary he appeared to be giving up on it. And although in his first days at the front he had felt a certain nostalgia for the "circle of luminous intelligence in which I lived in Florence," a year later he confessed that he no longer had any "faith in political movements favored by intellectuals like us." Even more unsettling was the fact that he had begun to feel an enormous emotional distance from his former collaborators. Returning to Florence, he found Palazzeschi remote and depressed, and Papini "absent from the war—I don't mean as a soldier but in his mind."[12] When he read in a newspaper of Slataper's death in December 1915, he cried out in pain, but in a letter to Soffici ten days later, he admitted that the event had ultimately moved him very little.[13] Similarly, when Giovanni Boine died a year later he confessed to being "upset that I don't feel a deep sadness." And when he thought about his own future, he imagined himself as an editor, busy but disengaged from the contemporary political fray and without his former collaborators. It would be "better to start over again and not take up the legacy of La Voce with all these intellectuals who are so unhappy, testy, full of resentments, rancorous, evil, gossipy, self-centered—despite all their talents and good qualities in other respects."[14]

In short, the war that Prezzolini had imagined in 1912 as a "magnificent event" that would "elevate all hearts" and restore a sense of "grandeur" to public life had actually produced just the opposite effect, exposing all the ills of Italian life and leading him to vow that after the war he would make a clean break with his avant-garde past. The one Florentine avant-gardist with whom he did keep in close touch throughout the war was Soffici, whose war diaries present an utterly different view of the war.

On an "icy-cold and gray morning" in December 1915, Soffici trekked the twelve miles from Poggio a Caiano to Pistoia to begin training as a second lieutenant in the infantry. "So ended my long advance toward the appointed goal; I entered the war, and with the war a world also ended."[15] Yet, unlike his more serious friend, Soffici was able to transfer enough of the spirit of the avant-garde world into his new one to keep himself endlessly fascinated by it and, for the most part, exhilarated as well. Soffici spent two and a half years at the front until the armistice of November 1918. Twice wounded, he would be decorated with a Silver Medal for bravery, and his three war diaries of 1917 are among the most vivid and detailed descriptions we have of life on the Italian front.[16]

The second of the diaries, *Kobilek*, which covers two intense weeks in August between Soffici's return from one hospital stay and his departure for another, has been called "a 'ludic' vision of the war events" and, with its images of the beauty and speed of battle, a specifically "futurist" vision as well.[17] Yet this judgment, though true as far as it goes, misses the fact that *Kobilek* contains none of the derisiveness and arrogance that so permeated Soffici's contributions to *Lacerba*. The tone of the war diary is softer, more reflective, and much more reverent, especially in its awe-struck depiction of the silent majesty of the Alpine landscape as a setting for so much death and destruction. For example, as Soffici made his way down the mountainside after taking a piece of shrapnel near his left eye, he found himself entering

a semicircle of immense, pale rocks that rose straight up toward a vast background of sky whitened by the midday heat. It was a kind of fabulous amphitheater that displayed itself as an ever-widening curve to the right and left, to the back of trenches on one side, and to Mount Jelenik, powerful and bare, on the other. The sun, which had just begun to turn toward the west, threw into that great limestone shell its most intense flames, producing a red-hot, dazzling light and flashes of heat that were nowhere diminished by shadows. Only inside some of the rock overhangs was a bit of shadow thrown off. It was in order to take shelter from that insufferable heat that all the soldiers who came into this place climbed up into the overhangs where they perched themselves birdlike, leaning against the curved walls, one next to the other by the thousands, arousing in my mind the image of a flock of vultures resting after some fantastic flight. And the whole multitude was screaming, incessantly repeating a single word: water! water! water! It was an imposing chorus and stage, an Aeschylean festival that stirred the soul, as if some heroic moment of ancient history had suddenly come back to repeat itself, or as if the last act of some great tragedy was being staged. This theatrical image was acted out in the liveliest way by the group in the center, which I joined. The ground between us and the rocks was level, forming a kind of platform or stone proscenium that seemed perfectly placed for the principal actors in the drama. In fact, sitting on the stones were the protagonists: first, Major [Alessandro] Casati, still in the joyous afterglow of the objective that had been achieved; then Major Foglietta, some other commanders I did not know, and Captain Borri . . . All of them greeted me cordially, marveling at the state to which I had been reduced, but without yet realizing how much I still suffered.[18]

Throughout, Soffici seemed to want to immerse himself in natural and human immediacies and to plumb their symbolic significance. No doubt he wanted to ensure that they would remain deeply etched in his memory.[19] But he also self-consciously sought to lose himself in reality, to become immanent to it in the manner of Baudelaire and Rimbaud. *Kobilek* is a celebration of war as a poetic fusion of art and life, a plunge into the primal that seeks to escape all traces of bourgeois identity. For Soffici, the war was the moral equivalent of Rimbaud's move to Africa, and *Kobilek* is better described as a Rimbaudian text than a futurist one. Like Rimbaud, Soffici was determined not only literally to merge himself with the natural world of sensations, but also to make his way through it joyously, however hellish it might prove. "If someday I should receive a prize attesting to my courage, I would like it to be justified neither in terms of my hard work nor in view of the dangers I confronted; I would have it say only this: 'He was happy in the trenches of Kobilek.'"[20]

Nothing in the text is more insistent than its references to his efforts to be happy in the midst of adversity—and to the contradictions these efforts produced.[21] During one grenade attack when Soffici and his company were out in the open, they sought shelter in some abandoned Austrian dugouts. Nearby lay

three Austrian cadavers, swollen, bruised, their faces and hands so singed that they were no longer recognizably human. They looked like three piles of rags or trash around which flies buzzed and millions of insects swarmed. Beside the one closest to me lay a book—new but with its print starting to fade—that I later picked up and took with me. It was *The World as Will and Idea* by Schopenhauer, in one of those disgustingly neat and correct editions that suit the German taste. If the spectacle before me had not been so grievous, it would have been laughable to see what fate had befallen this pessimistic reader! But no, it was not the time to laugh. Death in battle is so close to everyone that one feels drawn to respect it even amid the enemy.[22]

Yet Soffici's urge toward black humor and his purported "happiness" in the trenches should not be taken to mean that he spent the war in ribald fraternization with the masses of peasant foot soldiers. On the contrary, the image that emerges both from photographs of Soffici at the front and from his diaries is that of an officer who led the troops from a distance, who insisted upon military formalities of rank.[23] His contempt for "fat and sweaty Tuscans" is no longer in evidence, and the *popolo* are now idealized as loyal and good, but they are still considered "ignorant" and in need of being shaped by active leadership.[24] As the scene in the rocky Alpine "theater" suggests, Soffici identified strongly with the commanders on the proscenium and regarded the troops as so many birdlike spectators. That is why we find none of the brazen *teppismo* of a Rosai in Soffici's conception of his military role. Perhaps that too is why Soffici would emerge from the war as a kind of father figure for young avant-gardists like Rosai, but one who carefully guarded his distance from them and refused to be drawn into their midst.

Soffici would dedicate the last of his diaries, which told the grim story of the post-Caporetto retreat, "to Generals Cadorna and Capello, with loyalty." His portraits of these men, as well as of his own immediate commander, Alessandro Casati (the very same Casati with whom he had been friends in the Milan of *Il Commento*) were admiring in the extreme and nowhere evidenced the kind of contempt that Prezzolini had expressed about Cadorna. The only central figure among the officer corps whom Soffici criticized was Leonida Bissolati, the leader of reformist socialism, whom he found too abstract and ideological in his efforts to rally the troops. Yet even Bissolati is described as a man whose "air" was one of "modesty and cordiality," whose face shone with "goodness" and "intelligence," and "whose warmth and sincerity had moved" a group of officers at dinner.[25]

This attitude toward rulers and followers, which Soffici would later describe to Prezzolini as "populist . . . in the Machiavellian manner . . . [with] everyone in his proper place," helps us to understand why he emerged from the war with the cultural outlook of a man of order, despite the sense of wild exhilaration he had felt at the front.[26] Looking back on the dramatic collapse of the Italian forces at Caporetto and the subsequent sixty-mile flight across the river valleys of Friuli to Monte Grappa, Soffici claimed to have little taste for argument about who had been at fault.[27] But in a letter to Prezzolini he did venture the view that "the common soldier is largely innocent of all that happened; the fault must rather be shared by all those who are above the people"—political leaders as well as military commanders.[28] Of the war's enduring legacies for Soffici, none was greater than his conviction that new political leadership for Italy was necessary and that those who had the greatest right to rule were the officers like himself who had "lived in vital, bodily contact with the great masses of simple people" during those eventful years.[29]

In contrast to Prezzolini, who wrote of the war critically and with emotional distance, Soffici was almost completely immersed in the immediacies and particulars of the experience, and with the notable exception of the pages he devoted to Caporetto, he thought little about its larger historical meaning. Yet his diaries appear reflective and detached when compared with those of Ottone Rosai, the self-styled Tuscan *teppista* who depicted his participation in the war as a nearly unceasing, antiheroic escapade of revelry, practical jokes, and heavy drinking.[30]

Born into an artisan family in Florence in 1895 (his father was a cabinetmaker and engraver), Rosai considered himself the walking paradigm of *toscanità* who, from his earliest days as an art student, had devoted himself to portraying the folklore, customs, and street life of those quarters of Florence "where the few bourgeois who enter do so by mistake."[31] At eighteen he had met Papini and Soffici at *Lacerba*'s futurist exhibition, and over the next year he became a mainstay at the Giubbe Rosse, even if his articles and drawings graced *Lacerba* only occasionally. "As a young man," Viviani later recalled, "Rosai was a great loafer. He had a curve in his spine and was misproportioned and ungraceful, but his countenance was unmistakably that of a Florentine brawler, and neither the years nor bitter experience ever softened it. Only his eyes always remained boyish: limpid and opened wide to the world."[32] Despite his shortcomings, Rosai quickly made a distinctive mark. When he published his first poem in *Lacerba*, Soffici introduced the young man of nineteen as "my friend Rosai, painter and Tuscan bad boy," and he later confessed that, for him, Rosai was "not a man, but a representation, a symbol," the living incarnation of the populist artisan whom all the *lacerbiani* wished to be but none were and, therefore, whom "we would have had to invent if had he not existed."[33]

Having imagined military service as an extension of the brawling street life he lived in Florence, Rosai had volunteered for the élite *arditi* in January 1915. However, the reality of military life quickly proved less glamorous than he had imagined it. According to his account in *Il libro di un teppista* (1919), even as he walked down a Florence street to be inducted he felt that the light rain was "jeering" him, and he thought with some nostalgia about his erstwhile liberty as he was being led to a mass haircut, ironically, in a huge room of the Goldoni Theater. Amid the piles of hair, he noticed that "between the true bourgeois and us, there was already something that set us apart," and from the "contempt" he felt for these native enemies in his midst was born a new camaraderie with "my companions."[34]

Rosai's new world was one of intense class divisions—between ordinary foot soldiers and the officer corps, between foot soldiers and the *imboscati* (the "war shirkers" whose factory jobs exempted them from military service), and between foot soldiers and those few "bourgeois" who had entered their ranks. These divisions provoked a scornful attitude in Rosai but also, because of his identification with the commoners, a more lighthearted one. His book begins with the announcement that "a mess kit and a spoon were the essentials in my military equipment," and it was toting these, rather than a rifle or a box of grenades, that he had gone to the Giubbe Rosse for a post-induction gathering. There "Palazzeschi, Soffici, Papini, and other friends greeted me with a terrific outburst of laughter and . . . I breathed my last big mouthfuls of intelligent air."[35] At the railroad station the next day, Rosai felt new anger at the officials who threw him "inside like a load of baggage," but, waving to the crowd of relatives and friends, he and his fellow recruits cheered themselves on and raised clenched fists. As they rode toward training camp in Rome, the cheering and songs continued, and they replenished their wine supplies at every whistle stop. Once in Rome, however, they gained a kind of grudging respect for their superiors, who threatened such lax behavior with a night in the brig.

This interplay of conviviality and contempt would remain a defining characteristic of Rosai's military experience. On the day Italy declared war on Austria, he was again in Florence living it up at the Giubbe Rosse; the very next day he boarded another troop train, this time for the front. A few days later he was part of the eastward march toward the Isonzo River that opened the battle against Austria. Despite some grim and anxious moments during this initial period of sparring before the opposing lines became better established, Rosai and his friends managed to continue to amuse themselves in the "soft mud of the trenches." His diary entry of August 1 presents the following conversation: "What day is it?" "Thursday, I think." "Get off it, it's Saturday." "Isn't it like a Monday? What time is it?" "Umh, how should I know?" "I killed four of them." "Four what?" "Four lice." Although the amusement of lice hunting was mostly confined to the hours after dark, Rosai's companions seemed always to be eating and making merry as enemy fire landed. "5 August . . . We go to the yard, the beans are cooked, and we eat them as the guns go off; they are still going off as we digest . . . 6 August . . . We eat potatoes and fall to the rear at the sound of gunfire. 7 August. Today pasta. We digest as we play tombola in the trenches twenty meters from the enemy. 8 August. The usual things. The Austrians respect the holiday."[36]

As the weeks and months dragged on and his letters to friends in Florence often went unanswered, Rosai felt the estrangement from those at home typical of the front-line soldier. There were also days when he doubted whether "it is worth risking our lives for a mountain of rocks and rusting iron."[37] But for the most part his tale played itself out in the same terms and spirit as at the beginning. Meals, firefights, a comrade's death, lice hunting, games of tombola, brief respites in nearby towns and more occasional ones in Bologna or Florence—these are what fill his account of three more years of war. Perhaps this sameness explains why Rosai devoted less than forty pages to those years, as compared with the seventy he gave to his first six months. In any case, his book closes, not with any assessment of what all this had meant, but only with the story of his transfer back to Florence at the end of 1918, where his *teppismo* would be quickly adapted to yet another battle.

Among Rosai's old friends in Florence was Papini, who had never gone to the front despite having been very active in the intervention campaign. When he collected many of his pro-intervention articles and republished them in the book *La paga del sabato* at the end of 1915, Papini added a new introduction somewhat disarmingly titled "My Cowardice."[38] It began by stating what he imagined others must be thinking—that "I favored the war but did not go to war; I wanted the war and did not enlist; I wrote for the war and yet remained at home, writing other things. Surely I am a coward, a scoundrel, an *imboscato*." Apparently this was an implication he felt compelled to confront, for the introduction went on at length with a variety of counterarguments. Their gist was that he had supported the war for "ideal" reasons rather than "material" ones and that it therefore made sense for him to stay home and write further about those ideals. Moreover, being at the front lines was not the only way to wage war; the great thinkers of the Risorgimento had not literally fought either. Finally, it made no sense to get himself killed as had other intellectuals like Péguy and Renato Serra. The fact that he remained at home did not necessarily mean he was merely "sleeping or amusing himself."

Yet by the time this essay was written, there were many signs that such arguments were little more than a pose, that Papini had become deeply depressed by the enduring slaughter, and that he no longer regarded the "warm bath of black blood" as a useful rite. Certainly, as his articles on the first anniversary of the war had made clear, he had long ceased to "love" this particular bloodbath or to believe that it could change the "popular spirit and make it more moral."[39] But the signs that

Papini's heart was no longer in the Italian war effort went well beyond what he wrote directly about it. In his private life and in much of the rest of his writing, he was clearly returning to his other "soul"—to the one that had worked toward a "religion of nature" before he had abandoned it for the iconoclasm and bombast of *Lacerba*. In his three years at the forefront of *Lacerba*, he had published exactly one poem in its pages.[40] Now, having given up his role as an active cultural organizer, his verses appeared in nearly every issue of Giuseppe De Robertis' more literary *La Voce*. They revealed a spirit that had become far quieter, more meditative, less urban, and far less irreverent than the one that had prevailed in "futurist Florence."

In the Tuscany of 1913, perhaps the cultural initiative most diametrically opposed to *Lacerba* was the Catholic reactionary *La Torre* of Siena, a journal whose tone toward "futurists" was no less vituperative than the one *Lacerba* reserved for the most boorish bourgeois.[41] But now, as Papini opened up his private, religious side, he and *La Torre*'s former editor, Domenico Giuliotti, began an intellectual correspondence that soon blossomed into friendship. Under Giuliotti's influence, Papini turned increasingly to nineteenth-century writers such as Joseph de Maistre, Louis de Bonald, Juan Donoso Cortés, Louis Veuillot, Ernest Hello, and Léon Bloy.[42] Bloy, of course, was the figure whose traditionalism had proved such a disappointment to Soffici when the troubled young avant-gardist had visited him at the height of his spiritual crisis of 1907. Yet now, with all the enthusiasm of a fresh discovery, Papini called Bloy "the greatest living writer in the French language."[43]

One condition that had much facilitated Papini's correspondence with Giuliotti was that the latter went off to war only in May 1916 and then, after a year at the front, moved to Rome with the War Ministry (just as Prezzolini had). Meanwhile, Papini had also drawn closer to another man who stayed home, Filippo Naldi, editor during the war of Bologna's *Il Resto del Carlino*. Naldi was a somewhat shadowy figure, whose ties with industrialists had enabled him to provide funding for Mussolini's *Il Popolo d'Italia* in its first months—until Mussolini got wind of his secret connections with Salandra's government.[44] Recognizing Papini's talent and availability, Naldi had encouraged him to write for the *Carlino*, and Papini in fact devoted a great deal of time during the war to writing for it on a wide variety of subjects. When Naldi moved to Rome in December 1917 to begin a new daily, *Il Tempo*, Papini seized the opportunity to be among so many friends and went to Rome himself as literary editor. The association was short-lived (Papini left Rome in mid-April), but his few months in the shadow of the Vatican may have added some momentum to the emerging forces in his life.

The effect of Papini's new interest in Catholic thought in the context of an enduring world war is fully evident in the articles he wrote for *Il Resto del Carlino* and *Il Tempo*. Just as before the war he had personalized the meaning of the coming conflict in terms of an Italian spiritual "revolution," by the fall of 1915 he saw "a pious atmosphere of new faith" settling over the battlefields, one that strongly suggested the possibility of "a rebirth of Catholic Christianity." Indeed, he went so far as to predict that "after the age of iron and depopulated religion will come the age of silver and religion restored."[45] But as the war entered its third year in the summer of 1916, this triumphal spirit gave way to the blackest pessimism. Papini now offered the war as evidence that "human nature had not changed in seven thousand years of known history" and that all those nineteenth-century hopes of a progressive, secular civilization had been the bitterest of illusions.[46]

Throughout the rest of the war, this black mood so permeated Papini's writing that the historical arrival of the war and the idea of a rebirth of the old Catholic order appeared almost to fuse for him as a single great event. For example, to commemorate Easter in 1917, he devoted an article to that holiday's "deepest" meaning, which he claimed was "the slaughter of innocents." The reason why "the sweetest, purest, and simplest little animal was deliberately chosen as the victim of this eternal and forever renewed sacrifice" was that "the gods of the first ages wanted the blood of innocents. From time immemorial, by a frightening law that appears to have been desired and invented by Satan, it has been determined that the innocent must die in order for the guilty to be saved. The war is one of the rites of this tremendous law. When peoples are decimated the truly guilty seldom die, but how many innocents . . . have lost their lives among woods and rocks when men arise who so hate each other!"[47]

Was the war, then, some horrible punishment that God had visited upon secular civilization? Might it have been avoided if the traditional Catholic world had been preserved from modern intrusions such as the French Revolution? Should we now embrace Catholicism and return to the traditional society in which it was the reigning principle of order? Such questions hung like a pall over Papini's articles of 1917 and early 1918, but his answers remained elusive—in large measure because it was still unclear whether he had come to embrace Catholicism as a personal faith. Then, in May 1918, he put a new twist on his by then familiar invective about "internal enemies":

The forms of betrayal are infinite and the traitors innumerable. Traitors are not just spies, deserters, renegades, enemy agents, arsonists, and others who prepare our defeat. It is time to admit that incapable generals, inept ministers, rapacious industrialists, thieving merchants, dishonest employees, big-time smugglers, lightweight novelists, pessimists by calculation or stupidity, fanatics by thickheadedness or love of phrases, adulterers, greedy suppliers, unskilled censors, stubborn and astute *imboscati*, and draft dodgers—all those who directly or indirectly increase discontent, hunger, sadness, misery, deceit, and disorder—are the real traitors, and that as traitors they should be marked out for disgrace by all those citizens who are not the accomplices of these serpents but their victims. He who truly loves does not betray. But had there been love in the world—had Christianity truly been Europe's common faith—this war would not have been. Christianity is the acute consciousness of the originary wickedness of man and the effort to conquer and rule over it with love. But redemption is only proclaimed and few fulfill it. Is there today, even in Rome, a single true Christian?[48]

A few days later, in a letter to the Catholic literary critic Cesare Angelini, then at the front as an army chaplain, Papini spoke about the "slow but profound spiritual mutation" that had finally overwhelmed him. "Appearances notwithstanding, I have always been at heart a mystic; but I am now becoming, and not only in theory, a Christian. The events of this year have brought home to me the great discovery that, while everyone knows the Gospel, almost no one applies it and lives it."[49] For Papini it was the moment of his "second birth," the moment at which his "futurist" soul was declared dead and buried in order that his poetic one might live. Although he never felt the heat of enemy fire or saw a fellow soldier killed, there was no one upon whom the war had a more profound or lasting effect.

The War at Home and the Politicization of the Avant-Garde

In September 1914, as the battle for Italian intervention was warming up, Papini wrote in *Lacerba* that "for peasants, tenant farmers, workers, and bourgeois . . . the only value of their lives consists in facing death. The others, the brainy ones, those who create and think and provide moral encouragement, are also working for their country, and they have no need to go and kill when those who are worth less and mean less than they do can go and kill with better results."[50] It was an arrogant and cynical remark, but it also proved largely accurate as a prediction of the social reality of the coming war. While we do not have figures for war participation and combat deaths that break down cleanly by social class, the figures we do have for provinces within Tuscany certainly support the notion that peasants and tenant farmers (though not workers and probably not "bourgeois") were more likely both to serve and to die in the war than were urban intellectuals.[51]

Current estimates suggest that of the nearly 6 million Italian men who served in the First World War, about 600,000 died, another 500,000 were permanently disabled, and a million more were wounded. For Tuscany, the corresponding figures are about 450,000 men in arms and 47,000 deaths. When one adjusts the former figure to reflect those actually present at the front, the chances that a Tuscan would never return from battle appear to have been about one in six. Moreover, that those who stayed at home also faced hardships is suggested by a much higher than normal rate of infant mortality during the war years, as well as large numbers of deaths from the *spagnola* (influenza outbreak) that swept across Europe in 1918 and 1919.

But casualty and population figures only begin to measure the human toll of the war. The general population in Tuscany, as in the rest of Italy, experienced severe hardships. Agricultural production fell precipitously, in part because of the conscription of so much farm labor, and much of what was produced had to be requisitioned by the government for the army. Commodity prices also fell relative to the soaring general rate of inflation, and this meant that agricultural workers dependent on wages (as against tenants who had barter arrangements with their landlords) saw their standard of living fall as well. Meanwhile, city dwellers had to stand in long lines even for basic goods such as bread, milk, and eggs and were forced to pay high prices for them—when they were available. The inevitable black market that accompanied such a situation made urban life still more embittered.

All of this might have been bearable had Italian military success been greater. But in a slow-moving war of attrition there was little moral uplift to be gained from the daily news. Moreover, those who returned from the front were often demoralized by the terrible conditions they had experienced, as well as by the fact that the trenches were seen, as one returning Tuscan peasant soldier put it, merely as a place "where one goes to die without any hope of profit."[52] This sense of desperation, compounded by anger and indignation that so many factory workers were able to avoid military duty, produced an atmosphere of burning moral outrage even before the rout at Caporetto.

The idea of Italian intervention had never been popular among the masses of ordinary Tuscans, but the intensity of the intellectual minority's support for the war in 1915 had helped to push the government into such a policy. By the summer of 1916, however, not only had intellectual support for the war nearly evaporated, but protest demonstrations against it had become a common sight across Italy, and nowhere more so than in Florence.[53] By 1917, and especially after Caporetto, the government was forced to make extravagant promises about land reform in order to continue to recruit sufficient manpower for the front lines. Thus, when the war ended in November 1918, the Tuscan masses seethed not only with outrage against what they had endured for three years, but also with a sense that the government owed them a much improved situation as compensation for the war effort. When the government failed to deliver on its promises, Tuscan society became a tinderbox in which the slightest spark sufficed to produce a social explosion.

The political situation created by the war, then, was in many ways the "revolutionary" one that the prewar avant-garde had predicted and sought, even if it threatened in 1919 to turn in a more socialist and less "spiritual" direction than they had envisioned. Yet, with the limited exception of Soffici, the generation born in the 1880s that had brought that avant-garde into being had lost its stomach for revolutionary change once the reality of the war had arrived. As if to symbolize this development, *La Voce* continued in two versions during the early months of the war, but neither of them any longer represented either the modernist project of cultural renewal or the individuals originally associated with it. *La Voce politica* was always a rather narrowly focused organ of interventionism, and although it did not cease publication until December 1915, Prezzolini no longer wrote for it after July. And while De Robertis' *La Voce* survived until the end of 1916, it was an inward-looking venture that aimed to reinterpret literary classics and lacked any avant-garde aspiration to make an immediate impact on the moral climate surrounding it.

After the war many intellectuals saw De Robertis' *La Voce* as the harbinger of a necessary return to classical order, and sought to emulate that return with new journals that pursued a similarly pure intellectualism while avoiding potentially compromising social entanglements.[54] But in the midst of the First World War, a new group of intellectuals a half-generation younger than the *vociani* suddenly thrust themselves into public life, and they had their own ideas about how Italy could be spiritually regenerated.

Although it never achieved the prestige of *La Voce* or the notoriety of *Lacerba*, the journal *L'Italia futurista*, created by a group of young Florentines born in the early 1890s, was certainly cognizant of its predecessors when its first biweekly issue appeared in June 1916.[55] Yet as the journal's name indicates, this was a group with close ties to Marinetti, and that fact, coupled with its self-consciousness as a rising generation, led *L'Italia futurista* to repudiate earlier Florentine efforts at futurism such as *Lacerba*. As its coeditor, Emilio Settimelli, wrote in its opening manifesto:

> We do not continue *Lacerba* and we are proud to say so. In fact, being ill-mannered and using bad words (the self-styled audacities of medieval university students) have nothing to do with futurism. We hold strongly to our refined and elegant geniality, which though modern does not exclude fisticuffs and smacks on the ears, as well as to our divine virility. *L'Italia futurista* will be the first dynamic Italian journal. It will have writer-combatants, subscribers from the trenches, and critics who frequent taverns (which are safe from airplane raids) as well as aviator propagandists.[56]

The same idea was repeated years later by a sometime contributor to the journal, the artist Primo Conti, who wrote that "compared with us, the futurists of *Lacerba* appeared a bit like converted professors . . . like the remains of a traditionalist baggage to be discarded. This is why *L'Italia futurista*, even in its typography, wanted to make a self-conscious choice in opposition to the Soffician taste for creating anew within tradition."[57]

Naturally, the idea of being ousted from the cultural limelight was not a pleasing one to the *lacerbiani*, even if they themselves were no longer willing to fill it. Thus, when Papini informed the readers of the *Mercure de France* that "the futurist group has founded a new review in Florence," he added immediately that "after the separation of the most original and exciting artists, such as Carrà, Palazzeschi, Papini, and Soffici, and the death of Boccioni (who fell from a horse while he was doing his service in the artillery near Verona), the movement has lost much of its importance and influence."[58] Still, some younger *lacerbiani* like Ugo Tommei did contribute to it, and even Soffici sent it one article in 1917.[59]

In addition to Settimelli, the main figures in the *Italia futurista* group were the brothers Bruno and Arnaldo Ginanni-Corradini (who adopted the pen names of Bruno Corra and Arnaldo Ginna), Mario Carli, Remo Chiti, Maria Crisi Ginanni, and another set of brothers, Vieri and Neri Nannetti. Corra was the journal's other coeditor (except for a few months in 1917 when he was spelled by Ginna), and Crisi Ginanni, who was married to Ginna, directed its small press. Of the group as a whole, the most artistically talented was probably Ginna. He was its only painter, and he did film, photography, and poetry as well. His *Vita futurista* (1916), which is generally recognized as the first futurist film, involved nearly everyone in the group in some capacity. Although it is no longer extant, we know from a detailed scene-by-scene summary in *L'Italia futurista*, as well as from still photos, that it broke with any continuous narrative line and was also highly experimental in cinematic technique.[60]

Despite the hostility between the *Italia futurista* group and at least the older *lacerbiani*, there were inevitably some continuities between the two journals. They shared many of the same enemies—above all the historicist philosophy of Croce and the decadentism of D'Annunzio—and they drew from many of the same French sources, especially Rimbaud. Like *Lacerba*, *L'Italia futurista* condemned "seriousness" and "rationality," and was no less fond of creating scandal, appealing to the virtues of regenerative violence, or denigrating the *popolo*. It also drew upon *Lacerba*'s antifeminist rhetoric of "virility," even if it permitted one particularly talented woman to join its tight-knit fraternity. Moreover, although the journal's typography was indeed somewhat different from *Lacerba*'s (its multicolumned pages created a much denser look), it shared the same enthusiasm for wild poetic exhibitions of *parole in libertà*.

One major difference between the two journals was the overwhelming presence of Marinetti in *L'Italia futurista*, which far exceeded what *Lacerba*—more zealous in protecting the individual autonomy of its various resident "geniuses"—had ever permitted, even in the heyday of its alliance with the Milanese. Marinetti's name dominated its front page—the most straightforwardly political page of the four that made up a typical issue and the place where manifestos and articles by "futurists at the front" almost always appeared. But in addition to according Marinetti top billing, *L'Italia futurista* shared his fondness for the modern technics of speed and flight to a far greater extent than the *lacerbiani* ever had, and this enthusiasm was frequently apparent in the poems, serialized novels, and reviews of theater, film, and books that formed the journal's interior.[61] The enthusiasm for film, which had been almost non-existent in *Lacerba*, probably also derived from the greater interest of the younger generation in exploring the potential of modern technology for art.

Several other, lesser differences between the two journals help to convey what was distinctive about *L'Italia futurista*. First, and most obviously, it had an actual war (rather than the idea of a coming war) to provide the basis for its rhetoric, and many of its participants actually made their contributions from the front.[62] In fact Carli, despite a myopia nearly as serious as Papini's, managed to fight virtually the entire war for the *arditi* and still function as one of the journal's prime contributors. Second, unlike the *lacerbiani* (and also unlike Marinetti), *L'Italia futurista* had a strong interest in dreams, the unconscious, and the forces of the surreal—somewhat in the manner of the dadaists then operating in

9. An early issue of *L'Italia futurista* (26 August 1916), announcing the death of the futurist painter Umberto Boccioni.

Zürich, although the two groups appear to have been working independently.[63] Third, *L'Italia futurista* was much less receptive toward foreigners and cultural developments outside Italy. Thus, in 1917 Corra even attacked Apollinaire (whose father was Italian) as too "French" to comprehend current developments in futurism, while more generally maintaining that "Italian futurist art is increasingly detaching itself from every foreign current."[64]

Of all the differences between *Lacerba* and *L'Italia futurista*, however, none was so significant as the way they conceived of themselves as functioning groups. The best-known photograph of *L'Italia futurista*'s inner circle, taken by Mario Nunes Vais in 1919, shows eight of its members (including Marinetti), all similarly dressed in dandyish fashion and staring ahead at right angles to the camera with nearly identical, stern and unblinking expressions. The image has an unmistakable aura of military bearing and resolve, of individualism subordinated to collective will in a manner completely unlike the older generation of Florentine avant-gardists. Thus even if, to critics like Prezzolini, the group's image also appeared to be one of "vanity, the small vanity of self-advertisement . . . [by] people who do not think except about themselves," it was still undeniable that they had marshaled themselves as a political unit, as a protopolitical party, in a way Prezzolini's generation never had.[65]

10. The collaborators on *L'Italia futurista* (from left: Remo Chiti, Neri Nannetti, Bruno Corra, Emilio Settimelli, Arnaldo Ginna, Maria Ginanni, Trilluci, and F. T. Marinetti) in a photograph by Mario Nunes Vais, 1919.

That *L'Italia futurista* sprang up in Florence rather than in Milan or Rome is testimony to its roots in the city's formidable avant-garde tradition. Yet it went one step further than had any of its predecessors. *Leonardo, La Voce,* and *Lacerba* had all preached "discipline," but they had never been able to apply the value to their own internal conduct as groups. Only with the generation that came of age during the war was Florentine modernism politicized in the sense that the political ends of the group came to take precedence over the intellectual itineraries of its individual members. Although this presentation of a unified face to the world was relatively short-lived—*L'Italia futurista* ended in February 1918—it is significant that its last issue featured Marinetti's "Manifesto of the Italian Futurist Party," and that the group went on to play a key role in the establishment of the early postwar *fasci* in Florence and Rome.

When Carli and Settimelli moved to Rome in the fall of 1918 to begin yet another journal, *Roma futurista,* their paths nearly crossed with Prezzolini's. A year earlier, after *Il Popolo d'Italia* had strengthened its operations in Rome and had begun to produce both a Milan and a Rome edition, Prezzolini had resumed his work on Mussolini's daily, and during the first half of 1918 he had given it a great deal of his attention. But in September he returned to the front to try to bolster Italy's flagging, post-Caporetto army just as the two Florentine futurists were arriving. They in turn would soon begin to make occasional contributions to *Il Popolo d'Italia* and to become absorbed into the incipiently fascist cultural politics that Prezzolini had left.

With his contributions to *Il Popolo d'Italia* of 1918, Prezzolini can be seen as having made his own "politicization of modernism," for even though he did not subordinate his identity to that of any group, he did make his earlier cultural message available in a more politicized form and for an enterprise not entirely unlike the earlier Florentine journals. And even if Mussolini's newspaper was too much the mass-circulation daily to be properly thought of as avant-garde, it did have avant-garde elements. Although its main thrust after the intervention campaign had been to act as the exuberant cheerleader for the Italian cause, it also made constant efforts to appeal to a popular readership by printing local news from small towns across Italy, long lists of soldiers who had recently died at the front, and even a few serialized novels.[66] As Margherita Sarfatti later recalled, it was "a journal at once bohemian, full of rage, and sumptuous . . . without any emotionally disengaged and anonymous articles and editorials. [It had] short columns of large type separated by spaces that made the columns appear as firing lines; headlines that were battle cries recording loves and hates in block letters at the top of every page and then, in smaller letters, over each of its six columns; and that electrifying signature that one's eyes darted about to find: *Mussolini,* brief and apodictic, following his agitated and imperious words."[67]

In its rhetoric, moreover, the *Popolo d'Italia* of 1916 and 1917 had conducted a tireless campaign against Italy's many "internal enemies" and had sought to counterpose the Italy of the common people, who deserved whatever fruits victory might bring, with the Italy of the government, which was held responsible (along with the church) for whatever failures the Italian war effort had suffered. These were, of course, continuations of the thrust Papini and Prezzolini had given *Il Popolo* in 1915. But it was with Prezzolini's more coherently argued contributions of 1918 that this rhetoric received its fullest expression.

In reacting to Caporetto, Prezzolini cut loose the themes of his prewar writing from their embeddedness in the cultural modernism of those years and distilled their political essence for a readership that had little interest in Bergson, Croce, Nietzsche, or Rolland.[68] The basic message was simple. Every society has a political class, but Italy's had never offered real leadership. Before the war it was completely ignorant of the *popolo* it ruled, and now it had "abandoned" them in the midst of crisis.[69] Its lack of leadership was especially evident in the moral domain, but it suffered from a lack of ideas in every domain and had no notion even of what it means to lead. Moreover, rooted as it was in the materialistic bourgeoisie, its ignorance was willful. It was, in short, "a head that has no idea how to communicate to its body those movements that can be born only of a vision of reality and a consciousness of things."[70]

In his book on Caporetto, which he wrote just days after the retreat began, Prezzolini pressed the same indictment, but with a relentlessness and attention to detail that made it read like a legal brief. Although Cadorna as commander-in-chief was surely at fault, "catastrophes like the present one can never be exhaustively explained by an occasional cause, but are the result of multiple and complex underlying factors."[71] These factors—all traceable to the nation's ruling class—included the lack of military preparedness in 1915, the failure to develop any strategic concept, the neglect of troop morale and adequate troop training, a prevailing moral climate that encouraged *imboscati* and bureaucratic sabotage, a "system of lies" in the press, and a lack of discipline everywhere. The disaster of Caporetto had been not so much a military as a moral one, the result of the "moral disintegration" of the Italian "system" as a whole. Caporetto was—as he concluded in a formulation that would become the basis for a major myth—nothing less than "a *labor strike*, which is to say, in wartime, a suicide."[72]

What, then, was the remedy for Italian society in 1918? Not surprisingly, Prezzolini fell back on the concept to which he had devoted so much attention in his "Words of a Modern Man": that of discipline. But now, instead of thinking it through only in philosophical and religious terms, he tried to specify the social and political context that would be truly supportive of a modern discipline:

> Italy suffers with respect to what in military jargon are called cadres [*quadri*] . . . In military life cadres are the officers, their immediate subordinates, and the noncommissioned officers. They organize [*inquadrano*] the mass of simple soldiers. They shape them and guide them . . . In civilian life there are also cadres, even if their roles are not specifically indicated. There are the cadres of the bureaucracy and also those of the professional world, business, and agriculture: cadres for economic life and, when they participate in it, for political life . . . To organize for industrial life is also to organize for military life. Once one is accustomed to discipline, one is accustomed to discipline forever. Discipline is, I would say, an inclination, a taste that one assumes just as one assumes other tastes and more material inclinations. One of the great cadres that few manage to resist is the Catholic church . . . Other cadres are those the working masses have created in the last twenty-five years: the Chambers of Labor, the Leagues, the Craft Federations . . . But all these cadres are scarce. They fail to hold the masses together. Leaders are scarce in every aspect of Italian life. Every time some enterprise is attempted, the same names are proposed. Our political life is impoverished, in comparison with that of France or England, because of the scarcity of men.[73]

But, for Prezzolini's analysis, one key problem lingered. If Italy had benefited from some new "cadres" in recent years and yet still remained ineffective in producing leadership, how might further cadres be developed that would succeed in providing the necessary discipline for postwar life? In the prewar period, Prezzolini had looked to the avant-garde to play this role, but this possibility—implicit in the very existence of *Il Popolo d'Italia*—was not discussed, nor did Prezzolini try to push the journal to play such a role. While he did hint that cadres might somehow come out of the war experience, he did not make clear how this might occur. Thus, the crucial link in his analysis remained obscure. The existing political class was hopeless, and the "second Italy" was potentially ready to displace it. But without some new groups or institutions to organize and discipline that new Italy, it would remain permanently waiting in the wings. One might have imagined, reading Prezzolini in the *Popolo d'Italia* of 1918, that all of this would have led him to support the fascist movement when it began to emerge early the following year. But by then his political voice had become oddly silent.

The Emerging Culture of Florentine Fascism

After the armistice of November 1918, many of Florence's artists and writers drifted back to the same cafés around the Piazza Vittorio from which they had spawned the interventionist movement four years before. Although a few of those who had been most active then were notably absent, two members of the old *Lacerba* group—Rosai and Agnoletti—once again became the leading figures. Beside them were mostly the members of a new futurist political party whose founding manifesto had appeared in *L'Italia futurista* the previous February and which had been formed in Rome in September. These included Settimelli, Carli, Chiti, and the Nannetti brothers from the *Italia futurista* group, as well as another figure who had written both for their journal and for *Il Popolo d'Italia:* Enrico Rocca. Together they now formed a local party section called the Fascio Politico Futurista, with Agnoletti at its head.

The new *fascio* met regularly on the second floor of the Caffè Gambrinus and, by the spring of 1919, was producing a journal aptly named *L'Assalto*.[74] A few blocks away on the Piazza Ottaviani stood the Florentine headquarters of another new political organization—a veterans' group called the Associazione Nazionale dei Combattenti—which had its own independent journal, *Il Giornale dei Combattenti,* and which had also chosen Agnoletti as its leader. The two small and overlapping groups combined to form the Fascio Fiorentino di Combattimento just before the first rally of the national movement of the same name, which Mussolini held in Milan's Piazza San Sepolcro on March 23, 1919.

Such an alliance of futurists and war veterans had a certain logic within an avant-garde culture that had come to identify modernity with war and regenerative violence. Yet in the wake of the armistice, the mood of confidence and exhilaration that had prevailed when that equation was first proposed earlier in the decade had given way to one of doubt and anger. How was it exactly that Italy had won a victory in this war? Victory for whom and for what? For big capitalist firms and war profiteers, who had made fortunes? For the *imboscati,* who had spent the war in the comfort of their homes? Perhaps there was yet another war to be waged to ensure a true victory and not a "mutilated" one.[75]

One of those young Florentines who would soon be loudly raising such questions and threats, but who remained with his army unit in Albania until the middle of 1919, was Umberto Banchelli. It is difficult to learn much about this obscure figure beyond the fact that he had a brief correspondence with Prezzolini in 1923 after the latter had given his memoirs on the early days of Tuscan fascism a favorable review.[76] But the book is one of the best documents we have on those events as well as on the mentality that prevailed in them. This is how it begins:

> Our war of 1915 against the German Empires was the first national war a unified Italy had fought since the fall of the Roman Empire 1,600 years before. It should have been the historical cementing of our spirit and the complete material unification of our lands, the fulfillment after centuries of the desires and efforts of martyrs, thinkers, and unknown heroes. Dante's mission. It should have been the manifestation of the material and moral force of those social and political classes who for fifty years have arrogated to themselves the right to lead, without any possibility of challenge from those with different ideas. It should have been the final examination for our legislators, lawyers, teachers, professors, thinkers, philosophers, materialists, and pseudo-idealists; first the baptism of fire, then the consecration before sacred fire of our glory and the death of a whole period of social-democratic literature and its authors. Teachers and disciples should have been able to march, renewing the glories of Achilles and the conquests of Caesar. Instead what happened, first with the neutralism of 1914, then from 1915 to 1918, and finally from 1918 to the international conference at Geneva, is well known . . . The internal enemies, by means of their poisonous propaganda, have taken Truth and Nation and prostituted them to the gold of various external Lenins and internal eunuchs.

And it was to rooting out those internal enemies, overthrowing the political class that had allowed them to flower, and dismantling "the whole system that governs us" that, Banchelli believed, he and his fascist comrades were dedicated.[77]

In Banchelli's view, then, fascism was a movement to right the wrongs of the war years, to achieve the moral regeneration that the war should have brought to fruition but that, instead, it had squandered shamefully. While it is not clear who may have had direct influence upon his ideas, the mark of both Prezzolini and Papini upon them—from the idea of the war as a moral "final examination," to the rhetoric of the "internal enemy," to the concept of the "political class" and the idea that the war experience was an indictment of the entire Italian "system"—is not hard to divine. That is a point to which we shall return. But what was most typical about his view was an element he probably derived from them only indirectly (through the rhetoric of the internal enemy), and that was the tendency to blame the disappointments of war and the ills of Italian society upon those Italian-socialist "eunuchs" who followed "external Lenins."

As the Florentine *fascio* made its first moves into the piazza during the fall and winter of 1918–19, it almost invariably chose socialist rallies as their setting. Thus, as Rosai recalled in 1922:

[Our] first battle was fought and won in November 1918 in the Piazza San Gallo. There had been a leftist political meeting there that day presided over by Pescetti and Pieraccini and involving 8,000 participants. Our minuscule band [of 13] went in there with a big flag, a megaphone, and lots of faith in our hearts . . . Having arrived in San Gallo, we sat down under the "arch of triumph" and at the right moment, at the signal of our leader, Enrico Rocca, we slashed our way without hesitating [shooting off revolvers in the air and swinging sticks] in the midst of the crowd of brutes who, terrified, tried to save themselves by fleeing. Their leaders were the first to sneak away, and the followers did not lose much time in falling in behind them despite their aching ribs.[78]

Yet despite the braggadocio, Rosai's "minuscule band" made little impact during the "red years" of 1919 and 1920 on a city that was very much at the center of the Italian socialist movement. Even by the time of the first fascist congress, held in Florence in October 1919, Rosai could reckon the membership of the local *fascio* at only sixty.[79]

The one bright spot on the horizon for Tuscan fascism in 1919 was the organization that spring of an Alleanza di Difesa Contadina (Peasant Defense League), the membership of which (according to Banchelli's estimate) soon reached 25,000.[80] Yet while it is certainly true that Tuscan fascism would become dramatically more powerful as it radiated out into the countryside, it is very unlikely that Banchelli's estimate is accurate for 1919 or that any such number could truly be counted as supporters of fascism before the spring of 1921. A better indication of the movement's early support is that, in the parliamentary elections of November 1919, the fascists failed to win a single seat regionally or nationally. Even in Milan, Mussolini's movement managed to get only 5,000 votes, less than 2 percent of the electorate.

Between the election and the next fascist congress of May 1920 in Milan, Tuscan fascism underwent considerable change. Almost all the futurists—including Settimelli, Chiti, Carli, and the Nannetti brothers—defected that spring, in part because of what they perceived as a conservative drift in Mussolini but also, and just as importantly, because they themselves had grown weary of the messiness of actual politics and anxious to return to the uncompromising world of pure culture.[81] Taking the place of the *Italia futurista* group was a new and more sinister (often gangsterish) element typified by Amerigo Dùmini, an Italian-American who had come to Italy as a war volunteer, drifted into Florence from the Albanian front with Banchelli, and then worked as a leader of its emerging "squadrist" underworld. In 1924 he would be responsible for the most famous political murder in postwar Italian history, that of the socialist deputy Giacomo Matteotti.[82]

In 1920 Dùmini spent much of his time preaching his political gospel from Florentine street corners. As part of his performance he would ask passersby in threatening tones, "Are you Italian?" and then pin a miniature tricolor flag to their shirts where a socialist red carnation had been, or might otherwise be. He also edited a journal called the *Sassaiola fiorentina* (Florentine Volley of Stones), to which Agnoletti, Rosai, and Soffici contributed, and which appeared irregularly from 1920 until 1923.[83] Occasionally he even sent articles to *Il Popolo d'Italia*.[84] The role for which he was best known, however, was that of the paramilitary *squadrista* who, beginning with an attack in the agricultural center of Montespertoli in October 1920, led an increasing number of "punitive expeditions" in which buildings identified as "socialist" were trashed or burned and their occupants terrorized and, not infrequently, killed. Dùmini called his squad "Me ne frego"—the "I don't give a damn" squad—a nickname that recalled a common soldier's refrain from the war but that derived ultimately from a famous bit of Papinian rhetoric in *Lacerba*.[85]

The immediate context for the rise of Tuscan *squadrismo* was the rapidly deteriorating labor situation in the spring and summer of 1920. Agricultural strikes had run at five times the prewar level in 1919; they doubled again in 1920.[86] Industrial labor disputes were rising at a similarly breakneck pace and would reach their apex in September 1920 when the famous "occupation of the factories" was declared across the nation. In Florence, tension reached the breaking point on August 10, when an army ammunition dump was blown sky-high, killing ten people. "Socialists" were suspected of having started the fire that set it off. Then, on August 29, came "tragic Sunday," when the city police chief was shot dead during efforts to quell rioting in which three young workers also lost their lives. As a result, a general strike was declared, and this then merged seamlessly into the factory occupation that began on September 2.

For the entire month of September, as the red flag flew over every factory in Pignone, Rifredi, and Sesto Fiorentino, as well as throughout the older working-class quarters of Santa Croce and San Frediano, fear blanketed the rest of the city. One young fascist recalled: "My father told me, 'We have reached the end, Mario,' there is no longer any hope, they have occupied the plants, the worker soviets are already functioning, they have placed armed pickets in the workshops as if another state had already taken over, and the disorganization of the government has reached new heights."[87] The *squadrismo* that followed in October, and that continued unabated in 1921—even after police opened fire on the *squadristi* at Sarzana in July, killing eighteen—was very much a reaction to the September drama, a retribution for what many on the left would later regard as their failure to outlast the government by carrying the factory occupation through to the bitter end.

In many cases, the attacks were direct reprisals for socialist victories. Thus, the expedition to Montespertoli had followed a day of municipal elections in which socialists had won impressively, and similar attacks soon followed socialist victories in the working-class quarters of Florence, in nearby towns such as Empoli and Scandicci, and as far away as Pisa, Volterra, and even Perugia. But at other times the attacks seemed almost randomly timed. On the last Sunday in February 1921, a bomb was thrown into a procession of liberal students as they approached the Piazza dell'Unità, where they intended to place flowers on the monument to those who had died fighting for Italian independence. Two people died, and twenty or more were injured. Later the same day fascist gunmen approached the socialist union leader and editor Spartaco Lavagnini as he was working in his office, shot him at point-blank range, and left a lighted cigarette dangling from the dead man's mouth.

Over the next few days the city moved to the brink of civil war as one socialist Casa del Popolo was burned down, barricades were rapidly thrown up in working-class quarters, and fighting ensued that killed fifteen and wounded more than a hundred. To bring the violence to an end, the authorities ultimately broke the socialist barricades with tanks and other armored vehicles. Clearly, the fascist tactic had been to ignite atavistic fears, both among the authorities and in the general population, and by nearly every measure they were strikingly successful. Whereas in March 1921 only about 500 Florentines were identified as fascist by the national party, two months later the figure had leaped to 6,353. And a year later, after a similar springtime growth spurt, the number would soar to 20,880. Similarly, whereas only about 3 percent of Italian fascists were Tuscan in March 1921 (out of a national population in which Tuscans represented 8 percent), by May 1922 Tuscany had 16 percent of the national total and Florence had become second only to Bologna as a leading center of urban fascism in Italy.[88]

Despite these dramatic increases of support, however, Tuscan fascism never became anything like a mass movement. Even with 50,000 members in May 1922, the movement had less than 2 percent of the region's population. Nor were its recruits held together by social or political background. On the contrary, they came from every class and from among liberals, Catholics, futurists, monarchists, D'Annunzians, anarchists, republicans, masons, and socialists. While to some extent this was true everywhere in Italy, Tuscany lacked the large groups of *braccianti* (agricultural wage-laborers) that gave coherence to fascist recruitment in other core areas of support such as Emilia-Romagna. As historians of the subject have suggested, that is probably why Tuscan fascism was more dependent than its counterparts elsewhere on urban elements such as artisans, the unemployed, and criminals; why it was among the most violent fascist movements in Italy; and why it was so dependent for its success on the complicity of the local authorities, who not only looked the other way but even supplied the *squadristi* with arms.[89]

Yet there is one further implication in the fact that Tuscan fascism was an eclectic and minoritarian movement, an implication that is still more important from the vantage point of this book. Although its *squadrismo* was undoubtedly rooted in the social reality of a potential socialist takeover, Tuscan fascism had always drawn considerable energy from the idealism of the intellectuals in its midst, and, like the interventionist movement in Florence in 1915, it was both stimulated and legitimized by the tradition of violent rhetoric that it inherited from Florentine cultural avant-gardism. Thus, even though the former members of the *Italia futurista* group dropped out of the *fascio* by mid-1920, they had provided it with important direction during its crucial first year and a half. And even though many non-intellectuals became central to its leadership over the next two years, Rosai and Agnoletti remained central players in the *fascio* throughout the years of fascist ascendancy. Indeed, disillusionment did not strike Rosai until the Matteotti murder of June 1924, and Agnoletti continued even after that as a leader in the effort to promote a "second wave" of revolutionary idealism within the fascist movement. Their continued presence at the center of Florentine fascism attests that it was in many ways the fruit of a tradition of avant-garde activity and rhetoric that stretched back from their own roots in *Lacerba* to the days of *Leonardo*.

Another figure who is indicative of this unbroken tradition and who, like Agnoletti, was central to the Tuscan "second wave" was a young intellectual from Prato named Kurt Erich Suckert, who would later become famous in Italy as the novelist Curzio Malaparte.[90] On September 20, 1922, just five weeks before the March on Rome, Malaparte took out formal membership in the Florentine *fascio*. Then twenty-four, he was already experienced well beyond his years and was fast becoming the most important single individual to carry the Florentine avant-garde tradition into fascism.

In the words of Ugo Ojetti, Malaparte was "a handsome young man with shining black hair, black eyes, and long black eyelashes that appeared artificial, a young man of intelligence, nimble, well-dressed, and self-confident."[91] As a high-school student in 1914, he had occasionally gone to the Giubbe Rosse with his favorite teacher, Bino Binazzi, a poet and sometime contributor to *Lacerba*. There he had met Papini and Soffici. Rebelling against the control of his father (a German immigrant who worked in Prato as a master dyemaker), he had run off to the Argonne region of France in February 1915 to fight with the *Garibaldini*. Once Italy intervened in the war, he had joined the fighting along the Piave River, but he returned with his Italian unit to France in the spring of 1918. After the war he first went to Belgium as an aide to an Italian general, and then, with the Italian diplomatic corps, to Warsaw. While in Eastern Europe, his adventuresome spirit also took him to the revolutionary sites of Berlin and Budapest. Almost as if they were also part of some grand tour, he also made brief stops at the University of Rome and at the Sorbonne in these years, although he was too busy with his own projects ever to contemplate earning a degree.

In his first book, written in 1920, Malaparte took up Prezzolini's thesis that Caporetto had amounted to a "labor strike" by Italy's peasant soldiers. Unlike Prezzolini, however, he aggressively pursued the image of a rising "second Italy" in an effort to make it useful to the fascist movement. But by the time the book was published in 1921, its message had become anathema to a fascist movement that was becoming more and more conservative as it sought to gain more power within the existing system, and the book created a major scandal among fascists. When Malaparte brought the book out again in 1923, he changed the title from *Viva Caporetto* to *La rivolta dei santi maledetti* (The Revolt of the Damned Saints) and tried to give it a more conservative coloration. In this regard he was aided by Soffici, who added a vituperatively right-wing preface. Very likely the name change to Malaparte, which followed shortly thereafter, was also an attempt to silence fascist attacks on him by making him appear more Italian and by avoiding possible associations with Germany and Judaism.[92]

In *Viva Caporetto* Malaparte showed himself to be no less the populist than Agnoletti or Rosai, and although he recognized that the revolt had been too anarchic and undisciplined to succeed, he did not draw the élitist implications from Caporetto that Prezzolini did. It was Malaparte's populism that appears to have led him into the fascist movement and to have made him into a fervent *squadrista* once he was in it.[93] It also stood at the center of his understanding of the March on Rome. Indeed, the man whom Piero Gobetti would soon call "fascism's mightiest pen" provided one of the most lyrical celebrations of fascist populism ever written when, as a member of the Tuscan delegation that took part in the March on Rome, he described the entrance of the various "black legions" into the city:

> We were "the provinces." We had risen up against Rome. We had brought our dead, Giovanni Berta with his hands cut, Annibale Foscari with his open abdomen, Dante Rossi with his head cut off, all our dead on our backs, from Lombardy, from the Veneto, from Romagna, from Tuscany, from Umbria, from Abruzzo, from Campania, to Rome, into Rome, into the inner rooms of Roman houses. With wooden crosses high over the black people. With long rods like pikes or prods. With black banners . . . People from the earth, children of the earth, the most ancient generation of the earth, humble masters of the earth, of all our land, all our fields, all our stones, all our meadows, our woods, our rivers; eaters of earth, drinkers of rivers, rustic people mystical and fierce, a peasant people, a warrior people, a people of executioners, a people of combatants. Children of the earth, natural generations carrying out justice, thirsty for justice, in the name of God, *in nomine Dei, in nomine Virginis, in nomine Sanctorum omnium,* in the name of all the saints, solitary saints, healing saints, peaceful saints, warrior saints, avenging saints. The cross and the knife . . . And Rome there in the distance, absolutely white in the reflected light . . . Rome, with the statues of its warriors, its Caesars, its legislators, martyrs, saints, and prophets, immobile and dramatic in the changeless serenity of its ancient ambience. Rome, resounding with fountains, the rushing waters for which arrived from the country by aqueduct and underground channel, felt an immense and profound pressure from under the pavement of its streets, the stones of its *piazze,* and the floors of its churches, as the identical, heavy steps of the black Legions beat their rhythm on the roads of the Consuls.[94]

Unlike Soffici, who had pictured himself at the front sharing center stage with his fellow officers while the common soldiers were mere spectators, and even more unlike Prezzolini, Malaparte imaged himself as just another participant in a secular-religious procession of fascist peasants entering Rome to reinvigorate an ancient imperial civilization. For Malaparte at that moment, there was no doubt that the "cultural renewal" of Italy was finally at hand.[95]

Modernism and the Postwar "Recall to Order"

Prezzolini was also in Rome on those fateful days at the end of October 1922. He had been living there for most of the war and postwar period and, because of the spiraling postwar inflation, had recently taken a position as a correspondent for the Foreign Press Service of New York.

In this capacity he undoubtedly watched the ragtag brigades of black-shirts who paraded for six hours past the Palazzo del Quirinale on October 31 and then moved on to Mussolini's hotel to hail the new prime minister. But he certainly did not take part in it, and in his diary entry for that day he confessed that the event left him "perplexed." "I see very clearly the cowardice and the mental and moral impoverishment of those who oppose fascism. I recognize the youth of fascism and the possibility of beginning something new without having the old cliques to please . . . On the other hand, fascism is coarse and uncultivated; it runs roughshod over liberty and threatens disasters in foreign policy. Overall, then, I don't feel I can take a clear-cut position."[96]

The private thoughts of Soffici and Papini during the March on Rome have left no comparable traces. Although Soffici's writings of the time make clear that he backed the event with enthusiasm, he remained at home in Poggio a Caiano and went to Rome only two months later to work on some of the new fascist journals that were founded in the wake of the movement's coming to power.[97] His continued enthusiasm for the early days of the regime led him to remain in Rome for much of the next year and a half. Papini, however, appears to have been relatively un-moved by fascism's arrival in power. At the time of the March, he had just returned to Florence from Bulciano, where he had spent most of the summer and fall at work on his sections of a "dictionary of the savage man"—an ironic guide to the ruralist Catholic culture he now shared with Giuliotti, the book's coauthor.[98]

Would Papini, Prezzolini, and Soffici have recognized their own prewar modernist rhetoric of cultural renewal in Malaparte's hyperbolic image of a triumphal funeral procession of peasants demanding justice before an ancient imperial throne? That is a complex question that must be answered somewhat differently in each individual case, but it will prove useful to bear it in mind as we consider their various postwar cultural itineraries.

Papini's conversion to Catholicism in the spring of 1918 was clearly the decisive event that shaped the rest of his life, and it had intellectual consequences that ultimately turned him against both avant-gardism and modernism and deepened his disenchantment with contemporary politics of every ideological hue. Yet these consequences were not immediate. That Italy had fought the war on the side of the French culture he had always so deeply admired, and that their joint forces appeared increasingly likely in 1918 to emerge victorious, produced for him a new dream. As he wrote in June, "Italy and France, already bound by an alliance that will not end with the war, ought to become leaders of . . . [a] Latin superstate. They ought to attract Spain, Portugal, and Belgium to their side and create [a new economic and political union of] Western Europe in opposition to Central Europe."[99]

This dream of a new "Latin superstate" led Papini to launch *La Vraie Italie*, a monthly he hoped would refurbish the cultural prestige of a victorious Italy for the French. As its title suggests, the journal was written wholly in French and, though produced in Florence, was to be distributed primarily to French subscribers. Its intention, as expressed in its maiden issue of February 1919, was to "examine, rectify, and refute the writings on Italian matters that are produced for foreign consumption," to be "an intellectual guidebook for the Italy of today, that is, for a country whose true spirit is no less unknown to foreigners than those of China or Brazil."[100] In a sense, then, *La Vraie Italie* simply reversed the formulas of the prewar *La Voce* and *Lacerba*. Rather than import French culture for the edification (or titillation) of Italians, it aimed to inform the French about Italian cultural developments that deserved their serious attention. Yet in making this reversal, Papini abandoned all modernist notions of providing civilization with renewed cultural foundations and set his sights more modestly on defending the Italian culture that already existed in order to enhance his nation's prestige within Europe.

Just before the first issue appeared, Papini had written to Prezzolini in Rome, apparently in hopes of interesting him in the enterprise and luring some contributions.[101] But Prezzolini was suspicious of it as a potential new *Lacerba*, and he not only declined to contribute but declared in his diary that "I have split . . . from Papini and Soffici, in silence about the most intimate things. I go toward the unknown."[102] As these words suggested, Soffici did participate in *La Vraie Italie*—Papini even declared them jointly responsible for it in the first issue—but their collaboration proved difficult. For while Papini's aims for the journal made him take a rather cool and objective stance, Soffici was interested in using it to promote the avant-garde goal of a new moral environment of *italianità*. When D'Annunzio and his troops took Fiume that September, the action symbolized for Soffici precisely what he was after, while for Papini it was a "betrayal" of Italy's "universal and human spirit." Bitterly, Papini complained to him that "your political simplemindedness has become passion and fanaticism," and he concluded that it had therefore become "useless to continue" their collaboration.[103] On the same day he wrote to Prezzolini about Soffici that "you can't reason with him: I tried to write him about D'Annunzio, and instead of responding to my arguments he put forward a creed."[104]

After the October issue, *La Vraie Italie* would appear only one more time, in May 1920. Yet Papini's differences with Soffici were not the only

11. Papini with his daughters, Gioconda (left) and Viola, in 1921, shortly before publication of his *Storia di Cristo.*

reason for its demise. Just as significant was the fact that it had never reached its targeted audience. As Papini admitted when he bade his readers farewell, three-quarters of them had been Italian.[105] Moreover, his attention was being increasingly diverted from the journal by a project that he regarded as more important and that would certainly prove more rewarding. This was the *Storia di Cristo,* a book on which he had been hard at work since August and that, after its appearance in an Italian edition in 1921, would be translated into more than twenty languages in order to meet a worldwide demand.

Ironically, in view of its commercial success, *The Story of Christ* contained a polemic against capitalism that was so deeply embedded as to suggest that modern civilization as a whole had been a tragic mistake. Papini's Jesus was a simple rustic, a carpenter who worked with wood before he became a "workman of the spirit," and who regarded the "trades of the peasant, the mason, the smith, and the carpenter . . . as those most infused with the life of man, the most innocent and religious. The warrior degenerates into a bandit, the sailor into a pirate, the merchant into an adventurer, but the peasant, mason, smith, and carpenter do not betray, cannot betray, do not become corrupt." That was why Jesus "took his language from the country," why "he almost never used learned expressions, abstract concepts, colorless and general terms," and why Papini, too, took pride in having written his book "almost entirely in the country, and in a remote and untamed country."[106]

For Papini, Jesus was the creator of a new culture based on "love," a value unknown in the ancient world. His only aim was to "transform men from beasts to saints by means of love." His command to "love your enemies" was an effort to "remake the whole man, to create a new man . . . to extirpate the most tenacious center of the old man." But Papini's Jesus certainly did not counsel turning one's other cheek toward the demonic forces of money ("the Devil's dung") and commerce. "Jesus is the enemy of the [material] world, of the bestial life of the many . . . He was born to change the world and to conquer it . . . to drive Satan from the earth as His father drove him from heaven." For Jesus, "business— that modern god—is a form of theft," and "a marketplace is therefore a cave of obsequious brigands, of tolerated robbers."[107]

Reading Papini's *Story of Christ*, it is difficult to escape the impression that the modern world had arrived at a stark and terrifying choice between continuing with the self-destruction and self-abasement of its materialist civilization or returning to the "savage" roots represented by the original Christian vision. In his introduction to the book, Papini recalled the "nineteenth-century" devotion to creating secular religions—"the religions of Truth, the Spirit, the Proletariat, the Hero, Humanity, Nationalism, Imperialism, Reason, Beauty, Nature, Solidarity, Power, the Act, Peace, Pain, Pity, the Ego, the Future," as well as those specific to "Freemasons, spiritualists, Theosophists, occultists, and scientists." But he argued that these "religions for the irreligious" (a notion that Prezzolini had deployed positively in his *Words of a Modern Man*) were but "frozen abstractions" that could not and did not "fill the hearts that had renounced Jesus." That was why Christianity, which had never been "expelled from the earth either by the ravages of time or the efforts of men," was still an active choice.[108] It remained only to be seen whether modern civilization as a whole could recognize its error and return to the true way.

For Papini, then, the embrace of Christianity was also the recognition that his own earlier secular-religious wanderings—in pragmatism, futurism, a religion of nature, and elsewhere—had been inadequate, and that modernist attempts to renew culture on a secular basis would necessarily fail even if they managed to reach primal depths in human nature and experience. Moreover, while the choice posed by Christianity in the modern context was a profoundly political one, its dimensions were such as to dwarf even the political concerns with which he had begun *La Vraie Italie*. In the same letter to Prezzolini in which he complained of Soffici's political fanaticism—a letter written after he had spent six weeks of nearly uninterrupted work on *Storia di Cristo*—Papini confessed that "it has become increasingly difficult for me to become impassioned about what is generally called 'politics.'" In the present context,

> liberty will be sacrificed and diminished, whichever class wins. The intellectuals who become partisans of one or the other side will have steadily less influence in the world. The rich people buy them off when they need them, and the poor distrust them. The most honest ones, like Bissolati and Turati, who try to build bridges, are misunderstood and will have to hide themselves. Excuse all these speeches—things that you know and perhaps think too. Although you, an old Hegelian, probably believe in an immanent justice in history and a series of overcomings toward what is better, I believe that the only overcoming would consist in changing man. If this problem is insoluble, then all the others are as well.[109]

Very likely it was this antipolitical attitude that stood behind the indifference toward fascism that Papini manifested in a 1921 interview with *Il Popolo d'Italia*.[110] Similarly, in the summer of 1922 he wrote in a notebook, "I am thinking about writing an open letter to Mussolini on fascism. I began it, then gave it up."[111] For while fascism, for Malaparte, was certainly an expression of religious need and an effort to create a "new man"—a view that, as we will see, Soffici shared—for Papini it was only the latest in a long line of secular religions that were doomed to fail. Only in the 1930s, after fascism reconciled itself with the papacy and became much more normalized as a regime, would Papini begin to pay it the kind of respect that Malaparte accorded it at the time of its initial triumph.[112] Thus, while it is unclear whether Papini recognized the fruits of his early modernist efforts at cultural renewal in the March on Rome, what is clear is that the question no longer mattered to him, since he now repudiated all secular forms of cultural politics.

Among those who never really accepted Papini's conversion as genuine and who was most dismayed by his attack on secular religion and by the withdrawal from active engagement with the conditions of modern life that his Christianity appeared to represent was his old friend Prezzolini. For, despite all the doubts he had experienced during the war and early postwar years, Prezzolini remained committed to the notion that Christianity was dead and that the modern world could satisfy its spiritual cravings only by pursuing a secular surrogate. As he wrote to Papini in January 1920, it was a pity they had missed each other recently in Florence, since "I would have been pleased to talk again about your attitude toward Christianity—about your conversion, as they say—in order to tell you again that it gives me no satisfaction whatsoever either in itself or with respect to who you are."[113]

Yet even if Prezzolini shuddered at the idea of a born-again Papini, there was no denying that Christianity had finally given his friend the firm and unambiguous self-definition that he had hitherto always lacked. In contrast, Prezzolini appeared to live out the early postwar years in a kind of self-imposed limbo. His connections with Florence had languished as he stayed on in Rome, but he now also removed himself from the center of the nation's cultural and political life. Rather than continuing to work for *Il Popolo d'Italia*, for example, he devoted himself to the more isolated activities of running *La Voce*'s press, which he transferred to the capital in 1919, and writing for a foreign audience for whom his articles were mere reportage.

A good indication of the convictions Prezzolini held in early 1920 is provided by the preface to a short book he wrote on the postwar political situation.[114] It opened with a very chastened appraisal of what one could hope for on the Italian scene. Efforts by intellectual critics to press the nation for reform had become useless. The best one could do would be to ally with the few like-minded critics one might find and then "separate yourselves from the rest of the country, rather than get dragged into a sterile act of protest or an unequal struggle that would probably drain even those forces of enthusiasm and renewal that exist in a minority." In effect, Prezzolini was embracing the kind of disengagement from cultural politics that, back in the days of *Leonardo* and *La Voce*, he had criticized so harshly in the older generation of D'Annunzian aestheticists, like those of *Il Marzocco*.

Yet if "remaking the Italians" was doomed to failure, perhaps there was some room for hope at the "supranational" level of culture and politics. "Humanity, unsatisfied by the egoisms of state and nation, is moving toward new solutions. The national problem is not the principal one today, and, above all, it is not the key problem. National problems can be solved only by adopting a sincerely supranational vision." Yet when Prezzolini then turned to articulate the principal problems that a supranationalism would need to address, the possibility of "new solutions" appeared to fall into a huge abyss between the utopian hope of a league of nations and the present futility of more localized action. For humanity's greatest problem remained the lack of spiritual principles upon which to base a modern culture. "It is said that this war represented the failure of the democratic ideologies, but I would say rather that it represented the failure of every ideology and every ideal." Short of a utopian solution, all "we can do that is both possible and relatively sensible is the patient and humble work of trying to sublimate as much as possible, of debarbarizing, intellectualizing, making conscious and refined that necessary explosion of barbarity that has been called, perhaps, to bring us all up for air and cure us of too much civilization."

Despite his great pessimism, then, Prezzolini's counsel was precisely the opposite of Papini's Christian "savagery." For him there was no "sensible" choice other than to press on with the project of creating a viable form of modern cultural life, while also—as Freud would argue a decade later in *Civilization and Its Discontents*—acknowledging the strains that recent experience had made evident and seeking to sublimate them in ways that would be both psychically satisfying and socially fruitful. In this sense Prezzolini's modernist faith persisted, even as he rejected his earlier avant-gardist methods of acting upon it. Not surprisingly, this did not prove a happy combination.

Much as Prezzolini might have wished to escape his immediate Italian context in supranationalist flights of fancy—or, as he put it in another place, by becoming a "good European"—he was in fact unable to avoid reflecting upon the cultural renewal that in his judgment Italy still desperately needed but to which he now felt incapable of contributing.[115] In 1921 he published a bitterly ironic pamphlet on the cultural "code of Italian life" which, in contrast to the book on Italian culture that he and Papini had coauthored in 1906, offered no hope of "intellectual and moral reform."[116] According to his new analysis, the citizens of Italy could be divided into two categories—"the *furbi* [clever ones] and the *fessi* [fools]." While their membership might change, the possibility of eradicating them altogether was nil. For the *furbi* were *furbi* precisely in the sense that they pursued their personal advantage at the expense of the community ("what belongs to everyone—offices, the furnishings in them, railway cars, libraries, gardens, museums. . .—belongs to no one"), and the *fessi* were too *fessi* even to notice, let alone to force a constructive change.[117]

Moreover, it was not easy for Prezzolini to escape his avant-garde past. The younger generation of intellectuals who had grown up as admiring readers of *La Voce*—men like Gobetti and his communist friend Antonio Gramsci—continued to press him for an activist solution to Italy's postwar crisis. Thus Gramsci invited him to speak to a group of Turinese workers in 1921, and Gobetti demanded his contribution to the *La Rivoluzione liberale*, the journal he edited in Turin a few doors down from Gramsci's *L'Ordine nuovo*.[118] But when Prezzolini finally responded to Gobetti's prodding in the fall of 1922, the most hopeful idea he could come up with was for the establishment of a "società degli apoti"—literally, a "society for those who do not drink"—to which those intellectuals who were critical of both fascism and bolshevism might devote themselves. To Gobetti the suggestion smacked of scholasticism and privatism. It amounted to a pitiful admission of defeat.[119]

Yet what Gobetti and other antifascist activists in the younger generation saw as Prezzolini's unconscionable aloofness and indifference toward a looming fascist victory was no less rooted in moral and political reflection than were their more outspoken responses. As Prezzolini explained in a letter to Gobetti early in 1923, "fascism is realizing many of our ideas [from the days of *La Voce*], just as Giolitti did with [expanded] suffrage and Sonnino with the war . . . The methods of fascism disgust me. Many of its men are repugnant. But the others on the opposite side are repugnant to me too. The fascists have stirred things up; Giolitti and Nitti did not take risks and exercise will the way they do. They have their defects. But what about the others? *Who is better than they are in Italy?*"[120] In short, Prezzolini refused to forget that he had spent much of his early adult life railing against the failures of Italian liberalism in power, and since he recognized that Mussolini's fascism was a legitimate heir to his own earlier avant-garde modernism, he believed it would be hypocritical for him now to condemn it and embrace its liberal critics.

In light of this attitude, it seems likely that Prezzolini would have recognized his prewar ideal of cultural renewal in Malaparte's description of the March on Rome, even if he had become too much the skeptic to participate in any such secular-religious observance. Indeed, even in the wake of the Matteotti murder and Mussolini's assumption of dictatorial powers in early 1925, Prezzolini refused to repudiate fascism or to deny that he and his fellow prewar avant-gardists were in no small measure responsible for its existence. Thus, despite the fact that the "counter-manifesto" of the antifascist intellectuals was written in 1925 by Croce—the thinker for whom he continued to have the highest regard—he not only refused to sign it but treated it as simply a competing "mythology" to the one Gentile had proposed in his "Manifesto of the Fascist Intellectuals."[121] This was undoubtedly a convenient position, since his esteem for Gentile and (above all) for Mussolini was also very great, but it did rest upon an important conviction. As he argued in an article of May 1925, "many intellectual opponents [of fascism] today forget that fascism was created in May 1915. In reality, *fascism was born with the war, is a natural child of the war, which, like the Risorgimento, was desired only by a minority.* Only those who opposed the war have the moral right today to oppose fascism, while those who wanted the war either ought to accept fascism, seeking to actualize through it as many ideas useful to the country as possible, or they ought to stand aloof from the partisan battle and contribute only where they can do something useful without assuming political responsibility."[122]

In fact Prezzolini himself took neither of the latter two roads but chose rather to avoid the continuing pain of facing them—and perhaps also to do penance for the overblown quality of his prewar rhetoric—by going into exile. In the fall of 1925 he moved to Paris, where for the next four years he would head the press section of the Institute of Intellectual Cooperation (one of the agencies of the League of Nations); and late in 1929 he moved on to New York, where he joined the faculty of Columbia University. But despite his distance from the regime in Italy, he continued to insist upon his own personal responsibility for it, even to the point of admitting that "everything I did in Florence after 1908" was "a great error and a vain effort."[123] Thus, when in March 1928 Soffici published an article that attacked Prezzolini's politics as "naive and bumbling" but also acknowledged their joint responsibility for the advent of fascism, Prezzolini responded with enthusiasm.[124] "You have put things properly and I am grateful to you. You know what I think about what I did [in prewar Florence]: it amounted to nothing, and I therefore take dispassionately—even as a penitence for past sins of pride—all the condemnations and ostracisms."[125]

In the same letter to Soffici, Prezzolini included a copy of one he had received from Mussolini in November 1914, in which the latter had invited him to join *Il Popolo d'Italia*. At that moment, Prezzolini suggested, when Mussolini was more profoundly in need of new support than at any other time in his political career, "he had turned to all of us on *La Voce*: not to *L'Impero* . . . or to *L'Idea Nazionale*, or to Paolo Orano's *La Lupa*, or to [Massimo] Bontempelli's *Cronache letterarie*." In that sense, "all of us prepared the way for both the good and the bad of today." And, while he and Soffici had never apportioned that "good and bad" in the same way, they were now in full agreement that the Florentine avant-garde they and Papini had founded had played a key role in fascism's prewar cultural origins.

When Prezzolini returned to Florence for a brief visit later that spring, he found Soffici "increasingly critical of fascism," but that was very much a recent departure from what had been, until then, a posture of fervent intellectual support.[126] Indeed, as we have seen, Papini had found him "fanatical" in his postwar politics, and certainly Soffici's early writings on fascism show none of the Prezzolini's doubts about it.[127] Yet if we turn back to 1918, differences between the political standpoints and activities of Prezzolini and Soffici were not very apparent, and one inevitably wonders where to locate the beginnings of the separation between two men who, by their own agreement in 1928, had participated together in the cultural origins of Mussolini's movement.

One of the factors that tied together those Florentine intellectuals like Agnoletti, Rosai, and Malaparte who were strongest in their support for fascism was their populism and self-identification as "men of the people." During the first two and a half years of Italian participation in the war, Soffici clearly did not share this attitude, but there are signs that his perspective may have changed in 1918. For example, in order to rally the spirits of the post-Caporetto Italian army, he had put together in the spring of that year a humor magazine for the troops called *La Ghirba*.[128] Not only do extant photographs of Soffici and his co-workers on *La Ghirba* picture them as a closely knit group spanning ranks and ages, but the journal itself, with its many cartoons, jokes, and ribald dialogues drawn from the daily experience of the common soldiers, could have been produced only by someone who appreciated the popular imagination.[129]

The same impression is conveyed in an article on art that Soffici wrote after a visit to Tuscany in those very same months:

I returned to observe the workers around me. And I recognized that, if the gestures they made while at rest were harmonious, the movements that they made while at work were still more beautiful. There was a rhythm in every one of their movements; evidently it was even a law of an aesthetic nature. He who hammered at stone, he who mixed lime in a barrel and then ladled it over stone, he who shoveled earth and loaded into the wheelbarrow, all acted with order, with care, according to a principle that is not natural but originates in a spirit refined by a long civilizing process . . . Having arrived at this view, I concluded that, since every civilized people had absorbed little by little and put into action the principles of art, all men were destined to become artists over time, and therefore that artistic expression in the proper sense of the word would ultimately become useless and cease.[130]

Of course, Soffici had been interested in the Tuscan peasantry as artistic subject matter since his first trips home from Paris over a decade before, but only now did he begin to shed his contempt for their inferiority as people. Certainly he had never before acknowledged that they were in any sense his artistic equals. In his painting over the next few years, Soffici would not only depict Tuscan scenes but exhibit them as evidence for the proposition that "Mediterranean" civilization was superior to its northern counterparts—including the Parisian one he had been so captivated by in his youth.

By the fall of 1920, Prezzolini was noting in his diary that he and

Soffici "were always arguing, and that what divides us above all is our evaluation of the Italian people." Yet there was at least one other sign that Soffici had been traveling down a political road very different from Prezzolini's for much of the previous year. In his articles for *Il Popolo d'Italia* in 1918, Prezzolini had sharply criticized the traditional liberal ruling class, but he had neither embraced fascism nor castigated its socialist opposition, and his contributions ceased once the fascist movement took off. In contrast, the articles Soffici wrote for Mussolini's paper in August 1919 were full of invective about internal enemies directed not so much against any élite as against a specific segment of the Italian population: working-class socialists.[131] In this respect the articles shared the dominant mindset of the emerging fascist intelligentsia, and although Soffici would not openly declare himself a fascist until 1921, they clearly signaled his departure from the more guarded political views of his two closest Florentine friends. Indeed, as they were written at a time when Papini was privately defending socialist leaders like Turati and Bissolati as "honest" men, it seems likely that Soffici's antisocialist attitude played a role in the crisis of *La Vraie Italie* that September.

Despite the inflation of his rhetoric, however, there is no evidence that Soffici participated actively in Tuscan *squadrismo*. Indeed, there were many outward signs of a new, even "bourgeois," respectability in his life. In June 1919 he had married Maria Sdrigotti, a young woman he met while in Udine with the army, and by April 1920 he was the father of a baby daughter. Moreover, from March through December of that year he devoted himself to producing a new artistic journal called *Rete mediterranea,* which, though not entirely devoid of political content, remained very much above the contemporary fray.

In its four issues, which Soffici compiled single-handedly, *Rete mediterranea* recalled many aspects of his international avant-garde background, such as his associations with Léon Bloy, Rémy de Gourmont, Apollinaire, futurism, and the interventionist movement of 1915.[132] Yet his object was not to revive this avant-garde but to insist that its "intellectual and aesthetic anarchy" had been historically superseded by the more conservative values of contemporary Italian art.[133] As he argued in an "apology for futurism":

We have had even bolder experiences than other peoples have had; and they have had to follow us, imitate us. Europe, France, have taken up the futurist model; they dress themselves according to our fashion magazines. From this moral and practical point of view, we have triumphed. Today, today we can concern ourselves seriously with serious and grand things, without distractions, with our minds free of petty preoccupations. And we can let the others break their necks on the road to the abyss where they have arrived following us, and where we now see them tumbling among their "dadas," while we have stopped to build our own house.[134]

For Soffici, those "artists of talent" like his old friend Picasso, who continued to pursue the avant-garde adventure of the artist as an "other" isolated from these peasant masses, were "happily treading down a false path." The fundamental need of contemporary culture was restorative, and, for that, the best hope was a "retro-garde" art that celebrated the activities of everyday life in the natural world in order to inspire a social and moral "recall to order."[135]

Although Soffici genuinely believed that in the postwar world the old avant-garde had become outmoded while the "retro-garde" had moved to culture's cutting edge, the paradox must nonetheless have come as a shock to all readers old enough to remember his excesses in *Lacerba*. He therefore sought to explain to them in the opening article of *Rete mediterranea* how he

had returned from the war another man . . . At the moment when the war took Europe by surprise, I found myself, along with a certain number of the artists of my generation, in a full boil of ideas and lyrical enthusiasms, which we tried to express in continually new forms with the audacity of a second youth that is more effervescent than the first one. We aimed, then, at the creation in Italy of a new literary and artistic school that would be absolutely modern . . . This was "the period of uncontrolled Dionysian liberty . . . that came just before the storm and seemed to contain a presentiment of it" . . . Today it is no longer necessary to establish what the results of that revolutionary orgy were. It is enough to say that no principle of tradition, no established rule of taste, no standard was found worthy of respect, capable of containing our mad dash, and we therefore came to believe—as Rimbaud had, and perhaps even more than he—that the disorder of our own spirits was sacred . . . But then came the moment of action that we had called for, and from there my trans-formation began . . . Truly, it was not without surprise that I soon noticed a group of people whom I had until then scorned as the paradigm of every idiocy, baseness, vulgarity, and cowardice, and whom I now found beside me as colleagues and superiors and who were quite different from my prior image of them . . . This war taught a lot of us . . . how much humanity, beauty, spontaneity of life and of the senses one can find beyond our artificial bounda-ries among those ordinary but still dignified masses that are almost the whole of humankind and that we had scornfully christened en bloc as "bourgeoisie!" . . . Besides, some of those who had been among my companions at work, people who were supposed to be of a mentality and character similar to mine, men whom I had even considered friends, had participated in the bastardizing and the universal contamination of the spirit. I confess that for me that realization came as a rude shock . . . I began to ask myself if the negation of so many traditional principles, and the proclaiming of an intellectual and aesthetic anarchy that I had delighted in, did not in the end represent an enormous risk . . . That doubt then led naturally to another: . . . that to have so noisily discredited and repudiated those principles [of moral and social order] might have been, in essence, an act of recklessness, a tremendous mistake, committed with the best of intentions certainly, but an error owing to a certain immaturity of judgment and also somewhat to a silly desire to appear courageous and extraordinary.[136]

Still, the irony of a newly married and comfortably "retro-garde" *lacerbiano* was not lost on Prezzolini, who laughed aloud in an article of 1922: "Look at Soffici, who thinks he has become a disciplined and bourgeois man, even though he cannot find a single review, a single journal, a single group with whom he is in agreement, and who is reduced to realizing, as a man, the dream that was always his as a youth, that of a review that is his alone."[137]

It may have been in part to escape this isolation that Soffici became involved, in 1921, with local fascist journals such as the *Sassaiola fiorentina* and, in 1922, with Mussolini's new journal, *Gerarchia*. Yet this collaboration, to which he was sufficiently committed to move to Rome for fifteen months in the first days of the fascist regime, was also a natural outgrowth of the activist spirit that had originally propelled him into Florentine modernism, as well as of his newer commitments to populism and a "recall to order." Of course, it was not clear that all these ideals could be made to cohere, especially since Soffici continued to pursue his own artistic program, the independence of which he jealously guarded. Could one be a member of the fascist movement and also an independent artist? Could a "fascist art" create the conditions for a return to order and yet remain tied to the modernist movement in culture? These were difficult questions both politically and intellectually.

Perhaps Soffici's fullest attempt to answer them was an article that appeared in *Gerarchia* a month before the March on Rome.[138] Essentially, his strategy there was to strike a balance, however precarious, at every fork in the road. Thus, on the one hand, he argued that artists should maintain their individualism: any "political control over the free manifestation of the genius who creates beauty" was out of the question. But, on the other hand, it was also clear to him that no genius who creates beauty could possibly embrace the "vulgar materialist" and "sentimentalist" forms associated with artists of "socialist" inspiration, a standard presumably designed to declare off limits all those still working in the realist and naturalist traditions, as well as to make fascism congenial to those like himself who had been reared in the "spiritual revolutionary" traditions of Italian modernism. Indeed, Soffici's definition of fascism as "a movement aimed at total regeneration," rather than as "a political party," made it virtually coterminous with modernism. Yet how could it be modernist and still effect a return to order? Here Soffici attempted to balance the idea that fascism ought to "love the past and antiquity" with the commitment not to make it "an enemy of modernity." "Fascism, which is a revolutionary movement but not a subversive or extremist one, aims not at a transvaluation of values but rather at their clarification; it does not admit anarchy or arbitrariness but, on the contrary, wants to restabilize and reinforce the law." Thus it should foster an art that is "neither reactionary nor revolutionary, since it unifies the experience of the past with the promise of the future."

For Soffici, then, fascism was something less than a fully modernist "transvaluation of all values," but it nonetheless contained modernist elements. And nowhere was this more true than in its pageantry as a secular-religious movement. In a passage less emotional but no less committed than the description of the March on Rome by his young friend Malaparte, Soffici wrote in *Il Popolo d'Italia* a few days after the event:

> It is no small glory for fascism that it has brought the religious sense into its ceremonies, along with that picturesque touch of theater which so disgusts our more funereal and Quakerish Italians. One sees that the leaders of fascism have profoundly understood the spirit of our race, as well as the usefulness that every kind of liturgical pomp can have and has had. Until now, only Roman Catholicism and the army have known how to captivate the hearts and imaginations of the Italian people in their functions and parades, and thereby blend the souls of the people together in a communion of ardent unity. Fascism, following tradition, renews the miracle of human solidarity around austere and magnificent symbols.[139]

It is necessary to add, however, that although Soffici admired this new religion, he did not practice it with great zeal. In 1925 he dutifully signed Gentile's manifesto, and over the next decade and a half he lent himself to fascism on every ceremonial occasion, including his own induction into the Italian Academy in 1939. But in relation to the activists of the younger generation in Tuscany who created a fascist cultural movement around journals such as Mino Maccari's *Il Selvaggio*, Soffici was mostly just the patron saint who symbolized their continuity with the glory days of prewar Florentine avant-gardism. As one of Maccari's young writers advised in late 1924, with regard to a proposed new "institute or circle

12. Prezzolini, Papini, and Soffici in 1928 at the Caffè Aurora in the hills of Fiesole above Florence.

of Tuscan fascist culture . . . the secret for the success of any such initiative lies in the wisdom of those who would preside over it. And here it is appropriate to mention the name of Soffici, the Tuscan and fascist who ought to be the teacher of all of us and to whom we ought to entrust the guidance of our intellectual movement. Soffici's work is among those that will endure, and his influence on our generation has been extremely great and beneficial."[140]

Though still only in his mid-forties, Soffici had become a grand old man of Tuscan avant-gardism, a fate in many ways shared by his two closest former collaborators in Florence, even if the constituencies for whom they were grand were somewhat different in each case. Indeed, from the vantage point of Mussolini's war in Ethiopia a decade later, which all three men supported with great national pride, the differences between Soffici's fascism, Papini's "savage" Christianity, and Prezzolini's guilt-ridden agnosticism did not appear very great. While Soffici alone had believed in the early years of fascism that it represented the realization of the secular religion he had dreamed of in his youth, he had long since come to recognize that fascism was a regime change rather than a new form of civilization. Moreover, like the others, he had come to believe that his prewar modernist vision was seriously flawed, that the project of "cultural renewal" or a "transvaluation of values" through a revolution in art had failed and would never succeed. Like the others too, he had lived the fascist years in a kind of intellectual exile from the centers of cultural activity in Italy, preferring to cultivate his own private spiritual garden rather than to continue the search for any "great party of intellectuals." Finally, like the others, he took on the somewhat paradoxical attitude of at once rejecting his prewar past and yet spending much of his later years collecting the documents and recording the memories that would immortalize that era in the cultural history of post-independence Italy.

Conclusion

The Cultural Politics of Florentine Modernism

Looking back upon the world of *Leonardo* and *La Voce* from the vantage point of the late 1950s, Prezzolini marveled that it had become a "literary myth" for the "new generations" despite the fact that "the 'success' of those two 'periodicals of ideas' was in their own time rather mediocre and barely sufficient to allow them to last five and nine years with hardships and sacrifices."[1] Yet surely there was much about the avant-garde culture of that Florentine *bell'època* that made perfectly explicable its newly won mythic status. For it was a world that had dazzled with the sheer extravagance of its intellectual aims: to overthrow the reigning culture of scientific positivism, academic stuffiness, and commercial vulgarity—in Prezzolini's words of 1903, that "entire stench of poisonous acid, flabbiness, and vanity" in which he and his generation had been reared; to put in its place nothing less than a new secular religion drawn from the most advanced philosophical thought of the day; to fulfill De Sanctis' vision of "intellectual and moral redemption" by becoming the "torch" that would "burn and brighten" the path to a new Italy; to discard "decadentist" overrefinement and to articulate and live out the moral virtues that would allow primal individuality to be recovered from beneath the dross of a staid and poorly modernized, backwater society. Moreover, all this was conceived by a group of young people who were autodidacts and outsiders in their own city, and who yet dared to take on Paris and to rub shoulders with the likes of Henri Bergson and William James. Their early years may have been "the end of a world," as the title of a volume of Soffici's memoirs had it, or "a remote past" of long Sunday-afternoon walks in the Cascine, as in Papini's related image; but they were also the scene of an extraordinary crusade to force the birth of a new cultural world.

Of course, the extravagant scope of these modernist dreams could become an embarrassment for those who lived out their "transvaluation" in the nightmare of the "great war." There is no reason to doubt the unanimous judgment of the Florentine avant-gardists that they had never known the common people whose cultural lives they had plotted to "renew," until after the débacle their propagandistic efforts helped to foment. They had indeed lived as élitist Jean-Christophes, narcissistic "new aristocrats" who held their fellow citizens in contempt. Their ideals were sometimes almost ludicrously self-aggrandizing, as in the case of the "Italy of the thinkers" Prezzolini had foreseen in 1906. Yet, had they been wrong to laugh at and feel shamed by the steam-powered streetcar they were forced to ride to Poggio a Caiano? Had they not responded to their early spiritual crises by infusing their detached ideals with a dose of native *toscanità?* Had they not taken a serious turn toward genuine social involvement with the early *La Voce?* Had they not made candid reassessments of their early failings in their autobiographies of 1912? Had they not been right to recognize that "when God no longer exists for a people, He will necessarily be rediscovered," and right to try to give real intellectual substance to the form that rediscovery would take?

Moreover, had they not made remarkable progress in creating a new "party of the intellectuals" in a city still living off Renaissance glories and utterly closed to cultural innovation? *Leonardo* was created overnight by a small band of intellectual unknowns; yet only three years later, its editor was being called a "genius" and "the most radical conceiver of pragmatism to be found anywhere" by one of the foremost thinkers in the Western world. True, the journal itself fared less well. It was always more a vehicle for personal soul-searching than the engine for cultural renewal its editors had hoped to make it, but they had recovered within a year of its demise to launch a new journal that met the latter goal with much greater success. Although *La Voce* was not equally satisfying to everyone in its inner circle, it did produce real solidarity among its dozen stalwarts and two dozen more occasional but highly loyal contributors, and it was soon recognized as the most important avant-garde journal in Italy. While that solidarity was broken by disagreements over the Italian involvement in Libya, and then languished in the years of Florentine futurism, it was largely restored during the intervention campaign, the success of which was owed in no small measure to the formidable propagandistic skills of Florentine intellectuals. Moreover, even in the years in which *Lacerba* and *La Voce* merely coexisted, the cultural achievements of the avant-garde that these journals made manifest were quite impressive. Indeed, the division of labor between Prezzolini's high road of philosophical education and *Lacerba*'s low road of irrationalist buffoonery, though certainly unplanned, managed nonetheless to bring Florence a combination of intellectual prestige and cultural notoriety that was quite unprecedented in its recent history.

How are we to account for this explosion of intellectual vitality which, in light of that history, seemed to come almost out of nowhere? Clearly one source lay in the character of Florentine society. The city's old aristocratic élite and its patronizing culture of *moderatismo* had prevented the emergence of anything approaching a civil society, and the changes Florence had undergone in the late nineteenth century had actually moved the city even further away from being a genuine public space. Thus were planted the seeds not only of an avant-garde counter-culture but of a potent working-class opposition and, as would become fully apparent in 1921, a peasant-based opposition as well. Moreover, in resting on its Renaissance laurels, the city's élite had helped to turn it into a mecca for foreigners. Ultimately, this was bound to fuel the resentment of those tired of seeing their city regarded as a "museum" and a "hotel for honeymoon trips" where one heard only the "abominable Anglicized or Frenchified" version of one's language, if one heard it at all. Even in creating a university, the old Florentine élite had been so out of touch with the more advanced currents of European intellectual life that it had cultivated positivism precisely at the time when this outlook was elsewhere declining. In this sluggish, provincial climate, the avant-garde that the Istituto quite unintentionally helped to spawn counterattacked against positivism with ideals of virile self-assertion and spiritual discipline, ideals necessary, in its view, for overcoming the reigning obsession with material well-being and restoring a sense of greatness to the public world.

Yet the shortcomings of the Florentine élite were also in some ways merely indicative of a more general failure in post-Risorgimento Italy. Nowhere in the newly independent nation had there been a serious attempt by public officials to "make Italians." And nowhere was there the kind of grass-roots "nationalization of the masses" that George Mosse has portrayed so vividly in the civic life of nineteenth-century Germany, with its gymnastic and folk-dance groups, male choirs, sharpshooting societies, and the like.[2] This was not, however, because the secular-religious needs such institutions sought to fulfill were absent in Italy, as the emergence of the Florentine avant-garde clearly attests. Rather the fact that few such secular-religious institutions existed in the public world the young Florentines found made them all the more acutely aware of how starved it was for such a "new politics." Their efforts in the years before the war, however narrowly intellectualistic and disconnected from the masses, can be understood as their attempt to create a true national spirit as well as a more spiritual nation. Yet despite their occasionally explicit calls for public festivals and the like—as in the articles by Enrico Ruta and Jean-Richard Bloch that Prezzolini published in 1914—they really did not know how to translate such goals into practice, except of course by plunging Italy into a "great war."

Another source of the vitality of the Florentine avant-garde lay in the increasingly stimulating course of events after 1900, above all the war in Libya, which set ablaze the passions of nationalism and the cult of violence, and created the frenzied atmosphere in which a journal like *Lacerba* could be born and thrive. Yet there was very little in *Lacerba*'s rhetoric that had not already been displayed in *Leonardo,* and it seems only fair to credit the ingenuity of the young Florentines themselves as a primary source of the prestige and notoriety that they would gain. For if the restrictive policies and narrow thinking of both the Florentine élite and its other regional and national counterparts set the context for the emergence of an avant-garde, and if events like the Libyan invasion fueled its development, it was the prescient clarity with which the avant-gardists themselves articulated the public's aspirations to join the cultural mainstream of modern Europe, to invigorate domestic life with new energy and activity, and to meet unsatisfied spiritual needs through war, that best accounts both for the success it achieved at the time and for the mythic status it would attain for later Italian generations.

But of course there were also great shortcomings in the aspirations and activities of the Florentine avant-garde, shortcomings that made it a central cultural building block in the rise and ultimate triumph of Tuscan *squadrismo* and Mussolinian fascism. First and foremost among these shortcomings was the attitude of its participants toward politics. From their earliest days in *Leonardo,* when they attempted to separate its philosophical and spiritual concerns from the more political ones of *Il Regno,* to Prezzolini's *Progetto* for *La Voce,* in which he tried to separate its educational mission from any involvement in real politics, to Papini's "we don't give a damn about politics" in *Lacerba,* they continually swore off overt political activity as if it threatened their intellectual purity. Had they aspired only to the conventional role of reinterpreting the received textual and artistic canon or of merely commenting upon present cultural life in light of that tradition, this would not have mattered. But given that they deployed their inflammatory rhetoric in constant incitements to action, their attitude toward politics could only encourage irresponsibility. For they were able to accuse, criticize, propose, and incite, without the corresponding need to convince potential alliance partners of the importance and feasibility of their ideas and ideals, or to translate them into concrete political programs, institutions, and policies.

The apparent exception to this point, of course, was the decision by both *Lacerba* and *La Voce* in 1914 to press for Italian intervention in the First World War. But it is only apparently an exception, because even though they then pursued a concrete political goal, they merely raised a Sorelian myth rather than seriously reflecting upon the probable domestic effects of an interventionist policy or the wishes of the Italian people. And once those effects and wishes became apparent, they disowned for the most part what they had done. Moreover, although their goal for Italy had in one central respect become politically concrete, they still had no answer to the question of what sort of political institutions and programs the war was supposed to create and what the postwar Italian political order should be. In these respects, they remained as utopian as in the days before August 1914 when they had hoped to forge a new Italy by cultural means alone.

A second shortcoming of Florentine avant-garde culture lay in the rhetoric of the moral virtues that it derived from Carducci, Nietzsche, Weininger, and Rimbaud, and that it deployed as part of an Oedipal revolt against D'Annunzio and decadentism. For this rhetoric not only led the avant-garde to appeal to regenerative violence, misogyny, and war; it also produced other vague and emotionally charged ideals such as Soffici's Rimbaudian "deregulation of sensory experience" and Papini's "masculinism," ideals that in their self-absorption could only further blind them to the concrete social needs of their fellow citizens and the real prospects for meeting them.

Third, although the "militant idealism" of Prezzolini was inspired by quite different sources, its blinding effect was arguably no less or very different. Of all the *vociani*, Prezzolini was always the most insistent and acute on the importance of educating the Italian masses, and on this point he was undoubtedly right. As the best contemporary historians of Italian fascism continue to argue, no structural condition was more important in fascism's rise than the lack of civic consciousness in Italian society and the profound disjuncture between that society and the nation's more advanced parliamentary institutions.[3] But even though Prezzolini was right in his diagnosis, it is hard now to see, removed as we are from the heady days of 1913 and 1914, why he imagined that the philosophical idealisms of Croce and Gentile were the essential basis for educating the Italians. Indeed, it is arguable that the notion that Gentile particularly encouraged—namely, that social problems could actually be resolved at the level of philosophical reflection and, in this sense, that the distinction between theory and practice could be completely collapsed—lay at the heart of Prezzolini's terrible miscalculation about the effects of Italian entry into the First World War.

Finally, another related weakness in Florentine modernist rhetoric was its tendency to descend from the heights of abstractions about secular religions and moral virtues to personalistic political answers—the need for "a man" or for *teppisti* who did not "wear white gloves"—without regard for the more complex intermediate levels of problem-specific and institution-oriented thinking, where genuine answers were more likely to be found. The cultural politics of Florentine modernism involved such a cosmic perspective on the issues being faced that any and all solutions produced by democratic processes of reform were bound to appear to be anemic half-measures. Since a return to "traditional" ways was also judged negatively, the only "true" solutions became "charismatic" ones in which perceived political goods coincided with the spiritual and often psychological needs of the modernists themselves. And it was precisely this combination of philosophical reflection with appeals to charisma that made it so plausible for sincere fascists like Malaparte to believe in 1922 that "the future discipline now in formation," which Prezzolini had foreseen in 1913, had finally arrived.

Of course, not all the Florentine modernists aided the fascist movement or even accepted its arrival in power as legitimate. Indeed, at least one of the central participants in *La Voce*, Giovanni Amendola, played a leading role in the constitutional opposition to the fascist regime. From his position as editor of the antifascist newspaper *Il Mondo* and, beginning in April 1924, as a parliamentary deputy, Amendola led the Aventine Secession after the Matteotti murder, published Croce's 1925 antifascist manifesto, and was generally a thorn in Mussolini's side until he, like Gobetti, died in 1926 from fascist assaults. One thinks too of Guido De Ruggiero, who, though less an activist than Amendola, published his *History of European Liberalism* in 1925, a provocative act of symbolic politics that earned him the wrath of the regime and ultimately cost him a university position. Yet among the *vociani* who did not embrace fascism the more typical response was that of Papini and Prezzolini: remaining aloof. Prezzolini, as we have seen, had a principled justification for his aloofness. Yet even as his postwar disillusionment led him to reverse the activism of his prewar militant idealism, his new stance displayed the same tendency to balk at dirtying his hands in the messy business of an institutionally specific politics. Precisely for that reason it is difficult not to sympathize with those like Amendola and

Gobetti who criticized him for not taking an active role in opposing the fascist state, even if Prezzolini was right to believe that the damage he had done in earlier years to stimulate the fascist movement could not now be very easily repaired.

What all the *vociani* could agree upon in the postwar years was that, in effect if not in intention, they had built the ideological bomb set off by the war and the postwar "red years." We have already seen that Tuscan fascism displayed continuities with the earlier avant-garde both in personnel and rhetoric. But such continuities also existed between Florentine modernism and Mussolini's rhetoric of fascism: the "cultural renewal" and "spiritual revolution" the avant-garde championed was precisely what Mussolini claimed to be carrying out in the 1920s. The difference between the two positions lay not in rhetoric but in the fact that Mussolini was willing to engage in the political action necessary to translate ideals into reality. While to demonstrate this point fully would take us beyond the scope of this book, and even to render it plausible moves us outside the context of Florence, I want now to attempt to do the latter, since it is only by pursuing the connection between the rhetorics of Mussolini and the *vociani* that the significance of Florentine avant-garde modernism can be fully appreciated.[4]

The Rhetoric of Mussolini

We have seen that even in his "socialist" period Mussolini shared many experiences and cultural attitudes with his generational counterparts in Florence and, in particular, their agenda of spiritual and cultural renewal. Yet it was in the four and a half years between his open break with the Socialist Party and his launching of the fascist movement in Milan's Piazza San Sepolcro that this influence became central to his political rhetoric. And it was toward the end of that period that he first explicitly acknowledged, in a letter to Prezzolini, how he had been "made and remade, first by the words of *Leonardo* and then by those of *La Voce*," and how "I am therefore indebted to you for many things."[5]

One of those debts was to the interventionist rhetoric that Prezzolini and Papini had developed before they joined the early *Popolo d'Italia*. Just as Prezzolini had written in 1912 that "war is the general examination to which peoples are called every so often by history, where everything that is healthy, even if hidden, is revealed," so Mussolini now defended Italian entry into the First World War on the grounds that "war is the examination of peoples" in which "they reveal their naked selves."[6] Yet not only did Mussolini's version of the "great war" myth view war as a moral and spiritual test in the manner of *La Voce*, but he also utilized the same overall framework that the writers for *La Voce* had given it: two Italies poised for a confrontation, with the incumbent, decadent Italy understood as an "internal enemy," the real enemy against which war must be waged.[7]

Still more significant, however, was Mussolini's debt to the manner in which the writers for *La Voce*—including Prezzolini, Papini, and Soffici, but also Slataper, Jahier, and Boine—had moved back and forth between, or even fused, an anarchic, risk-taking, and destructive attitude and a more conservative attitude devoted to values such as discipline, work, duty, and order. It is interesting that Mussolini would later claim to have been most influenced by Soffici, Slataper, and Jahier—precisely those in whom this combination was liveliest.[8] Yet, with regard to the former attitude, it was much more to Slataper's vitalism than to Soffici's Rimbaudian style in *Lacerba* that Mussolini's version can be likened; and, with regard to the latter, his greatest debt was clearly to Prezzolini's concept of discipline.

Mussolini's attraction to risk-taking and destruction was a large part of what drew him to Nietzsche, about whose transvaluation of values he wrote approvingly in 1908 that it was the product of "savage egoisms in revolt . . . who find neither limit, nor restraint, nor moderation in the hitherto reigning morality."[9] In the years of the intervention campaign and the war, which he regarded as having the potential for just such a transvaluation, he was fond of spurring his own troops on through hortatory articles with exclamatory titles such as "Audacity!" and "Dare!"[10] In these articles he argued that what was wrong with Italy's political class was precisely its lack of these virtues. "Many of the men who govern us have a static mentality," he wrote toward the end of the war. "They are afraid of novelty. 'Risk' does not attract them. Even the conviction that the war would be brief has 'weighed' on the way in which they have conducted the war."[11] In contrast, during the intervention campaign he celebrated his own "squads of men" as "an organism full of life and capable of living," whose mode of organization not only lacked the "rigidity" of a political party but also allowed them to exploit "the faculty of intuition that grasps the sense and importance of a situation" and to capitalize on their "hatred of the status quo, scorn for 'philistinism,' love of effort, and search for risk."[12]

However, at the same time that he was celebrating his "squads" for their intuition and daring, he was also demanding of them an interior, spiritual discipline that would set an example for the general population. In 1915 he criticized the way the government was using a concept of discipline to support its neutrality, arguing that it had no "right to require the discipline and the silence of Italian citizens" when "the causes of the 'nervousness' of moral indiscipline lie in the political system followed by Italy's rulers . . . To demand the 'discipline' of a people it is necessary to enlighten it."[13] Then, in 1922, as he was about to step into power, he told his fascist *squadristi* that "we have to impose on ourselves the most iron discipline because otherwise we will not have the right to impose it on the nation."[14]

In 1924 Prezzolini tried to separate his own concept of discipline from Mussolini's by claiming that the latter was merely military, while his own was simultaneously personal, spiritual, social, and military.[15] Yet Mussolini's actual use of the concept makes it clear that he was much in Prezzolini's debt, particularly in his emphasis on the spiritual-religious dimension of discipline. This was most explicit in 1925, when he used it to justify his new dictatorship:

> Never in the world has a parliamentary majority, composed largely of sensible, passionate men, like the [present] fascist majority, given such a majestic example of discipline. Here it is clear—like the light of the sun—that the discipline of fascism truly has aspects of a religion. Here is revealed in their unmistakable stigmata the face and soul of a people that learned in the trenches to conjugate, in all its forms and tenses, the sacred verb of all religions: obey! Here is the sign of the new Italy that detaches itself once and for all from the old anarchist and rebellious mentality and intuits that only in the silent coordination of all forces, under the order of a single man, can the perennial secret of every victory be found.[16]

But the spiritual-religious as well as the social aspect of Mussolini's concept of discipline had been fully evident in earlier years.[17] In fact in 1918, a few months after Prezzolini had attempted to spell out in *Il Popolo d'Italia* how "cadres" might be developed to forge discipline in each of society's many institutional arenas, Mussolini indelicately appropriated Prezzolini's concept to meet the concrete problem of the nearly 225,000 reserve officers who were about to be discharged from the army and who were thereby threatened with the loss of the high status and pay to which they had become accustomed.[18] Mussolini's suggestion was that the government supervise their redeployment into new civilian roles in which they could organize the "powerful and inert masses" and make themselves into "the élite of the new aristocracy, of the Italian trenchocracy."[19]

In addition to discipline, Mussolini made many appeals to related values such as order, duty, work, and hierarchy.[20] Indeed, once he was in power he proclaimed that "men are perhaps tired of liberty; they have made an orgy of it. Today liberty is only the chaste and strict virgin for whom the generations of the first half of the last century fought and died. For the intrepid, restless, and hardened young who face the dawn of new history there are other words that exercise a much greater fascination, and these are order, hierarchy, and discipline."[21]

Moreover, all these moral virtues were associated in Mussolini's mind with precisely the same goal that Prezzolini had before the war when he declared that "the spiritually fundamental fact of modern times" was the need to create secular "substitutes for the social, intellectual, and emotional functions carried out until the French Revolution by the church."[22] In 1918 Mussolini proclaimed: "We want the spiritual republic. And the *arditi* should be our pure air, our festive assault, thought with muscles, truth without slippers, religion without the clergy, life without listlessness, death without shame."[23] Two years later he drew out the historical implications of his movement in still grander terms:

> Two religions contend today for dominion over the human spirit and the world: the black and the red. Today their encyclicals come from two Vaticans: the one in Rome and the other in Moscow. We are the heretics of these two religions. We alone are immune to their contagion. The outcome of this battle is, for us, of secondary import. For us the combat has its prize in the combat itself, even if it is not crowned by victory. The world today is strangely analogous to that of Julian the Apostate. Will the "Galileo of the red hair" win once again? Or will the mongol Galileo of the Kremlin win? Will there be a "transvaluation" of all values, as there was in the twilight of Rome?[24]

Clearly, Mussolini himself aimed to bring about such a transvaluation, not only through the religious language of his speeches but also through those political rituals and festivals of public life that, as Bloch had argued in *La Voce*, could alone restore an aura of grand spectacle to an increasingly impersonal world.

By 1922 the theme of a spiritual revolution to restore public life had become perhaps Mussolini's single most important rhetorical appeal.[25] In February he wrote that "spiritual creation of every sort—beginning with religious creations—will move to center stage, and nobody will dare persist in the anticlericalism that has been the favorite democratic occupation in the Western world for so many decades. When we say that God is returning, we mean that spiritual values are returning."[26] And as the moment of the March on Rome approached, Mussolini found himself before the crowd at Udine evoking the image of "one of the world's few cities of the spirit," whose "seven history-laden hills" had witnessed "one of the great spiritual wonders that history records. There an Eastern religion, foreign to us, was transformed into a universal religion that recovered in new form that empire that the consular legions of Rome had driven to the ends of the earth. Now we aspire to make of Rome the city of our spirit, a city purged, cleansed of all the elements that have corrupted and violated her; we aspire to make of Rome the pulsating heart, the active spirit of the imperial Italy of our dreams."[27] Finally, from Naples on the eve of the march, he declared: "We have created our myth. The myth is a faith, a passion . . . Our myth is the nation, our myth is the greatness of the nation! And to this myth, to this greatness, which we want to translate into a full reality, we subordinate everything else. For us the nation is above all spirit and is not just territory . . . A nation is great when it translates the force of its spirit into reality."[28]

So strong was Mussolini's aspiration to make fascism into the new secular religion that would satisfy the spiritual needs of modern society, and so indebted was he to Prezzolini for this notion, that the latter's reluctance to follow him from *Il Popolo d'Italia* into fascism will always remain something of a puzzle. We have seen that Prezzolini considered its methods "disgusting" and "many of its men . . . repugnant," yet also no other group, in his view, was more capable of leading Italy out its postwar crisis. It seems that Prezzolini simply could not make himself accept the idea that his dreams were being realized by *squadristi* even as he recognized that they were his dreams. While neither he nor Papini had been afraid to call for violence in the prewar years as a necessary means of rousing the "second Italy," both of them hesitated to join those who deployed it in the name of the new Italy once the possibility was truly at hand.

We have noted that Mussolini was more politically adept than any of the Florentine avant-gardists, that he took care to make clear to himself who his agents were and what tactics and alliances were necessary for him to achieve his goals. Yet there is a related difference that can be illustrated by the way he deployed Papini's concept of the "internal enemy." In Papini's view, war against an external enemy was the means for overcoming a decadent first Italy, his internal enemy, but he refused to go so far as to advocate war against the internal enemy. From within the same general position, Mussolini simply dropped this inhibition. Just as Prezzolini had taken a step Croce refused, arguing that Italian discipline could be achieved best through war, so Mussolini took a step Papini (and Prezzolini and, it appears, even Soffici) refused, arguing that the discipline of war could be turned simultaneously against the internal enemy. And it was his willingness to proclaim the need for and actually to use violence against an internal enemy that most clearly divided his fascist position from that of the *vociani* with whom he otherwise shared so much.[29]

In essence, then, the key difference between Mussolini and the Florentine avant-gardists had to do with attitudes toward politics and acceptable political means. Much of this difference can be traced to the fact that they were unwilling to become part of a movement that would have forced them to commingle with the uncultured peasant masses, while Mussolini, though far from a true populist, certainly recognized the need for building the popular strength of his movement in order to reach power. Yet it was Prezzolini who, perhaps more than anyone, had encouraged Mussolini to renounce socialism in 1914 and build a movement of "spiritual revolution." Together with Papini and Soffici, he had then aided Mussolini on *Il Popolo d'Italia* until the dawning fascist movement became explicit, and Soffici had proudly continued this association until the late 1920s. Other Florentine avant-gardists such as Agnoletti and Rosai had played still more important organizational roles in early Tuscan fascism. And all of them together, in over a decade of cultural barnstorming, had created the cultural context for fascist ideology before the war. Although some of them were then ashamed to recognize themselves in what they had produced, this shame reflected their political reticence and élitism far more than it did any disagreement over fundamental ideals and goals. Moreover, regardless of their intentions, their creation of a potent rhetoric of cultural renewal ultimately played into the hands of fascism, which, in need of intellectual credibility, appropriated this rhetoric and adapted it to more politically explicit but also more culturally impoverished and dangerous ends.

The Florentine Avant-Garde between Two Worlds

During the war De Ruggiero, who had been active in the "militant-idealist" phase of *La Voce*, wrote that to his great disappointment "none of the great moral forces of humanity . . . raise the tone of the struggle. Ancient religion, which has excited so many idea-forces in its millenarian history, has disappeared from our souls, and no new spiritual force— or new spirit in the old—has been able to substitute for it or revive it."[30] In this sense of being between two worlds, he was echoing a sentiment widespread in the period.[31] Even before the war, Durkheim had lamented that "the old gods are growing old or already dead, and others are not yet born," although he had been relatively sanguine about the prospects of overcoming "this state of incertitude and confused agitation" while maintaining a liberal order.[32] Other intellectuals, especially those like Thomas Mann who lived where liberalism was weaker, located one of its chief deficiencies in the fact that it was too prone to try to "separate religion from politics." Those who have "lost metaphysical religion," Mann recognized in 1915, were apt to put "the religious element into the social sphere," elevating "social life to religious consecration," in spite of liberalism's traditional hostility to such profanation.[33]

After the war, many intellectuals continued to believe that they were witnessing a profound transition between two worlds. Thus Freud wrote to a friend late in 1918 that "these are days of terrible tension. That the old should die is good, but the new is not yet there."[34] And over the next few years the theologian Friedrich Gogarten would conclude that it was the "destiny of our generation to stand between the times . . . in an empty space," while the poet and dramatist Béla Balázs would write that "we are already walking in the shadow of fresh green foliage, but the ground under our feet is still covered with a litter of dry, long-dead leaves."[35] From his prison cell in 1930, Gramsci would famously describe the "modern crisis" as consisting "precisely in the fact that the old is dying and the new cannot be born" and that "in this interregnum a great variety of morbid symptoms appear."[36]

This image was hardly foreign to Papini, Prezzolini, and Soffici, each of whom recognized in his own way how a traditional world based on ancient faiths had come to an end. Indeed, Prezzolini had invoked the image explicitly in his "Words of a Modern Man" when he spoke of the "destruction of the old Catholic discipline" and of a "future discipline now in formation." Moreover, the fact that they oscillated so widely between contradictory imperatives of spontaneity and discipline, will and order—as did Prezzolini with his "Bergsonian" and "Crocean" phases, Papini with his "two souls," and Soffici with his "full boil of lyrical enthusiasms" in *Lacerba* and his postwar "recall to order"—is certainly made more explicable by their perception of a crisis of world-historical proportions.

Yet the fact that this image of crisis was being forged in identical terms by so many of their contemporaries elsewhere in Europe—and from widely varying positions in their respective cultural and political fields— requires us to pause before concluding that the rhetoric of the Florentine avant-gardists was necessarily the cultural concomitant of the rise of a radical right. Might they not have moved to the left instead, had the left not seemed to them so culturally philistine, so threateningly closed off in its working-class ghettos, so unrealistic in its political aspirations, and so devoid of the forceful leadership that would have been necessary for it to gain power? After all, Prezzolini had shown an early interest in syndicalism and had collaborated with Salvemini on the early *La Voce*, Papini and Soffici had been receptive to Bissolati during the war, and the fascist Soffici sometimes expressed admiration for Lenin even as he caustically attacked Italian exponents of Bolshevik ideals.[37]

Moreover, might not their ideas and ideals have been put to use by the left, had the left instead of the right come to power in Italy in the early 1920s? Certainly, as we have seen, there were important Italian leftists such as Gramsci and Gobetti who had been deeply impressed by *La Voce*. It can even be shown that Gramsci appropriated the structure of his moral vocabulary from *La Voce*, that the dialectic of spontaneity and discipline evident in Florentine rhetoric and in Mussolini's was also very much his.[38]

Still, the history of modernist avant-gardism in Florence suggests that its trajectory toward the right was much stronger than any it might have had toward the left. The avant-garde intellectuals of the generation of 1880 in Florence had a hostility toward socialism that was rooted in events they had witnessed in the early years of the century, and their modernist aspirations were bound up from the beginning with a spiritualist conception of nationalism. Deeply rooted too were the élitist convictions that they drew from Pareto and Oriani and that seemed to relegate any notion of a truly democratic order to the historical dustbin. Moreover, their ideas of spiritual, cultural, and moral renewal were always undergirded by an animus against materialism, and this alone disposed them against the notion that a leftist movement could ultimately satisfy modern cravings for meaning. Finally, the Florentine avant-garde had such a deep-seated rhetoric of resentment—against academics and bureaucrats, against feminists, women, and D'Annunzian decadents, against *imboscati* and other internal enemies—and a discourse so frequently inflamed by anger and vituperation that it is difficult to imagine its partisans becoming aligned with people who pursued soft-minded ideals like equality, peace, and cooperation.

Some of the recent literature on the cultural origins of fascism elsewhere in Europe confirms this judgment. In *Rites of Spring*, for example, Modris Eksteins has argued that Nazism was at a "popular level" what the international avant-garde had been at "the level of 'high art.'"[39] This was because Nazism sought to "aestheticize politics" by marrying its irrationalism to an ideal of technical efficiency, turning history into myth, and transforming political institutions and rituals into theater, art, and "grand spectacle." In Eksteins' view, both cultural avant-gardism and Nazism preferred "perpetual motion, vitalism, and revolt" to "rules, platforms, and agendas"; both replaced "ethics" with "action" and attempts "to live dangerously"; and both nurtured an "urge to create" that became an "urge to destroy."[40] Yet all these commonalities could be derived just as credibly from the Florentine avant-garde as from its Parisian counterpart, upon which Eksteins primarily relies.

In studying the connection between modernist avant-gardism and Nazism, Eksteins considers only the anarchic dimension of the former and not its complementary dimension of discipline, which we have found so pronounced in the Florentine case. However, other historians have recently studied this dimension as well, most notably Isaiah Berlin in his effort to trace the intellectual origins of fascism to Joseph de Maistre.[41] What allows Berlin to make this apparently tenuous historical link is de Maistre's insistence on the need to exterminate "enemies" as well as on precisely whom he counted as enemies: "Protestants and Jansenists . . . deists and atheists, Freemasons and Jews, scientists and democrats, Jacobins, liberals, utilitarians, anticlericals, egalitarians, perfectibilians, materialists, idealists, lawyers, journalists, secular reformers, and intellectuals of every breed."[42] While the Florentine avant-gardists who came a century after de Maistre differed from him in seeking to appropriate the rhetoric of revolution for their side and mostly abandoning his hope of reviving ancient religious faiths, many of his enemies evidently remained theirs. Moreover, in a way that very much reinforces the connection between de Maistre and the Florentines, Berlin locates the essence of a fascist view of life in de Maistre's "tough-minded" view of the world as "full of sin, cruelty and suffering, and only able to survive through the violent repression exercised by the chosen instruments of power." Not for him any more than for them, the "softness" of romanticism and post-romanticism.[43] Like his, theirs was a ferocious world, a world that demanded ruthlessness even as it cried out for spiritual replenishment.

Against the received view of de Maistre, Berlin insists that he was in many ways modern, that "his doctrine, and still more his attitude of mind, had to wait a century before they came . . . into their own," that he "may have spoken the language of the past" but "the content of what he had to say presaged the future," and that he "understood . . . that the old world was dying" and tried to shape "the new world that was coming into place."[44] Regardless of whether we accept his entire thesis about de Maistre, Berlin is clearly right to question the tradition that began in the nineteenth century, and that still persists, of regarding all reactionary thought as necessarily backward-looking and antimodern.

Still more persuasively than Berlin's de Maistre, the Florentine avant-gardists present us with a case in which modernity was championed in the name of ideals and visions that were profoundly opposed to what many took modernity to mean then and what it has come to mean since. Their vision of modernity was one in which life would be reinvigorated by a new culture embodying a new spirituality, one that would make possible the full development of human creativity in technology, industry, science, and the arts, while also discarding the "bourgeois" crassness and the outmoded intellectual and political forms of positivism and democracy that were continuing to deform and enfeeble modern life in general, and its development in Italy in particular. Like Mussolini, who declared in 1920 that "the century of democracy" had "expired with the world war" and that "new kinds of aristocracy" were in the process of creating a "century of antidemocracy," they were convinced that theirs were the truly modern ideals and that, even as they stood between two worlds, the future surely lay with them.[45] Their only difference with Mussolini in this respect was that their hour of greatest confidence had come not after but just before the nineteenth-century world into which they were born had arrived at its nightmarish finale.

Notes

Bibliography

Index

Notes

Sources are cited below in shortened form. Full citations are provided in the Bibliography.

Introduction

1. *Leonardo* (4 Jan. 1903); emphasis in original. Except where otherwise noted, all translations are my own.

2. For my approach to political rhetoric, see Adamson, "The Language of Opposition in Early Twentieth-Century Italy."

3. See, for example, Herf, *Reactionary Modernism;* Mosse, *The Nationalization of the Masses;* Sternhell, *Neither Right nor Left;* and Timms and Collier, *Visions and Blueprints.*

4. For *decadentismo*—a concept sometimes used in the sense in which modernism is used in this book, sometimes in the sense of late nineteenth-century aestheticism, and sometimes in a sense that encompasses both modernism and aestheticism—see Binni, *La poetica del decadentismo;* Praz, *The Romantic Agony;* Salinari, *Miti e coscienza del decadentismo italiano;* and Seroni, *Il decadentismo.* For fascist ideology, see De Grand, *The Italian Nationalist Association and the Rise of Fascism in Italy;* E. Gentile, *Le origini dell'ideologia fascista (1918–1925);* Ledeen, *The First Duce;* Papa, *Fascismo e cultura;* Roberts, *The Syndicalist Tradition and Italian Fascism;* and Zunino, *L'ideologia del fascismo.*

5. See Croce, *Storia d'Europa nel secolo decimono,* 301.

6. Quoted in Mangoni, *L'interventismo della cultura,* 62.

7. See G. Gentile, *Il fascismo al governo della scuola,* 307–327.

8. In addition to the works by Bourdieu listed in the Bibliography, upon which the discussion in the text is based, Loïc J. D. Wacquant's "How to Read Bourdieu," in Bourdieu and Wacquant, *An Invitation to Reflexive Sociology,* 261–264, is a useful guide to Bourdieu's now voluminous and widely dispersed opus. See also my discussion of Bourdieu in *Marx and the Disillusionment of Marxism,* 216–223. For an extension of Bourdieu to history, see Ringer, *Fields of Knowledge,* 1–25, which includes a detailed and cogent (if somewhat too objectivist) reading of Bourdieu's method.

9. See the helpful diagram of these relations among fields in Bourdieu, "The Field of Cultural Production, or: The Economic Field Reversed," 319.

10. On the distinction between the documentary and the worklike, see LaCapra, *Rethinking Intellectual History*, 29–30.

11. See Trilling, *Beyond Culture*, especially xi–xviii; and Calinescu, *Faces of Modernity*, especially 4–5.

12. Spender, *The Struggle of the Modern*, 71, 60; for a complementary view, see Broch, *Hugo von Hofmannsthal and His Time*.

13. Spender, *The Struggle of the Modern*, 259, 209.

14. Ibid., 78, 106, 37–38, 144–146, 257, 83–92.

15. See Gluck, *Georg Lukács and His Generation, 1900–1918;* Jelavich, *Munich and Theatrical Modernism;* and Wilde, *Horizons of Assent.*

16. Images of civilization as a covering over of primal forces are rampant in the literature of the period. Often this is understood as a covering over of the physical, as in the poignant scene from Gide's *The Immoralist* (1902) in which the protagonist Michel, having discovered the need for a "new ethic" in North Africa, bares his chest to the hot sun of the Italian Amalfi coast. At other times civilization is understood to have covered over a primal language that can be best unearthed through poetry. This notion is pervasive in the thinking of symbolists such as Mallarmé and remains evident in later philosophical critics influenced by them such as Walter Benjamin. For a related discussion of modernism as uncovering, see Schwartz, *The Matrix of Modernism*, especially 4–6.

17. Baudelaire, *The Painter of Modern Life*, 13.

18. The idea of a great "party of intellectuals" was articulated by Papini as early as 1900; see his *Diario 1900*, 181–182; see also his letter to Prezzolini of 10 November 1907, now in their *Storia di un'amicizia*, 1:135–136.

19. For a fuller discussion of this concept of civil society, see Adamson, "Gramsci and the Politics of Civil Society."

20. Georg Simmel, "The Metropolis and Mental Life."

21. See Soffici's letter to Prezzolini of 20 September 1909, in *Lettere a Prezzolini*, 31, and his "Broderies Vénitiennes," *La Plume* (1 June 1904).

22. These are the famous words of Vittorio Emanuele II, King of Piedmont and then of Italy until 1878, quoted in Croce, *Storia d'Italia*, 2.

1. Sources of Avant-Gardism in Nineteenth-Century Florence

1. Prezzolini, "I miei fiorentini," *La Voce* (7 and 21 April, 14 July 1910).

2. See Papini's letter of 15 July 1910 in Papini and Prezzolini, *Storia di un'amicizia*, 1:256; and Soffici's letter of 10 April 1910 in Prezzolini and Soffici, *Carteggio*, 1:108.

3. Stendhal, *Rome Naples and Florence*, 311; Prezzolini quotes the original French.

4. On *mezzadria* see Snowden, *The Fascist Revolution in Tuscany, 1919–1922*, 7–117.

5. Less famously, the death penalty was restored in 1793 and remained in effect until 1853; see Davis, *Conflict and Control*, 129.

6. Turi, *"Viva Maria."*

7. Arthur Young, *Travels during the Years 1787, 1788 and 1789 Undertaken More*

Particularly with a View of Ascertaining the Cultivation, Wealth, Resources and National Prosperity of the Kingdom of France, 2 vols. (London, 1794), 2:156.

8. Woolf, *The Poor in Western Europe in the Eighteenth and Nineteenth Centuries*, 47–157; and Snowden, *Fascist Revolution in Tuscany*, 20–33.

9. Clark, *Modern Italy, 1871–1982*, 14.

10. Antonio Anzilotti, "La Toscana del secondo Leopoldo," *La Voce* (29 Sept. 1910).

11. Mazzini, "Dell'amor patrio di Dante," now in his *Pensiero e azione*, 69–85.

12. Letter to Giannetta Rosselli of September 1870 in Mazzini, *Scritti editi e inediti*, 90:49.

13. Papini, "Campagna per il forzato risveglio," *Leonardo* (Aug. 1906).

14. Papini, *Un uomo finito*, 148–149.

15. Soffici wrote to Papini on 5 December 1907: "One thing is certain: *we* are the men of Mazzini!" See their *Carteggio*, 161.

16. Mazzini, "'La Réforme intellectuelle et morale' d'Ernesto Renan," now in *Scritti editi e inediti*, 93:227–262.

17. Renan, *La Réforme intellectuelle et morale*.

18. Sergio Landucci has written: "'La scienza e la vita' and the memorable parliamentary discourses of 1874 and 1878 might be titled *La Réforme intellectuelle et morale de l'Italie*. All of these texts are animated by the same animus that had inspired the celebrated book of Ernest Renan, with their demand that Italy undergo what Renan had hoped for in his country: 'a reform of the Prussian variety, I mean . . . a strong and vigorous national education.'" See his *Cultura e ideologia in Francesco De Sanctis*, 406. The essay "La scienza e la vita," De Sanctis' inaugural lecture for the 1872–73 academic year at the University of Naples, is included in De Sanctis, *L'arte, la scienza e la vita*, 316–340.

19. Prezzolini, "Relazione del primo anno della 'Voce,'" *La Voce* (11 Nov. 1909).

20. Quoted in Noether, "Francesco De Sanctis," 6.

21. De Sanctis, "La scienza e la vita," 329–330.

22. Ibid., 339.

23. Papini, "Carducci è solo," *Leonardo* (Aug. 1906).

24. Carducci, "Moderatucoli," in *Edizione nazionale delle opere*, 25:113.

25. Papini, *L'uomo Carducci*, 32, 52–53.

26. See Carocci, "La polemica antidecadentista di Giosuè Carducci," 264.

27. Carducci, "Prefazione al 'Promoteo Liberato' di Percy Bysshe Shelley" (1894), in *Edizione nazionale delle opere*, 25:360.

28. Letter from Carducci to Emilio Teza of 20 June 1861 in *Edizione nazionale delle opere. Lettere*, 2:277–278.

29. Papini, *L'uomo Carducci*, 186.

30. Prezzolini, *Italia 1912*, 58.

31. This rhetoric is particularly pronounced in Prezzolini. For some good examples, see his "L'esperienza di Cristo," *Leonardo* (Feb. 1905) ("Stare a mezza via come noi . . ."); and "Parole d'un uomo moderno," *La Voce* (25 Sept. 1913) ("Il mondo moderno è distruzione della vecchia disciplina . . .").

32. Papini, *L'uomo Carducci*, 99.

33. Papini, "Carduccianismo," *La Voce* (18 March 1909); and Soffici, "Giosuè Carducci," *La Voce* (22 Dec. 1910).

34. Papini, *L'uomo Carducci*, 9–12.

35. Soffici, *Ricordi di vita artistica e letteraria*, in *Opere*, 6:33.

36. Prezzolini, *L'Italiano inutile*, 14, 24, 29.

37. Papini, "Le due tradizioni letterarie," *La Voce* (4 Jan. 1912).

38. Papini, "Miele e pietra" [Honey and Stone], *La Voce* (11 Aug. 1910). For the same theme in Prezzolini, see his review of Mario Morasso's *La nuova arma* in *Leonardo* (Nov. 1904).

39. Papini, *L'uomo Carducci*, 6.

40. The journal appeared in 144 issues grouped as 48 quarterly volumes, each of which ran about 500 pages; the first issue appeared in January 1821, the last in December 1832.

41. See Strelsky, "Dostoevsky a Firenze."

42. See Bargellini, *Florence the Magnificent: A History*, 3:376–377.

43. Francesco Protonotari, "La Nuova Antologia," *Nuova Antologia* (31 Jan. 1866).

44. See the prefatory note he added to G. B. Giorgini, "La chiesa e il partito liberale in Italia," *Nuova Antologia* (31 March 1866).

45. See Spadolini, *Firenze fra '800 e '900*, 68–73. Carducci wrote ten articles for *Nuova Antologia* from 1866 to 1872.

46. Landucci, *Cultura e ideologia in Francesco De Sanctis*, 236. For a complete accounting of these articles, see Francesco De Sanctis, *Lettere alla "Nuova Antologia,"* 14.

47. Much of this study is available in Sonnino, *Scritti e discorsi extraparlamentari, 1870–1902*, 101–192.

48. "Presentazione della 'Rassegna settimanale'" (6 Jan. 1878), now in Sonnino, *Scritti e discorsi extraparlamentari*, 215. The similarity of this standpoint to that adopted by *La Voce* was not lost on Prezzolini, who counted the *Rassegna settimanale* as its earliest "precursor"; see his *La Voce 1908–1913*, 14.

49. One exception was the *Rassegna nazionale*, which began in 1879 and persevered through the Giolittian era. It was the journal of the moderate Catholics who aimed at reconciliation with the new Italian state, though from a more conservative position than later Christian democrats such as Romulo Murri. For a general survey of all Florentine journals in this period, see Rotondi, "Giornali fiorentini dal 1880 al 1900."

50. Prezzolini, "I miei fiorentini," *La Voce* (14 July 1910).

51. A literal translation would be Institute of Professional and Specialized Higher Education. Florence had had a university during much of the Renaissance, but it was suppressed in 1503. After the restoration of the Medici in 1512, the university was reopened, but at Pisa. For a brief account of this experience, see Brucker, "Renaissance Florence."

52. Garin, *La cultura italiana tra '800 e '900*, 29–101.

53. Tocco wrote regularly for the *Nuova Antologia* in the 1890s and published widely in the history of philosophy until his death in 1911. Papini recalled: "One of the professors that I followed most conscientiously was Felice Tocco, who taught the history of philosophy. He lectured in the afternoon and I was one of the first to sit down in the black benches of the first row . . . I enjoyed the lucidity of his thought, despite the fitful, almost angry restlessness of his speech, and I greatly admired him for having studied the medieval heretics and Giordano Bruno." See Papini, *Passato remoto*, in *Tutte le opere*, 9:798–799.

54. Garin, *La cultura italiana tra '800 e '900*, 80–81.

55. Prezzolini, "Pasqualino," *Leonardo* (April 1905).

56. Stendhal, *Rome Naples and Florence*, 317.

57. Jules and Edmond de Goncourt, *L'Italie d'hier: Notes de Voyages 1855–1856* (Paris, 1894), 73.

58. Aldo Palazzeschi, "Vecchie inglesi," in *Stampe dell'800*, 61–62.

59. Jessie White Mario, *Vita di Garibaldi* (1884; reprint, Udine, 1986).

60. Pinzani, *La crisi politica di fine secolo in Toscana*, 33.

61. See Richard Ellmann, *Oscar Wilde* (New York, 1988), 54–56; Donald A. Prater, *A Ringing Glass: The Life of Rainer Maria Rilke* (Oxford, 1986), 46; and Gide, *The Journals*, 1:45–51.

62. On *A Szellem* and Lukács' view of Florence, see Arpad Kadarkay, *Georg Lukács* (Oxford, 1991), 72–73. Lukács' apparent aloofness was not shared by his friend and fellow Florence resident Lajos Fülep, who edited the journal with Lukács. Fülep became quite friendly with Giovanni Amendola, knew Giovanni Papini, Gaetano Salvemini, and probably many other *vociani*, and even contributed one short piece to *L'Anima*, the journal edited by Amendola and Papini in 1911. See G. Amendola, *Carteggio, 1897–1912*, 2:5–6, 38, 54, 141, 146, 211, 304–305, 329; and Lajos Fülep, "Suso," *L'Anima* (July 1911).

63. Soffici, *Il salto vitale*, in *Opere*, 7 (Part 2):79.

64. Papini, "Contro Firenze," *Lacerba* (15 Dec. 1913).

65. Estimates of Florence's population in 1865 range from 118,000 (Spadolini, *Firenze mille anni*, 225–226) to 150,000 (Fanelli, *Firenze*, 199).

66. Fei, *Nascita e sviluppo di Firenze città borghese*, 193–197.

67. For Ricasoli's attitude, see Spadolini, *Firenze mille anni*, 232–233.

68. The account of Florence's transformation that follows is based primarily on Pesci, *Firenze capitale (1865–1870);* Aranguren, "Il volto di Firenze dal 1870 al 1900"; Fei, *Nascita e sviluppo di Firenze città borghese;* and Fanelli, *Firenze*.

69. The first telephone lines were built in 1882, but they came into very little use until after 1885. See Mori, *La Toscana*, 136–143. The major streetcar line, spanning three kilometers between the city and the hills of Fiesole to the north, became a mainstay of local life in the 1890s.

70. The figures are for the province of Florence; see Pinzani, *Crisi politica*, 95.

71. This account of the turn-of-the-century crisis in Florence draws above all on Pinzani, *Crisi politica*.

72. Ibid., 12.

73. See, for example, Pasquale Villari, "I disordini universitari," *Nuova Antologia* (16 Feb. 1897): "Everywhere in the world there exist students who have no desire to study. Who can deny it? But elsewhere they go for strolls or practice fencing, gymnastics, rowing or cricket. Only in Italy do we find the strange phenomenon of students who are not content to cut classes, something they can do very freely, but . . . who wish to force classes to come to a halt."

74. It may seem odd to ban an intransigent-Catholic newspaper after a working-class uprising, since its editors were anything but working class in their basic orientation. Nonetheless, in the eyes of the national government, to maintain the position that the Italian state was illegitimate, and that good Catholics therefore should not vote, was certainly to appear subversive. As if to acknowledge the connection, *L'Unità cattolica*, which had come to Florence in 1893, would move to

working-class Prato in the midst of the general strike of 29 August–3 September 1902.

75. Pinzani, *Crisi politica*, 137.

76. The first major syndicalist-inspired general strike began two years later on 16 September 1904 in Milan, spreading first through the northern cities and, eventually, to major cities throughout the peninsula.

77. See Tosi, "D'Annunzio découvre Nietzsche (1892–1894)." The *Revue Blanche* article by Jean de Néthy (April 1892) excerpted and summarized Nietzsche mostly on the basis of *The Genealogy of Morals*. It was followed by extracts from *Beyond Good and Evil* (in August), from *Thus Spake Zarathustra* (in November), and from "The Problem of Socrates," *The Twilight of the Idols*, and *Nietzsche contra Wagner* (in 1897). All are now available in reprint editions (Geneva: Slatkine, 1968).

78. For the articles, see D'Annunzio, *Pagine disperse*, especially 544–588.

79. See especially Stelio's opening speech in *Il fuoco*.

80. Quoted in Alatri, *Gabriele D'Annunzio*, 196. The circumstances and meaning of the declaration have been widely misunderstood. Regarding the former, Alatri notes that the declaration came at a conference of the left held after parliament and was "not made in the assembly hall as is so often erroneously claimed." Regarding the latter, it is noteworthy that even though D'Annunzio would run with socialist support and under their banner, he never claimed to be a socialist ideologically; he declared for socialist energy, not for its principles. See the discussion in Alatri, 196–199.

81. The range extended from Gargàno, born in 1859, to Morasso and Adolfo Orvieto, born in 1871. One exception was Laura Orvieto, a cousin of the two brothers who would marry Angiolo in 1899. Born in 1876, she became a substantial contributor to *Il Marzocco* beginning in 1905. Among her contributions were a number of articles on feminism.

82. Oliva, *I nobili spiriti*, 153–176.

83. *Il Marzocco* (2 Feb. 1896).

84. On the "politics of nostalgia" in Umbertian Italy (1878–1900), see Drake, *Byzantium for Rome*.

85. See, for example, Angiolo Orvieto, "Sacrilegio!" *Il Marzocco* (17 Oct. 1897); and the unsigned "La réclame," *Il Marzocco* (23 July 1899) and "I tubi del telefono" (27 Sept. 1903).

86. "Conservatori in ritardo," *Il Marzocco* (22 May 1898). The article was unsigned. Pascoli's description came in an undated letter to Angiolo Orvieto. See Oliva, *I nobili spiriti*, 5.

87. The inaugural column appeared on 3 June 1900; all were unsigned.

88. Morasso's ideas were summed up in his *L'imperialismo artistico*.

89. Morasso, "La politica dei letterati. I. Il pregiudizio dell'astensione," *Il Marzocco* (2 May 1897), and "La politica dei letterati. II. La teoria dei partiti politici e la lotta futura," *Il Marzocco* (9 May 1897).

90. Diego Garoglio, "Politica e arte," *Il Marzocco* (23 May 1897). Orvieto's somewhat less reflective response was "Ancora della politica dei letterati," *Il Marzocco* (16 May 1897).

91. Enrico Corradini, "L'inchiesta del *Marzocco*," *Il Marzocco* (6 June 1897). For a fuller treatment of this episode see Drake, *Byzantium for Rome*, 187–212.

92. See Papini's account in *Passato remoto*, in *Tutte le opere*, 9:779–784; and in his *Diario 1900*, 10, 180–182.

93. See Prezzolini, "Al *Marzocco,*" *La Voce* (7 Jan. 1909), and the three articles titled "*Il Marzocco,*" in *La Voce* (29 April, 13 May, and 1 July 1909). Prezzolini's favorable attitude toward Conti was signaled in his very first article for *Leonardo,* "Vita trionfante," *Leonardo* (4 Jan. 1903), which was dedicated to him.

94. Prezzolini, review of Morasso's *La nuova arma* in *Leonardo* (Nov. 1904).

95. See Prezzolini, *Italia 1912,* 58.

96. Soffici, *Il salto vitale,* in *Opere,* 7 (Part 2):29–30. Related incidents are recounted in *Ricordi di vita artistica e letteraria,* in *Opere,* 6:31–32.

97. Soffici, *Il salto vitale,* in *Opere,* 7 (Part 2):40–43. Soffici's attitude toward D'Annunzio was less one-sidedly negative than Papini's, but by 1905 at least he did come to share the latter's view that D'Annunzio was "not the new man." See his letter to Papini of 23 September 1905 in their *Carteggio,* 79.

98. Prezzolini, *L'Italiano inutile,* 110.

99. Papini, *Passato remoto,* in *Tutte le opere,* 9:857.

100. Ibid., 855–856.

101. Papini, "Il D'Annunzianismo," in Papini and Prezzolini, *La coltura italiana,* 81–85.

102. Ibid., 81–82.

103. Ibid., 83–85.

2. The *Leonardo* Years

1. Papini, *Passato remoto,* in *Tutte le opere,* 9:725–727. Papini added that he later became certain the man was Nietzsche when he learned that, at just that time in 1885, Paolo Lanzki, who managed a hotel in the forests of Vallombroso and who admired Nietzsche, had invited him to stay, and that at the end of his stay Nietzsche had spent a few days in Florence.

2. Ibid., 736.

3. Papini, *Un uomo finito,* 63–64.

4. Papini, *Passato remoto,* in *Tutte le opere,* 9:736.

5. Papini, *Un uomo finito,* 3–4, 10–11.

6. Ibid., 13–14.

7. Gide, *Journals* (2 Jan. 1907), 1:196; Soffici, *Il salto vitale,* in *Opere,* 7 (Part 2):353.

8. See Papini, *Un uomo finito,* 39, 4.

9. Viviani, *Gianfalco,* 32–33.

10. Papini, *Passato remoto,* in *Tutte le opere,* 9:773–775.

11. Letter to Prezzolini of 31 July 1900, quoted in Papini and Prezzolini, *Storia di un'amicizia,* 1:17.

12. Papini, *Un uomo finito,* 17–21.

13. Papini, *Diario 1900,* 67.

14. Ibid., 181–182, 293–294.

15. Papini, *Passato remoto,* in *Tutte le opere,* 9:779–784.

16. Ibid., 803.

17. See Prezzolini's account of his childhood in *L'Italiano inutile,* 14–47.

18. Prezzolini, *Diario 1900–1941,* 27.

19. See Prezzolini, *L'Italiano inutile,* 36.

20. Prezzolini, "La mia Firenze," in Spadolini, *Firenze fra '800 e '900,* 302–304.

21. Papini, *Diario 1900,* 330, 49.

22. Romain Rolland, *Journal inédit* (March 1910), in Giordan, *Romain Rolland et le Mouvement Florentin de La Voce*, 199–200.

23. Prezzolini, *Diario 1900–1941*, 24.

24. Prezzolini, "La mia Firenze," 303.

25. Prezzolini, *L'Italiano inutile*, 97. Prezzolini commented: "When we published *Leonardo* these pseudonyms had been our names for quite a while, but not for reasons of secrecy or aestheticism, as might have been the case for other literary or political types. Our pseudonyms were already our intimate names; they were our sect names, which we used in public almost to celebrate a new personality, no longer one of family or state—in short, of a history that had made us, but of a new history that we believed we might remake without ancestors, completely without roots, without commitments and obligations toward anyone, confronting only the future that ought to be ours, because the individual was enough to make it—however he wanted it made. Will, freedom: Gian Falco, Giuliano il Sofista." In his diary entry of 8 January 1901, Prezzolini had written that Julian the Apostate had been "the first anti-Christian," while Julien Sorel was "the first individualist." See *Diario 1900–1941*, 31.

26. Prezzolini, "La mia Firenze," 304.

27. This became even more true after Papini's father died in the fall of 1902, for not only was his family much less well off than Prezzolini's but also, since his mother lived on for three more decades, he could draw upon no inheritance.

28. Prezzolini, *Diario 1900–1941*, 45–49.

29. See Papini and Prezzolini, *Storia di un'amicizia*, 1:43.

30. Soffici, *Il salto vitale*, in *Opere*, 7 (Part 2):23. Fattori had been central to the *macchiaioli* school of Florentine painting, which was based on techniques loosely derived from French impressionism. By the late 1890s it had become a fairly staid academic style.

31. Soffici, *Passi fra le rovine*, in *Opere*, 7 (Part 1):364–365.

32. Soffici, *Il salto vitale*, in *Opere*, 7 (Part 2):78–81.

33. Cavallo, *Soffici*, 15.

34. Soffici, *Il salto vitale*, in *Opere*, 7 (Part 2):415.

35. Ibid., 101.

36. Soffici, *Passi fra le rovine*, in *Opere*, 7 (Part 1):374–376.

37. Soffici, *Il salto vitale*, in *Opere*, 7 (Part 2):23. Late in 1907 Denis would actually come to Florence for several weeks of painting in the hills of Fiesole. There he would meet with Soffici as well as Papini and Prezzolini. See Papini's letters to Soffici of 21 and 28 December 1907 and Denis's letters to Soffici of 30 January and 10 February 1908 in Papini and Soffici, *Carteggio*, 166–167, 445–448. See also Prezzolini's letter to Soffici of 19 December 1907 in Prezzolini and Soffici, *Carteggio*, 1:3–4.

38. Soffici, *Il salto vitale*, in *Opere*, 7 (Part 2):90–91.

39. Letter from Costetti to Soffici of 16 September 1900, reproduced in Cavallo, *Soffici*, 16.

40. Soffici, *Il salto vitale*, in *Opere*, 7 (Part 2):150–151.

41. Ibid., 155 and generally 152–175.

42. See Cavallo, *Soffici*, 26–30, 56–58.

43. Soffici, *Il salto vitale*, in *Opere*, 7 (Part 2):296, 235, 298–301.

44. The design would remain on the cover of *La Plume*'s next two issues as well.

45. Soffici, *Il salto vitale*, in *Opere*, 7 (Part 2):192, 225.

46. Ibid., 216, 243. When Papini visited Soffici in Paris at the end of 1906, the two went together to the Bateau-Lavoir.

47. See Soffici, *Fine di un mondo*, 382–384.

48. Soffici, *Il salto vitale*, in *Opere*, 7 (Part 2):181–182.

49. For the early impressions of *Leonardo*, see ibid., 352–353. For the plug see *La Plume* (15 Feb. 1903) and *Leonardo* (8 March 1903). Soffici criticized *Il Marzocco* still more forcefully in a letter to Papini of 1906, asserting that it evidenced "the mediocrity and unspeakable poverty of the Italian spirit in these last years." Although the letter bears no date, it appears to have been written at the end of May or beginning of June. See their *Carteggio*, 103.

50. Soffici wrote two letters to the *Leonardo* circle, on 7 November 1902 and 20 February 1903; they are addressed to "Callistène Agonista," probably because he did not yet know specific names. The first letter from Papini to Soffici is dated 15 April 1903; the first from Soffici to Papini is dated 17 April. See their *Carteggio*, 39–40, 411–415.

51. Ruggero Jacobbi, "Ardengo Soffici tra tradizione e rinnovamento," in *Ardengo Soffici: L'artista e lo scrittore nella cultura del '900*, 23.

52. Soffici, *Il salto vitale*, in *Opere*, 7 (Part 2):323.

53. On "La Baronne," see Olivier, *Picasso et ses amis*, 217–218.

54. Richter, *La formazione francese di Ardengo Soffici, 1900–1914*, 73 n.224.

55. Olivier, *Picasso et ses amis*, 217; and Cavallo, *Soffici*, 52.

56. Soffici himself commented upon the resemblance in a letter to Papini of 28 August 1908. See their *Carteggio*, 332.

57. Soffici, "Le Salon d'Automne, Considérations," 334.

58. Earlier, in his letter to "Callistène Agonista" of 20 February 1903, Soffici had written: "there is nothing that is closer to Art than Mathematics, my dear friend." See Papini and Soffici, *Carteggio*, 415.

59. Letter from Soffici to Papini of 17 January 1904 in their *Carteggio*, 47–48.

60. Letter from Soffici to Papini (undated but apparently written in January 1905) in their *Carteggio*, 67. A few years later Soffici wrote to Miguel de Unamuno (16 Dec. 1908) that "I was seven years in Paris and it was there that I learned to love Italy all the more tenaciously. Without ever being a gallophobe and even loving many French poets—among others Verlaine, and especially Baudelaire, the least French and the most misunderstood in France, *malgré tout*—I know that race as one of the most foolish and superficial in the world." See Papini and Soffici, *Carteggio*, 456.

61. Soffici, "Ultima lettera agli amici," *Leonardo* (Feb. 1907).

62. The letter is undated but was probably written about March 1907. It reads in part: "Lately I have begun a deep study of Spanish with the intention of going to Spain this year. I have therefore bought a kind of anthology of the *meyores autores modernos* in which I found an absolutely beautiful short story by Unamuno." See Papini and Soffici, *Carteggio*, 120–121.

63. Papini, *Diario 1900*, 181–182; Prezzolini, *Diario 1900–1941*, 26, 44.

64. Papini, *Passato remoto*, in *Tutte le opere*, 9:812.

65. Papini, *Diario 1900*, 20–21.

66. Papini and Prezzolini, *Storia di un'amicizia*, 1:62. In retrospect it would be clear that Papini had romanticized (or badly gauged) both the size and coherence of his group. Most of the central articles for *Leonardo* would be written by him and Prezzolini.

67. Papini, *Un uomo finito*, 92.

68. Ibid., 102.

69. In addition to Gian Falco and Giuliano il Sofista, the pseudonyms included Perseo (Costetti) and La Compiuta Donzella (The Finished Damsel) for the one woman in the original group, Amy Bernardy. Bernardy's participation, however, was quite infrequent; she contributed only to the fifth issue in 1903 and to the penultimate one in 1907, most of her efforts being devoted to *Il Marzocco*, to which she became a major contributor during the decade before the war.

70. Papini, *Un uomo finito*, 103.

71. Ibid., 97. Prezzolini later commented: "The title *Leonardo* derived from Papini's reaction against the specialization and technicism of the time; with his encyclopedic and venturesome taste, Papini was bored with people who were acquainted with only one shopwindow, even if they knew it quite well." See *L'Italiano inutile*, 107.

72. Papini, "Il segreto di Leonardo," *Leonardo* (19 April 1903).

73. Prezzolini, *Diario 1900–1941*, 56.

74. Prezzolini, "Alle sorgenti dello spirito," *Leonardo* (19 April 1903).

75. This ambition is already implicit in a paper Croce wrote in 1898, "Francesco De Sanctis e i suoi critici recenti," later reprinted in *Una famiglia di patrioti ed altri saggi storici e critici*, 189–236. Prezzolini made much of the connection in his 1909 book *Benedetto Croce*, 27–32.

76. Croce, "Per la rinascita dell'idealismo" (1908), in *Cultura e vita morale*, 36.

77. Prezzolini, *Benedetto Croce*, 79, 90–93.

78. Prezzolini, "L'uomo Dio," *Leonardo* (27 Jan. 1903). Prezzolini would return frequently to the idea of the *uomo dio* in the next half-decade. See, for example, his essay on Novalis in *Studi e capricci sui mistici tedeschi*, 98, where he criticized Christianity as "rigid, ferociously egoistic, and aiming to possess a unique absolute" rather than "admit plurality," as do those who base their faith on an *uomo dio*. Papini would defend the same concept, though with no acknowledged debt to Croce and in a more pragmatist vein, in "Dall'uomo a Dio," *Leonardo* (Feb. 1906).

79. Papini, "Risposta a Benedetto Croce," *Leonardo* (10 Nov. 1903).

80. Croce, "*Leonardo*," *La Critica* (20 July 1903). The visit is reported in Ridolfi, *Vita di Giovanni Papini*, 395.

81. Ridolfi, *Vita di Giovanni Papini*, 395.

82. Papini, "La Logica di B. Croce," *Leonardo* (June–Aug. 1905).

83. Prezzolini, *L'Italiano inutile*, 92. For another view of the relation between Bergson and European modernism, see Schwartz, *The Matrix of Modernism*, 21–57.

84. Papini would review the volume very favorably in the very last issue of *Leonardo* (Aug. 1907). Shortly before, William James had written Papini calling "Bergson's new book . . . perhaps the divinest thing in philosophy since Plato" and one "which has killed intellectualism stone-dead, at last!" The letter, dated 13 June 1907, is held at the Fondazione Primo Conti in Fiesole. For two accounts of the way Bergson's lectures at the Collège de France soon became Friday-afternoon cultural events, see Papini, *Passato remoto*, in *Tutte le opere*, 9:877–878; and Halévy, *Péguy and Les Cahiers de la Quinzaine*, 78.

85. Bergson, *Essai sur les Données Immédiates de la Conscience*, in *Oeuvres*, 1–157.

86. Bergson, *Matière et Mémoire, Le Rire*, and "Le Rêve," in *Oeuvres*, 159–379, 381–486, and 878–897.

87. Prezzolini, "Vita trionfante," *Leonardo* (4 Jan. 1903).

88. Prezzolini, *Vita intima*, 9, 25.

89. *Leonardo* (10 Nov. 1903).

90. Prezzolini, "Vita trionfante" and *Vita intima*, 21.

91. Prezzolini, "Novalis," in *Studi e capricci sui mistici* 81–107. See also the passage from Novalis, titled "L'idealismo magico," that Prezzolini translated and reprinted in *Leonardo* (Feb. 1906). The passage was one of many he translated and published in Novalis, *Frammenti*, ed. G. Prezzolini (Milan: Libreria Editrice Lombarda, 1906).

92. Papini met both Sorel and Péguy in late 1906 during a visit to Paris, and from letters held at the Archivio Prezzolini in Lugano, it appears that Prezzolini began a correspondence with Sorel in May 1908 and with Péguy in April 1910, the year in which he met both men in Paris. Prezzolini clearly knew of their work, however, at least from the time of Papini's visit.

93. Papini, *Passato remoto*, in *Tutte le opere*, 9:876–881.

94. Ibid., 877.

95. James, *The Will to Believe and Other Essays in Popular Philosophy*, 29.

96. The philosophies of Bergson and James appear to have developed independently, but there were many affinities between them. Perhaps sensing them, Bergson sent James a copy of his *Matière et Mémoire* in 1898, but James did not recognize its significance until 1902, at which point he began their correspondence in a serious way. The two would meet at the end of May 1905 as James returned home from the Fifth International Congress of Psychology in Rome where he had met Papini.

97. Schiller, *Humanism*, xx, 13–14.

98. Papini, *Passato remoto*, in *Tutte le opere*, 9:907–908, is one of many places where Papini comments on the importance of James's "The Will to Believe" for his conception of pragmatism. See also Prezzolini's review of James's *The Varieties of Religious Experience* in *Leonardo* (June 1904), where the essay is singled out for its importance.

99. Prezzolini, "Scetticismo e sofistica (lettere ad uno scettico)," *Leonardo* (20 Dec. 1903); "Il David della filosofia inglese (F. C. S. Schiller)," *Leonardo* (March 1904); and "Un compagno di scavi (F. C. S. Schiller)," *Leonardo* (June 1904). The "Goliaths" in the second of these articles (F. H. Bradley, J. M. E. McTaggert, and J. B. Baillie) were being slain by a man who "cannot abide the professors of philosophy," an overstatement Schiller apparently found somewhat embarrassing. "Will you please remember," he pleaded in a letter of 29 March 1904 (Archivio Prezzolini), "that I too am a teacher of philosophy? So is James. We may be unlike the bulk of our confrères but the fact remains . . . And Bradley on the other hand has never taught."

100. *Leonardo* (June 1904).

101. Prezzolini, "Professionisti e dilettanti di filosofia in Italia," *Leonardo* (10 Nov. 1903).

102. Papini, "La filosofia che muore," *Leonardo* (10 Nov. 1903). Prezzolini also complained of the "mediocre eunuchism" of contemporary academic culture in *La coltura italiana*, 166.

103. Papini, *Un uomo finito*, 116.

104. Papini, "La filosofia che muore."

105. Papini, "Introduzione al pragmatismo," *Leonardo* (Feb. 1907). On pragma-

tism's ability to create truth, see his "Il pragmatismo messo in ordine," *Leonardo* (April 1905).

106. Papini, "Il pragmatismo messo in ordine."

107. For Papini, particularity correlated with activism, universalism with passivity. See "Atena e Faust," *Leonardo* (Feb. 1905).

108. Papini, "Morte e resurrezione della filosofia," *Leonardo* (20 Dec. 1903). The early Prezzolini also explicitly favored conceiving philosophy as a kind of *giuoco;* see his "La miseria dei logici," *Leonardo* (8 March 1903).

109. Papini, "Il pragmatismo messo in ordine."

110. Papini, "La volontà di credere" (1906), in *Pragmatismo*, 140.

111. The comparison was recognized by Papini himself in "Il pragmatismo messo in ordine," 46, and in *Il crepusculo dei filosofi*, 135.

112. James, "G. Papini and the Pragmatist Movement in Italy," 338. James also cited Papini several times in *Pragmatism:* 6, 32 (the "corridor theory"); 43, 78 ("my friend G. Papini"); and 123 ("Signor Papini, the leader of Italian pragmatism").

113. Letter from James to Papini of 27 April 1906, now held at the Fondazione Primo Conti (emphasis in original), reprinted in Luti, *Firenze corpo 8*, 38–39; all but a few lines may be found in Perry, *The Thought and Character of William James*, 2:571–572.

114. Papini, *Diario 1900*, 20–21.

115. The book would be published only in 1913, three years after James's death and long after it had become for Papini the mere academic exercise it had been designed to overthrow. For Papini's own account of this publication history, see *Sul pragmatismo*, vii–xii.

116. The one significant exception to this turning away from philosophy was the review *L'Anima*, which he edited with Giovanni Amendola in 1911. But his contributions there involved little fresh thinking, and were mostly just a Jamesian pragmatism recycled from the *Leonardo* period.

117. Papini, *Un uomo finito*, 297.

118. See Karl Marx, "Toward the Critique of Hegel's Philosophy of Law: Introduction," in *Writings of the Young Marx on Philosophy and Society*, ed. L. D. Easton and K. H. Guddat (Garden City, N.Y., 1967), 261.

119. In an editorial preface to "Marta e Maria (dalla contemplazione all'azione)," *Leonardo* (March 1904), Papini wrote: "For some time there has been arising even in Italy a reaction against intellectualism and a movement toward life and action. In the first issue of *Leonardo*, Giuliano il Sofista spoke of 'life triumphant' and in the last I posed as the new character and task of philosophy the remaking of the world rather than the contemplating of it."

120. Papini, "Mazzini è stato tradito," *Leonardo* (June–Aug. 1905).

121. The ninety-five issues of *Il Regno* appeared from 29 November 1903 through 25 December 1906; for a selection from and complete index of the review, see Frigessi, *La cultura italiana del '900 attraverso le riviste*.

122. See "Prefazione" and "Leonardo" in ibid., 369–371, 373–374.

123. Papini, "La coltura e la vita italiana," *Leonardo* (Oct.–Dec. 1905), republished as the introduction to Papini and Prezzolini, *La coltura italiana*, 5–12.

124. Papini, "La coltura e la vita italiana."

125. Ibid.

126. Papini and Prezzolini, *La coltura italiana*, 63.

127. Ibid., 160–172.

128. Ibid., 16. See also Prezzolini, *Il centivio*, 20–21.

129. Papini, "Atena e Faust," *Leonardo* (Feb. 1905). Later in *La Voce*, Papini would link the idea of cultural renewal as regaining the "nudity of man" with the virtue of sincerity, and credit Nietzsche with rediscovering "the courage of psychical nudity." See Papini, "Sincerità," *La Voce* (25 Nov. 1909). Finally, in 1912, Papini would return to the theme of a "nudity of mind" in *Un uomo finito*, 86, 116.

130. Nor did this faith weaken when Soffici returned to Tuscany fulltime in 1907. In a letter to Papini of 31 May or 1 June 1908, he wrote: "I am becoming ever more enthusiastic about our country and our people [*popolo*], the only one in Europe that is healthy in mind and body, clean, and capable of doing something . . . I have been thinking about this while looking at our children—our marvelous children with their strong limbs, well tanned and well formed; their hair strong, full of curls, and smelling like pigeon feathers; their faces well carved; their eyes pure and large; their whole persons straight and solid like bronze." See their *Carteggio*, 237–238.

131. For the reference to Gide, see Papini's review of his *Saul, Le Roi Candaule*, in *Leonardo* (June 1904).

132. In his memoirs, Prezzolini claimed to love the common people, whom he identified as those who rode third class on trains. "Even today, when I return from abroad, one of the greatest pleasures that awaits me in Italy is traveling third class, and I enter one of those crowded compartments with the expectation of an adventure like those had by romantic heroes." See *L'Italiano inutile*, 99.

133. Papini wrote revealingly a few years later that "I never knew them [men], and as a result I could only fail. One doesn't make listen those who do not wish to listen. I was a stranger among them, and they do not understand the language of strangers. They cannot love someone who is not consumed with love for them. Humanity is a woman who is moved only by those who love her or who make her afraid." See *Un uomo finito*, 230.

134. Papini, "Campagna per il forzato risveglio," *Leonardo* (Aug. 1906).

135. Already on 9 September 1905, Papini had written to Soffici: "I want to become truly—can I entrust this to you by now?—the spiritual guide of the young, very young and future Italy . . . D'Annunzio is not the new man. Carducci was a bold figure, a beautiful continuation of our classical stream but nothing more. Mazzini was not understood, and he did not much understand the Italians. I would like therefore to be the spiritual reorganizer of this old race." Two years later, on 10 November 1907, he wrote to Prezzolini about his "party of intellectuals," reviving an idea he had articulated as early as 1900. Prezzolini's response was complex and, as we will see Chapter 3, culminated in the founding of *La Voce*. Finally, on 5 December 1907 Soffici wrote Papini about the possibility of "our projected movement" (of a "party of the soul"), one that would allow them to overcome Catholic "pessimism" and to act on the fact that "*we are the men of Mazzini!*" See Papini and Soffici, *Carteggio*, 78, 161–162, 352; and Papini and Prezzolini, *Storia di un'amicizia*, 1:135–136.

136. The program appeared in print only a decade later when Papini and Prezzolini recycled their early "spiritual-nationalist" and antisocialist writings for the intervention campaign of 1914–15. See Papini, "Un programma nazionalista," in Papini and Prezzolini, *Vecchio e nuovo nazionalismo*, 1–36; long extracts from it have been translated in Lyttelton, *Italian Fascisms from Pareto to Gentile*, 99–119.

137. See Papini, "Chi sono i socialisti?" *Leonardo* (22 Feb. and 8 March 1903); Prezzolini, "Decadenza borghese," *Leonardo* (22 Feb. 1903); idem, "La Biblioteca

Nazionale di Firenze," *Leonardo* (22 Feb. 1903); and idem, "Maurice Barrès," *Leonardo* (10 May 1903).

138. Prezzolini, *Manifesto dei conservatori*, 80.

139. Prezzolini, "L'aristocrazia dei briganti," *Il Regno* (13 Dec. 1903), now in Frigessi, *La cultura italiana del '900 attraverso le riviste*, 2:455–460.

140. Prezzolini, *Il tempo della Voce*, 51.

141. Prezzolini, "L'aristocrazia dei briganti," 459. The letter, dated 17 December 1903, is reprinted in *Il tempo della Voce*, 53–56. On 31 December Pareto wrote a fuller reply that became the basis for an exchange with Prezzolini in *Il Regno* (10 Jan. 1904), now in Frigessi, *La cultura italiana*, 2:467–471.

142. Prezzolini, "La borghesia può risorgere? Una risposta a Pareto," *Il Regno* (10 Jan. 1904), now in Frigessi, *La cultura italiana*, 2:469–470. Emphasis in original.

143. Papini gives an account of the visit and of his knowledge of Pareto at the time in *Passato remoto*, in *Tutte le opere*, 9:873–875.

144. Papini, *L'uomo Carducci*, 186.

145. Letter from Pareto to Prezzolini of 17 December 1903 in Prezzolini, *Il tempo della Voce*, 54.

146. Alfredo Oriani, "L'aristocrazia nuova," *Leonardo* (Feb. 1907).

147. Prezzolini, "Le due Italie," *Il Regno* (22 May 1904), now in Frigessi, *La cultura italiana*, 2:500–503.

148. The novelty of Prezzolini's effort here was not so much in the opposition of the "two Italies" itself (which traded upon the long-standing distinction between a "real" and "legal" Italy) as in the way in which the distinction was drawn in generational terms and in order to proclaim the educational and cultural mission of the new generation. According to one historian, the distinction between a "legal" and a "real" Italy was first drawn by the conservative Count Stefano Jacini (1827–1891) and became a mainstay of the polemical literature in the early years after independence. See Seton-Watson, *Italy from Liberalism to Fascism, 1870–1925*, 25.

149. Prezzolini, "La menzogna parlamentare," *Il Regno* (5 June 1905), now in Papini and Prezzolini, *Vecchio e nuovo nazionalismo*, 75–81.

150. Papini, "Campagna per il forzato risveglio."

151. Prezzolini, "La borghesia può risorgere? Una risposta a Pareto," *Il Regno* (10 Jan. 1904), now in Frigessi, *La cultura italiana*, 2:470.

152. Papini, "Un programma nazionalista," in *Vecchio e nuovo nazionalismo*, 9, 10.

153. Papini, "Due nemici," *Il Popolo d'Italia* (9 Feb. 1915).

154. Prezzolini, "Decadenza borghese," *Leonardo* (22 Feb. 1903).

155. Prezzolini, "Elogia della violenza," *Leonardo* (June 1904).

156. Papini, "Siamo reazionari?" *Il Regno* (4 Sept. 1904).

157. Papini, "L'ideale imperialista," *Leonardo* (4 Jan. 1903). "Interiority" was also an important value for Prezzolini in this period; see, for example, *Vita intima*, 18–19.

158. Papini, "Chi sono i socialisti?" *Leonardo* (8 March 1903).

159. Papini, "Il D'Annunzianismo," in Papini and Prezzolini, *La coltura italiana*, 63, 79–85. See also Papini's letter of 18 June 1908 to Soffici in their *Carteggio*, 251–253.

160. See "Federico Nietzsche," *Leonardo* (June–Aug. 1905).

161. In his "Preghiera per Nietzsche," *La Voce* (20 Jan. 1910), Papini portrayed

him as a "virile" man who loved "danger, risk, and evil" and in whose life "woman played only a very small role." Six months later, Papini would embrace Weininger's antifeminism in "Miele e pietra," *La Voce* (11 Aug. 1910). A year and a half after that, he would contrast the "masculine art" of Dante's tradition with the "feminine art" of Petrarch's; see his "Le due tradizioni letterarie," *La Voce* (4 Jan. 1912).

162. In 1915, Papini would collect various polemical articles from the 1909–1915 period in a volume titled *Maschilità* (Masculinity). For the wider European context of this masculinism, see Dijkstra, *Idols of Perversity;* and Showalter, *Sexual Anarchy.*

163. In his memoirs, Prezzolini mentioned "the vogue of Nietzsche" prevalent at the time of Croce's *Estetica* (1902) and suggested that *Leonardo* was Nietzschean in tone, as in its founding manifesto that embraced "paganism" while condemning "Nazarene sheepishness" and "plebeian servitude." See *L'Italiano inutile,* 101, and *Manifesto dei conservatori,* 79. Moreover, his own early work alludes to Nietzsche (see, for example, *Vita intima,* 14), reflects Nietzschean attitudes (as in the claim of the "Elogio della violenza" that the "violence we employ has to do not with hatred for others but with love of ourselves"), and is frequently written in a Nietzschean, aphoristic style. Later he would recognize the debt he owed to Nietzsche's discussion of "discipline" in the third essay of *The Genealogy of Morals;* see his "Prefazione" (1971) to Giovanni Boine, *Carteggio,* 1:xv. But it is not clear whether he knew this aspect of Nietzsche in the *Leonardo* years.

164. See, for example, Prezzolini's review of Mario Morasso's *La nuova arma* in *Leonardo* (Nov. 1904).

165. See Weininger, *Sex and Character,* 7, 48, 91, 64, 181–183, 263, 266, 148, 177, 302, 317, 321, 338. Weininger was himself of Jewish origin, although his book explicitly stated (312) that he had an Aryan "tendency of mind."

166. Letter of 17 April 1906 from Munich, in Croce and Prezzolini, *Carteggio (1904–1945),* 1:52. Although he wrote "Vaihinger" (Hans Vaihinger was a relatively staid neo-Kantian one generation older than and a world apart from Weininger), Prezzolini was almost certainly referring to Weininger.

167. Prezzolini, "Nemico della femmina," *Leonardo* (Oct.–Dec. 1906).

168. Letter from Prezzolini to Rolland of 2 April 1908 in Giordan, *Romain Rolland et le Mouvement Florentin de La Voce,* 123–125. Prezzolini goes on to recommend that Rolland read Weininger's book. Shortly thereafter, Prezzolini wrote to Croce seeking his help in getting Weininger translated into Italian. See his letter of 29 June 1908 in Croce and Prezzolini, *Carteggio (1904–1945),* 1:116.

169. Papini, "Campagna per il forzato risveglio"; emphasis in original.

170. Péguy's concept of a "revolution of sincerity" is discussed in "La crise e le Parti Socialiste," in *Oeuvres en prose complètes,* 1:209–217. See also Bourdieu's analysis of the role of the virtue of sincerity in Verlaine's self-positioning relative to Mallarmé in "The Field of Cultural Production, or: The Economic World Reversed," 348. Like Péguy and the Florentines, Verlaine used sincerity as way of affirming his relatively more modest social background and lack of cultural capital.

171. See Prezzolini, "La nostra promessa," *La Voce* (27 Dec. 1908).

172. Papini, "Il pragmatismo messo in ordine," *Leonardo* (April 1905).

173. Letter from Prezzolini to Papini of 9 February 1905, in *Storia di un'amicizia,* 1:73.

174. Prezzolini, *L'Italiano inutile,* 163. Soffici's account of his first impressions of Prezzolini in 1907 is contained in *Fine di un mondo,* 17.

175. Soffici so claimed in his *Ricordi di vita artistica e letteraria*, in *Opere*, 6:151. Mario Richter has supported this idea with a quotation about suicide from Soffici's *Arcobaleno*, an autobiographical poem of 1915, which, in Richter's view, refers back to 1907. See his *La formazione francese di Ardengo Soffici, 1900–1914*, 97.

176. Soffici, *Il salto vitale*, in *Opere*, 7 (Part 2):440.

177. Ibid., 438.

178. See the letter from Soffici to Papini of 1 March 1907 in their *Carteggio*, 122–123.

179. The text of the letters exchanged by Soffici (24 or 25 March 1907) and Bloy (27 March), as well as Soffici's impressions of the event, may be found in his *Ricordi di vita artistica e letteraria*, in *Opere*, 6:150–167. Daniel Halévy described Bloy as "an eccentric believer given to much violence and abuse" but also as a powerful personality responsible, for example, for Jacques Maritain's early conversion from Protestantism to Catholicism; see his *Péguy and Les Cahiers de la Quinzaine*, 226. Bloy had written for *La Plume* in the early 1890s and continued as an occasional participant in the circle's soirées for many years thereafter, thus gaining access to many avant-garde intellectuals. He is supposed to have made a strong impression on J.-K. Huysmans and Georges Rouault, among others.

180. Soffici, *Fine di un mondo*, 18.

181. For Soffici's original notes from his conversation with Bloy, including this quotation, see Cavallo, *Soffici*, 80–81.

182. Soffici, *Fine di un mondo*, 18.

183. Soffici, "Pittori e scultori sacri," *Leonardo* (April–June 1907).

184. Soffici, "Rentrée," *Leonardo* (Aug. 1907).

185. Papini, "Miguel de Unamuno," *Leonardo* (Oct.–Dec. 1906). Papini sent a copy of his article to Unamuno, whose book on Don Quixote had appeared in 1905.

186. In a published reply to Papini's article, Unamuno argued that Catholicism had become rationalistic and unspiritual, in effect allied with atheism and materialism, and that although some noble Catholics had overcome this tendency, secular idealism was today the best road to spiritual renewal. See his "Sobre el Quijotismo," *Leonardo* (Feb. 1907).

187. Soffici, "Don Chisciotte in Toscana," *La Riviera ligure* (Dec. 1908), reprinted in Bellini, *Studi su Ardengo Soffici*, 207–218. A first letter from Soffici to Unamuno, which is undated but appears to have been written in early December 1908, is reprinted in Cavallo, *Soffici*, 94–97. Unamuno's reply of 12 December 1908 was followed by two more from him and four from Soffici over the next year; all are held at the Fondazione Primo Conti and are now reprinted in Papini and Soffici, *Carteggio*, 449–465. For Soffici's remembrances of this interchange, see his *Ricordi di vita artistica e letteraria*, in *Opere*, 6:377–383.

188. Letter from Soffici to Papini of 7 September 1908 in their *Carteggio*, 341–342; emphasis in original. The phrase translated here as "who judges and dispatches them as he wishes" is from Dante's *Inferno*, Canto V, line 6.

189. Letter from Papini to Prezzolini of 19 April 1907 in *Storia di un'amicizia*, 1:134.

190. In his letter to Soffici of 29 March 1906, which came at the end of this period, Papini mentioned that he had been diagnosed as suffering from "cerebral anemia." See their *Carteggio*, 100.

191. Letter from Papini to Prezzolini of 4 May 1906, in *Storia di un'amicizia*,

1:120–121. Papini had expressed this self-dissatisfaction and temptation to suicide before and in print; see his "Non voglio più essere ciò chi sono," *Leonardo* (April 1905).

192. Papini, "In quante maniere non ha capito L'Italia," *Leonardo* (Oct.–Dec. 1906).

193. Papini, *Un uomo finito*, 226.

194. Letter from Papini to Soffici of 22 January 1907 in their *Carteggio*, 116–117.

195. Letter from Papini to Soffici of 23 May 1908 in their *Carteggio*, 225; letter from Papini to Prezzolini of 18 May 1908 in *Storia di un'amicizia*, 1:207.

196. Papini, *Un uomo finito*, 271.

197. Carducci, "Giambi ed Epodi," in *Edizione nazionale delle opere di Giosuè Carducci*, 3:5. Papini spent virtually every summer at Bulciano and, especially in the 1908–1911 period, much of the rest of the year as well.

198. Papini, *Un uomo finito*, 274–275.

199. Prezzolini, *L'Italiano inutile*, 112.

200. Letter from Prezzolini to Papini of 18 April 1905 in their *Storia di un'amicizia*, 1:91; also in Prezzolini, *Diario 1900–1941*, 69.

201. Prezzolini, *L'Italiano inutile*, 113.

202. Letter from Prezzolini to Papini of 18 April 1905 in their *Storia di un'amicizia*, 1:91–92; also in Prezzolini, *Diario 1900–1941*, 69–70; emphasis in original.

203. See especially his letter to Prezzolini of 9 October 1905 in their *Carteggio (1904–1945)*, 1:41–42.

204. Papini and Prezzolini, *Storia di un'amicizia*, 1:71.

205. Prezzolini wrote an essay on "Rudolf Kassner," *Leonardo* (Feb. 1907). Hebbel was of course no longer strictly contemporary, but Prezzolini received him almost as if he were. He praised Hebbel's play *Judith* in a letter to Papini of 12 February 1907, the same letter in which he first mentioned Claudel; see *Storia di un'amicizia*, 1:125. Kierkegaard, who was completely unknown in Italy until an essay on him appeared in the April–June 1906 issue of *Leonardo*, is mentioned in the Kassner essay; Prezzolini had come to know his work through Knud Ferlov, a Danish professor then living in Rome, who was attracted to *Leonardo*. A translation by Ferlov of one of Kierkegaard's short essays, "The Most Unhappy Man," appeared in *Leonardo* (Aug. 1907). Interestingly, three of the figures who most concerned Prezzolini at this point—Novalis, Kassner, and Kierkegaard—would also appear centrally in Georg Lukács, *Soul and Form* (1910).

206. Prezzolini, "L'esperienza del Cristo," *Leonardo* (June–Aug. 1905).

207. See Papini's letter of 19 April 1907 in *Storia di un'amicizia*, 1:133–135. The obituary is "La fine," *Leonardo* (Aug. 1907).

208. The point was borne out by *Leonardo*'s circulation, which was never greater than 500 (no more than 200 of those being paid subscriptions). See Frigessi, *La cultura italiana*, 1:37; and Papini and Prezzolini, *Storia di un'amicizia*, 1:233.

3. La Voce

1. Papini had been doing occasional articles for *Il Giornale d'Italia* beginning in 1904, for *La Gazzetta dell'Emilia* and *La Riviera ligure* beginning in 1906, and for *La Stampa* beginning in 1907. In 1908 he reviewed Prezzolini's *Il cattolicismo rosso*

and wrote on Walt Whitman for *Nuova Antologia*. Both he and Prezzolini had also contributed to the *Revue du Nord*, a French-language journal of literary and art criticism that began in Florence in 1904, moved to Rome in mid-1905, and ceased publication in December 1906. Prezzolini treated the *Revue du Nord* as a precursor of *La Voce* in his *La Voce 1908–1913*, 20–23.

2. Letters of 3 and 8 January 1908 in Papini and Soffici, *Carteggio*, 173, 178.

3. Papini and Prezzolini, *Storia di un'amicizia*, 1: 144.

4. *Poesia* was published as a monthly from February 1905 through October 1909. Marinetti's first futurist manifesto, which had appeared in *Le Figaro* in February 1909, was translated for its July–August 1909 issue.

5. Concerning the influence of *La nuova arma: La macchina* (1905) on Marinetti, see Salaris, *Storia del futurismo*, 15–16; and Ossani, *Mario Morasso*, 167–207. The book had been harshly reviewed by Prezzolini in *Leonardo* (Nov. 1904).

6. Both Soffici and Marinetti had close ties to the Parisian avant-garde, but those ties were quite different. Marinetti's Paris was that of Verhaeren and Jarry, Soffici's that of Picasso, Apollinaire, and Max Jacob, the one group dramatic and demonstrative in its approach to culture, the other more cerebral and reflective, the one in awe of the marvels of modern technology, the other inspired by the need to reinvigorate modernity with a sense of the mythic and primal.

7. Their excommunications would force the shutting down of *Il Rinnovamento* in December 1909, bringing its three years of publication to a close.

8. Ridolfi, *Vita di Giovanni Papini*, 122.

9. Contorbia has reprinted the issue with a critical introduction; for the untitled prologue, see his *Il Commento (1908)*, 71; emphasis in original.

10. In a letter of 21 February to Papini, Prezzolini indicated he had written a long critique of *Il Commento* but had torn it up because the journal was not worth correcting. Still, the gist of his critique is quite clear both here and in a subsequent letter of 28 February. See Gentili, "Prezzolini e Soffici a Papini (1902, 1908, 1912)," 227 n.4.

11. Ridolfi, *Vita di Giovanni Papini*, 124.

12. Right then, in fact, Prezzolini was debating Soffici about current French art; see Prezzolini, "La teoria e l'arte di Beuron," *Vita d'arte* (April and Aug. 1908).

13. Prezzolini and his wife visited Naples from 10 to 21 April 1908. A good indication of the dramatic effect the visit had upon him can be found in his letter to Croce of 22 May, now in their *Carteggio 1904–1945*, 1:104–105.

14. Prezzolini, *La teoria sindicalista*, 31–32.

15. Ibid., 34.

16. Prezzolini, *L'Italiano inutile*, 118.

17. Prezzolini, "La vita o la filosofia," *Leonardo* (Aug. 1907).

18. Prezzolini, *La teoria sindicalista*, 16–17, and *Benedetto Croce*, 79.

19. Each book refers to the other at crucial points in the argument; see Prezzolini, *La teoria sindacalista*, 16–18, and *Benedetto Croce*, 25–26.

20. On the origins in 1908 of his relationship with Salvemini, see Prezzolini, *Il tempo della Voce*, 429. For some examples of his more left-leaning articles of 1909 and 1910, see "Perché siamo anticlericali," *La Voce* (21 Jan. 1909), and "Che fare?" *La Voce* (23 June 1910). Both of them show a Salveminian influence, particularly in their positive attitude toward democracy.

21. Prezzolini, *La teoria sindacalista*, 7–9.

22. See Papini's letter of 8 January 1908 in *Storia di un'amicizia*, 1:143–144, which indicated that he was then writing a book on the subject.

23. Papini's attitude toward the syndicalist action at Parma is unclear, but we know that its moral force was still impressing Prezzolini four years later when he was condemning syndicalist leaders as insincere. See Prezzolini, *Italia 1912*, 75–76.

24. Mostly for this reason, Soffici continually tried to talk Prezzolini out of his Croceanism. See, for example, his letter of 11 August 1909 in his *Lettere a Prezzolini, 1908–1920*, 22–23. Papini's disdain for the "Crocean rigidity of degrees of spirit" is evident in his letter to Prezzolini of 2 March 1908 in *Storia d'un amicizia*, 1:165.

25. The principle was expressed rather wryly as follows: "I have never criticized anyone for preferring Barolo to Chianti, and I promise not to become irritated if I hear it said that Gozzoli is not an artist or that Brangwyn is a preserved cadaver—provided, however, that we have a well-established understanding that such an affirmation has the same value as my own when I put risotto on top of macaroni." See Prezzolini's letter of 6 March 1908 to Papini in *Storia d'un amicizia*, 1:181.

26. See Prezzolini's letters to Papini of 12 April in *Storia di un'amicizia*, 1:194–196, and to Soffici of 16 April 1908 in their *Carteggio*, 1:11–12.

27. Long lost, the "Progetto di una rivista di pensiero in Italia" is now reprinted in Prezzolini, *Italia 1912*, 97–103.

28. Dated 12 May 1908, the letter is reprinted in Gentili, "Prezzolini e Soffici a Papini," 226–228.

29. In his letter to Prezzolini of 18 May 1908 in *Storia d'un amicizia*, 1:203–219, Papini remarked: "You say that this review would be distinguished from *La Critica* by the fact that no one would have to subscribe to any philosophical credo. Only up to a point, however. From what you have written me about Croce and from some sentences in the program it seems that if you are not a Crocean, you are very close to being one . . . I think the review will be, speaking approximately, a more open *La Critica*, a slightly more liberal *La Critica*, but still *La Critica*."

30. Letter from Papini to Prezzolini of 18 May 1908 in *Storia di un'amicizia*, 1:212–215.

31. See Prezzolini's letter of 28 May to Papini in Gentili, "Prezzolini e Soffici a Papini," 229–230.

32. Letter from Papini to Soffici of 23 May 1908 in their *Carteggio*, 225.

33. See Soffici's account in his letter to Papini of 13 July 1908 in their *Carteggio*, 264–265.

34. See his letter of 23 September in his *Lettere a Prezzolini, 1908–1920*, 6–10. The list ranged from simple—*L'Appello* (The Cry) or *La Riforma spirituale* (Spiritual Reform)—to more elaborate possibilities such as *La Favola del Paese* (The Talk of the Town) or *La Lanterna di Diogene* (Diogenes' Lamp).

35. See Prezzolini, *Il sarto spirituale*, 85. Although we do not know exactly when the choice was made, we do have an interesting passage that reflects what the phrase may have connoted for Prezzolini. It occurs in a diary entry he made while in Munich in 1906: "To be an artist or philosopher is nothing other than letting one's *voice* [*voce*] speak and doing nothing to lower it. People may be divided between those who have a voice and those who do not, between those who let it speak and those who stifle it." See his *Diario 1900–1941*, 75; emphasis in original.

36. Prezzolini, *Diario 1900–1941*, 84.

37. The circular, dated 18 October 1908, is reprinted in Luti, *Firenze corpo 8*, 46–47.

38. Prezzolini, *Diario 1900–1941*, 91.

39. On the speech, see Salomone, *Italian Democracy in the Making*, 56.

40. Papini's comment came in an unsigned piece for *Lacerba* (15 Jan. 1914), now reprinted as "Sem Benelli" in *Stroncature*, 111.

41. See Prezzolini, *L'Italiano inutile*, 166. The only available alternative was a horse-drawn coach, but this was much more costly and so they tended to avoid it except when one of Soffici's somewhat more prosperous friends, such as the sculptor and painter Medardo Rosso, offered to pay their fares.

42. Ibid., 130.

43. Ibid., 126.

44. The Thursday ritual began with the fourth issue of 7 January 1909, the previous three issues having appeared on Sunday. *La Voce* appeared twenty-two times as a biweekly in 1914 and then continued as a less avant-garde, more purely literary journal under Giuseppe De Robertis in 1915 and 1916, first as a biweekly and then, after May 1915, as a monthly.

45. Occasionally *La Voce* went to six or even eight pages, but four was the norm; in the five years of its existence as a weekly there were 1,232 pages in all.

46. See *La Voce* (31 March 1910).

47. Gramsci, *Quaderni del carcere*, 4:2188–89.

48. For Prezzolini's reckonings concerning *La Voce*'s readership, see *La Voce* (11 Nov. 1909) and (29 Dec. 1910), as well as his *La Voce 1908–1913*, 9–10.

49. For a list of the cities in which *La Voce* could initially be purchased, see the issue of 8 April 1909. Early in 1913 *La Voce* was forced to increase its price to twenty cents an issue, but even then its pricing policy was in marked contrast to the one that had governed *Leonardo*. The earlier journal had started out at fifteen cents an issue, increased to fifty cents by late 1904, and doubled to a full lira by 1905.

50. Besides Grey and Sarfatti, two other women who contributed to *La Voce* were Neera, the pen name of Anna Radius Zuccari, and Sibilla Aleramo, author of *Una donna*. During the *La Voce* years, Aleramo would have brief romantic involvements with Papini and Boine.

51. Soffici, *Fine di un mondo*, 68.

52. Prezzolini, *Italia 1912*, 83–85.

53. Ibid., 83–86.

54. Prezzolini, "La nostra promessa," *La Voce* (27 Dec. 1908).

55. Alberto Vedrani, "I giudizi su Cesare Lombroso," *La Voce* (25 Nov. 1909), and "Cesare Lombroso," *La Voce* (9 and 23 Dec. 1909). Vedrani directed a psychiatric hospital in Lucca.

56. See Prezzolini's prefatory note to Giuseppe Gallico, "Il siciliano," *La Voce* (30 Sept. 1909), and his response to Giovanni Borelli, "Ancora e sempre contro Roma," *La Voce* (1 Sept. 1910).

57. Papini, "L'Italia risponde," *La Voce* (20 Dec. 1909). The article impressed Romain Rolland, who translated it into French.

58. Soffici, "L'impressionismo e la pittura italiana," *La Voce* (6 May 1909).

59. Giorgio Sorel, "Il valore sociale della castità," and Roberto G. Assagioli, "Le idee di Sigmund Freud sulla sessualità," *La Voce* (10 Feb. 1910). The issue also contained discussions of Otto Weininger by Giulio A. Levi, of clerical celibacy by Romolo Murri, and of female sexuality by Margherita Sarfatti, among many other articles and features.

60. Giannotto Bastianelli, "La musica a Firenze: Gino Bellio," *La Voce* (5 May 1910).

61. Letter from Papini to Rolland of 2 April 1909 in Giordan, *Romain Rolland et le Mouvement Florentin de La Voce*, 173–174; emphasis in original. Likewise, Prezzolini had written in his very first article for *La Voce* that "fortunately for us, France is not Paris, nor is all Paris on display in its boulevards or for sale in its shop windows and fashionable department stores"; see his "La politica francese," *La Voce* (20 Dec. 1908).

62. See, for example, Romain Rolland, "Jean-Christophe è con noi," *La Voce* (23 Dec. 1909); Giorgio Sorel, "Il risveglio dell'anima francese," *La Voce* (14 April 1910); and Charles Péguy, "La tapisserie de Sainte Geneviève et de Jeanne d'Arc," *La Voce* (21 Nov. 1912).

63. Rolland's extensive contact with the *vociani* is documented in Giordan, *Romain Rolland et le Mouvement Florentin de La Voce;* his relations with Bloch are documented in their *Deux Hommes se Rencontrent*. We do not know with certainty how Bloch met Prezzolini, but Rolland appears to have been the intermediary; see, above all, his letter of 29 March 1910 to Prezzolini in Giordan, 210–211. In any case, *La Voce* was recommending *L'Effort* to its readers by the time of its issue of 1 September 1910, 388. From Prezzolini's letter to Soffici of 29 September 1910, in which he mentioned that *L'Effort* had printed translations of Soffici's two articles on the Impressionist Exhibition in Florence, we can surmise that the correspondence between Bloch and Prezzolini had begun by then. See Prezzolini and Soffici, *Carteggio*, 1:132–133.

64. The visit to Péguy and Sorel is mentioned in a letter from Soffici to Papini of 11 March 1910 (held at the Fondazione Primo Conti) as well as in Prezzolini's diary entry of 10 March 1910, *Diario 1900–1941*, 90. Regarding the visit to Rolland, see the marvelous description in Soffici, *Fine di un mondo*, 186–187.

65. Initial publicity for the show in *La Voce* (3 March 1910) promised works by Picasso as well, but none was finally included.

66. Prezzolini, "L'Esposizione di Venezia," *La Voce* (28 April 1910), compared the Florence exhibition favorably with one organized in Venice the previous fall.

67. See Scipio Slataper, "'Giuditta' di F. Hebbel," *La Voce* (24 Nov. 1910); Papini, "Miele e pietra," *La Voce* (11 Aug. 1910); Giulio Levi, "Ottone Weininger," *La Voce* (10 Feb. 1910); and Italo Tavolato, "Frank Wedekind," *La Voce* (30 May 1912). Later, in the 12 August 1914 issue of *Il Resto del Carlino*, Giovanni Boine added yet another discussion of the tormented young Viennese "genius."

68. The review appeared in *La Stampa* (31 Dec. 1912); it is reprinted in Papini, *Stroncature*, 257–265.

69. In 1912 Aleramo was involved in a tempestuous love affair with Papini, and his attitude toward Weininger was clearly a major issue in the relationship. See Aleramo's letters to Papini of 2 and 12 October 1912 in Conti and Morino, *Sibilla Aleramo e il suo tempo*, 74–77.

70. See Sibilla Aleramo, "La pensierosa," *Il Marzocco* (18 Jan. 1914), where she argued that "the famous 'pure thought' does not exist for a woman," and "Apologia dello spirito femminile," *Il Marzocco* (9 April 1911), where the retreat from a socially oriented feminism is already explicit, though without the connection to Weininger. The articles are reprinted in her *Andando e stando*, 59–69 and 126–141. See also Alba Andreini, "Weininger e weiningeriani nella riflessione e nella biografia di Sibilla Aleramo," in Buttafuoco and Zancan, *Svelamento*, 120–136.

71. Soffici, "Anna Gerebzova," *La Voce* (30 Jan 1913).

72. See Prezzolini, "La guerra pietosa," *La Voce* (26 Oct. 1911); and Papini, "La guerra vittoriosa," *La Voce* (19 Oct. 1912).

73. Falea de Calcedonia, "La morte del socialismo (discorrendo con Benedetto Croce)," *La Voce* (9 Feb. 1911). Though cast as an interview, the article was in fact written out in advance by Croce; Falea de Calcedonia is a pseudonym.

74. Prezzolini, "Perché siamo anticlericali," *La Voce* (21 Jan. 1909).

75. Gaetano Salvemini, "I radicali alla Camera," "Documenti elettorali meridionali e radicali," and "L'indennità dell'on. F. S. Nitti," *La Voce* (15 April 1909).

76. "Da Giolitti a Sonnino," *La Voce* (16 Dec. 1909); signed "La Voce," the article is clearly Prezzolini's.

77. Ibid.

78. Ibid.

79. When Oriani died in 1909, Prezzolini wrote a moving obituary in *La Voce* (21 Oct.) praising him for his "force of character arising out of quasi-religious convictions," and in 1912 he reissued *La lotta politica in Italia* under the auspices of *La Voce*'s press.

80. Prezzolini, "Caccia all'uomo," *La Voce* (3 June 1909).

81. Papini, "Nazionalismo," *La Voce* (22 April 1909).

82. Prezzolini, "Che fare?" *La Voce* (23 June 1910). For *La Voce*'s critique of nationalism at the time of its founding convention, see Prezzolini, "Nel VII anniversario della nascita" del "Regno"; and Giovanni Amendola, "Il convegno nazionale," *La Voce* (1 Dec. 1910). Here the accent is on the claim that the ANI's nationalism would "change nothing in the realm of spirit and life" (Amendola), that it would never offer the "interior renewal that is needed" (Prezzolini).

83. Papini, *Passato remoto*, in *Tutte le opere*, 9:920.

84. For the bulk of their correspondence, see Prezzolini, *Amendola e "La Voce,"* 31–183. In the final letter, dated 29 September 1924, Amendola wrote Prezzolini to break off their relationship because of what he believed to be Prezzolini's solidarity with the profascist writer Luigi Pirandello. Prezzolini considered this a misunderstanding of his views but made no reply.

85. At the Giubbe Rosse one day in 1904, Papini had struck up a friendship with Jurgis Baltrusaitis, a Lithuanian poet living in Florence. From him he learned about a Moscow circle around the journal *Vesy* that included Valery Bryusov and Andrey Bely in addition to Baltrusaitis himself. This sparked Papini's interest sufficiently to produce a brief article on them for *Leonardo;* see Papini, "La Bilancia (Viessy)," *Leonardo* (Feb. 1905). Thus, when Amendola came to Moscow, he had a letter of introduction from Papini and was able to fall in with the circle immediately, even producing one article for *Vesy*. See Papini, *Passato remoto*, in *Tutte le opere*, 9:865–870; his letter to Amendola of 7 July 1905 in G. Amendola, *Carteggio, 1897–1912*, 1:149; and his letter of 26 October 1904 to Soffici in Paris in their *Carteggio*, 59. For the correspondence between Amendola and William James, see G. Amendola, *Carteggio, 1897–1912*, 1:158, 203–204, 269–271.

86. Letter of 22 October 1906 from Amendola to Papini in G. Amendola, *Carteggio, 1897–1912*, 1:251.

87. Ibid.; see also E. Amendola, *Vita con Giovanni Amendola*, 83, where a page from his notes at a lecture by Wundt is reproduced.

88. See Papini, *Passato remoto*, in *Tutte le opere*, 9:921. Eva Kühn Amendola published the essay "Ottimismo trascendentale di A. Schopenhauer" in a 1907 issue

of *Coenobio*, a journal edited in Lugano. See her *Vita con Giovanni Amendola*, 8, 43–44.

89. Papini, *Passato remoto*, in *Tutte le opere*, 9:922.

90. Letter of 8 December 1911 from Scipio Slataper to Elody in his *Lettere*, 2:95.

91. See Giovanni Amendola, "Maine de Biran e Kant," *L'Anima* (Jan. 1911), and *Maine de Biran*, the book into which the article was subsumed.

92. G. Amendola, *La volontà e il bene*, now in *Etica e biografia*, 25.

93. Twelve issues of *L'Anima* (The Soul) were produced from January through December 1911. Besides Papini and Amendola, contributors included Henri Bergson, Giovanni Boine, Italo Tavolato, and Theodor Däubler.

94. Prezzolini, *Quattro scoperte*, 179–181.

95. For the comparison of the two southerners from which this quotation is drawn, see Prezzolini, *Amici*, 120–122.

96. Ernesto Rossi, quoted in Origo, *A Need to Testify*, 131.

97. See his letter of 3 June 1908 in Salvemini, *Carteggi*, 1:386–387.

98. Salvemini's most famous attack on Giolitti was as the "minister of the under-world"; his book bearing that title *(Il ministro della mala vita)* was published by *La Voce* in 1910.

99. See Prezzolini, *Il tempo della Voce*, 429.

100. See Salvemini's letter to Prezzolini of 6 October 1911 in his *Carteggi*, 1:522.

101. *L'Unità* was published as a weekly from 16 December 1911 until 31 December 1920, with a three-month interruption in the fall of 1914 and then a longer one from the end of May 1915 until December 1916, during which time Salvemini served as a volunteer at the front. It was published in Florence except in 1917–18, when it was located in Rome.

102. See Croce, *A History of Italy, 1871–1915*, 251. For Salvemini's later career, see Hughes, *The Sea Change*, 91–100.

103. Letter of 20 July 1910, quoted in Prezzolini, *La Voce 1908–1913*, 774.

104. See Ferdinando Pasini, "L'università italiana a Trieste," *La Voce* (2 Jan. 1913).

105. Soffici, *Fine di un mondo*, 70.

106. Stuparich, *Scipio Slataper*, 91.

107. The three volumes of Scipio Slataper, *Lettere*, were written respectively to Anna (a suicide victim in May 1910, to whom he dedicated his autobiographical novel, *Il mio carso*), Elody (later the wife of Giani Stuparich), and Gigetta (whom he would marry in 1913).

108. Slataper, "Lettere triestine," *La Voce* (11 and 25 Feb., 11 and 25 March, 22 April, 29 July, 9 Sept. 1909).

109. Slataper, *Ibsen*, 223.

110. Slataper, *Appunti e note di diario* (19 Feb. 1911), 133.

111. Slataper, "Ai giovani intelligenti d'Italia," *La Voce* (26 Aug. 1909).

112. Letter from Slapater to Gigetta of 10 December 1911 in Slataper, *Lettere*, 3:117–118. Slataper's Prezzolini is of course the Prezzolini of *La Voce*, not the anarchic individualist of *Leonardo* or the rebel Prezzolini remembered himself as having been in high school.

113. For the value of "barbarity" in Slataper, see his "Quando Roma era Bisanzio," *La Voce* (20 April 1911).

114. Slataper, "Il silenzio," *La Voce* (24 March 1910).

115. Stuparich, *Scipio Slataper*, 99.

116. Aleramo, "Scipio Slataper," in *Andando e stando,* 159.

117. Jahier was actually born in Genoa in 1884, but this was, as Prezzolini later put it, "only by accident . . . He is a man from the mountains of Piedmont who speaks Tuscan, and his countries are two: the Waldensian valley for the ancestors on his father's side and Florence for the language he uses" (his mother's family was Florentine). See Prezzolini, *Amici,* 37.

118. For Boine's debt to de Maistre, see Isnenghi, *Il mito della grande guerra,* 71. Boine was also, however, a Catholic modernist quite critical of the lack of spirituality in the contemporary church. For more on his reactionary view of the state, see his "Gobineau e la razza," *La Rassegna contemporanea* (10 Aug. 1914):394–413. In 1911 he had opposed the widening of the suffrage; see his letter to Prezzolini of 24 April in his *Carteggio,* 1:156.

119. See Piero Jahier, "Paul Claudel" and "Partage de Midi," *La Voce* (11 April and 13 June 1912).

120. See Soffici, "Il claudellismo," *La Voce* (10 Oct. 1912); Jahier, "Claudellismo e lemmonismo," *La Voce* (17 Oct. 1912); and Soffici, "Claudellismo ancora," *La Voce* (24 Oct. 1912).

121. Papini, "Giovanni Boine," *Il Resto del Carlino* (20 May 1917), excerpted in Prezzolini, *La Voce 1908–1913,* 484.

122. See Boine, "San Giovanni della Croce," *Il Rinnovamento* (Nov.–Dec. 1907 and March 1908), reprinted in *Il peccato e le altre opere,* 519–548.

123. Some of Unamuno's letters to Boine are reprinted in the third volume of Boine, *Carteggio.* The Kierkegaard recommendation came in his letter of 18 January 1907 (3:41), and there is a reference to it in Boine's review of his *Vida de D. Quijote y Sancho,* in *Il Rinnovamento* (Feb. 1907), which suggests that he pursued it. Papini and Soffici also corresponded with Unamuno in this period, but for them he figured primarily as an intellectual stimulus for their pursuit of *toscanità,* while for Boine (as for Amendola, who also wrote to Unamuno at this time) his importance had more to do with the possibility of Christian faith.

124. See Boine's letter of 25 May 1910 to Alessandro Casati in Boine, *Carteggio,* 3:401–402.

125. Boine, *Il peccato e le altre opere,* 7. For Boine's theorization of "fragmentism," see his "Un ignoto," *La Voce* (8 Feb. 1912).

126. Boine, "Che fare?" *La Voce* (25 Aug. 1910), a reply to Prezzolini, "Che fare?" *La Voce* (23 June 1910). There Prezzolini had written, in phrases that may remind us of the more famous ones later penned by William Butler Yeats: "Everything is falling. Every ideal is vanishing. Parties no longer exist, only little groups and their clients. The sad state of parliament has repercussions throughout the country . . . Everything is fragmenting . . . The disgust is enormous. The best no longer have any confidence."

127. Boine, "La ferita non chiusa," *La Voce* (23 March 1911).

128. Boine, "L'estetica dell'ignoto," *La Voce* (29 Feb. 1912). For Croce's reply, in which he defended the virtues of clarity and order as well as individuality, see his "Amori con le nuvole," *La Voce* (4 April 1912). Boine then responded with "Amori con l'onestà,'" *La Voce* (11 April 1912), a defense of "mystery" rather than "clarity" as central to a proper understanding of the world. From this time on, Boine became extremely antagonistic to Croce, claiming, for example, in a letter of 13 April 1914 to their mutual friend Alessandro Casati that Croce "mortifies the spirit." See Boine, *Carteggio,* 3:832.

129. Boine, "Don Chisciotte in Toscana," *La Voce* (18 April 1912).

130. Prezzolini, *Il tempo della Voce*, 130.

131. Benito Mussolini, "La lotta linguistica nel Trentino" and "Il Trentino," *La Voce* (6 Jan. and 15 Dec. 1910); these were reissued from *La Voce*'s press in May 1911 as a small volume, *Il Trentino veduto da un socialista.*

132. See Mussolini, "La mia vita dal 29 luglio 1883 al 23 novembre 1911," in *Opera omnia*, 33:256. In November 1907 Mussolini took up study in Bologna toward a diploma in French, and in the spring and summer of 1908 he taught French in a school in Oneglia on the Italian Riviera.

133. The young Mussolini's relation to Marxism is a deeply contentious point among scholars. For an argument that he was "as orthodox a Marxist as any in the ranks of the Italian Socialist Party," see Gregor, *Young Mussolini and the Intellectual Origins of Fascism*, 41–42, 53. The difficulty with this argument is that although Mussolini sometimes wrote with conviction about Marx, he also wrote with equal or greater conviction about anti-Marxist rebels such as Nietzsche. In this respect, the judgment of his friend and comrade Angelica Balabanoff rings true, despite the animosity she felt toward him by the time she delivered it. Mussolini, she wrote, was a revolutionary not because of any essentially intellectual commitment but because of "his own sense of indignity and frustration, his passion to assert his own ego, and from a determination for personal revenge." See Balabanoff, *My Life as a Rebel*, 45. See also R. De Felice, *Mussolini*, 1:38–42; and Croce, *A History of Italy, 1871–1915*, 266–267.

134. See Mussolini's letter to Prezzolini of 4 January 1909 in E. Gentile, *Mussolini e "La Voce*," 35; see also Mussolini's article "La Voce," *Vita trentina* (3 April 1909), reprinted in the same volume, 83–87, in which *Leonardo* is discussed at some length.

135. Mussolini, "La filosofia della forza," *Il Pensiero romagnolo* (13 Dec. 1908), now in *Scritti politici di Benito Mussolini*, 109.

136. Simonini, *Il linguaggio di Mussolini*, 158. The novel, written that year, appeared serially from January through May 1910.

137. Letter from Mussolini to Prezzolini of 1 October 1909, now in E. Gentile, *Mussolini e "La Voce*," 43.

138. Prezzolini continued: "Mussolini is one of us. He is a *vociano*." See R. De Felice, *Intellettuali di fronte al fascismo*, 103.

139. For two of Mussolini's unsuccessful efforts to publish in *La Voce*, see E. Gentile, *Mussolini e "La Voce*," 35 and 39–40.

140. Mussolini, "La Voce," 86. The passage quoted comes from Papini and Prezzolini, *La coltura italiana*, 172.

141. See De Begnac, *Palazzo Venezia*, 131. The statement was made in May 1935.

142. Mussolini, "La teoria sindacalista,"in *Scritti politici*, 114. According to R. De Felice, "Mussolini was never a revolutionary syndicalist in the strict sense of the term, that is, in the political-organizational sense." See his *Mussolini*, 1:41.

143. Mussolini clearly shared Prezzolini's view that syndicalism's weakness was its failure to produce strong leadership, and he echoed Prezzolini's doubts about the syndicalists' frequenting of fashionable cafés. Even the review's final note of hope— that a "new human character" might still arise out of the "mass of workers once they are purified of syndicalist practice"—was somewhat less than syndicalist, since the idea of a "new human character" was linked to "Alfredo Oriani and his

magnificent *La rivolta ideale*," a book that took the same skeptical view of the workers as did Prezzolini.

144. R. De Felice, *Mussolini*, 1:85–87, 284. Mussolini was publicly explicit about *La Voce*'s importance for him on at least three occasions: in 1912, 1917, and 1935. See E. Gentile, *Il mito dello Stato nuovo dall'antigiolittismo al fascismo*, 105.

145. See Mussolini's letter of 5 November 1914 to Prezzolini asking him, Papini, and Slataper to join *Il Popolo d'Italia*, now in E. Gentile, *Mussolini e "La Voce,"* 63–64.

146. See Mussolini's letter to Prezzolini of 25 March 1914, now in ibid., 62. *Utopia* appeared in ten issues from November 1913 through December 1914. During the war years Mussolini again refocused his search for a "new aristocracy," this time turning to the "men of the trenches" in hopes of a future *trincerocrazia* (trenchocracy), clearly a prototype for fascism. See his "Trincerocrazia" (15 Dec. 1917), in *Scritti politici*, 171–173.

147. See Prezzolini's brief annotation to the announcement of *Utopia* in *La Voce* (4 Dec. 1913), in which he added that "the enterprise seems to us to exceed even the many resources of Benito Mussolini. This man is *a man*, and he stands out all the more in a world of stick figures and of consciousnesses frayed like so many worn-out elastic bands." See also Mussolini's reply, "L'impresa disperata (a Prezzolini)," *Utopia* (15 Jan. 1914):1–5.

148. The declaration, made to Yvon De Begnac, is quoted in Veneziani, *La rivoluzione conservatrice in Italia*, 152.

149. See Segrè, *Fourth Shore*.

150. For an interesting effort to capture this mood, see Renato Serra, "Partenza di un gruppo di soldati per la Libia," *Scritti*, 2:523–534. The piece originally appeared in *Il Cittadino* (21 April 1912) of Cesena, Serra's hometown newspaper.

151. Giovanni Amendola, "La guerra," *La Voce* (28 Dec. 1911).

152. In Prezzolini, "L'illusione tripolina," *La Voce* (18 May 1911), the focus is a counterattack against Corradini and *L'Idea Nazionale;* in the unsigned editorial "Perché non si deve andare a Tripoli," *La Voce* (17 Aug. 1991), it is on calculating Libya's economic value; the two points are then combined in another editorial, "Tripoli e Triplice," *La Voce* (21 Sept. 1911).

153. See the editorial "A Tripoli" and Slataper, "E i cipressi di San Guido?" *La Voce* (5 Oct. 1911).

154. Papini, "La guerra vittoriosa," *La Voce* (19 Oct. 1911); emphasis in original.

155. "La guerra pietosa," *La Voce* (26 Oct. 1911); the editorial was unsigned but almost certainly written by Amendola.

156. G. Amendola, "La guerra."

157. Antonio Anzilotti, "La nostra tradizione e il Nazionalismo," *La Voce* (4 July 1912).

158. Riccardo Bacchelli, "La disciplina degli italiani," *La Voce* (18 July 1912).

159. Prezzolini, "Voce della nuova generazione," *La Voce* (5 Dec. 1912); emphasis in original. The close association of war and discipline had already been expressed in the editorial in which *La Voce* first declared itself in favor of the Libyan enterprise; see "A Tripoli," *La Voce* (5 Oct. 1911).

160. See Prezzolini, *Italia 1912*, 82–87. The same usage occurs in a letter to Jean-Richard Bloch of 20 February 1912 (Archivio Prezzolini) in which Prezzolini spoke of what was almost certainly his *Italia 1912* project as a *cahier* for a French

audience: "P.S. In the *Cahier* I would speak of *La Voce* only incidentally, putting it in its 'historical' context."

161. Letter from Papini to Prezzolini of 7 August 1909, excerpted in Prezzolini, *La Voce 1908–1913*, 309–310. See also Papini's more direct criticisms of *La Voce* in his letter to Soffici of 30 December 1908 in their *Carteggio*, 408.

162. See the exchange between Soffici and Prezzolini from 9 to 15 June in their *Carteggio*, 1:184–189. See also Soffici's complaints about Prezzolini's incomprehension of art and about the "professorism" of the early *La Voce* in his letters to Papini of 28 August and 26 December 1908 in their *Carteggio*, 334, 406.

163. Diary entry of 10 April 1910, cited in E. Gentile, *La Voce e l'età giolittiana*, 157.

164. Letter from Prezzolini to Salvemini of 11 July 1911 in Salvemini, *Carteggi*, 1:491–492.

165. See Casati's letter to Prezzolini of 15 April 1911 in their *Carteggio*, 2:277–278.

166. See Slataper's letter to Prezzolini of 21 April 1911 in Prezzolini, *Il tempo della Voce*, 395–398.

167. Papini, "Il significato del futurismo," *Lacerba* (1 Feb. 1913).

168. Soffici, "La ricetta di Ribi Buffone," *La Voce* (1 April 1909).

169. Soffici, "Arte libera e pittura futurista," *La Voce* (22 June 1911).

170. The incident is retold in Soffici, *Fine di un mondo*, 196–204; and in Carrà, *La mia vita*, 149–151.

171. "Avviso a chi tocca," *La Voce* (6 July 1911). Appearing in large print and in a box on the issue's final page, this "warning to those who come next" was unsigned, but privately Prezzolini acknowledged having written it.

172. See Amendola's letters of 6 and 7 July 1911 in Prezzolini, *Il tempo della Voce*, 407–408. Later Prezzolini would take it as indicative of Amendola's uniquely moralistic character that he would formally "resign" from *La Voce*. See Prezzolini, *Amendola e "La Voce*," 11.

173. See Amendola's letter of 10 July 1911 to Salvemini in Salvemini, *Carteggi*, 491.

174. Letter of 7 July 1911 from Salvemini in Rome to Prezzolini, ibid., 484–488; emphasis in original.

175. Letter of 5 July 1911 from Prezzolini to Salvemini, ibid., 484.

176. Letter of 7 July 1911 from Prezzolini to Salvemini, ibid., 488–489.

177. Ibid., 498–499.

178. Letter of 28 September 1911 from Salvemini to Prezzolini, ibid., 506–509.

179. See especially the letter of 29 September 1911 from Amendola to Salvemini, ibid., 512–514.

180. Salvemini's resignation letter to Prezzolini is reprinted both in ibid., 521–524, and in Prezzolini, *Il tempo della Voce*, 441–447.

181. Letter of 20 October 1911 from Prezzolini to Salvemini in Salvemini, *Carteggi*, 539.

182. E. Amendola, *Vita con Giovanni Amendola*, 292, 309; emphasis in original. Included among the participants, Amendola made clear, would be Salvemini, even though "his democratic formulas repel me." Salvemini spoke of the same idea in a letter that summer to Giuseppe Lombardo-Radice: "We would like—Prezzolini and I—to hold a private gathering in Florence of a dozen reliable men: to discuss the fundamental problems of contemporary Italy; to specify a group of concrete ideas

that we hold in common; to separate out the individual questions for appropriate study and to dedicate a year of *La Voce* to a continual campaign for our common ideas; and so to prepare for September 1912 a Florence Congress of the friends of *La Voce* and to launch the program and create the organization of a new party." Cited in Golzio and Guerra, *La cultura italiana del '900 attraverso le riviste*, 5:49 n.1.

183. Papini, "Schegge," *Lacerba* (15 Sept. 1913).

4. Culture Wars and War for Culture

1. *Lacerba* (1 Dec. 1913).
2. Viviani, *Giubbe Rosse*, 65. In addition to Viviani's book, this account of the futurist exhibition and *serata* in Florence is based on the recollections of Soffici in *Fine di un mondo*, 327–333; the newspaper story in *Il Corriere della Sera* (13 Dec. 1913), now reprinted in Vassalli, *L'alcova elettrica*, 140; the reportage in *Lacerba* (15 Dec. 1913); and the secondary accounts in Manghetti, *Futurismo a Firenze 1910–1920*, 167–172, Tisdall and Bozzolla, *Futurism*, 92, and Bargellini, *Florence the Magnificent*, 4:141–145.
3. Viviani, *Giubbe Rosse*, 66.
4. *Il Corriere della Sera* (13 Dec. 1913), reprinted in Vassalli, *L'alcova elettrica*, 140.
5. Soffici, *Fine di un mondo*, 328.
6. Viviani, *Giubbe Rosse*, 70.
7. Aldo Palazzeschi, letter to *Lacerba* (15 Dec. 1913).
8. One of Marinetti's most original manifestos, "Distruzione della sintassi, immaginazione senza fili, parole in libertà," appeared in Milan on 11 May 1913. A slightly abbreviated version was reprinted in *Lacerba* (15 June 1913).
9. For the letters, see Cavallo, *5 xilografie e 4 puntesecche di Ardengo Soffici con le lettere di Picasso*.
10. Letter from Soffici to Papini of 9 December 1909 (Fondazione Primo Conti, Fiesole).
11. Letter from Soffici to Papini of 28 December 1910 (Fondazione Primo Conti).
12. Letter from Soffici to Slataper of 3 March 1910, now in Dedola, "'La Voce' e i 'Cahiers de la Quinzaine,'" 558.
13. See Soffici's letter of 8 August, Papini's reply of 12 August, and Soffici's reply to that on 16 August 1908 in their *Carteggio*, 286–311. The controversy was stimulated by Papini's "Walt Whitman," *Nuova Antologia* (16 July 1908), reprinted in *Tutte le opere*, 4:1077–1101.
14. Letter from Papini to Soffici of 11 September 1908 in their *Carteggio*, 353.
15. Letter from Soffici to Papini of 8 August 1908 in ibid., 286–287.
16. Soffici, *Arthur Rimbaud*, now in *Opere*, 1:63–195.
17. Ibid., 101, 126, 142. Soffici would later regard his own differences with Marinetti as being tantamount to those between Rimbaud and Mallarmé.
18. Ibid., 183, 187, 111.
19. Ibid., 65, 68, 91, 78, 98.
20. Soffici, "Picasso e Braque," *La Voce* (24 Aug. 1911).
21. Soffici wrote a futurist aesthetics—"Principî di un'estetica futurista," *La Voce* (31 Jan., 29 Feb., 31 March, 31 May, 31 July, and 31 Dec. 1916), continued in *L'Italia futurista* (27 Jan. 1918), *La Raccolta* (15 June and 15 Aug.–15 Oct. 1918),

and *Valori plastici* (Nov.–Dec. 1919), and republished as *Primi principî di una estetica futurista* by Vallecchi in 1920—but he never followed it in his own work. Indeed, by the time the book appeared, his painting had returned to a purely figurative style.

22. Soffici, *Ignoto toscano,* now in *Opere,* 2:8, 5.

23. Ibid., 10, 14, 22–23.

24. On the connection with Bloy's Marchenoir, see Richter, *La formazione francese di Ardengo Soffici, 1900–1914,* 99.

25. Soffici, *Lemmonio Boreo* (1912; revised and expanded, 1921), in *Opere,* 2:27–320.

26. Ibid., 29, 37, 49, 51, 57–58.

27. Ibid., 37, 62–63, 64, 115.

28. Isenghi, *Il mito della grande guerra,* 37.

29. Bellini, *Studi su Ardengo Soffici,* 64–112. The 1921 edition contains seventeen cantos.

30. Ibid., 104.

31. Letter from Prezzolini to Soffici of 1 February 1912 in their *Carteggio,* 1:215.

32. Papini, "Dove mettete la morale," *Nova et Vetera* (10–25 Aug. 1908), now in *Tutte le opere,* 6:17–21.

33. Papini, "La religione sta da sé," *Il Rinnovamento* (July 1908), now in *Tutte le opere,* 6:29–62; emphasis in original.

34. Papini, "I liberi cristiani," *Il Resto del Carlino* (13 Aug. 1910), now in *Tutte le opere,* 6:82–87; here Papini was frustrated enough with Catholic modernism to refer to it as "sterile and comical."

35. Papini, "Esistono cattolici?" *Lacerba* (15 Nov. 1913).

36. "Dacci oggi la nostra poesia quotidiana" appeared in the *La Voce* of 4 April 1912, Papini's maiden issue as editor.

37. For the sad story of this never completed manuscript, see Luigi Baldacci's introduction to Papini, *Rapporto sugli uomini,* 5–21.

38. Papini, "La toscana e la filosofia italiana," *La Cultura contemporanea* (April–May 1911), now in *Tutte le opere,* 8:835–836.

39. One exception was his Virgilian prose hymn, "La campagna," *La Voce* (5 Aug. 1909).

40. See the various letters of 1909 and 1910 in Papini and Prezzolini, *Storia di un'amicizia,* 1:235–257, above all that of 30 March 1910 in which Papini wrote: "There is another thing—much more grave. To put it briefly, I have begun to doubt the one thing that has allowed me to live: my creative powers."

41. Papini, *Un uomo finito,* 151.

42. At the proof stage, the book had a chapter titled "Ugliness," but Papini apparently suppressed it; see Ridolfi, *Vita di Giovanni Papini,* 144. Nonetheless, the theme of his physical ugliness plays an important role in the book in explaining his distance from others and his effort to triumph over them by virtue of his inner strength.

43. Ibid., 225.

44. Ibid., 281.

45. Ibid., 271–272.

46. Papini, *La seconda nascita* (1923), in *Tutte le opere,* 9:369–611.

47. Papini, *Un uomo finito,* 287.

48. Coedited with Federigo Tozzi, *La Torre* appeared as a biweekly for three

issues in 1913 (beginning on 6 November) and for five more in 1914 (the last two of which appeared on 6 and 21 May and were done in Florence).

49. Papini, "Diventar genio," *La Voce* (10 Oct. 1912).

50. Papini, "Introibo," *Lacerba* (1 Jan. 1913).

51. Giovanni Boine, "Epistola al tribunale," *La Voce* (21 Aug. 1913).

52. Letter from Amendola to Papini of 17 March 1913 in E. Amendola, *Vita con Giovanni Amendola*, 371.

53. See Prezzolini's letter to Papini of 17 July 1913 in their *Storia di un'amicizia*, 1:272, and Papini's reply of 22 July in the same volume, 280–282.

54. Prezzolini, *Discorso su Giovanni Papini* (speech delivered 10 Nov. 1914), now in his *Quattro scoperte*, 102.

55. Twenty-seven issues of *Les Soirées de Paris* appeared from February 1912 through August 1914. For approximately its last year the review was financed by Férat and Hélène d'Oettingen and housed in a flat they rented at Boulevard Raspail 278. In addition to their contributions and Apollinaire's, the review published a good deal by Max Jacob. All of them would soon be contributing to *Lacerba* as well.

56. Soffici, "Ancora del futurismo," *La Voce* (11 July 1912).

57. In a letter of 10 April 1912 (Fondazione Primo Conti), he wrote: "A dozen times I have threatened to meet face to face with the futurists, and perhaps I should reconcile myself even with them."

58. The letter is quoted in Soffici, *Ricordi di vita artistica e letteraria*, in *Opere*, 6:27. Vallecchi gives a substantially similar account in his *Ricordi e idee di un editore vivente*, 115–116. In a letter replying to Papini sometime later in the month, Soffici wrote: "I am very happy with this sudden, unexpected decision and the fact that we have acted upon such an admirable design. I am finding in myself the enthusiasm and the passion I had when I was twenty. I feel the sacred fire shooting out from everywhere." See Richter, *La formazione francese di Ardengo Soffici*, 222 n.100.

59. See Papini's letter to Soffici of 31 January 1912 (Fondazione Primo Conti).

60. Letter from Papini to Soffici of 13 January 1913, quoted in Massimo Carrà, "Convergenze e difficoltà fra Milano e Firenze," in Bagatti, Manghetti, and Porto, *Futurismo a Firenze*, 11. The letter was in response to Soffici's conclusion announced in a letter earlier in the month: "I have now rethought the incident with futurism and am convinced that we absolutely must go forward. It is the only movement with which we can associate ourselves. Working with the others we can make it more serious, effective, and fertile. The futurists lack the qualities that can make them be something important and effective, and these are qualities that we possess and can usefully bring to that movement." See Mario Richter, "Soffici futurista," in Manghetti, *Futurismo a Firenze 1910–1920*, 93.

61. See Papini and Soffici, "*Lacerba*, il futurismo e *Lacerba*," *Lacerba* (1 Dec. 1914); and Papini's 1919 introduction to *L'esperienza futurista (1913–1914)*, 4.

62. The speech of 21 February is reprinted in *Lacerba* (1 March 1913).

63. Papini, "Puzzo di Cristianucci," *La Voce* (9 Jan. 1913).

64. Papini, "Contro il futurismo," *Lacerba* (15 March 1913).

65. See Soffici, *Fine di un mondo*, 282, where he comments that for him "L'acerba" had Etruscan (thus Tuscan) resonances and that he had omitted the apostrophe simply to put the reader off balance. In Italian the adjective *acerbo* means sour, unripe or immature, and bitter.

66. Papini did officially become *Lacerba*'s editor only in 1915, when it became

a weekly in order to pursue more closely its campaign for Italian intervention in the war.

67. Papini, "Introibo," *Lacerba* (1 Jan. 1913).

68. *Lacerba* appeared in twenty-four biweekly issues in 1913 and 1914, the only irregularities being an extra edition on 20 September 1914 and a skipped issue in mid-December. In 1915 the review appeared weekly on Sunday for ten issues, and then on Saturday for eleven more. Its final issue of 22 May 1915 appeared on the day that Italian military mobilization was finally ordered.

69. See Gramsci's 1923 letter to Trotsky on futurism in his *Selections from Cultural Writings*, 53.

70. Vallecchi, *Ricordi e idee di un editore vivente*, 119.

71. *Quartiere latino* appeared as a biweekly for seven issues from 24 October 1913 through 28 February 1914. A frequent contributor to *Lacerba* as well, Tommei would die in the last year of the war.

72. The column, which ran in twenty-three installments from 15 January through 15 December 1913, was republished as a book of the same title by *La Voce*'s press (then run by Vallecchi) in 1915.

73. Soffici, "Giornale di bordo," *Lacerba* (15 March 1913).

74. Soffici, *Fine di un mondo*, 283.

75. See Richter, *La formazione francese di Ardengo Soffici*, 238.

76. Soffici, "I pittori cubisti," *La Voce* (26 June 1913). Soffici's articles "Cubismo e oltre," *Lacerba* (1 Jan., 1 Feb., and 15 Feb. 1913), formed the basis of his *Cubismo e oltre*, which appeared from *La Voce*'s press later the same year.

77. Apollinaire, "Nos amis les futuristes" and "Lettres d'Alfred Jarry," *Les Soirées de Paris* (15 Feb. 1914); Soffici, "Caffè: Il nostro amico Apollinaire," *Lacerba* (15 March 1914).

78. Marinetti, "Il poeta futurista Aldo Palazzeschi," now in his *Teoria e invenzione futurista*, 54–56. Marinetti's aim at publicity for futurism was perhaps most evident in his claim that Palazzeschi—a mild-mannered and rather shy man with homosexual interests—"lives among the Beguinnes [a medieval religious order for women] in order to rape them."

79. See Soffici, *Fine di un mondo*, 284, for an account of Palazzeschi's role as mediator in an important meeting between the Florentines and the Milanese in February 1913.

80. Soffici, "Aldo Palazzeschi," *La Voce* (17 July 1913).

81. Aldo Palazzeschi, "Il controdolore: Manifesto futurista," *Lacerba* (15 Jan. 1914).

82. Palazzeschi's "resignation" was published in *La Voce* (28 April 1914).

83. See Palazzeschi's letter to Prezzolini of early May 1914 in their *Carteggio 1912–1973*, 16–19.

84. Aldo Palazzeschi, "Neutrale," *Lacerba* (1 Dec. 1914). When drafted in 1916, Palazzeschi accepted a noncombatant role in the Italian army's signal corps.

85. Italo Tavolato, "Elogio del caffè," *Lacerba* (15 March 1914).

86. Viviani, *Giubbe Rosse*, 95.

87. Italo Tavolato, "Contro la morale sessuale," *Lacerba* (1 Feb. 1913), "Glossa sopra il manifesto futurista della lussuria," *Lacerba* (15 March 1913), and "Elogio della prostituzione," *Lacerba* (1 May 1913). Later the same year the articles were republished by Ferrante Gonnelli in a slim volume titled *Contro la morale sessuale*.

88. On Saint-Point, see Salaris, *Storia del futurismo*, 53–56.

89. See Soffici, *Fine di un mondo*, 322.

90. Papini, "Morte ai morti," *Lacerba* (1 April 1913).

91. Papini, "Gesù peccatore," *Lacerba* (1 June 1913). On 1 April 1914 *Lacerba* carried an announcement that Papini had been acquitted by a local court of having "offended against the predominant religion of the state."

92. Papini, "I cari genitori," *Lacerba* (15 May 1913), and "Chiudiamo le scuole!" *Lacerba* (1 June 1914).

93. Papini, "Il massacro delle donne," *Lacerba* (1 April 1914).

94. See the untitled editorial "L'opera di *Lacerba*" and Papini and Soffici, "*Lacerba*, il futurismo e *Lacerba*," which covers the same points in more detail, in *Lacerba* (1 Dec. 1914).

95. Papini, "Il massacro delle donne," 99.

96. Papini, "La vita non è sacra," *Lacerba* (15 Oct. 1913). For similar rhetoric by Soffici, though somewhat later, see his "Per la guerra," *Lacerba* (1 Sept. 1914).

97. Papini, "Freghiamoci della politica," *Lacerba* (1 Oct. 1913). After war was declared, Papini would try to reconcile this attitude with his interventionism by adding: "I wrote, 'we don't give a damn about politics,' but by politics I meant the way it is played out today by political parties, and I never (NEVER) wrote that we don't give a damn about patriotism, Italy, etc." See Papini's letter of 21 August 1914 to Prezzolini in Luti, *Firenze corpo 8*, 65; emphasis in original.

98. Papini, "La necessità della rivoluzione," 74.

99. Papini, "Perché son futurista," *Lacerba* (1 Dec. 1913).

100. Papini, "Cerchi aperti," *Lacerba* (15 March 1914). Papini's ostensible reason for reaching the conclusion that futurism had become a "church" had to do with differences in the conception of art, Papini's conception being much more favorable toward reflective mediations in art than was Marinetti's. Yet, given that such a difference would have been apparent to Papini from the beginning, and that he had nonetheless gone along with the alliance for nearly a year, his real objection must have been more political than aesthetic in nature. Moreover, this conclusion is substantially confirmed by Soffici's later account, which presented the break with futurism as having been forced by Marinetti's nonnegotiable demand to have *Lacerba* print a series of his articles, articles the Florentines found to be of little intellectual merit. See Soffici, *Fine di un mondo*, 456–458.

101. Soffici, *Fine di un mondo*, 307–310.

102. Letter of 24 November 1921 in Carrà and Soffici, *Lettere 1913–1929*, 148; emphasis in original. The reference to Boccioni in the past tense reflects the fact that he died in the war in 1916.

103. The association of futurism and *teppismo* was constant. For some examples, see Papini's early "Discorso di Roma," *Lacerba* (1 March 1913); his "All'*Idea Nazionale*," *La Voce* (6 March 1913); and Ugo Tommei, "Elegia per il povero teppista," *Lacerba* (15 June 1914).

104. Letter from Prezzolini to Rolland mailed on 15 October 1912, now in Giordan, *Romain Rolland et le Mouvement Florentin de La Voce*, 307–310.

105. Rolland, "La guerra delle due rive," *La Voce* (7 Nov. 1912).

106. Even before *Lacerba* appeared, Prezzolini gave it a brief but courteous introduction in *La Voce* (26 Dec. 1913).

107. Letter of 8 February 1913 from Prezzolini to Soffici in their *Carteggio*, 1:245.

108. See *La Voce* (10 April 1913).

109. Prezzolini, "Alcune idee chiare intorno al futurismo," *La Voce* (10 April 1913).

110. For the distancing, see Prezzolini, "*La Voce e Lacerba*," *La Voce* (5 June 1913), and "Il processo a *Lacerba*," *La Voce* (3 July 1913). For the attack, see his "Un anno di *Lacerba*," *La Voce* (28 Jan., 28 Feb., and 28 March 1914).

111. The change was announced in Prezzolini, "*La Voce* nel 1914," *La Voce* (11 Dec. 1913), and the slogan was used as the journal's subtitle in each of the twenty-two issues of 1914 that were under Prezzolini's direction.

112. Among the high points of *La Voce* in 1913, besides Prezzolini's own very important five-part series, "Parole d'un uomo moderno," were a famous exchange between Croce and Gentile and a six-part series by De Ruggiero on the idealist concept of culture. See Benedetto Croce, "Intorno all'idealismo attuale," *La Voce* (13 Nov. 1913); Giovanni Gentile, "Intorno all'idealismo attuale (Ricordi e confessioni)," *La Voce* (11 Dec. 1913); and Guido De Ruggiero, "Critica del concetto di cultura," *La Voce* (26 Dec. 1912; 2, 9, and 30 Jan. and 6 and 13 Feb. 1913).

113. Prezzolini, *Italia 1912*, 51; emphasis added.

114. Ibid., 56, 65.

115. Ibid., 74, 78–79.

116. Prezzolini, "La vita nazionale," *La Voce* (6 Feb. 1913).

117. Prezzolini, "Parole d'un uomo moderno," *La Voce* (13 March, 24 April, 22 May, 14 Aug., and 25 Sept. 1913).

118. Giovanni Boine, "Parole d'un uomo moderno," *La Voce* (1 May 1913).

119. Despite De Ruggiero's renown as a historian of liberalism and a liberal opponent of fascism, his prewar thinking was strongly influenced by his teacher Gentile. For this background, see Sasso, "Considerazioni sulla filosofia di De Ruggiero."

120. "World as theater" *(il mondo-teatro)* was a central concept in Enrico Ruta, "Il mito e il fatto," *La Voce* (13 and 28 May 1914).

121. Prezzolini, "Impressioni: Le sorprese della storia," *La Voce* (7 Nov. 1912).

122. Prezzolini, "Ringraziamenti," *La Voce* (13 April 1914); emphasis in original.

123. Ruta, "Il mito e il fatto."

124. Jean-Richard Bloch, "La democrazia e le feste," *La Voce* (28 July 1914). The article had previously appeared in *L'Effort Libre*, the journal Bloch then edited in Poitiers, although it may have been written in Florence, where he spent six months from the end of 1913 through the spring of 1914.

125. Prezzolini, "Sciopero generale," *La Voce* (28 June 1914); Papini, "I fatti di Giugno," *Lacerba* (15 June 1914). Both authors used the metaphor of disease to characterize the state of Italy in their concluding paragraphs.

126. Prezzolini, "Sciopero generale."

127. Prezzolini's new preface to their *Vecchio e nuovo nazionalismo* is dated April 1914.

128. See Prezzolini, *Diario 1900–1941*, 138, and his "Io, Soffici, Papini," *La Voce* (28 July 1914).

129. See Soffici, *Ricordi di vita artistica e letteraria*, in *Opere*, 6:112, and *Fine di un mondo*, 425–427.

130. Letter of 6 August 1914, quoted in Luti, *Firenze corpo 8*, 186; Papini, untitled preface and "Il dovere dell'Italia," and Soffici, "Intorno alla gran bestia,"

Lacerba (15 Aug. 1914). Papini's article was republished in 1915 with the censored passages restored in *La paga del sabato*, now in *Tutte le opere*, 8:273–282.

131. Prezzolini, "Facciamo la guerra," *La Voce* (28 Aug. 1914). See also his letter to Alessandro Casati of 8 August 1914 in their *Carteggio*, 2:402.

132. Prezzolini and Soffici, *Carteggio*, 1:255. Among Soffici's subsequent articles on the war was a series, "Per la guerra," *Lacerba* (1, 15, and 20 Sept., 1 and 15 Oct. 1914).

133. Papini, *La paga del sabato*, in *Tutte le opere*, 8:279.

134. See, above all, Mann, *Reflections of a Nonpolitical Man*.

135. Prezzolini, "Facciamo la guerra."

136. See Giordan, *Romain Rolland et le Mouvement Florentin de La Voce*, 335–336.

137. Romain Rolland, "Protesta per la distruzione di Lovanio," *La Voce* (13 Sept. 1914); despite the Italian title, the letter itself was left in the original French.

138. In elections held on 24 January 1915, Florentines did support interventionist parties by a margin of 7,000 votes over their neutralist opponents. But of 60,000 eligible voters, only 27,000 actually cast a ballot.

139. The referendum results appeared on the final page of *Lacerba*'s issue of 1 November, the special supplement on 15 November.

140. See Prezzolini, *Il tempo della Voce*, 199. where Agnoletti's journal, *La Riscossa latina (The Latin Uprising)*, is described as "nationalist, artistic, and incredibility ill suited to that public." It appeared in twenty-three issues from January through September 1909, partly as a result of encouragement from Giovanni Pascoli, with whom Agnoletti had had a lively correspondence in the previous three years.

141. Fernando Agnoletti, "Canto per Trento e Trieste," *Lacerba* (1 Nov. 1914).

142. Soffici, *Fine di un mondo*, 431; and Vallecchi, *Ricordi e idee*, 123.

143. See, for example, Papini, "Ciò che dobbiamo alla Francia," *Lacerba* (1 Sept. 1914), and "L'antitalia," *Lacerba* (1 Nov. 1914).

144. Papini, "Amiamo la guerra," *Lacerba* (1 Oct. 1914).

145. See, for example, Prezzolini "La guerra tradita," *La Voce* (28 Sept. 1914), prefaced by a long quotation from Arthur Schopenhauer on "eternal justice."

146. Croce and Prezzolini, *Carteggio (1904–1945)*, 2:433–434; emphasis in original.

147. Prezzolini, "I socialisti non sono neutrali," *La Voce* (13 Oct. 1914); the article was signed "La Voce," but there is no doubt that Prezzolini wrote it.

148. Mussolini, "Dalla neutralità assoluta alla neutralità attiva ed operante," now in *Opera omnia*, 6:393–403. For a close analysis of the article, see R. De Felice, *Mussolini*, 1:258–264.

149. From 24 October to 8 November (the day Prezzolini accepted Mussolini's invitation to join *Il Popolo d'Italia*), Mussolini wrote four letters to Prezzolini, reprinted in E. Gentile, *Mussolini e "La Voce,"* 63–64, the last two of which were straightforward invitations. Prezzolini went to Rome immediately, and the last issue of *La Voce* he edited appeared on 28 November.

150. See Prezzolini's 8 November entry ("Mussolini is starting a newspaper and has asked me to collaborate. I accept.") in *Diario 1900–1941*, 140, his opening letter in *La Voce* of 28 November, and his "La pagina di Prezzolini," *La Voce* (15 Dec. 1914), the first issue of *La Voce* under the editorship of Giuseppe De Robertis.

151. Prezzolini, *L'Italiano inutile*, 204.

152. Letter from Prezzolini to Soffici of 5 December 1914 in their *Carteggio*, 1:256.

153. Mussolini called for the gathering in his article "L'adunata," *Il Popolo d'Italia* (24 Jan. 1915), which appeared under the banner headline "I fasci interventisti a raccolta!" Prezzolini wrote an editorial for the issue expressing certainty that the government would be forced to intervene in the war.

154. Prezzolini, *Diario 1900–1941*, 140–41.

155. Letter from Prezzolini to Papini of 15 December 1914 in their *Storia di un'amicizia*, 1:285–286.

156. Prezzolini, "L'Italia può essere grande?" *Il Popolo d'Italia* (13 Dec. 1914).

157. Prezzolini, "L'insegnamento di Oberdan," *Il Popolo d'Italia* (20 Dec. 1914).

158. See, for instance, the editorial "La necessità dell'intervento pervade la conscienza del popolo," *Il Popolo d'Italia* (23 Nov. 1914).

159. Letter from Prezzolini to Soffici of 5 December 1914 in their *Carteggio*, 1:256.

160. In "Non sono irredentista!" *La Voce* (30 Dec. 1914). Prezzolini aimed to correct the impression that might have been left by his earlier article "Basta con la Libia e a Trento e Trieste," *Il Popolo d'Italia* (28 Nov. 1914), namely, that he was an irredentist.

161. Mussolini also made an effort to recruit Slataper, but Slataper turned him down in favor of becoming associated with *Il Resto del Carlino*.

162. Prezzolini, "Giolitti vende l'Italia alla [Banca] Commerciale," and Papini, "Due nemici," *Il Popolo d'Italia* (9 Feb. 1915).

163. Following Papini's lead, writers for *Il Popolo d'Italia* began referring to Giolitti and his followers as the "German party in Italy." See, for example, Francesco Paoloni, "Lo sviluppo logico del giolittismo, partito tedesco in Italia," *Il Popolo d'Italia* (29 Jan. 1916). Later the same year Paoloni produced a book, *Il giolittismo: Partito tedesco in Italia*. By 1917, the notion of internal enemy was widened to include the "war shirkers" *(imboscati)*. By 1919, D'Annunzio was employing it in his irredentist campaign; see his "Letter to the Dalmatians," in Lyttelton, *Italian Fascisms from Pareto to Gentile*, 184. It remained a central notion in the heyday of *squadrismo*, 1920–1922. For an exemplary usage in a *squadrista* memoir, see Banchelli, *Le memorie di un fascista, 1919–1922*, 2–3. See also the discussion in E. Gentile, *Storia del partito fascista*, 499–503.

164. Papini, "Due nemici," reprinted in *Tutte le opere*, 8:313.

165. True to form, Papini denounced D'Annunzio's motives and style even as he shared the same political ends; see his "I mille e lo zero," *Lacerba* (8 May 1915).

166. *La Voce politica* appeared in fourteen biweekly issues from May 7 through December 31, 1915. But Prezzolini edited only its first six, at which point he left the journal to begin his military service.

167. Prezzolini, "La rivoluzione antigiolittiana," *La Voce politica* (22 May 1915).

168. Papini, "Abbiamo vinto," *Lacerba* (22 May 1915).

169. Prezzolini, "Vigiliamo," *La Voce politica* (7 June 1915).

170. Prezzolini, "Noi e la guerra," *La Voce* (15 July 1915).

171. Papini, "E' finito l'anno," *Il Resto del Carlino* (1 Aug. 1915), reprinted in *Tutte le opere*, 8:450–455.

5. The Fate of the Florentine Avant-Garde

1. Papini, "La guerra vittoriosa," *La Voce* (19 Oct. 1911). For Papini, Libya was not such a war; he hoped for a better one.

2. Viviani, *Giubbe Rosse*, 161.

3. From Papini's letter to Soffici of 29 May 1915 (Fondazione Primo Conti, Fiesole), it is evident that he tried to enter the army as a second lieutenant just after Italian intervention was declared.

4. Eksteins, *Rites of Spring*, 171–186. For the wider European context of war hysteria among intellectuals in 1914 and their subsequent disenchantment, see Stromberg, *Redemption by War*.

5. Letter of 24 October 1915 from Prezzolini to Soffici in their *Carteggio*, 1:265.

6. Letter of 26 December 1915 from Prezzolini to Soffici, ibid., 265–267.

7. Prezzolini, *Diario 1900–1941*, 162–301.

8. Ibid., 162–163.

9. Ibid., 163, 210, 165, 167, 206, 278, 300.

10. Prezzolini, "La guerra e la coltura," *Nuova Antologia* (1 Aug. 1916).

11. Prezzolini, *Diario 1900–1941*, 180, 225–226, 210.

12. Ibid., 190, 164, 185, 202.

13. Ibid., 191; letter of 2 January 1916 from Prezzolini to Soffici in their *Carteggio*, 1:268.

14. Prezzolini, *Diario 1900–1941*, 264, 202, 209.

15. Soffici, *Fine di un mondo*, 464.

16. The first of the diaries in terms of the chronology covered, *Errore di coincidenza*, was published serially in the four issues of Soffici's journal of 1920, *Rete mediterranea*. The other two—*Kobilek* (1918] and *La ritirata del Fruili* (1919)—are now available in Soffici, *I diari della grande guerra*.

17. Bellini, *Studi su Ardengo Soffici*, 176.

18. Soffici, *I diari della grande guerra*, 185–186.

19. Immediately before the passage just quoted he wrote: "When after a few minutes I finally got hold of myself and looked around as best as I could, I saw a grand spectacle that will remain in my memory forever." This aspect of the experience of the First World War has been studied most carefully by Paul Fussell; see his *The Great War and Modern Memory*.

20. Soffici, *I diari della grande guerra*, 173–174.

21. Ibid., 76 ("I am almost happy . . ."), 81 ("The trenches are sometimes idyllic . . ."), 134 ("It is difficult to say how much happiness arose in Casati and me . . .").

22. Ibid., 178.

23. For the photos, see Cavallo, *Soffici*, 266–268.

24. Soffici, *I diari della grande guerra*, 253, 95.

25. Ibid., 93.

26. Letter of 6 March 1921 from Soffici to Prezzolini in their *Carteggio*, 2:25.

27. Soffici, *I diari della grande guerra*, 350–351.

28. Letter of 28 November 1917 in Soffici, *Lettere a Prezzolini, 1908–1920*, 123–124.

29. Soffici, *I diari della grande guerra*, 91.

30. Rosai, *Il libro di un teppista*, 52.

31. Rosai, *Via toscanella*, 17.

32. Viviani, *Giubbe Rosse*, 135.

33. Soffici, "Caffè," *Lacerba* (15 Feb. 1914), and "Prefazione," in Rosai, *Via toscanella*, 9.

34. Rosai, *Il libro di un teppista*, 13–14.

35. Ibid., 9, 15.

36. Ibid., 56–57, 61–62.

37. Ibid., 63, 70.

38. Papini, "La mia vigliaccheria," in *Tutte le opere*, 8:243–251.

39. Papini, "Salviamo l'intelligenza!" *Il Resto del Carlino* (25 July 1915), now in *Tutte le opere*, 8:1070, and "E' finito l'anno," ibid., 450–455.

40. Papini, "Quattro begli occhi," *Lacerba* (15 Jan. 1914).

41. See the editorial by Domenico Giuliotti in the first issue, quoted in Piantini, *Quaderno '70 sul Novecento*, 22, which speaks of a "futurist contagion."

42. See Giuliotti and Papini, *Carteggio, I (1913–1927)*.

43. Papini, "L'isola," *Il Resto del Carlino* (30 April 1916), now in *Tutte le opere*, 8:1092. For further discussion of Bloy, see idem, "Paradosso dello scrittore," *La Voce* (30 Sept. 1916), and *Diario*, in *Tutte le opere*, 10:8–9.

44. On Naldi, see R. De Felice, *Mussolini*, 1:273–277; and Prezzolini, *L'Italiano inutile*, 204–208.

45. Papini, "Ritorni divini," *Il Resto del Carlino* (7 November 1915), now in *Tutte le opere*, 6:839.

46. Papini, "Perché (Dopo due anni)," *Il Resto del Carlino* (30 July 1916), now in *Tutte le opere*, 8:1103.

47. Papini, "La festa dell'agnello," *Il Resto del Carlino* (8 April 1917), now in *Tutte le opere*, 6:845.

48. Papini, "La selva dei traditori," *Il Tempo* (12 May 1918), now in *Tutte le opere*, 8:1144–45.

49. Letter from Papini to Cesare Angelini of 16 May 1918, quoted in Ridolfi, *Vita di Giovanni Papini*, 196.

50. Papini, "Contro la neutralità," *Lacerba* (15 Sept. 1914).

51. See Simonetta Soldani, "La Grande guerra lontano dal fronte," in Mori, *La Toscana*, 359. This article is very valuable in general, and I have relied on it for my remarks on the social impact of the war in Tuscany. Also useful in this respect is Snowden, *The Fascist Revolution in Tuscany, 1919–1922*, 33–41.

52. Capacci, *Diario di guerra di un contadino toscano*, 44.

53. See Spriano, *Storia del Partito comunista italiano*, 1:8.

54. One of the most important of these was *La Ronda*, edited by Vincenzo Cardarelli, which appeared in Rome from 1919 until 1923.

55. *L'Italia futurista* became a weekly after February 1917 and continued as such until its last issue of 14 February 1918.

56. Emilio Settimelli, "L'Italia futurista," *L'Italia futurista* (1 June 1916).

57. P. Conti, *La gola del merlo*, 131.

58. Papini, "Lettres italiennes," *Mercure de France* (1 Oct. 1916).

59. Soffici, "L'Italia futurista al fronte," *L'Italia futurista* (29 Sept. 1917). Nine of Tommei's contributions are reprinted in Verdenelli, *Ugo Tommei*, 183–198; one of them was on Rosai and was signed "Ugo Tommei, futurist at the front."

60. See "Alcune parti del film *Vita futurista*," *L'Italia futurista* (15 Oct. 1916), and "Domanda di revisione cinematografica per la richiesta di nulla osta," *L'Italia futurista* (2 Dec. 1916). See also Mario Verdone, "Cinema e letteratura del futurismo," in Verdone and Lauretta, *Cinema e futurismo*, 9–10.

61. On this relation, see Silvia Porto, "Marinetti e *L'Italia futurista*," in Menichi, *Marinetti il futurista*, 31–68.

62. One example of the way the war become blended into the journal's art came in Marinetti's manifesto, "La danza futurista," *L'Italia futurista* (8 July 1917); its three featured dances were the shrapnel, the machine gun, and the aviatrix.

63. On this point see Maria Papini's introduction to *L'Italia futurista (1916–1918)*, 53–54.

64. *L'Italia futurista* (10 Feb. 1917), quoted in Sergio Zoppi, "L'avanguardia europea e il futurismo a Firenze," in Manghetti, *Futurismo a Firenze*, 35–36.

65. Letter from Prezzolini to Soffici of 26 September 1917 in their *Carteggio*, 295.

66. Two of the novels were Paolo Valera's *La folla* (1914–15) and Jules Valles' *L'insorto* (1915).

67. Quoted in Rauti, *Storia d'Italia nei discorsi di Mussolini, 1915–1945*, 1:34.

68. Prezzolini published at least twelve articles in *Il Popolo d'Italia* from 1 February to 1 August 1918, and then a last one for the year on 14 December. The most important were "La scoperta del popolo italiano" (7 Feb.), "Io guardo più là" (27 Feb.), "L'Italia non è qui!" (27 April), "La classe dirigente in Italia" (13 June), "L'ignoranza dirigente" (27 June), "Inquadrare l'Italia" (10 July), and "I problema dei dirigenti" (25 July).

69. Prezzolini, "La classe dirigente in Italia." For a good example of how this theme was pursued, see Enrico Rocca, "La crisi dell'élite dirigente in Italia," *Il Popolo d'Italia* (30 March 1919).

70. Prezzolini, "La scoperta del popolo italiano."

71. Prezzolini, *Dopo Caporetto*, 10.

72. Ibid., 10, 58; emphasis added.

73. Prezzolini, "Inquadrare l'Italia."

74. *L'Assalto* (The Assault) was produced irregularly from 20 April 1919 until the end of the year. The few remaining copies appear to have been lost in the 1966 flood of the Arno.

75. On the theme of the "mutilated victory," see Piazzesi, *Diario di uno squadrista toscano, 1919–1922*, 78.

76. Banchelli, *Le memorie di un fascista, 1919–1922*. In his letter to Prezzolini of 21 March 1923 (Archivio Prezzolini), Banchelli began: "For many days now I have wanted to thank you for your unbiased and very beautiful article on the memoirs of a fascist. Among the many reviews that the book has had, it is the first that is objective and honest."

77. Ibid., 1–3.

78. Ottone Rosai, "I primi fascisti" (3 December 1922), cited in Fornari, "Sulle origini del fascismo a Firenze," 249.

79. Ibid.

80. Banchelli, *Le memorie di un fascista, 1919–1922*, 7.

81. On the end of the futurist-fascist alliance, see the perceptive analysis in Emilio Gentile, "Il futurismo e la politica," in R. De Felice, *Futurismo, cultura e politica*, 136–139, 147–148, and 155–156.

82. For this story, see Dùmini, *Matteotti*.

83. On *Sassaiola fiorentina*, see Fornari, "I periodici fascisti a Firenze," 58–70, 75–85.

84. Ibid., 83.

85. See Cantagalli, *Storia del fascismo fiorentino 1919–1925*, 110. Papini's article was "Freghiamoci della politica," *Lacerba* (1 Oct. 1913).

86. See Marco Palla, "I fascisti toscani," in Mori, ed., *La Toscana*, 458.

87. Piazzesi, *Diario di uno squadrista toscano 1919–1922*, 80.

88. R. De Felice, *Mussolini*, 2:8–9; Ernesto Ragionieri, "Il partito fascista (appunti per una ricerca)," in *La Toscana nel regime fascista (1922–1939)*, 1:59–60; and Palla, "I fascisti toscani," 460–461.

89. On the last point, see Ragionieri, "Il partito fascista," 63, and Banchelli, *Le memorie di un fascista, 1919–1922*, 14; on the others, see Snowden, "On the Social Origins of Agrarian Fascism in Italy," 286–287; Palla, "I fascisti toscani," 473; and Adrian Lyttelton's remarks in *La Toscana nel regime fascista (1922–1939)*, 2:444–448.

90. The adopted name of Malaparte (a negative play on Napoleon Bonaparte or Buonaparte) is used here even though Suckert did not actually take it until 1925.

91. Quoted in Vannucci, *Storia di Firenze*, 423.

92. Some fascists were indeed suspicious of Malaparte as a Jew; see Banchelli, *Le memorie di un fascista, 1919–1922*, 208.

93. On Malaparte's *squadrismo*, see Cantagalli, *Storia del fascismo fiorentino 1919–1925*, 46.

94. Malaparte, "Ritratto delle cose d'Italia, degli eroi, del popolo, degli avvenimenti, delle experienze e inquietudini della nostra generazione" (1923), in *L'Europa vivente e altri saggi politici (1921–1931)*, 201–204. Gobetti's phrase, which appeared in his 1925 introduction to Malaparte's *Italia barbara* (an edition Gobetti published in Turin), is cited in *L'Europa vivente*, 653.

95. For an analysis of Malaparte's rhetoric of the March on Rome, which accents its secular-religious content, see Evans, "La croce e il coltello." For Malaparte's increasing disillusionment with fascism after 1930 and his postwar conversion to Communism, see Guerri, *L'arcitaliano*, 117–288.

96. Prezzolini, *Diario 1900–1941*, 363.

97. In going to Rome, Soffici was responding to the urging of his friend, the poet Giuseppe Ungaretti. See Ungaretti's letter of 8 November 1922 in his *Lettere a Soffici 1917–1930*, 101–102.

98. Papini and Giuliotti, *Dizionario dell'omo salvatico*.

99. Papini, "Mittel-Europa ed Europa Occidentale," *Il Tempo* (18 June 1918), now in *Tutte le opere*, 8:474.

100. Papini, "Déclarations," *La Vraie Italie* (Feb. 1919). The article is reprinted in Cavallo, *Soffici*, 289, which also furnishes a complete index to *La Vraie Italie* on 288.

101. Letter from Papini to Prezzolini of 25 January 1919 in their *Storia di un'amicizia*, 1:303–304.

102. Prezzolini, *Diario 1900–1941*, 311.

103. Letter from Papini to Soffici of 4 October 1919 (Fondazione Primo Conti).

104. *Storia di un'amicizia*, 1:318.

105. Papini, "Adieux," *La Vraie Italie* (May 1920).

106. Papini, *Storia di Cristo*, 41–42, 46, 9.

107. Ibid., 145, 149, 243, 76, 303.

108. Ibid., 2–3; and Prezzolini, "Parole d'un uomo moderno," *La Voce* (13 March 1913).

109. Letter from Papini to Prezzolini of 4 October 1919 in their *Storia di un'amicizia,* 1:317–318.

110. See Papini, *Diario,* in *Tutte le opere,* 10:43.

111. Cited in Ridolfi, *Vita di Giovanni Papini,* 212.

112. See, for example, Papini, *Italia mia* [1939], in *Tutte le opere,* 8:481–545.

113. Letter from Prezzolini to Papini of 4 January 1920, in *Storia di un'amicizia,* 1:318–319. The letter began a two-and-a-half-year silence in their correspondence. See also Prezzolini, *Diario 1900–1941,* 338, 340.

114. Prezzolini, *Vittorio Veneto,* now in *Il meglio di Giuseppe Prezzolini,* 307–324. Subsequent citations are from the preface, 307–312.

115. Prezzolini, "L'Europa se ne va," unpublished manuscript dated 24 January 1923 (Archivio Prezzolini).

116. Prezzolini, *Codice della vita italiana,* now in *Il meglio di Giuseppe Prezzolini,* 175–194.

117. Ibid., 178, 189.

118. On Prezzolini's visit to Gramsci's group in February 1921, see his *Diario 1900–1941,* 336.

119. Prezzolini, "Per una società degli apoti," *La Rivoluzione liberale* (21 Sept. 1922), and Gobetti, "Difendere la rivoluzione," *La Rivoluzione liberale* (25 Oct. 1922), now in Prezzolini, *Gobetti e "La Voce",* 58–64, 72–76.

120. Letter of 5 January 1923, in *Gobetti e "La Voce",* 94–95; emphasis in original. For similar statements of ambivalence, see Prezzolini, *Diario 1900–1941,* 362–363, 427.

121. Prezzolini, "Gli intellettuali e la politica," *Il Resto del Carlino* (26 May 1925), now in Prezzolini, *Sul fascismo,* 70.

122. Ibib., 71; emphasis in original.

123. Prezzolini, *Diario 1900–1941,* 415.

124. Soffici, "Firenze," *Il Selvaggio* (29 Feb. 1928).

125. Letter from Prezzolini to Soffici of 28 March 1928 in their *Carteggio,* 2:77.

126. Prezzolini, *Diario 1900–1941,* 416.

127. Most of Soffici's political writings from 1919 through 1923 are collected in his *Battaglia fra due vittorie.*

128. Twenty-nine issues of *La Ghirba* appeared from 7 April to 31 December 1918, first as the "newspaper for the soldiers of the Fifth Army," and then, when Soffici was transferred, for the Ninth Army.

129. On *La Ghirba,* see Cavallo, *Soffici,* 278 (includes a photograph), and Isnenghi, *Giornali di trincea (1915–1918),* 152–154.

130. Soffici, "Principî di un'estetica futurista," *La Raccolta* (15 Aug.–15 Oct. 1918). For a still more direct expression of his new-found "love for the people," see his "Io e il popolo" (1920), in his *Battaglia fra due vittorie,* 42–43.

131. See especially Soffici, "In guardia!" *Il Popolo d'Italia* (10 Aug. 1919) and "La vigliaccheria del'Pus,'" *Il Popolo d'Italia* (27 Aug. 1919), now in *Battaglia fra due vittorie,* 1–8 and 17–22. In Italian *pus* not only has the same meaning as in English but also serves as an acronymn for the socialists.

132. A complete index to *Rete mediterranea* is available in Cavallo, *Soffici,* 294.

133. Soffici, "Dichiarazione preliminare," *Rete mediterranea* (March 1920).

134. Soffici, "Apologia del futurismo," *Rete mediterranea* (Sept. 1920).

135. Letter from Soffici to Prezzolini of 27 November 1920 in their *Carteggio,* 2:19–20. The idea of a "recall to order" *(richiamo all'ordine),* typical for the period,

was central to all Soffici's postwar thinking on culture and society, and he used it as the subtitle to his 1928 collection, *Periplo dell'arte*.

136. Soffici, "Dichiarazione preliminare."

137. Prezzolini, *Amici*, 157.

138. Soffici, "Il fascismo e l'arte," *Gerarchia* (25 Sept. 1922).

139. Soffici, "Religiosità fascista," *Il Popolo d'Italia* (7 Nov. 1922), now in *Battaglia fra due vittorie*, 206–207.

140. Giovanni Tramontano, "Fascismo toscano," *Il Selvaggio* (21 Dec. 1924). See also Mino Maccari, "Spuntature," *Il Selvaggio* (1–14 March 1926), who argued that "if it had not been for *Lacerba*, fascism would not have gained men like Soffici, Rosai, Vallecchi, and many others, with their patrimony of geniality, honesty, and very Italian virtues."

Conclusion

1. Prezzolini, *Il tempo della Voce*, 11.

2. See Mosse, *The Nationalization of the Masses;* R. De Felice, *Fascism*, 40; Adamson, "Fascism and Culture," 415–417; and E. Gentile, *Il culto del littorio*, 15–25.

3. See, for example, Vivarelli, *Storia delle origini del fascismo*, 1:18.

4. For fuller discussions of the many sources of Mussolini's rhetoric, see Adamson, "The Language of Opposition in Early Twentieth-Century Italy"; and Simonini, *Il linguaggio di Mussolini*.

5. Letter from Mussolini to Prezzolini of 20 October 1917, now in E. Gentile, *Mussolini e "La Voce,"* 75.

6. Mussolini, "La prima guerra d'Italia," *Il Popolo d'Italia* (14 Feb. 1915), now in his *Opera omnia*, 7:197.

7. Thus, in a typical statement, Mussolini argued just as negotiations with the Austrians over territorial claims were getting underway in March 1915: "Either there will be war for the nation and civilization or there will be internal war. If the forces of the past—they are called Monarchy, Papacy, and Conservatism—do not leave the way open for us, then the forces of life will overturn the forces of death, the young will replace the old, and a great insurrectionary movement both necessary and fatal will redeem Italy in the face of the world." See his "Le forze vive rovesceranno le forze morte," *Il Popolo d'Italia* (15 March 1915), now in *Opera omnia*, 7:256.

8. See De Begnac, *Palazzo Venezia*, 131.

9. Mussolini, "La filosofia della forza," now in *Scritti politici di Benito Mussolini*, 101.

10. Mussolini, "Audacia!" *Il Popolo d'Italia* (15 Nov. 1914), and "Osare!" *Il Popolo d'Italia* (13 June 1918), now in his *Scritti politici*, 155–157 and 176–179.

11. Mussolini, "Osare!" in *Scritti politici*, 177.

12. Mussolini, "L'adunata," *Il Popolo d'Italia* (24 Jan. 1915), now in his *Opera omnia*, 7:141.

13. Mussolini, "Disciplina?" *Il Popolo d'Italia* (11 April 1915), now in *Opera omnia*, 7:323–325.

14. Mussolini, "L'azione e la dottrina fascista dinnanzi alle necessità storiche della nazione," *Il Popolo d'Italia* (20 Sept. 1922), now in *Opera omnia*, 18:413.

15. Prezzolini, *Benito Mussolini*, reprinted in *Quattro scoperte*, 158.

16. Mussolini, "Riesame critico della situazione" (Feb. 1925), quoted in Rauti, *Storia d'Italia nei discorsi di Mussolini, 1915–1945*, 1:510.

17. For some examples, see Mussolini, "Variazioni su vecchio motivo: Il fucile e la vanga," "Orientamenti," "Orientamenti e problemi," "Disciplina . . .," "Disciplina," "Disciplina assoluta," and "Ancora la disciplina," *Il Popolo d'Italia* (1 May, 12 June, 18 Aug. 1918; 12 Dec. 1920; 24 July 1921; 7 and 13 Sept. 1922).

18. Prezzolini, "Inquadrare l'Italia," *Il Popolo d'Italia* (10 July 1918); Mussolini, "I quadri della nuova Italia," *Il Popolo d'Italia* (27 Nov. 1918). See also the article on Prezzolini that Mussolini published less than two weeks before: "Le otto ore di lavoro: Una lettera di Prezzolini," *Il Popolo d'Italia* (16 Nov. 1918), now in *Opera omnia*, 12:9–10.

19. Mussolini, "I quadri della nuova Italia." Mussolini developed his concept of "trenchocracy" as one of his many solutions to the problem of where to locate the "new aristocracy." See his "Trincerocazia," *Il Popolo d'Italia* (15 Dec. 1917), now in his *Scritti politici*, 171–173.

20. In Mussolini's first speech to the Chamber of Deputies on 16 November 1922, he called for a three-part program of "economy, work, and discipline"; see his *Opera omnia*, 19:21.

21. Mussolini, "Forza e consenso," *Gerarchia* (March 1923), now in his *Scritti politici*, 227–228.

22. Prezzolini, "Parole d'un uomo moderno," *La Voce* (13 March 1913).

23. Mussolini, "Arditi," *Il Popolo d'Italia* (14 Nov. 1918); the article was signed "Uno qualunque," but it responded to a letter written to "Prof. Mussolini," and the connections with the letter make it virtually certain that Mussolini was the "anyone."

24. Mussolini, "Navigare necesse" (1 Jan. 1920), quoted in Rauti, *Storia d'Italia nei discorsi di Mussolini*, 1:264.

25. There were of course many aspects to this appeal, some conservative and defensive (restoring public order and taming the revolutionary left), others ostensibly more progressive (creating a nation of producers and a public life of grandeur worthy of those who had once presided over the Roman Empire). There were also clearly important elements of Mussolinian rhetoric, such as those related to improving economic efficiency and fulfilling Italy's territorial aspirations, that do not fall under the rubric of spiritual revolution. But the latter did not play as predominant a role in Mussolini's speeches as did those involving the theme of spiritual revolution.

26. Mussolini, "Da che parte va il mondo?" *Gerarchia* (25 Feb. 1922), now in his *Opera omnia*, 18:71.

27. "Dal discorso tenuto da Mussolini a Udine" (20 Sept. 1922), in Répaci, *La marcia su Roma*, 689.

28. Mussolini, "Il discorso di Napoli," *Il Popolo d'Italia* (25 Oct. 1922), now in his *Scritti politici*, 221.

29. For one of the first instances in which Mussolini took this step beyond Papini, see his "Verso l'azione," *Il Popolo d'Italia* (12 March 1915), now in *Opera omnia*, 7:251.

30. De Ruggiero, "Il pensiero italiano e la guerra," *Revue de Métaphysique et de Morale* (September 1916), now in his *Scritti politici 1912–1926*, 141–142.

31. See Wohl, *The Generation of 1914*, 203–237.

32. Durkheim, *The Elementary Forms of the Religious Life*, 475.

33. Mann, *Reflections of a Nonpolitical Man*, 237.

34. Letter of 25 October 1918 from Sigmund Freud to Sandor Ferenczi, quoted in the *Sigmund Freud-House Catalogue* (Vienna, 1975), 43.

35. Gogarten, "Between the Times," *Die Christliche Welt* (1920), now in J. M. Robinson, *The Beginnings of Dialectic Theology* (Richmond, Va., 1968), 277; and Béla Balázs, diary entry of 17 August 1921, quoted in Gluck, *Georg Lukács and His Generation*, 209.

36. Gramsci, *Quaderni del carcere*, 1:311.

37. For Soffici on Lenin, see his *Battaglia fra due vittorie*, 48–49, 103.

38. For an impressive demonstration of this point, see Ciliberto, "Gramsci e il linguaggio della 'vita.'"

39. Eksteins, *Rites of Spring*, 311.

40. Ibid., 311–315, 328.

41. Berlin, "Joseph de Maistre and the Origins of Fascism."

42. Ibid, 119.

43. Ibid, 158–159.

44. Ibid, 96, 102.

45. Mussolini, "Da che parte va il mondo?" *Gerarchia* (25 Feb. 1922), now in his *Opera omnia*, 18:71.

Bibliography

Archival Sources and Special Collections

Archivio Prezzolini, Biblioteca Cantonale, Lugano
Archivio Soffici, Poggio a Caiano
Bandy Archive, Vanderbilt University
Biblioteca Marucelliana, Florence
Biblioteca Nazionale, Florence
Fondo Palazzeschi, Facoltà di Lettere e Filosofia, Florence
Fondo Papini, Fondazione Primo Conti, Fiesole
Fondo Vallecchi, Palazzo Corsini Suarez, Florence
Gabinetto Gian Pietro Vieusseux, Florence
Hoover Institute, Stanford University
Houghton Library, Harvard University
Istituto Giangiacomo Feltrinelli, Milan

Newspapers and Periodicals (in chronological order)

Antologia, 1821–1832, Florence
Nuova Antologia, 1866–1933, Florence
Il Marzocco, 1896–1927, Florence
La Nazione, 1898–1927, Florence
Leonardo, 1903–1907, Florence (reprint ed. Bologna: Arnaldo Forni, 1981)
La Voce, 1908–1916, Florence (reprint ed. Bologna: Arnaldo Forni, 1985)
L'Anima, 1911, Florence
Les Soirées de Paris, 1912–1914, Paris (reprint ed. Geneva: Slatkine, 1971)
Lacerba, 1913–1915, Florence (reprint ed. Milan: Gabriele Mazzotta, 1970)
La Torre, 1913–1914, Siena
Mercure de France, 1913–1917, Paris
Quartiere latino, 1913–1914, Florence (reprint ed. Livorno: Belforte Editore Libraio, 1986)
Utopia, 1913–1914, Milan (reprint ed. Milan: Feltrinelli, n.d.)
Il Popolo d'Italia, 1914–1922, Milan and Rome
La Voce politica, 1915, Rome

L'Italia futurista, 1916–1918, Florence
La Vraie Italie, 1919–1920, Florence
Rete mediterranea, 1920, Florence
Il Selvaggio, 1924–1927, Colle Val d'Elsa and Florence (reprint ed. Florence: SPES, 1976)

Books and Articles

Adamson, Walter L. "The Language of Opposition in Early Twentieth-Century Italy: Rhetorical Continuities between Prewar Florentine Avant-Gardism and Mussolini's Fascism." *Journal of Modern History* 64 (1992):22–51.
———— "Modernism and Fascism: The Politics of Culture in Italy, 1903–1922." *American Historical Review* 95 (1990):359–390.
———— "Fascism and Culture: Avant-Gardes and Secular Religion in the Italian Case." *Journal of Contemporary History* 24 (1989):411–435.
———— "Gramsci and the Politics of Civil Society." *Praxis International* 7 (1987–88):320–339.
———— *Marx and the Disillusionment of Marxism.* Berkeley: University of California Press, 1985.
Alatri, Paolo. *Gabriele D'Annunzio.* Turin: UTET, 1983.
Aleramo, Sibilla. *Andando e stando.* Milan: Mondadori, 1942.
———— *A Woman.* 1906. Translated by R. Delmar. Reprint, Berkeley: University of California Press, 1980.
Amendola, Eva Kühn. *Vita con Giovanni Amendola.* 2nd ed. Florence: Parenti, 1961.
Amendola, Giovanni. *Carteggio, 1897–1912.* Edited by E. d'Auria. 2 vols. Bari: Laterza, 1986–1987.
———— *Etica e biografia.* Naples: Ricciardi, 1953.
———— *Maine de Biran.* Florence: Casa Editrice Italiana, 1911.
Apollinaire, Guillaume. *Méditations esthétiques: Les peintres cubistes.* 1913. Reprint, Paris: Hermann, 1980.
Aquarone, Alberto. *L'Italia giolittiana.* 2 vols. Bologna: Il Mulino, 1981.
Aranguren, Piero. "Il volto di Firenze dal 1870 al 1900." *Rassegna storica toscana* 10 (1964):109–115.
Ardengo Soffici: L'artista e lo scrittore nella cultura del '900. Atti del convegno di studi, Poggio a Caiano, Villa Medicea (7/8 giugno 1975). Florence: Centro Di, 1976.
Asor Rosa, Alberto. *Scrittori e popolo.* Rome: Savelli, 1976.
———— *Storia d'Italia.* Vol. 4: *Dall'Unità a oggi,* pt. 2: *La cultura.* Turin: Einaudi, 1975.
Bagatti, Fabrizio, Gloria Manghetti, and Silvia Porto. *Futurismo a Firenze: 1910–1920.* Florence: Sansoni, 1985.
Bagnoli, Paolo, ed. *Giovanni Papini: L'uomo impossibile.* Florence: Sansoni, 1982.
Balabanoff, Angelica. *My Life as a Rebel.* 1938. Reprint, Bloomington: Indiana University Press, 1973.
Banchelli, Umberto F. *Le memorie di un fascista, 1919–1922.* Florence: Sassaiola Fiorentina, 1922.
Bargellini, Piero. *Florence the Magnificent: A History.* 4 vols. Translated by B. Farson. Florence: Vallecchi, 1980.

———— "La città al principio di secolo." *Rassegna storica toscana* 20 (1974):155–165.

Baudelaire, Charles. *The Painter of Modern Life and Other Essays*. Translated by J. Mayne. London: Phaidon, 1964.

Bellamy, Richard. *Liberalism and Modern Society*. University Park: Penn State University Press, 1992.

———— *Modern Italian Social Theory: Ideology and Politics from Pareto to the Present*. Stanford: Stanford University Press, 1987.

Bellini, Eraldo. *Studi su Ardengo Soffici*. Milan: Vita e pensiero, 1987.

Bergson, Henri. *Oeuvres*. 2nd ed. Paris: Presses Universitaires de France, 1963.

Berlin, Isaiah. "Joseph de Maistre and the Origins of Fascism." In *The Crooked Timber of Humanity*, 91–174. London: John Murray, 1990.

Binni, Walter. *La poetica del decadentismo*. Florence: Sansoni, 1977.

Biondi, Mario, ed. *Ardengo Soffici: Un bilancio critico*. Florence: Festina Lente, 1990.

Bloch, Jean-Richard, and Romain Rolland. *Deux Hommes se rencontrent: Correspondance (1910–1918)*. Cahiers Romain Rolland, 15. Paris: Albin Michel, 1964.

Bobbio, Aurelia. *Le riviste fiorentine del principio del secolo (1903–1916)*. Florence: Sansoni, 1936.

Boine, Giovanni. *Carteggio*. 5 vols. Edited by M. Marchione and S. E. Scalia. Rome: Edizioni di Storia e Letteratura, 1971–1979.

———— *Il peccato e le altre opere*. Parma: Guanda, 1971.

———— *Discorsi militari*. Florence: Libreria della Voce, 1915.

Boni, Massimiliano. *Oriani e La Voce*. Bologna: Edizioni Italiane Moderne, 1988.

Borgese, G. A. *D'Annunzio*. 1909. Reprint, Milan: Mondadori, 1983.

Borghi, Lamberto. *Educazione e autorità nell'Italia moderna*. Florence: La Nuova Italia, 1951.

Bourdieu, Pierre. *In Other Words: Essays towards a Reflexive Sociology*. Translated by M. Adamson. Stanford: Stanford University Press, 1990.

———— "Social Space and Symbolic Power." *Sociological Theory* 7 (1989):14–25.

———— "Flaubert's Point of View." *Critical Inquiry* 14 (1988):539–562.

———— "The Field of Cultural Production, or: The Economic World Reversed." *Poetics* 12 (1983):311–356.

Bourdieu, Pierre, and Loïc J. D. Wacquant. *An Invitation to Reflexive Sociology*. Chicago: University of Chicago Press, 1992.

Bozzetti, Gherardo. *Mussolini direttore dell'"Avanti!"* Milan: Feltrinelli, 1979.

Broch, Herman. *Hugo von Hofmannsthal and His Time*. Translated by M. P. Steinberg. Chicago: University of Chicago Press, 1984.

Brucker, Gene. "Renaissance Florence: Who Needs a University?" In Thomas Bender, ed., *The University and the City*, 47–58. New York: Oxford University Press, 1988.

Buttafuoco, Annarita, and Marina Zancan, ed. *Svelamento: Sibilla Aleramo, una biografia intellettuale*. Milan: Feltrinelli, 1988.

Calinescu, Matei. *Faces of Modernity: Avant-Garde, Decadence, Kitsch*. Bloomington: Indiana University Press, 1977.

Campanile, Marina. *Prezzolini, l'intellettuale, "La Voce."* Naples: Loffredo, 1985.

Cantagalli, Roberto. *Storia del fascismo fiorentino 1919–1925*. Florence: Vallecchi, 1972.

Capacci, Giuseppe. *Diario di guerra di un contadino toscano.* Florence: Cultura, 1982.

Carducci, Giosuè. *Lettere scelte.* Edited by G. Ponte. Genoa: Tilgher, 1985.

——— *Edizione nazionale delle opere di Giosuè Carducci.* 30 vols. Bologna: Zanichelli, 1952–1957.

——— *Edizione nazionale delle opere. Lettere.* 22 vols. Bologna: Zanichelli, 1938–1968.

Caretti, Lanfranco. *Sul Novecento.* Pisa: Nistri-Lischi, 1976.

Caretti, Stefano. "Firenze nei mesi della neutralità." *Rassegna storica toscana* 23 (1977):67–100.

Carocci, Giampero. *Giolitti e l'età giolittiana.* Turin: Einaudi, 1961.

——— *Giovanni Amendola nella crisi dello Stato italiano, 1911–1925.* Milan: Feltrinelli, 1956.

——— "La polemica antidecadentista di Giosuè Carducci." *Belfagor* 4 (1949):263–282.

Carpi, Umberto. *Giornali vociani.* Rome: Bonacci, 1979.

——— *"La Voce": Letteratura e primato degli intellettuali.* Bari: De Donato, 1975.

——— *Letteratura e società nella Toscana del Risorgimento. Gli intellettuali dell'"Antologia."* Bari: De Donato, 1974.

Carrà, Carlo. *La mia vita.* 2nd ed. Milan: Rizzoli, 1945.

Carrà, Carlo, and Ardengo Soffici. *Lettere 1913–1929.* Edited by M. Carrà and V. Fagone. Milan: Feltrinelli, 1983.

Casati, Alessandro, and Giuseppe Prezzolini. *Carteggio.* 2 vols. Edited by D. Continati. Bellinzona-Rome: Dipartimento della Pubblica Educazione del Cantone Ticino and Edizioni di Storia e Letteratura, 1990.

Cassieri, Giuseppe, ed. *La Ronda 1919–1923.* Turin: Edizioni Rai Radiotelevisione Italiana, 1969.

Castelli, Alighieri, ed. *Pagine disperse di Gabriele D'Annunzio.* Rome: Bernardo Lux, 1913.

Castronovo, Valerio. *La stampa italiana dall'Unità al fascismo.* Bari: Laterza, 1973.

Cattaneo, Giulio. "G. Papini, prima della conversione e dopo." *Storia contemporanea* 2 (1971):905–917.

Cavaglion, Alberto. *Otto Weininger in Italia.* Rome: Casucci, 1982.

Cavallo, Luigi. *Soffici: Immagini e documenti (1879–1964).* Florence: Vallecchi, 1986.

——— *Ottone Rosai.* Milan: Galleria il Castello, 1973.

——— *5 xilografie e 4 puntesecche di Ardengo Soffici con le lettere di Picasso.* Milan: Edizioni d'Arte Grafica Uno, 1966.

Ceccuti, Cosimo. "Alle origini della università fiorentina: L'Istituto di Studi Superiori." *Rassegna storica toscana* 23 (1977):177–203.

Chiti, Luca. "1911: Crisi 'politica' della Voce." *Filologia e Letteratura* 15 (1969):174–216.

Ciampini, Raffaele. *Gian Pietro Vieusseux: I suoi viaggi, i suoi giornali, i suoi amici.* Turin: Einaudi, 1953.

Ciliberto, Michele. "Gramsci e il linguaggio della 'vita.'" *Studi storici* 30 (1989):679–699.

Clark, Martin. *Modern Italy, 1871–1982.* London and New York: Longman, 1984.

Cochrane, Eric W. *Florence in the Forgotten Centuries, 1527–1800.* Chicago: University of Chicago Press, 1973.

Conti, Bruna, and Alba Morino. *Sibilla Aleramo e il suo tempo*. Milan: Feltrinelli, 1981.

Conti, Giuseppe. *Firenze vecchia*. Florence: Vallecchi, 1985.

Conti, Primo. *La gola del merlo*. Florence: Sansoni, 1983.

Contorbia, Franco, ed. *Il Commento (1908)*. Genoa: Il Melangolo, 1976.

Corradini, Enrico. *Scritti e discorsi (1903–1914)*. Turin: Einaudi, 1980.

———— *Discorsi politici (1902–1923)*. Florence: Vallecchi, 1923.

Cortelazzo, Michele A. "La formazione della retorica mussoliniana tra il 1901 e il 1914." In D. Goldin, ed., *Retorica e politica: Atti del II convegno Italo-tedesco, Bressanone, 1974*, 179–188. Padua: Liviana, 1977.

Costanzo. Mario. *Giovanni Boine*. Milan: Mursia, 1961.

Croce, Benedetto. *Storia d'Europa nel secolo decimono*. Bari: Laterza, 1981.

———— *Lettere ad Alessandro Casati, 1907–1952*. Naples: Istituto Italiano per gli Studi Storici, 1969.

———— *Cultura e vita morale*. 3rd ed. Bari: Laterza, 1955.

———— *Storia d'Italia dal 1871 al 1915*. 1927. Reprint, Bari: Laterza, 1953. Translated as *A History of Italy, 1871–1915* by C. M. Ady. Oxford: Clarendon Press, 1929.

———— *Una famiglia di patrioti ed altri saggi storici e critici*. 1919. 3rd ed. Bari: Laterza, 1949.

———— *Estetica come scienza dell'espressione e linguistica generale: teoria e storia*. 1902. 9th ed. Bari: Laterza, 1950.

Croce, Benedetto, and Giuseppe Prezzolini. *Carteggio (1904–1945)*. 2 vols. Edited by E. Giammattei. Bellinzona-Rome: Dipartimento della Pubblica Educazione del Cantone Ticino and Edizioni di Storia e Letteratura, 1990.

D'Annunzio, Gabriele. *Tutte le opere*. 11 vols. Milan: Mondadori, 1939–1976.

———— *Pagine disperse*. Edited by A. Castelli. Rome: Lux, 1913.

Davis, John A. *Conflict and Control: Law and Order in Nineteenth-Century Italy*. Atlantic Highlands, N.J.: Humanities Press, 1988.

De Begnac, Yvon. *Palazzo Venezia: Storia di un regime*. Rome: La Rocca, 1950.

Dedola, Rosanna. "'La Voce' e i 'Cahiers de la Quinzaine': Una messa a punto." *Giornale storico della letteratura italiana* 96 (1979):548–563.

De Felice, Franco. "L'età giolittiana." *Studi storici* 10 (1969):114–190.

De Felice, Renzo, ed. *Futurismo, cultura e politica*. Turin: Edizioni della Fondazione Giovanni Agnelli, 1988.

———— *Intellettuali di fronte al fascismo*. Rome: Bonacci, 1985.

———— "Prezzolini, la guerra e il fascismo." *Storia contemporanea* 13 (1982):361–426.

———— *Interpretations of Fascism*. Cambridge, Mass.: Harvard University Press, 1977.

———— *Fascism: An Informal Introduction to Its Theory and Practice*. Edited by M. A. Ledeen. New Brunswick, N.J.: Transaction Books, 1976.

———— *Mussolini*. 5 vols. Turin: Einaudi, 1965–1981.

De Grand, Alexander J. *The Italian Nationalist Association and the Rise of Fascism in Italy*. Lincoln: University of Nebraska Press, 1978.

———— "Curzio Malaparte: The Illusion of the Fascist Revolution." *Journal of Contemporary History* 7 (1972):73–89.

Dello Vicario, Annagiulia. *Lettere Papini-Aleramo (1912–1943) e altri inediti*. Naples: Edizioni Scientifiche Italiane, 1988.

Del Noce, Augusto. "Prezzolini 'utile': La sua opera come documento primo per l'interpretazione della storia italiana del XX secolo." In Luciano Guarnieri, *Prezzolini*, 21–39. Florence: Cassa di Risparmio di Firenze, 1984.

——— "Prezzolini e il superamento del fascismo e dell'antifascismo." *L'Europa* (15 March 1972):75–96.

——— *L'epoca della secolarizzazione*. Milan: Giuffrè, 1970.

Del Vivo, Caterina, ed. *Il Marzocco, carteggi e cronache fra Ottocento e avanguardie (1887–1913). Atti del seminario di studi (12–14 dicembre 1983)*. Florence: Olschki, 1985.

Del Vivo, Caterina, and Marco Assirelli, eds. *Il Marzocco, carteggi e cronache fra Ottocento e avanguardie (1887–1913). Mostra documentaria*. Florence: Gabinetto G. P. Vieusseux and Comune di Firenze, 1983.

De Maria, Luciano. *La nascita dell'avanguardia: Saggi sul futurismo italiano*. Venice: Marsilio, 1986.

——— *Marinetti e il futurismo*. Milan: Mondadori, 1973.

De Ruggiero, Guido. *Scritti politici 1912–1926*. Edited by R. De Felice. Bologna: Cappelli, 1963.

De Sanctis, Francesco. *Lettere alla "Nuova Antologia."* Edited by G. Spadolini. Florence: Le Monnier, 1983.

——— *L'arte, la scienza e la vita*. Edited by M. T. Lanza. Turin: Einaudi, 1972.

Dijkstra, Bram. *Idols of Perversity: Fantasies of Feminine Evil in Fin-de-Siècle Culture*. New York: Oxford University Press, 1986.

Drake, Richard. "Decadence, Decadentism, and Decadent Romanticism in Italy: Toward a Theory of *Décadence*." *Journal of Contemporary History* 17 (1982):69–92.

——— "The Theory and Practice of Italian Nationalism." *Journal of Modern History* 53 (1981):213–241.

——— *Byzantium for Rome: The Politics of Nostalgia in Umbertian Italy, 1878–1900*. Chapel Hill: University of North Carolina Press, 1980.

Dùmini, Amerigo. *Matteotti: "Coups et blessures ayant entraîné la mort."* Paris: Julliard, 1973. Translation of *Diciasette colpi*. Milan: Longanesi, 1958.

Durkheim, Émile. *The Elementary Forms of the Religious Life*. 1912. Translated by J. W. Swain. New York: Free Press, 1965.

Eksteins, Modris. *Rites of Spring: The Great War and the Birth of the Modern Age*. New York: Doubleday/Anchor, 1989.

Evans, Arthur R. "La croce e il coltello." *Italian Quarterly* 23 (1982):47–51.

Falqui, Enrico. *Indice della "Voce" e di "Lacerba."* Florence: Vallecchi, 1966.

——— "Testimonianze francesi sulla 'Voce.'" *Nuova Antologia* 100 (1966):240–247.

Fanelli, Giovanni. *Firenze*. Rome and Bari: Laterza, 1980.

Fei, Silvano. *Firenze: 1881–1898: La grande operazione urbanistica*. Rome: Officina Edizione, 1977.

——— *Nascita e sviluppo di Firenze città borghese*. Florence: G. and G., 1971.

Firenze giolittiana. Florence: Bonechi, 1976.

Forgacs, David, ed. *Rethinking Italian Fascism*. London: Lawrence and Wishart, 1986.

Fornari, Luisa. "I periodici fascisti a Firenze: Tendenze e contrasti del primo fascismo fiorentino (1919–1922)." *Rassegna storica toscana* 17 (1971):51–119.

———— "Sulle origini del fascismo a Firenze." *Rassegna storica toscana* 16 (1970):215–255.

Frigessi, Delia, ed. *La cultura italiana del '900 attraverso le riviste*. Vols. 1–2: *Leonardo, Hermes, Il Regno*. Turin: Einaudi, 1960.

Fussell, Paul. *The Great War and Modern Memory*. New York: Oxford University Press, 1975.

Gaeta, Franco. *La crisi di fine secolo e l'età giolittiana*. Turin: UTET, 1982.

———— *La stampa nazionalista*. Rocca San Casciano: Cappelli, 1965.

Gambillo, Maria Drudi, and Teresa Fiori. *Archivi del futurismo*. 2 vols. Rome: De Luca, 1958.

Garin, Eugenio. *La cultura italiana tra '800 e '900. Studi e ricerche*. Bari: Laterza, 1963.

Gentile, Emilio. *Il culto del littorio: La sacralizzazione della politica nell'Italia fascista*. Rome and Bari: Laterza, 1993.

————"Fascism as Political Religion." *Journal of Contemporary History* 25 (1990):229–251.

———— *Storia del partito fascista, 1919–1922: Movimento e milizia*. Rome and Bari: Laterza, 1989.

———— "From the Cultural Revolt of the Giolittian Era to the Ideology of Fascism." In Frank J. Coppa, ed., *Studies in Modern Italian History*, 103–119. New York and Frankfurt: Peter Lang, 1986.

———— *Il mito dello Stato nuovo dall'antigiolittismo al fascismo*. Rome and Bari: Laterza, 1982.

———— *L'Italia giolittiana*. Rome and Bari: Laterza, 1977.

———— *Mussolini e "La Voce"*. Florence: Sansoni, 1976.

———— *Le origini dell'ideologia fascista (1918–1925)*. Bari: Laterza, 1975.

———— "La storia di Prezzolini." In G. Longo, ed., *Prezzolini 90*, 13–45. Milan: Quaderni dell'Osservatore, 1972.

———— *La Voce e l'età giolittiana*. Milan: Pan, 1972.

———— "Papini, Prezzolini, Pareto e le origini del nazionalismo italiano." *Clio* 7 (1971):113–142.

Gentile, Giovanni. *Gino Capponi e la cultura toscana nel secolo decimonono*. Florence: Sansoni, 1973.

———— "La dottrina del fascismo." *Enciclopedia Italiana* 14 (1932):847–851.

———— *Il fascismo al governo della scuola*. Palermo: R. Sandron, 1924.

———— *Teoria generale dello spirito come atto puro*. 1915. 6th ed. Florence: Sansoni, 1959.

Gentili, Sandro, ed. *G. Papini, atti del convegno di studio nel centenario della nascita, 1982*. Milan: Vita e Pensiero, 1983.

———— "Prezzolini e Soffici a Papini (1902, 1908, 1912)." In Paolo Bagnoli, ed., *Giovanni Papini: L'uomo impossibile*, 220–251. Florence: Sansoni, 1982.

Gide, André. *The Journals of André Gide*. 4 vols. Translated by J. O'Brien. New York: Alfred A. Knopf, 1947.

Giordan, Henri. *Paul Claudel en Italie, avec la Correspondance Paul Claudel/Piero Jahier*. Paris: Klincksieck, 1975.

———— *Romain Rolland et le Mouvement Florentin de La Voce*. Cahiers Romain Rolland, 16. Paris: Albin Michel, 1966.

———— "Contribution à l'histoire des 'Cahiers': Les premières réactions italiennes."

Cahiers de l'Amitié Charles Péguy. Vol. 19: *Actes du Colloque International d'Orléans, 7–9 Septembre 1964*, 336–346.

Giordano, Alberto. *Invito alla lettura di Jahier*. Milan: Mursia, 1973.

Giorgetti, Giorgio. "Sulle origini della società toscana contemporanea." *Studi storici* 15 (1974):671–693.

Giuliotti, Domenico, and Giovanni Papini. *Carteggio, I (1913–1927)*. Edited by N. Vian. Rome: Edizioni di Storia e Letteratura, 1984.

—— *Dizionario dell'uomo salvatico*. Florence: Vallecchi, 1923.

Gluck, Mary. "Towards a Historical Definition of Modernism: Georg Lukács and the Avant-Garde." *Journal of Modern History* 58 (1986):845–882.

—— *Georg Lukács and His Generation, 1900–1918*. Cambridge, Mass.: Harvard University Press, 1985.

Golzio, Francesco, and Augusto Guerra, eds. *La cultura italiana del '900 attraverso le riviste*. Vol. 5: *L'Unità, La Voce politica*. Turin: Einaudi, 1962.

Gramsci, Antonio. *Selections from Cultural Writings*. Edited by D. Forgacs and G. Nowell-Smith. Translated by W. Boelhower. Cambridge, Mass.: Harvard University Press, 1985.

—— *Quaderni del carcere*. 4 vols. Edited by V. Gerratana. Turin: Einaudi, 1975.

Grana, Giani. *Curzio Malaparte*. Florence: Il Castoro, 1967.

Gregor, A. James. *Young Mussolini and the Intellectual Origins of Fascism*. Berkeley: University of California Press, 1979.

—— *The Ideology of Fascism*. New York: Free Press, 1969.

Guerri, G. B. *L'arcitaliano: Vita di Curzio Malaparte*. Milan: Bompiani, 1980.

Halévy, Daniel. *Péguy and Les Cahiers de la Quinzaine*. New York and Toronto: Longmans, Green, 1947.

—— *La vie de Frédéric Nietzsche*. Paris: Calman-Lévy, 1922.

Hamilton, Alastair. *The Appeal of Fascism: A Study of Intellectuals and Fascism, 1919–1945*. New York: MacMillan, 1971.

Hancock, W. K. *Ricasoli and the Risorgimento in Tuscany*. London: Faber and Gwyer, 1926.

Hearder, Harry. *Italy in the Age of the Risorgimento, 1790–1870*. London and New York: Longman, 1983.

Herf, Jeffrey. *Reactionary Modernism*. New York: Cambridge University Press, 1984.

Hughes, H. Stuart. *The Sea Change: The Migration of Social Thought, 1930–1965*. New York: Harper and Row, 1975.

—— *Consciousness and Society: The Reorientation of European Social Thought, 1890–1930*. New York: Vintage Books, 1958.

Hulten, Karl Gunnar Pontus. *Futurism and Futurisms*. New York: Abbeville Press, 1986.

Isnenghi, Mario. *L'educazione dell'italiano: Il fascismo e l'organizzazione della cultura*. Bologna: Cappelli, 1979.

—— *Giornali di trincea (1915–1918)*. Turin: Einaudi, 1977.

—— *Il mito della grande guerra: Da Marinetti a Malaparte*. 2nd ed. Rome and Bari: Laterza, 1973.

—— *Giovanni Papini*. Florence: La Nuova Italia, 1972.

—— "Il piccolo borghese sovversivo." *Ideologie: Quaderni di storia contemporanea* 4 (1968):89–99.

Jacobbi, Ruggero. *L'avventura del Novecento*. Milan: Garzanti, 1984.

Jacobitti, Edmund. *Revolutionary Humanism and Historicism in Italy.* New Haven: Yale University Press, 1981.

Jahier, Piero. *Con me.* Rome: Editori Riuniti, 1983.

——— *Ragazzo [e] Con me e con gli alpini.* 1919. Reprint, Florence: Vallecchi, 1953.

James, William. *Essays in Radical Empiricism.* 1912. Reprint, New York: Longmans, Green, 1922.

——— *Pragmatism and the Meaning of Truth.* 1907 and 1909. Reprint, Cambridge, Mass.: Harvard University Press, 1978.

——— "The Energies of Men." *Philosophical Review* (January 1907):1–20. Translated into Italian in *Leonardo* (February 1907):1–25.

——— "G. Papini and the Pragmatist Movement in Italy." *Journal of Philosophy, Psychology and Scientific Methods* (21 June 1906):337–341.

——— *The Varieties of Religious Experience: A Study in Human Nature.* 1902. Reprint, New York: Macmillan, 1961.

——— *The Will to Believe and Other Essays in Popular Philosophy.* 1897. New York: Dover, 1956.

Jannini, P. A., ed. *Apollinaire e l'avanguardia: Quaderno del Novecento francese 1.* Rome: Bulzoni, 1980.

——— "La rivista 'Poesia' di Marinetti e la letteratura francese." *Rivista di letterature moderne e comparate* 19 (1966):210–219.

——— *La fortuna di Apollinaire in Italia.* Varese and Milan: Istituto Editoriale Cisalpino, 1965.

Jelavich, Peter. *Munich and Theatrical Modernism: Politics, Playwriting, and Performance, 1890–1914.* Cambridge, Mass.: Harvard University Press, 1985.

Jesi, Furio. *Cultura di destra.* Milan: Garzanti, 1979.

Kern, Stephen. *The Culture of Time and Space, 1880–1918.* Cambridge, Mass.: Harvard University Press, 1983.

Koon, Tracy H. *Believe, Obey, Fight: Political Socialization of Youth in Fascist Italy, 1922–1943.* Chapel Hill: University of North Carolina Press, 1985.

LaCapra, Dominick. *Rethinking Intellectual History: Texts, Contexts, Language.* Ithaca: Cornell University Press, 1983.

Landucci, Sergio. *Cultura e ideologia in Francesco De Sanctis.* Milan: Feltrinelli, 1977.

Langella, Giuseppe. *Da Firenze all'Europa: Studi sul Novecento letterario.* Milan: Vita e Pensiero, 1989.

——— "La prima 'Voce' prezzoliniana e gli intellettuali." *Critica letteraria* 5 (1977):121–145.

Ledeen, Michael. *The First Duce.* Baltimore: Johns Hopkins University Press, 1977.

Leone De Castris, Arcangelo. *Decadentismo e realismo.* Bari: Adriatica, 1959.

Lisci, Leonardo Ginori. "La società di Firenze (1900–1914)." *Rassegna storica toscana* 20 (1974):167–176.

Lovett, Clara M. *The Democratic Movement in Italy, 1830–1876.* Cambridge, Mass.: Harvard University Press, 1982.

Lovreglio, Janvier. *Giovanni Papini.* 2 vols. Paris: Lethielleux, 1973.

Luperini, Romano. *Il Novecento.* 2 vols. Turin: Loescher, 1981.

——— *La crisi degli intellettuali nell'età giolittiana.* Messina and Florence: G. D'Anna, 1978.

——— *Scipio Slataper.* Florence: La Nuova Italia, 1977.

———— *Gli esordi nel Novecento e l'esperienza della "Voce."* Rome and Bari: Laterza, 1976.

Luti, Giorgio. "Firenze e la Toscana." In Alberto Asor Rosa, ed., *Letteratura italiana: Storia e geografia,* vol. 3, 463–546. Turin: Einaudi, 1989.

———— *Momenti della cultura fiorentina tra Ottocento e Novecento.* Florence: Le Lettere, 1987.

———— *Firenze corpo 8: Scrittori, riviste, editori del '900.* Florence: Vallecchi, 1983.

Lyttleton, Adrian. "The Language of Political Conflict in Pre-Fascist Italy." *Johns Hopkins University, Bologna Center, Research Institute, Occasional Paper* 54 (1988):1–20.

———— *The Seizure of Power: Fascism in Italy, 1919–1929.* New York: Scribner, 1973.

———— ed. *Italian Fascisms from Pareto to Gentile.* London: Jonathan Cape, 1973.

Mack Smith, Denis. *Mussolini.* New York: Alfred A. Knopf, 1982.

———— *Italy: A Modern History.* Ann Arbor: University of Michigan Press, 1969.

Malaparte, Curzio. *L'Europa vivente e altri saggi politici (1921–1931).* Edited by E. Falqui. Florence: Vallecchi, 1961.

Manghetti, Gloria, ed. *Futurismo a Firenze 1910–1920.* Verona: Bi & Gi, 1984.

Mangoni, Luisa. *L'interventismo della cultura: Intellettuali e riviste del fascismo.* Bari: Laterza, 1974.

———— "Giuseppe Prezzolini (1908–1914)." *Belfagor* 24 (1969):324–349.

Mann, Thomas. *Reflections of a Nonpolitical Man.* Translated by W. D. Morris. New York: Ungar, 1983.

Marchetti, Giuseppe. *Ardengo Soffici.* Florence: La Nuova Italia, 1979.

Marchione, Margherita, ed. *Giuseppe Prezzolini: Ricordi, saggi, e testimonianze.* Prato: Edizioni del Palazzo, 1983.

———— *Prezzolini: Un secolo di attività.* Milan: Rusconi, 1982.

Marinetti, Filippo. *Taccuini, 1915–1921.* Edited by A. Bertoni. Bologna: Il Mulino, 1987.

———— *Selected Writings.* Translated by R. W. Flint and A. A. Coppotelli. New York: Farrar, Straus and Giroux, 1971.

———— *La grande Milano tradizionale e futurista: Una sensibilità italiana nata in Egitto.* Milan: Mondadori, 1969.

———— *Teoria e invenzione futurista.* Milan: Mondadori, 1968.

Marinetti, Filippo, and Aldo Palazzeschi. *Carteggio.* Edited by L. De Maria. Milan: Mondadori, 1978.

Martellini, Luigi. *Invito alla lettura di Malaparte.* Milan: Mursia, 1977.

Mazzini, Giuseppe. *Pensiero e azione.* Edited by A. Levi. Florence: La Nuova Italia, 1960.

———— *The Duties of Man and Other Essays.* Edited by T. Jones. London: J. M. Dent, 1955.

———— *Scritti editi e inediti.* 94 vols. Imola: Galeati, 1906–1943.

Melchionda, Roberto. *Firenze industriale nei suoi incerti arbori.* Florence: Le Monnier, 1988.

Memmo, Francesco Paolo. *Invito alla lettura di Aldo Palazzeschi.* Milan: Mursia, 1986.

Menichi, Carlo Vanni, ed. *Marinetti il futurista.* Florence: Tellini, 1988.

Minore, Renato. *Giovanni Boine.* Florence: La Nuova Italia, 1975.

Mistriorigo, Luigi. "Nietzsche et D'Annunzio." *Revue Générale Belge* 7 (1964):31–41.

Morasso, Mario. *La nuova arma: La macchina.* Turin: Bocca, 1905.

——— *L'imperialismo artistico.* Turin: Bocca, 1903.

Mori, Giorgio, ed. *La Toscana.* Turin: Einaudi, 1986.

Mori, Massimo. "L'interpretazione attivistica di James negli scritti di G. Papini." *Rivista di filosofia* 63 (1972):213–227.

Mosse, George L. *Nationalism and Sexuality.* New York: Howard Fertig, 1985.

——— *Masses and Man.* New York: Howard Fertig, 1980.

——— *The Nationalization of the Masses.* New York: Howard Fertig. 1975.

Mussolini, Benito. *Scritti politici di Benito Mussolini.* Edited by E. Santarelli. Milan: Feltrinelli, 1979.

——— *Opera omnia.* 35 vols. Edited by E. Susmel and D. Susmel. Florence: La Fenice, 1951–1963.

——— *I discorsi della rivoluzione.* Milan: Casa Editrice del Partito Nazionale Fascista, 1923.

Mutterle, Anco Marzio. *Scipio Slataper.* Milan: Mursia, 1981.

——— "Ardengo Soffici scrittore di guerra." In *Umanesimo e tecnica,* 117–136. Padua: Liviana, 1969.

Nanni, Torquato. *Benito Mussolini.* Florence: Libreria della Voce, 1915.

Noether, Emiliana P. "Francesco De Sanctis: Education for Citizenship." Paper presented at the International De Sanctis Conference, University of Naples, 1977.

Nozzoli, Anna, and Carlo Maria Simonetti. *Il tempo de "La Voce."* Florence: Vallecchi, 1982.

Oliva, Gianni. *I nobili spiriti: Pascoli, D'Annunzio, e le riviste dell'esteticismo fiorentino.* Bergamo: Minerva italica, 1979.

Olivier, Fernande. *Picasso et ses amis.* Paris: Delamain et Boutelleau, 1933.

Oriani, Alfredo. *La rivolta ideale.* 1908. 8th ed. Bologna: Cappelli, 1943.

——— *La lotta politica in Italia: Origini della lotta attuale (476–1887).* 3 vols. 1892. Reprint, Bologna: Cappelli, 1925.

Origo, Iris. *A Need to Testify: Portraits of Lauro de Bosis, Ruth Draper, Gaetano Salvemini, Ignazio Silone, and an Essay on Biography.* New York: Harcourt Brace Jovanovich, 1984.

Ossani, Anna T. *Mario Morasso.* Rome: Edizioni dell'Ateneo, 1983.

Ostenc, Michel. *Intellectuels italiens et fascisme (1915–1929).* Paris: Payot, 1983.

Palazzeschi, Aldo. *Il piacere della memoria.* Verona: Mondadori, 1964.

——— *Stampe dell'800.* Florence: Vallecchi, 1964.

——— *Il codice di Perelà.* 1911. Reprint, Florence: Vallecchi, 1920.

Palazzeschi, Aldo, and Giuseppe Prezzolini. *Carteggio 1912–1973.* Edited by M. Ferrario. Rome: Edizioni di Storia e Letteratura, 1987.

Paoloni, Francesco. *Il giolittismo: Partito tedesco in Italia.* Milan: Edizione del Popolo d'Italia, 1916.

Papa, Emilio R. *Fascismo e cultura.* Venice and Padua: Marsilio, 1974.

Papini, Giovanni. *Diario 1900.* Florence: Vallecchi, 1981.

———*Stroncature.* Florence: Vallecchi, 1978.

——— *Opere: Dal "Leonardo" al Futurismo.* Edited by L. Baldacci. Milan: Mondadori, 1977.

———— *Rapporto sugli uomini.* Milan: Rusconi, 1977.

———— *Città felicità, Firenze.* Edited by V. Paszkowski. Florence: Vallecchi, 1960.

———— *Tutte le opere.* 10 vols. Milan: Mondadori, 1958–1966.

———— *Storia di Cristo.* 1921. Reprint, Florence: Vallecchi, 1977. Translated by M. P. Agnetti as *The Story of Christ.* London: Hodder and Stoughton, 1923. Also translated by D. C. Fisher as *Life of Christ.* New York: Harcourt, Brace, 1923.

———— *L'esperienza futurista (1913–1914).* 1919. Reprint, Florence: Vallecchi, 1981.

———— *L'uomo Carducci.* 1918. 4th ed. Bologna: Zanichelli, 1924.

———— *Ardengo Soffici.* Bologna: Resto Carlino, 1916.

———— *Maschilità.* 1915. Reprint, Florence: Vallecchi, 1932.

———— *Sul pragmatismo.* Milan: Libreria Editrice Milanese, 1913.

———— *Un uomo finito.* 1913. Reprint, Florence: Vallecchi, 1929. Translated by V. Pope as *The Failure.* Westport, Conn.: Greenwood Press, 1972.

———— *Il crepuscolo dei filosofi.* Milan: Società Editrice Lombarda, 1906.

———— *Il tragico quotidiano.* Florence: Lumachi, 1906.

———— "Philosophy in Italy." *The Monist* 13 (1903):553–585.

Papini, Giovanni, and Giuseppe Prezzolini. *Storia di un'amicizia.* 2 vols. Florence: Vallecchi, 1966.

———— *Vecchio e nuovo nazionalismo.* Milan: Studio Editoriale Lombardo, 1914.

———— *La coltura italiana.* Florence: Lumachi, 1906.

Papini, Giovanni, and Ardengo Soffici. *Carteggio, I, 1903–1908: Dal "Leonardo" a "La Voce."* Edited by M. Richter. Rome: Edizioni di Storia e Letteratura, 1991.

Papini, Giovanni, and Armando Spadini. *Carteggio 1904–1925.* Edited by P. Spadini Debenedetti and V. Scheiwiller. Milan: Vanni Scheiwiller, 1984.

Papini, Giovanni, and Attilio Vallecchi. *Carteggio (1914–1941).* Florence: Vallecchi, 1984.

Papini, Maria C., ed. *L'Italia futurista (1916–1918).* Rome: Edizioni dell'Ateneo e Bizzarri, 1977.

Papini, settant'anni. Florence: Vallecchi, 1951.

Pareto, Vilfredo. *Les Systèmes socialistes.* 2 vols. Paris: Giard and Briet, 1902.

Parronchi, Alessandro. *Rosai oggi.* Florence: Pananti, 1982.

Péguy, Charles. *Oeuvres en prose complètes.* 2 vols. Paris: Gallimard, 1987.

Perfetti, Francesco. *Il movimento nazionalista in Italia (1903–1914).* Rome: Bonacci, 1984.

Perry, Ralph Barton. *The Thought and Character of William James.* 2 vols. Boston: Little, Brown, 1935.

Pesci, Ugo. *Firenze capitale (1865–1870).* Florence: Bemporad, 1904.

Piantini, Leandro, ed. *Quaderno '70 sul Novecento.* Padua: Liviana, 1970.

Piazzesi, Mario. *Diario di uno squadrista toscano 1919–1922.* Rome: Bonacci, 1981.

Pieri, Piero. *Ritratto del saltimbanco da giovane: Palazzeschi 1905–1914.* Bologna: Pàtron, 1980.

Pinzani, Carlo. *La crisi politica di fine secolo in Toscana.* Florence: Barbèra, 1963.

Poesio, Paolo Emilio. "La vita teatrale a Firenze nei primi anni del secolo XX." *Rassegna storica toscana* 20 (1974):191–204.

Poggioli, Renato. *The Theory of the Avant-Garde.* Translated by G. Fitzgerald. Cambridge, Mass.: Harvard University Press, 1968.

Pompeati, Arturo. "Il Marzocco." *Nuova Antologia* (16 June 1933):559–568.

Pongolini, Francesca Pino, ed. *Giuseppe Prezzolini, 1882–1982. Atti delle giornate di studio 27 gennaio e 6 febbraio 1982.* Bellinzona: Dipartimento della Pubblica Educazione, 1983.

———— ed. *I cento anni di Giuseppe Prezzolini. Catalogo della mostra bio-bibliografica.* Lugano: Biblioteca Cantonale, 1982.

Praz, Mario. *The Romantic Agony.* Translated by A. Davidson. London: Oxford University Press, 1933.

Preti, Luigi. *Mussolini giovane.* Milan: Rusconi, 1982.

Prezzolini, Giuseppe. *Italia 1912: Dieci anni di vita intellettuale (1903–1912).* Edited by C. M. Simonetti. Florence: Vallecchi, 1984.

———— *Il meglio di Giuseppe Prezzolini.* Milan: Longanesi, 1981.

———— *Diario 1900–1941.* Milan: Rusconi, 1978.

———— *Sul fascismo (1915–1975).* Milan: Pan, 1976.

———— *La Voce 1908–1913: Cronaca, antologia e fortuna di una rivista.* Milan: Rusconi, 1974.

———— *Amendola e "La Voce."* Florence: Sansoni, 1973.

———— *Manifesto dei conservatori.* Milan: Rusconi, 1972.

———— *Gobetti e "La Voce."* Florence: Sansoni, 1971.

———— "Un episodio del futurismo." *La Nazione* (14 August 1969).

———— *L'Italiano inutile.* 2nd ed. Florence: Vallecchi, 1964.

———— *Quattro scoperte: Croce, Papini, Mussolini, Amendola.* Rome: Edizioni di Storia e Letteratura, 1964.

———— *Il tempo della Voce.* Florence and Milan: Vallecchi and Longanesi, 1960.

———— *Fascism.* Translated by K. MacMillan. New York: E. P. Dutton, 1927.

———— *Giovanni Amendola.* Rome: A. F. Formiggini, 1925.

———— *Benito Mussolini.* Rome: A. F. Formiggini, 1924.

———— *La coltura italiana.* 1923. Reprint, Milan: Corbaccio, 1938.

———— *Io credo.* Turin: Pinerolo, 1923.

———— *Mi pare.* Fiume: Lloyd, 1923.

———— *Amici.* Florence: Vallecchi, 1922.

———— "Lo storicismo di un mistico." *La Rivoluzione liberale* 1 (7 December 1922):1.

———— *Codice della vita italiana.* Florence: La Voce, 1921.

———— *Vittorio Veneto.* Rome: La Voce, 1920.

———— *Dopo Caporetto.* Rome: La Voce, 1919.

———— *Paradossi educativi.* Rome: La Voce, 1919.

———— *Tutta la guerra: Antologia del popolo italiano sul fronte e nel paese.* 1918. Reprint, Milan: Longanesi, 1968.

———— *Uomini 22, città 3.* Florence: Vallecchi, n.d. [1918].

———— *Discorso su Giovanni Papini.* Florence: Libreria della Voce, 1915.

———— *La Dalmazia.* Florence: Libreria della Voce, 1913.

———— *La Francia e i francesi nel secolo XX, osservati da un italiano.* Milan: Treves, 1913.

———— *Studi e capricci sui mistici tedeschi.* Florence: Quattrini, 1912.

———— *Benedetto Croce.* Naples: Ricciardi, 1909.

———— *La teoria sindacalista.* Naples: Perrella, 1909.

———— *Il cattolicismo rosso.* Naples: Ricciardi, 1908.

———— *Cos'è il modernismo: Enciclica dell'8 sett. 1907 contro il modernismo.* Milan: Treves, 1908.

———— *L'arte di persuadere.* Florence: Lumachi, 1907.

———— *Il sarto spirituale: Mode e figurini per le anime della stagione corrente.* Florence: Lumachi, 1907.

———— *Il centivio.* Milan: Libreria Editrice Lombarda, 1906.

———— *Il linguaggio come causa di errore.* Florence: G. Spinelli, 1904.

———— *Vita intima.* Florence: G. Spinelli, 1903.

Prezzolini, Giuseppe, and Ardengo Soffici. *Carteggio.* Edited by M. E. Raffi and M. Richter. 2 vols. Rome: Edizioni di Storia e Letteratura, 1977–1982.

Ragionieri, Ernesto. *Un comune socialista: Sesto fiorentino.* Rome: Editori Riuniti, 1976.

Rauti, Pino. *Storia d'Italia nei discorsi di Mussolini, 1915–1945.* 2 vols. Rome: Centro Editoriale Nazionale, n.d.

Ravindranathan, T. R. *Bakunin and the Italians.* Kingston and Montreal: McGill-Queen's University Press, 1988.

Renan, Ernest. *La Réforme intellectuelle et morale.* Paris: Michel Levy, 1871.

Répaci, Antonino. *La marcia su Roma.* Milan: Rizzoli, 1972.

Ricci, Aldo G. "Michels e Mussolini." *Storia contemporanea* 15(1984):287– 294.

Riccio, Peter M. *On the Threshold of Fascism.* New York: Casa Italiana, Columbia University, 1929.

Richter, Mario. *La formazione francese di Ardengo Soffici, 1900–1914.* Milan: Vita e Pensiero, 1969.

Ridolfi, Roberto. *Vita di Giovanni Papini.* Verona: Mondadori, 1957.

Ringer, Fritz. *Fields of Knowledge: French Academic Culture in Comparative Perspective, 1890–1920.* New York and Paris: Cambridge University Press and Editions de la Maison des Sciences de l'Homme, 1992.

Risolo, Michele. "Firenze principio di secolo." *Rassegna storica toscana* 10 (1964):167–180.

Roberts, David D. *Benedetto Croce and the Uses of Historicism.* Berkeley: University of California Press, 1987.

———— *The Syndicalist Tradition and Italian Fascism.* Chapel Hill: University of North Carolina Press, 1979.

Rolland, Romain. *Jean-Christophe.* Translated by G. Cannan. New York: Modern Library, 1913.

Romagnoli, Ettore. *Polemica carducciana.* Florence: A. Quattrini, 1911.

Romanò, Angelo, ed. *La cultura italiana del '900 attraverso le riviste.* Vol. 3: *La Voce, 1908–1914.* Turin: Einaudi, 1960.

Rosai, Ottone. *Opere dal 1911 al 1957.* Edited by P. C. Santini. Florence: Vallecchi, 1983.

———— *Lettere 1914–1957.* Edited by V. Corti. Prato: Edizioni Galleria d'Arte Moderna Falsetti, 1974.

———— *Alla ditta: Soffici, Papini, e compagni.* Florence: Edizioni Fiorentini, 1931.

———— *Il libro di un teppista.* 1919. Reprint, Florence: Vallecchi, 1930.

———— *Via toscanella.* Florence: Vallecchi, 1930.

Rotondi, Clementina, ed. *Il Marzocco (Firenze 1896–1932): Indici.* 2 vols. Florence: Olschki, 1980.

Rotondi, Clementina. "Giornali fiorentini dal 1880 al 1900." *Rassegna storica toscana* 10 (1964):117–137.

Rumi, Giorgio. "'Il Popolo d'Italia' (1918–1925)." In Brunello Vigezzi, *Dopoguerra e fascismo: Politica e stampa in Italia,* 427–524. Bari: Laterza, 1965.

Saccone, Antonio. *Marinetti e il futurismo.* Naples: Liguori, 1984.

Salaris, Claudia. *Il futurismo e la pubblicità: Dalla pubblicità dell'arte all'arte della pubblicità.* Milan: Lugetti, 1986.

———— *Storia del futurismo: Libri, giornali, manifesti.* Rome: Editori Riuniti, 1985.

Salinari, Carlo. *Miti e coscienza del decadentismo italiano.* 2nd ed. Milan: Feltrinelli, 1973.

Salomone, A. William. *Italian Democracy in the Making: The Political Scene in the Giolittian Era, 1900–1914.* Philadelphia and London: University of Pennsylvania Press and Oxford University Press, 1945.

Salvemini, Gaetano. *Carteggi.* Vol. 1: *1895–1911.* Edited by E. Gencarelli. Milan: Feltrinelli, 1968.

———— *Come siamo andati in Libia e altri scritti dal 1900 al 1915.* Edited by A. Torre. Milan: Feltrinelli, 1963.

———— "La politica di Benedetto Croce." *Il Ponte* 10 (1954):1728–43.

Santucci, Antonio. *Il pragmatismo in Italia.* Bologna: Il Mulino, 1963.

Sasso, Gennaro. "Considerazioni sulla filosofia di De Ruggiero." *De Homine* 21 (1967):23–70.

Scalia, Gianni, ed. *La cultura italiana del '900 attraverso le riviste.* Vol. 4: *Lacerba, La Voce (1914–1916).* Turin: Einaudi, 1961.

Schiller, F. C. S. *Humanism: Philosophical Essays.* London: Macmillan, 1903.

Schorske, Carl. *Fin-de-Siècle Vienna.* New York: Alfred A. Knopf, 1980.

Schwartz, Sanford. *The Matrix of Modernism: Pound, Eliot, and Early Twentieth-Century Thought.* Princeton: Princeton University Press, 1985.

Segrè, Claudio G. *Fourth Shore: The Italian Colonization of Libya.* Chicago: University of Chicago Press, 1974.

Seigel, Jerrold. *Bohemian Paris: Culture, Politics, and the Boundaries of Bourgeois Life, 1830–1930.* New York: Viking, 1986.

Seroni, Adriano. *Il decadentismo.* Palermo: Palumbo, 1964.

Serra, Renato. *Le lettere.* Edited by U. Pirotti. Ravenna: Longo Editore, 1989.

———— *Scritti.* 2 vols. 2nd ed. Edited by G. De Robertis and A. Grilli. Florence: Le Monnier, 1958.

Seton-Watson, Christopher. *Italy from Liberalism to Fascism, 1870–1925.* London: Methuen, 1967.

Shattuck, Roger. *The Banquet Years.* New York: Harcourt, Brace, 1958.

Showalter, Elaine. *Sexual Anarchy: Gender and Culture at the Fin de Siècle.* New York: Viking, 1990.

Simmel, Georg. "The Metropolis and Mental Life." 1903. In *The Sociology of Georg Simmel,* 409–424. Edited and translated by K. H. Woolf. Glencoe, Ill.: Free Press, 1950.

Simonetti, Carlo Maria. *Le edizioni della Voce.* Florence: Giunta Regionale Toscana and La Nuova Italia Editrice, 1981.

Simonini, Augusto. *Il linguaggio di Mussolini.* Milan: Bompiani, 1978.

Slataper, Scipio. *Scritti politici 1914–1915.* Edited by Giorgio Barone. Trieste: Edizioni "Italo Svevo," 1977.

———— *Scritti letterari e critici.* Edited by G. Stuparich. Milan: Mondadori, 1956.

———— *Scritti politici.* Milan: Mondadori, 1954.

———— *Appunti e note di diario.* Edited by G. Stuparich. Milan: Mondadori, 1953.

———— *Lettere.* 3 vols. Edited by G. Stuparich. Turin: Buratti, 1931.

———— *Ibsen.* 1916. Reprint, Florence: Vallecchi, 1944.

————— *Il mio carso*. 1912. Reprint, Milan: Mondadori, 1980.

Snowden, Frank M. *The Fascist Revolution in Tuscany, 1919–1922*. New York: Cambridge University Press, 1989.

————— "On the Social Origins of Agrarian Fascism in Italy." *Archives Européenes de Sociologie* 13 (1972):268–295.

Soffici, Ardengo. *Lettere a Prezzolini, 1908–1920*. Edited by A. Manetti Piccinini. Florence: Vallecchi, 1988.

————— *I diari della grande guerra*. Edited by M. Bartoletti Poggi and M. Biondi. Florence: Vallecchi, 1986.

————— *Opere*. 7 vols. Florence: Vallecchi, 1959–1968.

————— *Fine di un mondo*. Florence: Vallecchi, 1955.

————— *Periplo dell'arte: Richiamo all'ordine*. Florence: Vallecchi, 1928.

————— *Battaglia fra due vittorie*. Florence: Soc. An. Ed. "La Voce," 1923.

————— *Primi principî di una estetica futurista*. Florence: Vallecchi, 1920.

————— *Giornale di bordo*. Florence: Libreria della Voce, 1915.

————— "Aprés la mort d'un héros (Constantin Meunier)." *La Plume* (15 April 1905):321–325.

————— "Broderies Vénitiennes." *La Plume* (1 June 1904):638–645.

————— "Le Salon d'Automne, Considérations." *L'Europe Artiste* (October–November 1904):333–339.

————— "Notes Italiennes." *La Plume* (15 February 1903):260–263.

Solinas, Stenio. *Giuseppe Prezzolini: Un testimone scomodo*. Rome: Giovanni Volpe, 1976.

Solmi, Sergio. "Nietzsche e D'Annunzio." *Il Verri: Rivista di Letteratura* 9 (1975):7–16.

Somalvico, Bruno. *Sorel e Prezzolini: Convergenze o malintesi? (1908–1911)*. Bellinzona: Archivio Storico Ticinese, 1982.

Sonnino, Sidney. *Scritti e discorsi extraparliamentari, 1870–1902*. Edited by B. F. Brown. Bari: Laterza, 1972.

Sorel, Georges. *From Georges Sorel: Essays in Socialism and Philosophy*. Edited by J. Stanley. New York: Oxford University Press, 1976.

Spadolini, Giovanni. *La Firenze di Pasquale Villari*. Florence: Le Monnier, 1989.

————— *La Firenze di Gino Capponi fra restaurazione e romanticismo: Gli anni dell'"Antologia."* Florence: Le Monnier, 1985.

————— *Giolitti: Un'epoca*. Milan: Longanesi, 1985.

————— *Firenze fra '800 e '900*. Florence: Le Monnier, 1984.

————— *Firenze mille anni*. Florence: Le Monnier, 1984.

————— *Fra Vieusseux e Ricasoli: Dalla vecchia alla "Nuova Antologia."* Florence: Le Monnier, 1982.

————— *Firenze capitale: Gli anni di Ricasoli*. Florence: Le Monnier, 1979.

Spender, Stephen. *The Struggle of the Modern*. London: Hamish Hamilton, 1963.

Spini, Giorgio, and Antonio Casali. *Firenze*. Rome and Bari: Laterza, 1986.

Spriano, Paolo. *Storia del Partito comunista italiano*. 5 vols. Turin: Einaudi, 1967–1975.

Stendhal [Henri Beyle]. *Rome Naples and Florence*. Translated by R. N. Coe. London: John Calder, 1959.

Sternhell, Zeev. *Neither Right nor Left: Fascist Ideology in France*. Translated by D. Maisel. Berkeley: University of California Press, 1986.

Strelsky, Katharine. "Dostoevsky a Firenze." *Rassegna storica toscana* 20 (1974):81–88.

Stromberg, Roland N. *Redemption by War: The Intellectuals and 1914*. Lawrence: Regents Press of Kansas, 1982.

Stuparich, Giani. *Scipio Slataper*. Milan: Mondadori, 1950.

Tarchi, Marco, ed. *Il Popolo d'Italia: Antologia 1914–1917*. Rome: Luciano Landi, 1982.

Tavolato, Italo. *Contro la morale sessuale*. Florence: Gonnelli, 1913.

Tenenbaum, Louis. "From Futurism to Pacifism: Aldo Palazzeschi and the First World War." *Italica* 63 (1986):386–395.

Thayer, John. *Italy and the Great War: Politics and Culture, 1870–1914*. Madison: University of Wisconsin Press, 1964.

Timms, Edward, and Peter Collier, eds. *Visions and Blueprints: Avant-Garde Culture and Radical Politics in Early Twentieth-Century Europe*. Manchester and New York: Manchester University Press and St. Martin's Press, 1988.

Tisdall, Caroline, and Angelo Bozzolla. *Futurism*. New York and Toronto: Oxford University Press, 1978.

La Toscana nel regime fascista (1922–1939). 2 vols. Florence: Olschki, 1971.

Tosi, Guy. "D'Annunzio découvre Nietzsche (1892–1894)." *Italianistica: Rivista di Letteratura italiana* 2 (1973):481–513.

Trilling, Lionel. *Beyond Culture*. London: Secker and Warburg, 1966.

Turi, Gabriele. *"Viva Maria": La reazione alle riforme leopoldine (1790–1799)*. Florence: Olschki, 1969.

Ungaretti, Giuseppe. *Lettere a Soffici 1917–1930*. Edited by P. Montefoschi and L. Piccioni. Florence: Sansoni, 1981.

Valesio, Paolo. "The Lion and the Ass: The Case for D'Annunzio's Novels." *Yale Italian Studies* 1 (1977):67–82.

Vallecchi, Attilio. *Ricordi e idee di un editore vivente*. Florence: Vallecchi, 1934.

Vannucci, Marcello. *Storia di Firenze*. Rome: Newton Compton, 1986.

Vassalli, Sebastiano. *L'alcova elettrica*. Turin: Einaudi, 1986.

Veneziani, Marcello. *La rivoluzione conservatrice in Italia: Genesi e sviluppo della "ideologia italiana."* Milan: Sugarco, 1987.

Verdenelli, Marcello. *Ugo Tommei (1894–1918)*. Florence: La Ginestra, 1989.

Verdone, Mario, and Enzo Lauretta. *Cinema e futurismo*. Agrigento: Centro di Ricerca per la Narrativa e il Cinema, 1987.

Vergelli, Anna, ed. *Castello in Aria: Carteggio inedito Agnoletti-Pascoli*. Rome: Bulzoni, 1985.

Vivarelli, Roberto. *Storia delle origini del fascismo*. 2 vols. Bologna: Il Mulino, 1991.

Viviani, Alberto. *Giubbe Rosse*. Florence: Vallecchi, 1983.

——— *Gianfalco*. Florence: Barbèra, 1934.

Wanrooij, Bruno. "The Rise and Fall of Italian Fascism as a Generational Revolt." *Journal of Contemporary History* 22 (1987):401–418.

Weininger, Otto. *Sex and Character*. 1903. New York: AMS, 1975.

Wilde, Alan. *Horizons of Assent: Modernism, Postmodernism, and the Ironic Imagination*. Baltimore: Johns Hopkins University Press, 1981.

Wilkinson, James. *The Intellectual Resistance in Europe*. Cambridge, Mass.: Harvard University Press, 1981.

Williams, Raymond. "When Was Modernism?" *New Left Review* 175 (1989):48–52.

Wohl, Robert. *The Generation of 1914*. Cambridge, Mass.: Harvard University Press, 1979.

Woolf, S. J. *The Poor in Western Europe in the Eighteenth and Nineteenth Centuries*. London: Methuen, 1986.

———— *A History of Italy, 1700–1869*. London: Methuen, 1979.

———— ed. *The Nature of Fascism*. London: Weidenfeld and Nicolson, 1968.

Zapponi, Niccolò. *I miti e le ideologie: Storia della cultura italiana 1870-1960*. Naples: Edizioni Scientifiche Italiane, 1981.

Zunino, Pier Giorgio. *L'ideologia del fascismo*. Turin: UTET, 1985.

Index

Nannetti, Vieri (1895–1957), 220, 227, 229

Napoleon I, Emperor of France, 80

Napoleon III, Emperor of France, 38

Nazione, La, 17, 29, 31, 32, 42, 144, 155, 196

Neera [Anna Radius Zuccari] (1846–1918), 288n50

New aristocracy, concept of, 86, 140, 184, 266, 294n146, 310n19

Nietzsche, Friedrich, 2, 8, 11, 13, 82, 89, 122, 158; in Italy, 52, 119, 133, 138, 140, 255, 258, 274n77, 275n1, 283n163

Nitti, Francesco Saverio (1868–1953), 129, 242

Novalis [Friedrich von Hardenberg], 90, 105

Nuova Antologia, 29–30, 207

Oberdan, Guglielmo (1858–1882), 132, 142, 200

Oettingen, Hélène d' [Roch Grey], 62, 116, 172

Ojetti, Ugo (1871–1946), 232

Orano, Paolo (1875–1945), 243

Ordine nuovo, L', 241

Oriani, Alfredo (1852–1909), 12, 86, 126, 140, 264, 290n79

Orvieto, Adolfo (1871–1952), 45, 46, 47

Orvieto, Angiolo (1869–1968) 45, 47

Orvieto, Laura (1876–1953), 274n81

Orvieto, Leone, 45

Palazzeschi, Aldo [Aldo Giurlani] (1885–1971), 34, 155, 169, 170, 173–175, 180, 220; and Prezzolini, 174–175; and First World War, 192, 208, 213

Panunzio, Sergio (1886–1944), 200

Paoloni, Francesco, 303n163

Papini, Giacinta Giovagnoli (1884–1967), 98, 102

Papini, Giovanni (1881–1956), 1, 15, 28, 47; on Carducci, 22, 24, 26, 27, 163; on Mazzini, 22, 79; on Florence, 36; on D'Annunzio and aestheticism, 48–51, 163, 303n165; youth of, 53–55; and concept of party of intellectuals, 55, 64, 82–83, 151, 281n135, 295n182; on Rome, 64; and *Leonardo*, 64–66, 93–94, 97–98, 108; and Croce, 70; and William James, 70, 74, 75–78, 278n84; and Bergson, 73–74, 85; and *La coltura italiana*, 80–81; and campaign for a reawakening by force, 82–83, 96; and Pareto, 85–86; and concept of internal enemy, 87, 177–178, 201–202, 261, 303n163; on Nietzsche, 89–90, 281n129; in Paris, 91, 98, 172, 279n92; in Milan, 102–105; and syndicalism, 107; and *La Voce*, 110–111, 116, 147, 162, 163, 287n29; and masculinism, 122–123, 177–178, 283nn161,162; and Amendolas, 128, 129–130; and futurism, 154–155, 162, 166, 167–168, 177–180, 197, 220, 300n100; and Christianity, 156–157, 162, 164, 177, 215–217, 235, 236–240, 241; and religion of nature, 162–163, 215; and autobiography of 1912, 163–165; and *Il Popolo d'Italia*, 201; and First World War, 203, 205, 208, 213, 214–217; and fascism, 235, 239, 256

Pareto, Vilfredo (1848–1923), 26, 84, 89, 140, 264

Parma, strike of 1908 in, 108, 287n23

Pascoli, Giovanni (1855–1912), 45, 46, 48, 103, 148, 302n140

Pater, Walter, 45

Péguy, Charles (1873–1914), 73, 91, 92, 121, 122, 150, 214

Peirce, Charles Sanders, 74, 76

Peruzzi, Ubaldino (1822–1891), 38

Pescetti, Giuseppe, 41, 42, 43, 112, 229

Picasso, Pablo, 2, 59, 61, 122, 156, 158–159, 246; and *La Voce*, 105, 115, 121, 147, 150; and *Lacerba*, 169, 172

Pieraccini, Gaetano, 43, 229

Pietro Leopoldo, Grand Duke of Tuscany (1747–1792), 18–19

Pirandello, Luigi (1867–1936), 31, 290n84

Pissarro, Camille, 122

Pius X, Pope (1835–1914), 103

Platen-Hallermünde, August, 142

Plume, La, 60–61, 63

Poesia, 103, 286n4

Popolo, concept of, 82, 85, 123, 136, 201, 211, 221, 225, 244–245, 281nn130,132,133

Popolo, Il, 141, 142

Popolo d'Italia, Il, 87, 200, 215, 230, 239; *vociani* and, 135, 198–199, 201, 224–225, 226, 243, 245, 248, 262

Prezzolini, Dolores Faconti (1881–1962), 99

Prezzolini, Giuseppe (1882–1983), 2, 11, 28, 39; on Florence, 15–18, 20, 31, 37; on De Sanctis, 22; on Carducci, 26–27; on *Il Marzocco*, 47–49; on D'Annunzio, 49; youth of, 55–58, 64; and Rolland, 56, 91, 104, 122, 181, 195; in Paris, 65, 70, 186, 243, 279n92, 289nn61,64; and

Slataper, Scipio (1888–1915): as *triestino*, 11, 33, 120, 131–133, 176, 200; and *La Voce*, 112, 116, 122, 129, 133–135, 137, 139, 141–142, 145, 147–148, 156, 187, 208, 258

Socialist Party, 112, 144, 191, 195, 198

Soffici, Ardengo (1879–1964), 2, 9, 15; on Carducci, 26–27; on Böcklin, 36; on D'Annunzio, 49, 275n97; in Paris, 49, 59–64, 94–95, 156, 166, 172, 277n60, 289n64; youth of, 58–61; and *Il Marzocco*, 61, 277n49; and religion of art, 96–97, 108, 156–159, 162; fascism of, 97, 159–161, 230, 233, 235, 236, 243–250; and *La Voce*, 111, 116, 119–120, 147; and Claudel, 136, 139; and Boine, 138–139; and Mussolini, 141, 201, 247, 249; and futurism, 148–149, 154–155, 161, 164, 166, 167, 169, 171–172, 174–175, 179, 180, 220, 296n21, 298n60; and First World War, 209–212, 213, 219; and "return to order," 244, 245–247, 308n135

Soffici, Maria Sdrigotti (1897–1974), 245

Soirées de Paris, Les, 166

Sonnino, Sidney (1847–1922), 30–31, 124–125, 202, 242

Sorel, Georges (1847–1922), 73, 91, 107, 118, 120, 121, 122, 140, 186, 192

Space, public, 10, 13, 31–32, 33, 37–40, 147, 190

Spadini, Armando (1883–1925), 56, 59, 65

Spaventa, Bertrando (1817–1883), 32

Spender, Stephen, 7–8

Stendhal [Henri Beyle], 15–16, 32, 34

Studio, The, 59

Stuparich, Giani (1891–1961), 11, 132, 134

Svevo, Italo [Ettore Schmitz] (1861–1928), 174

Tailhade, Laurent, 148

Tavolato, Italo (1889–1966), 11, 33, 154, 169, 172, 176–177

Tempo, Il, 215, 216

Teppismo, 154, 181, 191–192, 212, 214, 256, 300n103

Thovez, Enrico (1869–1925), 50

Tocco, Felice (1845–1911), 32, 272n53

Tommei, Ugo (1894–1918), 171, 199, 206, 220

Torre, La, 165, 215

Toscanità, 9–10, 92, 180; in Soffici, 9, 63–64, 82, 95–97, 108, 156, 159–160, 161;

in Papini, 98–99, 162, 163, 164; in Rosai, 212

Toulouse-Lautrec, Henri, 122

Trilluci, 223

Turati, Filippo (1857–1932), 112, 130, 239, 245

Tuscany: myth of, 18–21, 31; fascism in, 20, 230–232

Umberto I, King of Italy (1844–1900), 43, 54, 56, 83

Unamuno, Miguel de, 96, 137, 277nn60,62, 284nn186,187, 292n123

Ungaretti, Giuseppe (1888–1970), 307n97

Unità, L', 130, 131, 145, 291n101

Unità cattolica, L', 42, 273n74

Utopia, 142, 294n146

Vailati, Giovanni (1863–1909), 76, 94, 101

Vais, Mario Nunes (1856–1932), 223

Vallecchi, Attilio (1880–1946), 155, 167, 169, 171, 193, 197

Vasari, Giorgio, 40

Vedrani, Alberto (1872–1963), 116

Verga, Giovanni (1840–1922), 13

Verhaeren, Emile, 103, 148

Verlaine, Paul, 140, 277n60

Veuillot, Louis, 215

Vico, Giambattista, 8, 24

Vielé-Griffin, Francis, 148

Vieusseux, Gabinetto, 28

Vieusseux, Gian Pietro (1779–1863), 27–28

Villari, Pasquale (1826–1917), 31, 32, 33, 130

Violence and war, concepts of, 88–89, 123, 138, 145–146, 149, 178–179, 191–195, 197–198, 204, 227, 257

Vita nuova, 31

Vittorio Emanuele II, King of Italy, 40

"Viva Maria!" (1799), 19

Viviani, Alberto (1894–1970), 53, 153, 155, 176, 206, 212

Voce, La: circulation of and contributors to, 116–117, 127, 288n49; themes of, 118–120; political rhetoric in, 123–124; changes in 1911 and after, 151–152; and interventionism, 196, 204, 205; during First World War, 219

Voce politica, La, 202, 219

Vogüé, Eugène Melchior de, 50

Vraie Italie, La, 236, 245

Walden, Herwarth, 115

Weber, Max, 23

Weininger, Otto, 89, 90–91, 100, 122, 176, 255
Whitman, Walt, 137, 156
Wilde, Oscar [Fingal O'Flahertie Wills], 35, 72, 149
World as theater, concept of, 189–190, 301n120

World War, First: campaign for Italian intervention in, 151, 177, 189, 193–203, 217, 255; effects on Tuscany of, 217–219
Wundt, Wilhelm, 128